HERMENEUTICS AND CRITICAL THEORY IN ETHICS AND POLITICS

HERMENEUTICS AND CRITICAL THEORY
IN ETHICS AND POLITICS

edited by
MICHAEL KELLY

The MIT Press
Cambridge, Massachusetts
London, England

First MIT Press edition, 1990

This work originally appeared as volume 21, numbers 1–2, of the journal *The Philosophical Forum*. The essay by Carol Gould has been added for this edition.

This book was printed and bound in the United States of America.

Library of Congress Cataloging-in-Publication Data

Hermeneutics and Critical Theory in Ethics and Politics / edited by Michael Kelly. – 1st MIT Press ed.
     p.   cm.
    Published also as v. 21, nos. 1–2 of the Philosophical forum.
    Includes bibliographical references.
    ISBN 0-262-11154-3. – ISBN 0-262-61066-3 (pbk.)
    1. Hermeneutics. 2. Ethics. 3. Social sciences–Philosophy.
I. Kelly, Michael, 1954–
BD241.H367   1990   90-32190
121'.68--dc20   CIP

CONTENTS

CONTENTS

INTRODUCTION

MICHAEL KELLY

Critique is a principal purpose of philosophical reflection on the social practices of ethics and politics. Yet it has not received as much philosophical attention as the other purposes—clarification, expression, and especially justification, the counterpart in the human sciences of verification in the natural sciences. The result of this neglect, intentional or not, is that there is little philosophical understanding or agreement about what critique ought to be in ethics and politics. At the same time, there are many competing paradigms of ethical and political critique which, in the absence of any philosophical guidance, has meant that they, as well as the various models of ethics and politics themselves, seem incommensurable.

Hermeneutics and critical theory provide two distinct but related paradigms of critique, which are important for three reasons: each has developed a history of critique over the last fifty years—critical theory mainly in social-political theory and aesthetics, hermeneutics in literary criticism and philosophy in general—and can therefore bring valuable experience to the present problematic of ethical and political critique; each represents a mode of philosophical reflection which is aware of its historical conditionedness yet which demonstrates that such conditionedness is not only compatible with critique but even necessary for it; and each already inspires ethical and political critique in our present philosophical climate, one which is marked by a skepticism toward the very possibility of philosophy, as well as of ethics and politics. For these reasons, it is both likely and desirable that any philosophical notion of critique exercised or introduced today will be influenced in some essential way by hermeneutics or critical theory.

The essays here are written by twelve philosophers whose work in philosophical ethics or politics has been influenced, directly or indirectly, positively or critically, by the debates over the last twenty-five years in, about, and between hermeneutics and critical theory. Jürgen Habermas provides perhaps the best example of these influences, because he stems from the tradition of critical theory but he was allied with hermeneutics against positivism at an   early stage of his philosophical career; only later did he actively distance himself from hermeneutics in the well-known Gadamer/Habermas debate of the late 1960s, early 1970s. By now Habermas has succeeded in establishing this distance, yet at the same time he refers to his work as, in part, interpretive social science. Not all the work included here, however, would be described by its authors as belonging to hermeneutics or critical theory (at least so long as the latter is tied to the Frankfurt School). Michael Walzer, for example, is not typically associated with either tradition, but he employs certain hermeneutic concepts and argumentative strategies in his critique of universalist theories of justice and in his model of social criticism. This is clear, if implicit, in his essay included here, and it is made explicit in Georgia Warnke's defense of his *Spheres of Justice*.

The authors will not be explicitly addressing the debates around hermeneutics and critical theory. Yet all the articles presuppose those debates in the sense that the authors' current theoretical positions are indications of some of the possible strategies for critical ethics and politics since the debates transpired and if one or some combination of these paradigms is followed, if only in part. That is, once the historical conditions of the need for, as well as the philosophical conditions for the possibility of, ethical and political critique are taken seriously, then hermeneutics and critical theory will assume important, if at times indirect, roles. There is, however, no unified sense of ethical and political critique underlying the different articles, and no "fusion of [critical] horizons" is expected to emerge from them. Even if there is eventually some consensus on the methodological level of critique between the authors who are included or represented here, there will, of course, still be a plurality of conflicting interpretations on the level of substantive moral and political principles. Finally, although critique is not even the explicit theme in each article, all the concepts or issues discussed here—justice, solidarity, contingency, freedom, social meaning, evil, common interest, practical rationality—are central to that general problematic; for they determine the means and ends of critique. The hope is that, together, these essays contribute to the self-understanding of the general historical and methodological starting point of any contemporary form of ethical or political critique.

Seyla Benhabib discusses a series of objections to discourse or communicative ethics concerning the principle of universalizability, the priority of the right over the good, the relationship between morality and politics, the question of moral motivation and character, and the issue of the contextualization of judgment in ethics. After showing how these objections do and do not apply to communicative ethics, a new mode of cognitivist ethics, she argues that they have *not* delivered "a *coup de grâce* to a dialogically reformulated universalist ethical theory."

Carol C. Gould investigates the role of "common interest" in contemporary political philosophy, especially in democratic theory. After distinguishing three alternative models of common interest—aggregative, objectivist, and constructivist—she criticizes the current approaches to these models offered by social-choice theory, Rawls, and Habermas. The framework of this critique is provided by Gould's recent work on democracy, in particular by her notions of common activity, self-development, equal rights of participation, etc. These same notions are discussed in more detail in the last section where she proposes an alternative conception of common interest.

The notions of solidarity and justice are often thought to be diametrically opposed, leading to competing conceptions of ethical and social theory. Yet Jürgen Habermas argues that they can be integrated within his model of discourse ethics: "the procedure of discursive will formation takes account of the inner connection of . . . the autonomy of unique individuals [justice] and their prior embeddedness in intersubjectively shared forms of life [solidarity]." He defends this claim in the context of a discussion of Lawrence Kohlberg's theory of moral development and, at the same time, makes an insightful comparison between his own procedural conception of justice and those of John Rawls and Thomas Scanlon.

Agnes Heller, whose contribution here is part of her multi-volume work on ethics, develops a Kierkegaardian conception of philosophical ethics by focusing on the concepts of contingency and choice and the categories of difference and universality. Although she criticizes universalistic ethics, she nevertheless argues that moral philosophy cannot renounce its task of providing "guidelines for *all* kinds of possible moral advice to *any* actor who formulates the question, 'What is the right thing for me to do'?" To explain how this is possible, she analyzes the morally relevant, modern conditions that the philosopher and her addressees share.

In Michael Kelly's analysis of Alasdair MacIntyre's and Habermas's views on the relationship between practical rationality and tradition, he argues that, although their views seem diametrically opposed — MacIntyre emphasizing tradition and Habermas rejecting it—they may converge to some extent on a methodological level. His principal purpose is to demonstrate that these two philosophers make important contributions to the conception of a philosophical ethics which, like hermeneutic ethics, is tradition-bound, but which, like Kantian ethics, is also rational and critical.

Adi Ophir, departing from Walzer's theory of complex equality and pluralistic justice to develop a "discourse of evil" (which does not treat evil as the mere privation of good) and a conception of distributive spheres of evil with their own social meanings and rules of conversion, makes a plea for a hermeneutic ethics that identifies both evil and preventable suffering. He also advocates a notion of a social contract "reformulated as a model for an agreement regarding the forms and modes of conversion of socially organized and preventable suffering."

In a comparison between Donald Davidson's analytic action theory, MacIntyre's account of the rationality of tradition, and Habermas's model of rational explanation linked to his notion of the rationalization of the lifeworld, Kenneth Baynes defends Habermas's model by arguing that it is better able to provide a basis for critical social theory. He also shows how Habermas's model of social science integrates interpretive and causal analyses by combining a rational reconstruction of the internal perspective of the social actor with a functionalist or "systems-theoretical" perspective.

Thomas McCarthy's article is an expanded version of his commentary on Jacques Derrida's "Politics of Friendship," which was delivered at the 1988 American Philosophical Association Meeting in Washington and published in the *Journal of Philosophy* [LXXXV, 11 (1988)]. [We asked Derrida himself to contribute to this volume; he originally agreed but then, unfortunately, had to withdraw at a late stage, too late for us to ask anyone else to represent deconstruction.] McCarthy challenges both Derrida's attempt to model his general approach to politics on the politics of friendship, and his "deduction of the political via the thinking of *différance*." After analyzing what he calls Derrida's eleven "Theses on Heidegger," McCarthy argues that, while the radicality of deconstruction is perhaps harmless in the field of metaphysics, it is "seriously disabling where morals and politics are concerned."

What is the relationship between Kant's conception of interpretation and his approach to political history? This is the question guiding Rudolf Makkreel's reconstruction of Kant's *Critique of Judgment,* in which he focuses on reflective judgments because they are able to coordinate contingency and particularity with necessity and universality. The example Makkreel discusses to link his reconstruction with Kant's political philosophy is the French Revolution, "a contingent historical fact" that "can intimate a necessary human goal." Part of Makkreel's argument is also that a new hermeneutic understanding of Kant's third Critique is necessary if hermeneutics itself is ever going to provide the basis of critical reflection that its critics have charged it lacks.

In a general critique of constructed philosophical conversations, such as Rawls's "original position," Habermas's "ideal speech situation," and Bruce Ackerman's "liberal dialogue," Michael Walzer defends real talk against ideal speech. Real talk, "the conscious and critical part of the processes that generate our received ideas and reigning theories—reflection become articulate," takes place within the context of the other "features [political struggle, socialization, compromise] of the complex social process that produces consensus and shared understandings." This is the only context, he argues, in which we can conceptualize and hope to realize a just society.

In Georgia Warnke's response to Walzer's critique, she argues that his objections are based on an interpretation of constructed conversations "as philosophical fictions for grounding norms and beliefs." She sketches a different interpretation that mitigates Walzer's original objections: there may be a methodological convergence between Rawls and Walzer, and Habermas's "idealizing presuppositions" are perhaps more related to real talk than Walzer realizes. In her separate article, Warnke defends Walzer against three major objections to his *Spheres of Justice,* by arguing that they "derive from a disregard for the hermeneutic basis" of his position. Her defense is based on references to "insights [about the interpretation of shared social meanings] that have emerged within the hermeneutic schools of social and literary interpretation."

Freedom in the modern world, according to Albrecht Wellmer, "rests on a normative dualism of 'negative' versus 'positive', i.e., communal freedom." After discussing competing communalist and individualist theories of freedom, he defends a universalist notion of communal freedom: "freedom that—through the institutions and practices of a society, through the self-understanding, concern, and habits of its citizens—has become a common *objective,*" and has thus become the universal content of politics understood as democratic will formation.

The sign of a good interpretation, according to Hans-Georg Gadamer, is that it not be recognized as an interpretation. This does not mean that the interpretation has parity with that which it interprets; it means that the subject matter being interpreted has received its rightful preeminence. In light of this, the reason for emphasizing 'hermeneutics' and 'critical theory' in the title of this collection is not to propagate hermeneutics or critical theory or to label the authors as hermeneuticists or critical theorists. The objective is to attain a better self-understanding of the principles, methodology, and goals of contemporary ethical and political critique.

ACKNOWLEDGMENTS

I would like to thank *The Philosophical Forum* for permission to reprint all of the articles included here, except Carol Gould's, which is printed here for the first time; and Basil Blackwell for Agnes Heller's article, which is part of her *A Philosophy of Morals,* published since the Forum issue originally appeared.

IN THE SHADOW OF ARISTOTLE AND HEGEL: COMMUNICATIVE ETHICS AND CURRENT CONTROVERSIES IN PRACTICAL PHILOSOPHY*

SEYLA BENHABIB

Like the explanation versus understanding controversy, the recent dispute concerning "communicative" or "discourse" ethics is informed both by the Anglo-American and Continental traditions of thought and reflects a provocative interaction between the two. Communicative ethics, as formulated by Karl-Otto Apel and Jürgen Habermas, has been influenced by the work of such moral philosophers as Kurt Baier, Alan Gewirth, H. M. Hare, Marcus Singer, and Stephen Toulmin[1] on moral reasoning and universalizability in ethics. Above all, however, it is in John Rawls's[2] neo-Kantian constructivism and Lawrence Kohlberg's[3] cognitive-developmental moral theory that Apel and Habermas have found the most kindred projects of moral philosophy in the Anglo-American world.

The central insight of communicative or discourse ethics derives from modern theories of autonomy and of the social contract, as articulated by John Locke, Jean Jacques Rousseau, and in particular by Immanuel Kant. Only those norms and normative institutional arrangements are valid, it is claimed, which individuals can or would freely consent to as a result of engaging in certain argumentative practices. Apel maintains that such argumentative practices can be described as "an ideal community of communication" (*die ideale Kommunikationsgemeinschaft*), while Habermas calls them "practical discourses." Both agree, however, that such practices are the only plausible procedure in the light of which we can think of the Kantian principle of "universalizability" in ethics today. Instead of asking what an individual moral agent could or would will, without self-contradiction, to be a universal maxim for all, one asks: What norms or institutions would the members of an ideal or real communication community agree to as representing their common interests after engaging in a special kind of argumentation or conversation? The procedural model of an argumentative

1

praxis replaces the silent thought experiment enjoined by the Kantian universal-izability test.

The current mood concerning neo-Kantian, procedural, and formalistic ethical theories on both sides of the Atlantic is probably best captured by the following statement of Stanley Hauerwas and Alasdair MacIntyre:

> This is not the first time that ethics has been fashionable. And history suggests that in those periods when a social order becomes uneasy and even alarmed about the weakening of its moral bonds and the poverty of its moral inheritance and turns for aid to the moral philosopher and theologian, it may not find these disciplines flourishing in such a way as to be able to make available the kind of moral reflection and theory which the culture actually needs. Indeed on occasion it may be that the very causes which have led to the impoverishment of moral experience and the weakening of moral bonds will also themselves have contributed to the formation of a kind of moral theology and philosophy which are unable to provide the needed resources.[4]

If this statement can be viewed as a fairly accurate indication of the *Zeitgeist* concerning ethical theory today, as I believe is the case, then this certainly does not bode well for yet another program of ethical universalism and formalism. Such ethical formalism is considered a part of the Enlightenment project of rationalism and of the political project of liberalism, and it is argued that pre-cisely these intellectual and political legacies are an aspect, if not the main cause, of the contemporary crisis. If communicative or discourse ethics is to be at all credible, therefore, it must be able to meet the kind of challenges posed by MacIntyre and Hauerwas.

In this essay, I would like to acknowledge this challenge and anticipate a set of objections and criticisms that can be pressed against communicative ethics from a standpoint that I will roughly describe as "neo-Aristotelian" and "neo-Hegelian." Since Aristotle's criticism in his *Nicomachean Ethics* and *Politics*[5] of Plato's theory of the good and of the ideal state, and since Hegel's critique of Kantian ethics in his various writings,[6] formalist and universalist ethical theories have been continuously challenged in the name of some concrete historical-ethical community or, in Hegelian language, of some *Sittlichkeit*. In fact, Apel[7] and Habermas[8] admit that one cannot ignore the lessons of Hegel's critique of Kantian morality. Whether they have successfully integrated these lessons into communicative ethics, however, is worth examining more closely.

In recent discussions, 'neo-Aristotelianism' has been used to refer to three, not always clearly distinguished, strands of social analysis and philosophical argu-mentation. Particularly in the German context, this term has been identified with a neo-conservative social diagnosis of the problems of late-capitalist societies.[9]

Such societies are viewed as suffering from a loss of moral and almost civilizational orientation, caused by excessive individualism, libertarianism, and the general temerity of liberalism when faced with the task of establishing fundamental values. Neither capitalist economic and societal modernization nor technological changes are seen as basic causes of the current crisis; instead, political liberalism and moral pluralism are regarded as the chief causes of this situation. From Robert Spaemann to Allan Bloom, this position has found vigorous exponents today.

The term 'neo-Aristotelian' is also frequently used to designate the position of thinkers like MacIntyre, Michael Sandel, Charles Taylor, and Michael Walzer, who lament the decline of moral and political communities in contemporary societies.[10] Unlike the neo-conservatives, the "communitarian" neo-Aristotelians are critical of contemporary capitalism and technology. The recovery of "community" need not only or even necessarily mean the recovery of some fundamentalist value scheme; rather, communities can be reconstituted by the reassertion of democratic control over the run-away megastructures of modern capital and technology. The communitarians share with neo-conservatives the belief, however, that the formalist, ahistorical, and individualistic legacies of Enlightenment thinking have been historically implicated in developments that have led to the decline of community as a way of life. Particularly today, they argue, this Enlightenment legacy so constricts our imagination and impoverishes our moral vocabulary that we cannot even conceptualize solutions to the current crisis which would transcend the "rights/entitlement/distributive justice" trinity of political liberalism.

Finally, 'neo-Aristotelianism' refers to a hermeneutical philosophical ethics, centered around the Aristotelian understanding of phronesis. Hans-Georg Gadamer[11] was the first to turn to Aristotle's model of phronesis as a form of contextually embedded, and situationally sensitive judgment of particulars. Gadamer so powerfully synthesized Aristotle's ethical theory and Hegel's critique of Kant that, after his work, the two strands of argumentation became almost indistinguishable. From Aristotle's critique of Plato, Gadamer extricated the model of a situationally sensitive practical reason, always functioning against the background of the shared ethical understanding of a community.[12] From Hegel's critique of Kant, Gadamer borrowed the insight that all formalism presupposes a context from which it abstracts and that there is no formal ethics that does not have some material presuppositions concerning the self and social institutions.[13] Just as there can be no understanding that is not situated in some historical context, so there can be no "moral standpoint" that would not be dependent upon a shared ethos, be it that of the modern state. The Kantian moral point of view is only intelligible in light of the revolutions of modernity and the establishment of freedom as a principle of the modern world.

These three strands of a neo-conservative social diagnosis, a politics of community, and a philosophical ethics of a historically informed practical reason form the core elements of the contemporary neo-Aristotelian position. Here I shall be concerned with neo-Aristotelianism less as a social diagnosis or as a political philosophy and more as a philosophical ethic.

Let me now formulate a series of objections to communicative ethics. Some version of these has been voiced by thinkers inspired by Aristotle and Hegel against Kantian-type ethical theories at some point or another. My goal will be to show that these objections have not succeeded in delivering a *coup de grâce* to a dialogically reformulated universalist ethical theory. A serious exchange between such a universalist ethical theory, which suffers neither from the methodological individualism nor from the ahistoricism of traditional Kantian ethics, and a hermeneutically inspired neo-Aristotelianism can lead us to see that some traditional oppositions and exclusions in moral philosophy are no longer convincing. The oppositions within the confines of which much recent discussion has run—universalism versus historicity, an ethics of principle versus judgment in context, or ethical cognition versus moral motivation—are no longer compelling. Just as it is not the case that there can be no historically informed ethical universalism, it is equally not the case that all neo-Aristotelianism must defend a conservative theory of communal ethics. Here I am concerned to indicate how such false oppositions can be transformed into a more fruitful set of contentions between two types of ethical theorizing which have marked the Western philosophical tradition since its beginnings in Socrates's challenge to the Sophists and his condemnation to death by the city of Athens.

I. SKEPTICISM TOWARD THE PRINCIPLE OF UNIVERSALIZABILITY: IS IT AT BEST INCONSISTENT AND AT WORST EMPTY?

Hegel criticized the Kantian formula, "Act only on that maxim through which you can at the same time will that it should become a universal law," on numerous occasions as being inconsistent at best and empty at worst.[14] He argued that the test alone whether or not a maxim could be universalized could not determine its moral rightness. As he pointed out in his early essay on *Natural Law*,[15] whether or not I should return deposits entrusted to me is answered in the affirmative by Kant with the argument that it would be self-contradictory to will that deposits should not exist. The young Hegel answers that there is no contradiction in willing a situation in which deposits and property do not exist, unless of course we make some other assumptions about human needs, scarce resources, distributive justice, and the like. Out of the pure form of the moral law alone, no concrete maxims of action can follow and, if they do, it is because other unidentified premises have been smuggled into the argument.

In view of this Hegelian critique, which continues to influence discussions of Kantian ethics even today,[16] the response of Kantian moral theorists has been twofold: first, some have accepted Hegel's critique that the formal procedure of universalizability can yield no determinate test of the rightness of maxims; they admit that one must presuppose some minimally shared conception of human goods and desires as goals of action, and must test principles of action against this background. This line of response has weakened the Kantian distinction between autonomy and heteronomy by accepting that the goals of action may be dictated by contingent features of human nature rather than by the dictates of pure practical reason alone. Rawls's list of "basic goods," which rational agents are supposed to want whatever else they also want, is the best example of the introduction of material assumptions about human desires into the universalizability argument.[17] The test of universalizability is not about whether we want these goods but rather about the moral principles guiding their eventual distribution. Other Kantian moral philosophers, and most notably among them, Onora O'Neill and Gewirth, have refused to jettison the pure Kantian program, and have attempted to expand the principle of the noncontradiction of maxims by looking more closely at the *formal features of rational action.* O'Neill,[18] for example, distinguishes between "conceptual inconsistency" and "volitional inconsistency" in order to differentiate among types of incoherence in action. "The non-universalized maxim," she writes, "embodies a conceptual contradiction only if it *aims* at achieving mutually incompatible objectives and so cannot under any circumstances be acted on with success."[19] Volitional inconsistency, by contrast, occurs when a rational agent violates what O'Neill names "Principles of Rational Intending."[20] Applying universalizability to maxims of action both to test their conceptual consistency and their volitional consistency avoids, so O'Neill claims, "the dismal choice between triviality and implausible rigorism."[21] In a similar vein, Gewirth expands on the idea of the "rational conditions of action" in such a way as to generate nontrivial and intersubjectively binding maxims of moral action from them.[22]

Both strategies have problems: in the first case, by allowing material presuppositions about human nature and desires into the picture, one runs the risk of weakening the distinction between Kantian and types of utilitarian or Aristotelian moral theory. The result is a certain eclecticism in the structure of the theory. The second position runs a different danger: by focusing exclusively on the conditions of rational intending or acting, as O'Neill and Gewirth do, one can lose sight of the question of intersubjective moral validity. After all, the Kantian principle of universalizability is formulated in order to generate morally binding maxims of action which all can recognize. As MacIntyre shows in his sharp critique of Gewirth, from the premise that I as a rational agent require certain conditions of action to be fulfilled, it can never follow that you have an *obliga-*

tion not to hinder me from enjoying these conditions.[23] The grounds for this obligation are left unclear; but it was precisely such grounds that the universalizability requirement was intended to produce. Put in Apel and Habermas's terms, the analysis of the rational structure of action for a single agent produces an *egological* moral theory that cannot justify intersubjective moral validity. Instead of asking what I as a single rational moral agent can intend or will to be a universal maxim for all without contradiction, the communicative ethicist asks: What principles of action can we all recognize or agree to as being valid if we engage in practical discourse or a mutual search for justification?

With this reformulation, universalizability is defined as an intersubjective procedure of argumentation geared to attain communicative agreement. This reformulation brings with it several significant shifts: instead of thinking of universalizability as a test of *noncontradiction,* we think of universalizability as a test of *communicative agreement.* We do not search for what would be non-self-contradictory but rather for what would be mutually acceptable for all. Furthermore, there is also a shift from the model of the goal-oriented or strategic action of a single agent intending a specific outcome to the model of *communicative action,* which is speech and action to be shared with others.

What has been gained through this reformulation such as to counter the Hegelian objection? Have we not simply pushed the problem from one procedure onto another? Instead of deriving moral principles from some procedure of conceptual or volitional coherence, do we not simply derive them now from our definition of the conversational situation? Theorists can construct or design conversations to yield certain outcomes: the preconditions of conversation may guarantee that certain outcomes will result.[24] In an earlier article, I formulated this problem as follows: either models of practical discourse or the ideal communication community are defined so minimally as to be trivial in their implications, or there are more controversial substantive premises guiding their design which do not belong among the minimal conditions defining the argumentation situation, in which case they are inconsistent.[25] We are back to the "dismal choice" between triviality or inconsistency.

I now believe that the way out of this dilemma is to opt for a strong and possibly controversial construction of the conversational model which would nonetheless be able to avoid the charges of dogmatism and/or circularity.[26] My thinking is as follows: what Habermas has previously named the conditions of an "ideal speech situation," and which in the essay, "Discourse Ethics: A Proposal for a Program of Philosophical Justification," are called the "universal-pragmatic presuppositions"[27] of communicative action, entail, in my opinion, strong ethical assumptions. They require of us (1) that we recognize the right of all beings capable of speech and action to be participants in the moral conversation—I shall call this *the principle of universal moral respect;* (2) these conditions further stipulate that, within such conversations, each has the same symmetrical rights to various speech acts, to initiate new topics, to ask for reflection about the presuppositions of the conversation, etc. Let me call this *the principle of egalitarian reciprocity*. The very presuppositions of the argumentation situation then have a normative content that precedes the moral argument itself. But can one then really avoid the charges of circularity and dogmatism?

One of the central disagreements between Apel and Habermas concerns precisely this issue of the justification of the constraints of the moral conversation. Apel maintains that:

> If, on the one hand, a presupposition cannot be challenged in argumentation without actual performative self-contradiction, and if, on the other hand, it cannot be deductively grounded without formal-logical petitio principii, then it belongs to those transcendental-pragmatic presuppositions of argumentation that one must always (already) have accepted, if the language game of argumentation is to be meaningful.[28]

For Apel, the principles that all beings capable of speech and action are potential members of the same communication community with me and that they deserve equal and symmetrical treatment are two such conditions.

In view of this Apelian strategy of fundamental grounding or *Letztbegründung,* Habermas argues that such a strong justification of communicative ethics cannot succeed and may not even be necessary. Rather than view the normative constraints of the ideal communication community as being "disclosable" via an act of transcendental self-reflection, Habermas argues that we view them as "universal pragmatic presuppositions" of speech acts corresponding to the know-how of competent "moral" agents at the postconventional stage. But, as Thomas McCarthy[29] has pointed out, there is no univocal description of the "know-how" of moral actors who have reached the postconventional stage of moral reasoning. Habermas's description of this know-how is one among many others like those of Rawls and Kohlberg. At the stage of postconventional moral reasoning, reversibility, universalizability, and impartiality are, under some descriptions, all aspects of the moral point of view, but the real point of philosophical contention is the acceptable or adequate description of these formal constraints. The appeal to moral psychology and development brings no exemption from the justificatory process. Kohlberg was wrong in thinking that the "ought" can be deduced from the "is." The formal structure of postconventional moral reasoning allows a number of substantive moral interpretations, and these interpretations always take place by presupposing a hermeneutic horizon.

As opposed to Apel's strategy of *Letztbegründung* and Habermas's strategy of a "weak transcendental argument" based on the rational reconstruction of competencies, I would like to plead for a "historically self-conscious universalism." The principles of universal respect and egalitarian reciprocity are our philosophical clarification of the constituents of the moral point of view from within the normative hermeneutic horizon of modernity. These principles are neither the *only allowable* interpretation of the formal constituents of the competency of postconventional moral actors nor are they unequivocal transcendental presuppositions to which every rational agent, upon deep reflection, must concede. These principles are arrived at by a process of "reflective equilibrium," in Rawlsian terms, whereby one, as a philosopher, analyzes, refines, and judges culturally defined moral intuitions in light of articulated philosophical principles. What one reaches at the end of such a process of reflective equilibrium is a "thick description" of the moral presuppositions of the cultural horizon of modernity.

At one level, of course, the intuitive idea behind universalistic ethics is very ancient, and corresponds to the "Golden Rule" of the tradition—"Do unto others as you would have others do unto you." Universalizability enjoins that we reverse perspectives among members of a "moral community"; it asks us to judge from the other's point of view. Such reversibility is essential to the ties of reciprocity which bind human communities together. All human communities define some "significant others" in relation to which reversibility and reciprocity must be exercised—be they members of my kin group, my tribe, my city-state, my nation, my coreligionists. What distinguishes "modern" from "premodern" versions of universalistic ethical theories is the assumption of the former that the moral community is coextensive with all beings capable of speech and action, and potentially with all of humanity. In this sense, communicative ethics sets up a model of moral conversation among members of a modern ethical community, for whom the theological and ontological bases of the inequality among humans has been radically placed into question.

This is not an admission of dogmatism in favor of modernity, for even this "dogma" of modernity, if you wish, can be challenged within the moral conversation itself. The racist, the sexist, or the bigot can challenge the principle of universal moral respect and egalitarian reciprocity within the moral conversation, but if he wants to establish that his position is right not simply because it is mighty, he must convince with argument that this is so. The presuppositions of the moral conversation can be challenged within the conversation itself, but if they are altogether suspended or violated then might, violence, coercion, and suppression follow. One thus avoids the charge of circularity: by allowing that the presuppositions of the moral conversation can be challenged within the conversation itself, they are placed within the purview of questioning. But insofar as they are pragmatic rules necessary to keep the moral conversation going, we can bracket them in order to challenge them but cannot suspend them altogether. The shoe is really on the other foot. It is up to the critic of such egalitarian universalism to show, with good grounds, why some individuals should be effectively excluded from the moral conversation.

Of course, our moral and political world is characterized more by struggles unto death among moral opponents than by a conversation among them. This admission reveals the fragility of the moral point of view in a world of power and violence, but this is not an admission of irrelevance. Political ideologies as well as subtler forms of cultural hegemony have always sought to make plausible the continuation of violence and power to those who most suffered from their consequences. When such ideology and hegemony no longer serve to justify such relations, then struggles unto death for moral recognition can follow. As a critical social theorist, the philosopher is concerned with the unmasking of such mechanisms of continuing political ideology and cultural hegemony; as a moral theorist, the philosopher has one central task: to clarify and justify those normative standards in the light of which such social criticism is exercised.[30]

Let us return once more to the Hegelian objection: Can a universalist ethical theory, which views universalizability in ethics as a moral conversation governed by certain procedural constraints, avoid the "dismal choice" between triviality or inconsistency? Hegel's critique assumes but does not clarify a distinction between universalizability as a procedure for *testing* and universalizability as a procedure for *generating* maxims. As a procedure for testing the intersubjective validity of moral principles and norms of action, communicative ethics is neither trivial nor inconsistent; as a procedure for generating valid principles of action, the model of moral conversation is a necessary but insufficient test case that requires, in any given instance, adequate contextualization. In other words, we can say of a course of action, the principle of which has passed the test of conversational universalizability, that it is morally permissible, but also assert that it was the wrong thing to do under the circumstances. The universalizability test should produce standards of what is morally permissible and impermissible in general; however, such tests are by no means sufficient to establish what is morally meritorious in any given context.

Habermas formulates the test of universalizability thus:

. . . unless the consequences and side effects which the general observance of a controversial norm can be expected to have for the satisfaction of the interests of each individual can be freely accepted by all.[31]

What we are asking is not whether, from this procedure, the moral theorist can deduce concrete moral principles guiding action. The adoption of "all contents," writes Habermas, "no matter how fundamental the action norm involved may be, must be made dependent on real discourses (or advocatory discourses conducted as substitutes for them)."[32]

Even if this principle of universalizability (''U'') is not intended to generate concrete principles or norms of action, can it serve as a test procedure for determining what is morally permissible and impermissible? As a test procedure, ''U'' enjoins us to engage in a counterfactual thought experiment in which we enter into conversation with all who would be potentially affected by our actions. Let us consider some standard moral maxims to assess what has been gained by this reformulation. Take the example used by Kant, ''deposits once made must be returned for otherwise there would be no property.'' The relevant question is: Does the principle, ''there ought to be property,'' satisfy the test that ''the consequences and side effects which the general observance of a controversial norm can be expected to have for the satisfaction of the interests of each individual can be freely accepted by all?'' The answer is that both the existence of property relations and its opposite can be adopted as collective maxims of action by moral actors, if the consequences of such arrangements for the satisfaction of the interests of each can be freely accepted by all. In other words, the existence or nonexistence of property relations cannot be determined via a moral deduction. Contrary to what Kant assumed, as long as they serve the satisfaction of the interests of each individual and this can be freely accepted by all, numerous forms of property arrangements are morally permissible. Kant was wrong in attempting to generate a categorical imperative to uphold property relations; what is at stake is not property as such but other moral values, like general welfare and the correct mode of dispensing of scarce resources. To this extent, the universalizability procedure in communicative ethics upholds Hegel's critique of Kant.

Yet, as formulated by Habermas, ''U'' also leads to morally disturbing and counterintuitive consequences. Take the maxim, ''Do not inflict unnecessary suffering.'' Whether or not we are to inflict unnecessary suffering is to be determined by whether ''the consequences and side effects which the general observance of a controversial norm can be expected to have for the satisfaction of the interests of each individual can be freely accepted by all.'' Can we imagine a situation in which it would be in the interests of each individual and freely accepted by them that they would be not only perpetrators but receivers of unnecessary suffering? The answer to this question appears to depend on an equivocation concerning 'interests'. Suppose there are masochists and sadists among us who interpret their interests as consisting precisely in the opportunity to inflict and receive such suffering. Are we ready to say that, under these conditions, *Neminem laede* ceases to be a morally valid principle? In other words, what appears to be the virtue of ''U'' in the property example, i.e., its indeterminacy, is its weakness in the second case. But the least that a universalist ethical theory ought to do is to cover the same ground as what Kant had described as "negative duties," i.e. duties not to violate the rights of humanity in oneself and in others. Yet "U" does not appear to do this.

I believe the difficulty is that Habermas has given "U" such a *consequentialist* formulation that his theory is now subject to the kinds of arguments that deontological-rights theorists have always successfully brought against utilitarians. Without some stronger constraints about how we are to interpret "U," we run the risk of regressing behind the achievements of Kant's moral philosophy. The categorical imperative proves as morally impermissible what Kant names "negative duties," not to lie, not to harm, not to cheat, or otherwise to violate the dignity of the human moral person. Positive moral duties cannot be deduced from the universalizability test alone but require contextual moral judgment in their concretization.[33] I have suggested above that the communicative-ethics version of "U" must likewise deliver criteria for distinguishing among the morally permissible and the morally impermissible, without, however, being able to yield adequate criteria of the morally virtuous or appropriate action in any given circumstance.

Agnes Heller, Albrecht Wellmer, and Otfried Höffe have all recently expressed stronger criticisms of communicative ethics: even as a test procedure for what is intersubjectively permissible, "U," they argue, is either too indeterminate or too complex or too counterfactual. In Heller's sharp formulation: "Put bluntly, if we look to moral philosophy for guidance in our actions here and now, we cannot obtain any positive guidance from the Habermasian version of the categorical imperative. Rather, what we could get is a *substantive limitation* placed on our intellectual intuitions: we, as individuals, should only claim universal validity for those moral norms which we can assume would be accepted by everyone as valid in an ideal situation of symmetric reciprocity."[34] Wellmer writes: "If we interpret U as an explication of our preunderstanding of moral validity, then this means that in our moral convictions and in our moral judgments, only such judgments must be involved that the consequences and side-effects which the general observance of a specific norm would have for each individual could be *freely* (*zwanglos*) accepted by all. This, however, so it appears to me, would make justified moral judgment a total chimera (*ein Ding der Unmöglichkeit*)."[35]

Heller argues that the Habermasian theory cannot be saved, for it is, in effect, a theory of "legitimation rather than one of validation."[36] Wellmer recommends that we interpret the ideals of "rational consent" or "agreement" as regulative principles, but that, in the solution of *real* moral problems under real moral *conditions,* we can "only think of what the reasonable person or those competent judges or those affected by our actions *would* say if they were sufficiently reasonable, good willing and competent in judgment."[37] I think Wellmer's response weakens the distinction between justification and contextualization.

11

Although I agree that such contextualization is absolutely crucial for *moral judgment* in real situations, I think his response makes the test of the validity of moral judgment a matter of phronesis alone. I am interested in seeing whether there is anything at all, any guidelines, in the procedure of discourse ethics which could place a "substantive limitation on our intellectual intuition," in the way of necessary but insufficient criteria. Heller considers the placing of such limitations alone too minimal an achievement for moral theory. In my opinion, however, it would be quite sufficient for a universalist moral theory that is self-conscious about the historical horizon of modernity within which it is situated, if it could succeed in placing such a substantive limitation on our intuitions.

I want to suggest that "U" is actually redundant in Habermas's theory and that it adds little but consequentialist confusion to the basic premise of discourse ethics. "D" ("Every valid norm must be accepted by all those affected.") states that only those norms can claim to be valid which meet (or could meet) with the approval of all concerned in their capacity as participants in a practical discourse. "D," together with those rules of argument governing discourses, and the normative content which I summarized as the principles of universal moral respect and egalitarian reciprocity, are in my view quite adequate to serve as the only universalizability test.

The chief difference between my proposal and Habermas's is that for him "U" has the effect of guaranteeing consensus. Without having their interests violated, all could freely consent to some moral content. But the difficulty with consent theories is as old as Rousseau's dictum—"*On les forcera d'être libre.*" Consent alone can never be a criterion of anything, neither of truth nor of moral validity; rather, it is always the rationality of the procedure for attaining agreement which is of philosophical interest. We must interpret consent not as an end-goal but as a process for the cooperative generation of truth or validity. The core intuition behind modern universalizability procedures is not that everybody could or would agree to the same set of principles, but that these principles have been adopted as a result of a procedure, whether of moral reasoning or of public debate, that we are ready to deem "reasonable and fair." It is not the *result* of the process of moral judgment alone that counts but the *process* for the attainment of such judgment which plays a role in its validity and, I would say, moral worth. 'Consent' is a misleading term for capturing the core idea behind communicative ethics: namely, the processual generation of reasonable agreement about moral principles via an open-ended moral conversation. It is my claim that this core intuition, together with an interpretation of the normative constraints of argument in light of the principle of universal respect and egalitarian reciprocity, are sufficient to accomplish what "U" was intended to accomplish, but only at the price of consequentialist confusion.

Let us return once more to the principle, "Do not inflict unnecessary suffering,'' to test this claim.[38] According to my formula, we are to imagine whether, if I and all those whose actions would affect me and by whose actions I would be affected were to engage in a moral conversation, governed by the procedural constraints of universal respect and egalitarian reciprocity, we could adopt this as a principle of action. By adopting the infliction of unnecessary suffering as a norm of action, however, we would in effect be undermining the very idea of a moral dialogue in the first place. But it would be absurd to want to adopt as valid or correct a principle of action—the infliction of arbitrary suffering—such as would impair or jeopardize the very possibility of an ongoing conversation among us. Since such ongoing moral conversation involves sustaining relations of universal respect and egalitarian reciprocity, if we all were to engage in the infliction of unnecessary suffering among ourselves, we would undermine the very basis of our ongoing moral relationship. In this sense, universalizability is not only a *formal procedure* but involves the utopian projection of a way of life as well.

There is an interesting consequence here: when we shift the burden of the moral test in communicative ethics from consensus to the idea of an ongoing moral conversation, we begin to ask not what all would or could agree to as a result of practical discourses to be morally permissible or impermissible, but what would be allowed and perhaps even necessary from the standpoint of continuing and sustaining the practice of the moral conversation among us. The emphasis now is less on *rational agreement,* and more on sustaining those normative practices and moral relationships within which reasoned agreement *as a way of life* can flourish and continue.

II. THE RIGHT AND THE GOOD

Sympathetic critics of communicative ethics have persistently pointed out that this project formulates more a model of *political legitimacy* than one of *moral validity.* To ask whether certain normative institutional arrangements would or could be freely adopted by all as being in their common interests, it is argued, is precisely to continue the central idea of the modern natural-right and social-contract traditions from Locke and Rousseau to Kant.[39] Although many agree that such a principle of rational consent is fundamental to the modern ideas of democratic legitimacy and justice, equally many contest that it can serve as a moral procedure that would be relevant in guiding individual action and judgment.

I have argued above that, on my interpretation, the basic principle of discourse ethics, together with the normative constraints of argumentation, can serve as "substantive tests" of our moral intuitions. Furthermore, if we do not want to jettison the distinction between *contextualization* and *justification* in ethics altogether, we can still preserve the model of a moral conversation taking place under the constraints of discourses as a limiting test for our intuitions of the morally permissible and impermissible. Clearly, then, whether discourse ethics is a model of legitimacy or one of moral validity will depend on what implications and usefulness we think this model has for guiding individual moral action and judgment. Precisely because I think that it can have such implications when interpreted properly, I also want to suggest that, at this stage of the debate, the critics' arguments are not convincing.

Whereas some critics of discourse ethics want to regard it as a program of political legitimacy rather than as one of moral validity, others of a more neo-Aristotelian persuasion argue that no principles of legitimacy can be formulated without presupposing some substantive theory of the good life. Quite in line with Hegel's critique of Kant, these contemporary Aristotelians, and especially communitarian critics of liberalism, maintain that the very idea of a *minimal-universalist* ethic, which would be supposedly "neutral" vis-à-vis the multiplicity of ethical life forms, is untenable. Taylor's objections to communicative ethics have followed this line of argument.[40] I want to name this the issue of the "right" versus the "good."

From the outset, however, we must distinguish between the liberal-communitarian version of this controversy, on the one hand, and the controversy as it applies to communicative ethics, on the other. The first controversy concerns whether liberal principles of justice, as formulated by Rawls and Ronald Dworkin in particular, are "neutral" in the sense of allowing the coexistence of many forms of life in the polity, or whether these principles both presuppose and privilege a specific way of life—let us say an individualist one, centered around the virtues of the rule of law at the expense of solidarity, of privacy at the expense of community, and of justice at the expense of friendship. Whereas liberals continue to aspire to such neutrality, communitarians insist on the illusory quality of their search.[41]

This debate among liberals and communitarians cannot be simply extended to communicative ethics, for the obvious reason that neither Apel nor Habermas has developed a normative theory of justice out of communicative ethics, although communicative ethics has definite institutional implications (cf. section III below). When applied to communicative ethics, the issue of the "right" versus the "good" concerns not so much the alleged neutrality or non-neutrality of principles of justice, as the very basis of the distinction between "justice" and the "good life" within ethical theory itself.

The defense of a deontological outlook in Habermas's theory takes a different form from what we encounter in Rawls's *A Theory of Justice*.[42] Whereas Rawls distinguishes between justice as the basic virtue of a social system and the domain of moral theory at large in which a full theory of the good is at work,[43]

Habermas is committed to the stronger claim that, after the transition to modernity and the destruction of the teleological worldview, moral theory in fact can only be deontological and must focus on questions of justice. Following Kohlberg, he insists that this is not merely a historically contingent evolution, but that "judgments of justice" do indeed constitute the hard core of all moral judgments. Habermas writes: "Such an ethic . . . stylises questions of the good life, and of the good life together into *questions of justice,* in order to render practical questions accessible to cognitive processing by way of this abstraction."[44] It is not that deontology describes a kind of moral theory juxtaposed to a teleological one; for Habermas, deontological judgments about justice and rights claims define the moral domain insofar as we can say anything cognitively meaningful about this.

How can we, in fact, defend the thesis that judgments of justice and right constitute *the moral domain?* I can see two distinct arguments in Habermas's work on this issue. First, Habermas assumes that only judgments of justice possess a clearly discernible formal structure and thus can be studied along an evolutionary model.[45] Judgments concerning the good life are amorphous and do not lend themselves to the same kind of formal study. But of course this observation, far from justifying the restriction of the moral domain to matters of justice, could also lead to the conclusion that one needed to develop a less formalistic ethical theory. This is a view which has been successfully defended by Bernard Williams in his *Ethics and the Limits of Philosophy*[46] and by Taylor in various articles.[47]

Second, Habermas maintains that the evolution of judgments of justice is intimately tied to the evolution of self/other relations. Judgments of justice reflect various conceptions of self/other relations, which is to say that the formation of self-identity and moral judgments concerning justice are intimately linked. This is because justice is the social virtue par excellence.[48]

Again, however, it can be objected that the evolution of self/other relations must also be accompanied by the development of self-understanding and self-evaluation, and if justice is the sum of *other-regarding* virtues par excellence, this still does not preclude the consideration of *self-regarding* virtues and their significance for moral theory. If one understands Habermas's defense of deontological ethics as a claim concerning the *appropriate object domain* of moral theory, then I can see no plausible arguments in favor of such a restrictive view of what moral theory can hope to accomplish.

I concur, then, with communitarian critics of deontology, like Williams, Taylor, and Sandel, only to the extent that viewing justice as the center of morality unnecessarily restricts the domain of moral theory, thus distorting the nature of our moral experiences. But a universalist and communicative model of ethics need not be so strongly construed. Such a theory can be understood as defending a "weak" deontology; this means that valid moral norms must be able to stand the test of discursive justification. Since, however, practical discourses do not theoretically predefine the domain of moral debate and since individuals do not have to abstract from their everyday attachments and beliefs when they begin argumentation, we have to accept that not only matters of justice but those of the good life as well will become thematized in practical discourses. A model of communicative ethics, which views moral theory as a theory of argumentation, need not restrict itself to questions of justice. I see no reason why questions of the good life as well cannot become subject matters of practical discourses. It may very well be that discourses will not yield conceptions of the good life equally acceptable to all; however, there is a difference between assuming a priori that certain matters are questions of the good life and therefore inappropriate matters of moral argument, and assuming that a moral community will establish a line between individual conceptions of the good to be pursued freely and shared norms and values to be cultivated collectively. It is crucial that we view our conceptions of the good life as matters about which intersubjective debate is possible, even if intersubjective consensus, let alone legislation, remains unattainable in these areas. Only through such argumentative processes, however, can we draw the line between issues of justice and of the good life in an epistemically plausible manner, while rendering our conceptions of the good life accessible to moral reflection and moral transformation.

Of course, this is a far weaker result than may be preferred by a strong teleologist like MacIntyre, but it remains for such a teleologist to show that under conditions of modernity one can indeed formulate and defend a univocal conception of the human good. So far Habermas is right: under conditions of modernity and subsequent to the differentiation of the value spheres of science, aesthetics, jurisprudence, religion, and morals, we can no longer formulate an overarching vision of the human good. Indeed, as MacIntyre's definition of the good life—"the life spent in seeking the good life for man"[49]—very well reveals, as moderns we have to live with a variety of goodness. Whether the good life is to be fulfilled as an African famine relief fighter, a Warsaw ghetto resister, a Mother Teresa, or a Rosa Luxemburg, ethical theory cannot prejudge; at the most, modern moral theory provides us with some very general criteria by which to assess our intuitions about the basic validity of certain courses of action and the integrity of certain kinds of values. I regard neither the plurality and variety of goodness with which we have to live in a disenchanted universe nor the loss of certainty in moral theory to be a cause of distress. Under conditions of value differentiation, we have to conceive of the unity of reason not in the image of a homogeneous, transparent glass sphere into which we can fit all our cognitive and value commitments, but more as bits and pieces of dispersed crystals whose contours shine out from under the rubble.

III. ON THE DISTINCTION BETWEEN JUSTICE, MORALITY, AND POLITICS

The neo-Aristotelian and neo-Hegelian insistence on the centrality of a shared ethos or a concrete *Sittlichkeit* in the conceptualization and resolution of moral questions has unavoidable implications in the domain of political action as well. If this shared ethos and this *Sittlichkeit* are viewed not primarily as the unavoidable hermeneutical horizon over and against which moral questions and problems can be formulated, but if they are considered the normative standard in light of which to assess individual actions, then morality becomes subordinated to the collective ethos of a community.

As the young Hegel wistfully wrote of the polis:

As freemen the Greeks and Romans obeyed laws laid down by themselves, obeyed men whom they had themselves appointed to office, waged wars on which they had themselves decided, gave their property, exhausted their passions, and sacrificed their lives by thousands for an end which was their own . . . . In public as in private and domestic life, every individual was a freeman, one who lived by his own laws. The idea (Idee) of his country or of his state was the invisible and higher reality for which he strove, which impelled him to effort; it was the final end of *his* world or in his eyes the final end of *the* world, an end which he found manifested in the realities of his daily life or which he himself cooperated in manifesting and maintaining.[50]

Undoubtedly, this idealization of the Greek polis has to be viewed today more in light of German romantic attitudes toward Greek antiquity than judged as a historically accurate depiction of Greek society. As the mature Hegel himself recognized, the rights of subjective welfare and conscience are among the constituents of the moral freedom of the individual, and the individual's pursuits can never be wholly integrated within a concrete ethical totality. The split of ethical life into the family, civil society, and the state under conditions of modernity also means that potentially the dictates of individual conscience and welfare, on the one hand, and the claims of institutions—family, market, and the state—on the other, can always clash. In a famous passage of *The Philosophy of Right*, Hegel defended the rights of Anabaptists and Quakers to refuse military service in the modern state on the grounds that the modern state is strong enough to allow for dissent without crumbling in the face of it.[51] Both in his theory of representative institutions and even more so in his reflections on war and world history, however, Hegel made the "self-preservation" of the universal the *normative* goal to which morality had to be subordinated. Politics, understood as the sphere governed by the dictates of the self-preservation and welfare of collectivities, is juxtaposed by the mature Hegel to the "abstract cosmopolitanism" and "universalism" of Kantian ethics.

In contemporary debates, one can recognize this Hegelian antecedent in two charges that are frequently levelled against communicative ethics. First, communicative ethics is said to lead to anti-institutionalist and fundamentally anarchistic consequences in political life;[52] second, communicative ethics is said to be "moralistic" to the point of complete utopianism in the domain of politics. Imagine conducting a practical discourse on matters of international relations, state security, or maybe even banking and fiscal policy under the constraints of an ideal speech situation! The strategic and instrumental relation of the parties to each other is so fundamentally constitutive of these macro-institutions of political life that the kind of moralistic utopianism advocated by partisans of discourse ethics, so argues the political realist, would only result in confusion and insecurity. In the domain of politics, realism enlightened by an ethics of responsibility, in the Weberian sense, is the best approach.[53]

In the face of the charge of anti-institutionalism, it must be said that the discourse ethics is not a theory of institutions, although it has institutional implications. Whether we interpret them as principles of legitimacy or as principles of moral validity, neither "D" nor "U" can yield a concrete theory of institutions, but they have institutional implications.[54] Institutionalist thinkers like Herman Lübbe and Niklas Luhmann maintain that upholding any concrete institutions to the demands of such rational consensus would make life impossible. Within the constraints of institutions, decision procedures limited by space/time and scarce resources must be respected. To hope for the rational consensus of all under these circumstances would be to paralyze institutional life to the point of a breakdown.

This objection is justified, but it confuses levels: the discourse theory does not develop a positive model of functioning institutions, which after all will always be subject to space/time constraints as well as to those of scarce resources and personnel. The discourse theory develops a normative and critical criterion by which to judge existing institutional arrangements, insofar as these current arrangements suppress a "generalizable interest." This appeal to the "suppressed generalizable interest" need not be read along Rousseauian lines.[55] In complex societies, it is doubtful that there could be a definition and specification of the suppressed generalizable interest which would meet with the consent of all. But one can use this criterion as a critical yardstick by which to uncover the under-representation, exclusion, and silencing of *certain kinds* of interests. In other words, it is not so much the identification of the "general interest" which is at stake, as the uncovering of those partial interests which represent themselves as if they were general. The assumption is that institutions can function as channels of illegitimate exclusion and silencing, and the task of a critical discourse theory is to develop a moral presumption in favor of the radical democratization of such processes.

What institutionalists neglect is that power is not only a social resource to be distributed, say, like bread or automobiles. It is also a socio-cultural grid of interpretation and communication. Public dialogue is not external to but constitutive of power relations: paraphrasing Nancy Fraser,[56] there are officially recognized vocabularies in which one can press claims; idioms for interpreting and communicating one's needs; established narrative conventions for constructing individual and collective identities; paradigms of argumentation accepted as authoritative in adjudicating conflicting claims; the repertoire of available rhetorical devices, and the like. These constitute the "meta-politics of institutional dialogue" and, as a critical theorist, one is interested in identifying those social relations, power structures, and socio-cultural grids of communication and interpretation at the present which limit the identity of the parties to the dialogue, which set the agenda for what is considered appropriate or inappropriate matter of institutional debate, and which sanctify the speech of some over those of others as being the language of the public.

Certainly this is not the only point of view from which to understand and evaluate institutions; efficiency, stability, and predictability are also relevant criteria. To assume, though, that all discourses of legitimacy are counterproductive or anarchistic is to disguise political authoritarianism as a post-Enlightenment critique of the Enlightenment.

In "Is the Ideal Communication Community a Utopia?"[57] Apel deals extensively with the question of the utopian content and implications of communicative ethics. In his view, it would be utopian in the negative sense of extreme irrelevance to demand that all instances of strategic action, whether individual or collective, be governed by the norms of communicative action aimed at achieving mutual understanding and reciprocity. Nonetheless, it is both a moral and a political question to ask what the limits of individual and collective strategic action are, and to reflect on how to mediate between the requirements of self-interest, on the one hand, and the moral principles of mutual and cooperative understanding, on the other. Once we restate the problem in this fashion, a whole range of interesting considerations begins to emerge. The stark opposition between political utopianism and political realism is to be rejected. Communicative ethics anticipates nonviolent strategies of conflict resolution as well as encourages cooperative and associative methods of problem solving. It is a matter of political imagination as well as collective fantasy to project institutions, practices, and ways of life that promote nonviolent conflict-resolution strategies and associative problem-solving methods. Far from being utopian in the sense of being irrelevant, in a world of complete interdependence among peoples and nations, in which the alternatives are between nonviolent collaboration and nuclear annihilation, communicative ethics may supply our minds with just the right dose of fantasy such as to think beyond the old oppositions of utopia or realism, containment or conflict. Then, as today, we still can say, "*L'imagination au pouvoir*"!

IV. ON THE PROBLEM OF MORAL MOTIVATION AND CHARACTER

A major weakness of cognitive and proceduralist ethical theories since Kant has been their reductionist treatment of the emotional and affective bases of moral judgment and conduct. Twentieth-century neo-Kantian ethical theories have by and large rejected Kant's dualistic moral psychology and his repressive treatment of sensuality and the emotions, while retaining the distinction between "action done from the motive of duty" and "self-regarding actions." Nevertheless, this rejection of the Kantian treatment of the emotional and affective bases of ethics has not meant paying renewed attention to these issues. In recent years, it has been philosophers like Amelie Rorty, Martha Nussbaum, Annette Baier, and Lawrence Blum, on this side of the ocean, and Ursula Wolff, in Germany, as well as feminist moral theorists like Virginia Held and Sara Ruddick, who have developed a rich and significant body of work analyzing moral emotions and moral character.[58] Does the neglect of these issues by advocates of communicative ethics so far point not just to a weak spot in the theory but maybe to a blind spot altogether?

I would like to suggest that very often ethical cognitivism has been confused with ethical rationalism, and the neglect of the affective and emotive bases of ethics is a result of the narrow "rationalism" of most neo-Kantian theories. By 'ethical cognitivism', I understand the view that ethical judgments and principles have a cognitively articulable kernel, that they are neither mere statements of preference nor mere statements of taste, and that they imply validity claims of the following sort: "X is right," where by 'X' is meant a principle of action or a moral judgment, which means "I can justify to you with good grounds why one ought to respect, uphold, agree with X." In this sense, ethical cognitivism is opposed to ethical decisionism that reduces such principles and judgments to an 'I will' that cannot be further questioned. Ethical cognitivism is also opposed to ethical emotivism that conflates statements like 'Child molesting is wrong' with claims like 'I like Häagen-Dazs ice cream'.

By 'ethical rationalism', by contrast, I mean a theoretical position which views *moral judgments* as the core of moral theory, and which neglects that the moral self is not a moral geometer, but an embodied, finite, suffering, and emotive being. We are not born rational but we acquire rationality through contingent processes of socialization and identity formation. Neo-Aristotelians, as well as feminist theorists, have argued in recent years that we are children before we are adults, and that as human children we can only survive and develop within networks of dependence with others, and that these networks of dependence constitute the "moral bonds" that continue to bind us even as moral adults. In Held's words, by ignoring the genealogy of the moral self and the development of the moral person out of a network of dependencies, universalist theorists often view the moral agent as the autonomous, adult male head of household, transacting in the market place or in the polity with like others.[59] Since Rousseau, the demand has been to make *l'homme* whole again, either by making him wholly a *Burgher* or by making him a *citoyen*.

This "rationalist" bias of universalist theories in the Kantian tradition has at least two consequences: first, by ignoring or rather by abstracting away from the embedded, contingent, and finite aspects of human beings, these theories are blind to the variety and richness as well as significance of emotional and moral development. These are viewed as processes preceding the "genealogy" of the adult moral self; they seem to constitute the murky and shadowy background out of which the light of reason emerges.

Second, the neglect of the contingent beginnings of moral personality and character also leads to a distorted vision of certain human relationships and of their *moral texture*. Universalist and proceduralist ethical theorists often confuse the moral ideal of autonomy with the vision of the self "as a mushroom" (Hobbes).[60] Far from being a description of the "moral point of view," state-of-nature abstractions as well as visions of the "original position" are projections of the ideal of moral autonomy which only reflect the experience of the male head of household. But let us proceed cautiously here: I am *not* arguing that a truly universalist articulation of the moral point of view, one that includes the experiences of women and children, mothers and sisters, as well as brothers and fathers, is not possible. The gender blindness of much modern and contemporary universalist theory, in my opinion, does not compromise moral universalism as such, it only shows the need to judge universalism against its own ideals and to force it to make clear its own unjustified assumptions.

Current constructions of the "moral point of view" so lopsidedly privilege either the *homo economicus* or the *homo politicus* that they exclude all familial and other personal relations of dependence from their purview. Although to become an autonomous adult means asserting one's independence vis-à-vis these relations, the process of moral maturation need not be viewed along the fictive model of the nineteenth-century boy who leaves home to become "a self-made man" out "yonder" in the wide, wild world. Moral autonomy can also be understood as growth and change sustained by a network of relationships. Modern and contemporary constructions of the moral point of view are like the distorting lens of a camera: if you focus too badly, the scene in front of you not only becomes murky but can lose contours altogether and become unrecognizable. Likewise, the construction of those moral procedures which are to act as "substantive limits on our intuitions" must not be so out of focus that, by looking through them, we lose the moral contours and moral textures of such personal relationships. Moral vision is a moral virtue, and moral blindness implies not necessarily an evil or unprincipled person, but one who cannot see the moral texture of the situation confronting her.[61] Since the eighteenth-century, ethical rationalism has promoted a form of moral blindness with respect to the moral experience and claims of women, children, and other "nonautonomous others," and has rough handled the moral texture of the personal and the familial.

Communicative ethics, in my view, is a form of ethical cognitivism which has so far been presented as a form of ethical rationalism. Particularly the claim, discussed above, that judgments of justice constitute the hard core of all moral theory is an instance of such rationalism. As I have argued above (cf. section II), even from within the constraints of a discourse theory, this hard distinction between judgments of justice and those of the good life cannot be sustained. Neither can the privileging of moral judgments to the neglect of moral emotions and character. There is a curious inconsistency here. The theory of communicative competence develops a post-Enlightenment conception of reason, viewing it as the contingent acquisition of beings capable of language and action in order to articulate and sustain intersubjective validity claims.[62] The theory of communicative ethics, however, more often than not seems to perpetrate the Enlightenment illusions of the rational moral self as a moral geometer.

If this is so, how can I maintain, as I also did in the first part of this essay, that the model of a universalist moral dialogue, envisaged in accordance with the formal constraints of discourses, can serve as a defensible version of the "moral point of view"? My answer is that the less we view such discourses along the model of public fora or courts of appeal, and the more we understand them as the continuation of *ordinary moral conversations* in which we seek to come to terms with and appreciate the other's point of view, the less do we submit to the distorting lens of procedural universalism. To argue that the counterfactual ideals of reciprocity, equality, and the "gentle force of reason" are implicit in the very structures of communicative action is to argue that the "moral point of view" articulates more precisely those implicit structures of speech and action within which human life unfolds. Each time we say to a child, "But what if other kids pushed you into the sand, how would you feel then?", and each time we say to a mate, to a relative, "But let me see if I understand your point correctly," we are engaging in moral conversations of justification. And if I am correct that our goal is the process of such dialogue, conversation, and mutual understanding,

22

and not consensus, discourse theory can represent the moral point of view without having to invoke the fiction of the *homo economicus* or *homo politicus*. To know how to sustain an ongoing human relationship means to know what it means to be an "I" and a "me," to know that I am an "other" to you and that, likewise, you are an "I" to yourself but an "other" to me. Hegel named this structure that of "reciprocal recognition." Communicative actions are actions through which we sustain such human relationships and through which we practice the reversibility of perspectives implicit in adult human relationships. The development of this capacity for reversing perspectives and the development of the capacity to assume the moral point of view are intimately linked. In the final analysis, universalizability requires us to practice the reversibility of standpoints by extending this to the viewpoint of humanity. Such a capacity is essential to being a good partner in a moral conversation, and is itself furthered by the practice of moral conversation. In conversation, I must know how to listen, I must know how to understand your point of view, I must learn to represent to myself the world and the other as you see them. If I cannot listen, if I cannot understand, and if I cannot represent, the conversation stops, develops into an argument, or maybe never gets started. Discourse ethics projects such moral conversations, in which reciprocal recognition is exercised, onto a utopian community of humankind. But the ability and the willingness of individuals to do so begins with the admonition of the parent to the child: "What if others threw sand to your face or pushed you into the pool, how would you feel then?"

IV. JUDGING IN CONTEXT VERSUS PRINCIPLES RIGORISM

The last issue I would like to treat is the problem of phronesis or practical wisdom concerning particulars. Aristotle saw this as the crowning achievement of moral *paideia* and character. A common criticism of Kantian-type ethical theories is that they substitute an ethical rigorism of principles for the art of moral judgment.[63] Justifiable as this critique is, the discussion concerning moral judgment by either group of contenders in this debate has not advanced very far. The metaphor of the "archer hitting the mark" and the language of moral insight and blindness still dominate many recent treatments of the issue. If we can register a certain impatience with neo-Aristotelians in this respect, we must also admit that distinguishing between "justification" and "contextualization" cannot exempt the discourse theorists from analyzing what it is that we do when we supposedly contextualize moral principles and how this activity is related to the work of judging.[64] Obviously, there is a difference between the contextual application of a cookbook recipe in our kitchens, given the ingredients and the utensils we have, and the so-called "contextualization" of moral principles. If the discourse model is to succeed in acting as "a substantive limit on our intuitions" of the morally permissible and impermissible as well as guiding us in our vision of the morally required, we must be able to suggest how the procedural model of the moral conversation developed so far is involved in the process of moral judgment.

I would like to suggest that, if there are certain moral and cognitive skills involved in reaching perspicacious, appropriate, sensitive, and illuminating judgments, then they may bear a "family resemblance" to the conversational skills and virtues involved in the ongoing practice of moral dialogue and discourse. There is a cardinal requirement of contextual judgment, which most theorists from Kant to Arendt who have developed the problem of judgment have suggested, and this is the ability, in Arendt's words, for "representative thinking":

> The power of judgment rests on a potential agreement with others, and the thinking process which is active in judging something is not, like the thought process of pure reasoning, a dialogue between me and myself, but finds itself always and primarily, even if I am quite alone in making up my mind, in an anticipated communication with others with whom I know I must finally come to some agreement. From this potential agreement judgment derives its specific validity. This means, on the one hand, that such judgment must liberate itself from the "subjective private conditions," that is, from the idiosyncrasies which naturally determine the outlook of each individual in his privacy and are legitimate as long as they are only privately held opinions but which are not fit to enter the market place, and lack all validity in the public realm. And this enlarged way of thinking, which as judgment knows how to transcend its individual limitations, cannot function in strict isolation or solitude; it needs the presence of others "in whose place" it must think, whose perspectives it must take into consideration, and without whom it never has the opportunity to operate at all.[65]

In Kant's discovery of the "enlarged mentality" in his theory of reflective judgment, Arendt saw a model for the kind of intersubjective validity to which judgments had to be submitted in the public realm. Judgment involves the capacity to represent to oneself the multiplicity of viewpoints, the variety of perspectives, the layers of meaning, etc., that constitute a situation. This representational capacity is crucial for the kind of sensitivity to particulars, which most agree is central for good and perspicacious judgment. The more we can identify the different viewpoints from which a situation can be interpreted and construed, the more we will have sensitivity to the particularities of the perspectives involved. Put differently, judgment involves certain "interpretive" and "narrative" skills, which, in turn, entail the capacity for exercising an "enlarged mentality." This "enlarged mentality" can be described precisely as exercising the reversibility of perspectives which the discourse theory enjoins. The link, then, between a universalist model of moral conversation and the exercise of judgment is the capacity for the reversibility of moral perspectives, or what Kant and Arendt name the "enlarged mentality." Let me suggest in more detail why the narrative and interpretive skills involved in judging entail reversibility of moral perspectives.[66]

Moral judgment is crucial in at least three domains of moral interaction: the assessment of one's duties; the assessment of one's specific course of action as fulfilling these duties; and the assessment of one's maxims as embodied, expressed, or revealed in actions. In the assessment of one's duties, we are concerned with recognizing a particular situation as being one that calls forth a specific kind of moral duty. How do we know that this human situation calls forth the duty of honesty, or the virtue of loyalty or of generosity? What is it about a particular human situation that will allow us to identify it as being of a certain kind? I would like to suggest that here moral judgment is concerned first with the identification of human situations and circumstances as being "morally relevant." By 'morally relevant', I mean a situation or circumstance so defined that it would lead us to recognize a prima facie moral duty to act in a certain way. Although it is precisely the mark of one who has good moral judgment that she identifies this as being a situation of loyalty, of generosity, of courage, or of integrity, whatever else such judgment takes, it most certainly must involve the capacity for representative thinking or the reversibility of moral perspectives. Only one who is able imaginatively to represent to herself the variety and meaning of the human perspectives involved in a situation can also identify its moral relevance. For moral relevance in this context means understanding the moral descriptions, expectations, and interpretations that make up the narrative fabric of a human story.

What about the assessment of one's action? Whereas in the case of assessing moral duty we ask, "In what ways is this situation morally relevant for me?", now we are asking, "What is it that I must do to fulfill my duty to act morally once I have recognized it"? In other words, what I do, which course of action I choose, involves some interpretive ability to see my act under various act descriptions and to anticipate how action A may be viewed as one of generosity, whereas action B may be viewed as one of overbearing solicitude. I must have enough moral imagination to know the possible act descriptions or narratives in light of which an act embodying a maxim can be considered. Determining the identity of a moral action entails the exercise of moral imagination which activates our capacity for imagining possible narratives and descriptions in light of which our actions can be understood by others. Again, such moral imagination involves representative thinking, namely, the capacity to take the standpoint of others involved into account and to reason from their point of view.

Finally, let us look at the assessment of one's maxim, or principle of duty. There is often a clash between the moral intentions or principles guiding an agent and the interpretation of this by the world, once they are embodied in actions. In formulating moral intentions and maxims—"I recognize that I must be generous now"; "honesty is always my policy"—we project ourselves, our narrative history, into the world, and we want to be recognized as the doer of such and such. We identify our moral intentions and principles in terms of a narrative of which we ourselves are the author. This narrative also anticipates the meaning that such projection may or will have in the eyes of others. Assessing one's moral intentions and maxims, therefore, requires understanding the narrative history of the self who is the actor; this understanding exhibits both self-knowledge and knowledge of oneself as viewed by others. But, again, the narrative capacity for projecting a course of action, exhibiting and embodying our moral intentions and maxims, requires sensitivity to the many perspectives and interpretations in light of which our narrative and personal story will be construed. Reversibility of perspectives or the capacity for representative thinking are central in such formulations.

What I have suggested so far, then, is that, if we view discourses as a procedural model of conversations in which we exercise reversibility of perspectives either by actually listening to all involved or by representing to ourselves imaginatively the many perspectives of those involved, then this procedure is also an aspect of the skills of moral imagination and moral narrative which good judgment involves, whatever else it might involve. I do not therefore see a gaping gulf between moral intuition guided by an egalitarian and universalist model of moral conversation and the exercise of contextual judgment. Quite to the contrary, the kinds of interpretive and narrative skills I discussed above can also be easily used for "amoral" purposes. The exercise of good judgment can also mean manipulating people—presumably, good administrators, politicians, therapists, social workers, and even teachers of young children all exercise "good judgment," not always for the sake of moral reciprocity or with respect to enhancing the moral integrity of the one about whom such judgment is exercised. Moral judgment alone is not the totality of moral virtue. Here as well we need a "substantive limit" on our intuitions: only judgment guided by the principles of universal moral respect and reciprocity is "good" moral judgment, in the sense of being ethically right. Judgments that are not limited by such principles may be "brilliant," "right on the mark," "perspicacious," but also immoral or amoral. Saying this, however, is not to say that, in a fragmented universe of value, we are never in the situation of juggling moral principles against other political, artistic, and administrative ends. Kantian theories have paid little attention to this "fragmentation of value," and to the consequences that the fine tuning and balancing of our moral commitments with other value commitments have for the conduct of our lives.

Here we reach a frontier where moral theory flows into a larger theory of value and, I would say, into culture at large. Morality is a central domain in the universe of values that define cultures, and it is cultures that supply the motivational patterns and symbolic interpretations in light of which individuals think of narrative histories, project their visions of the good life, interpret their needs, and the like. Moral theory finds this material, so to speak, "given." Thus, moral theory is limited, on the one hand, by the macro-institutions of a polity, politics, administration, and the market, within the limits of which choices concerning justice are made. On the other hand, moral theory is limited by culture, its repertoire of interpretations of the good life, personality, and socialization patterns. These two domains form the larger ethical context of which morality is always but an aspect. Yet the relation between morality and this larger ethical context is not what neo-Aristotelians and the young Hegel would like us to think it is. Under conditions of modernity, as the old Hegel knew, the moral point of view always judges the institutions of which it is a part; and the modern individual exercises autonomy in distancing herself from the given cultural interpretation of social roles, needs, and conceptions of the good life. In this sense, the dispute between discourse theorists and neo-Aristotelians and neo-Hegelians is at heart a dispute about modernity, and about whether modern moral theory since Kant has been an accomplice in the process of the disintegration of personality and the fragmentation of value which are said to be our general condition today.[67] My intervention in this debate intended to show that, judged from within the confines of moral theory, and without delving into this larger issue about modernity and its discontents, the debate between neoAristotelians/neo-Hegelians and discourse theorists is still very much continuing. Although it is too trite to think that all philosophical debates lead to good endings, my own personal sense at this stage is that this confrontation has invigorated rather than weakened contemporary moral theory.

State University of New York/Stony Brook

NOTES

* This text will appear as the "Afterword" to *The Communicative Ethics Controversy,* Seyla Benhabib and Fred Dallmayr, eds. (Cambridge: MIT, forthcoming). I would like to thank my colleagues Kenneth Baynes and Dick Howard for their illuminating criticisms of an earlier draft.

SEYLA BENHABIB

1 See, respectively, *The Moral Point of View*. Abridged ed. (New York: Random House, 1965); *Reason and Morality* (Chicago: University Press, 1978); *Freedom and Reason* (New York: Oxford, 1963); *Generalizability in Ethics. An Essay in the Logic of Ethics with the Rudiments of a System of Moral Philosophy* (New York: Knopf, 1961); and *The Place of Reason in Ethics* (New York: Cambridge, 1953).

2 See *A Theory of Justice* (Cambridge: Harvard, 1971); "Kantian Constructivism in Moral Philosophy: The Dewey Memorial Lectures 1980," *Journal of Philosophy*, LXXVII, 9 (September 1980): 515-572.

3 *Essays on Moral Development, vol. 1*, and *The Psychology of Moral Development, vol. 2* (San Francisco: Harper & Row, 1984).

4 *Revisions* (Notre Dame: University Press, 1983).

5 In *The Basic Works of Aristotle*, Richard McKeon, ed. and trans. (New York: Random House, 1945).

6 For Hegel's early critique of Kant, see "The Spirit of Christianity and its Fate," in *Early Theological Writings*, T. M. Knox, trans. (Philadelphia: Pennsylvania UP, 1971), pp. 182-302; *The Phenomenology of Spirit*, A. V. Miller, trans. (New York: Oxford, 1977), ch. 6, sect. C; *The Philosophy of Right*, T. M. Knox, trans. (New York: Oxford, 1973), #40, Addition, pp. 39ff; *Science of Logic*, A. V. Miller, trans. (New York: Humanities, 1969), pp. 133ff.

7 "Kant, Hegel und das aktuelle Problem der normativen Grundlagen der Moral und Recht," in *Diskurs und Verantwortung* (Frankfurt: Suhrkamp, 1988), pp. 69-103; "Kann der postkantische Standpunkt noch einmal in substantielle Sittlichkeit aufgehoben werden?" in *ibid.*, pp. 103-154.

8 "Moralität und Sittlichkeit. Treffen Hegels Einwände gegen Kant auch auf die Diskursethik zu?" in *Moralität und Sittlichkeit: Das Problem Hegels und die Diskursethik*, Wolfgang Kuhlmann, ed. (Frankfurt: Suhrkamp, 1986), pp. 16-38.

9 Herbert Schnädelbach, "Was ist Neoaristotelismus?" in *Moralität und Sittlichkeit*, pp. 38-64; "What is Neo-Aristotelianism?" in *Praxis International*, VII, 3–4 (October-January 1987): 225-238.

10 For an excellent survey of the various strands of neo-Aristotelianism in contemporary discussions, and in particular for the serious differences between German and Anglophone neo-Aristotelian trends, see Maurizio Passerin d'Entreves, "Aristotle or Burke? Some Comments on H. Schnädelbach's 'What is neo-Aristotelianism?' " in *Praxis International*, VII, 3–4 (October 1987-January 1988): 238-246. I discuss communitarian philosophies in "Autonomy, Modernity and Community. An Exchange Between Communitarianism and Critical Social Theory," in *Zwischenbetrachtungen im Prozess der Aufklärung*, A. Honneth, T. McCarthy, Claus Offe, and Albrect Wellmer, eds. (Frankfurt: Suhrkamp, 1988), pp. 373-395.

11 *Truth and Method* (New York: Seabury, 1975).

12 "Hermeneutics as Practical Philosophy," in *Reason in the Age of Science*, Frederick G. Lawrence, trans. (Cambridge: MIT, 1981), pp. 88-113. I have not included Hannah Arendt's work under this categorization, because in matters of moral as opposed to political philosophy, she remained a Kantian thinker. I deal with some aspects of this admittedly not generally shared interpretation of her work in my "Judgment and the Moral Foundations of Politics in Hannah Arendt's Thought," in *Political Theory*, XVI, 1 (February 1988): 29-53.

13 Cf. "Hegel's Philosophy and its Aftereffects until Today" and "The Heritage of Hegel," in *Reason in the Age of Science*, pp. 21-38 and 38-69; and *Hegel's Dialectic*, P. Christopher Smith, trans. (New Haven: Yale, 1976).

14 Kant, *The Moral Law [Grundelgung der Metaphysik der Sitten]*, H. J. Paton, trans. (London: Hutchinson, 1953), p. 421.

15 T. M. Knox, trans. (Philadelphia: Pennsylvania UP, 1975), pp. 77–78.

28

16 For some recent considerations on Hegel's critique of Kantian ethics, see Jonathan Lear, "Moral Objectivity," in *Objectivity and Cultural Divergence*, S. C. Brown, ed. (New York: Cambridge, 1984), pp. 153-171.

17 The Kantian principle of universalizability does not, of course, dictate any specific content to the principles of justice; rather, it is operative in the construction of the "original position," as the privileged moral vantage point from which to enter into deliberations about matters of justice. Cf. Rawls, *A Theory of Justice*, passim.

18 "Consistency in Action," in *Morality and Universality*, Nelson T. Potter and Mark Timmons, eds. (Dordrecht: Reidel, 1985), pp. 159-186.

19 *Ibid.*, p. 168.

20 *Ibid.*, p. 169.

21 *Ibid.*

22 *Reason and Morality*, pp. 48-129.

23 *After Virtue* (Notre Dame: University Press, 1981), p. 67.

24 Cf. Michael Walzer, "A Critique of Philosophical Conversation," in this volume.

25 "The Methodological Illusions of Modern Political Theory: The Case of Rawls and Habermas," in *Neue Hefte für Philosophie*, XXI (Spring 1982): 47-74.

26 I have developed this argument more extensively in, "Liberal Dialogue vs. A Discourse Theory of Legitimacy," in *Liberalism and the Moral Life*, Nancy Rosenblum, ed. (Cambridge: Harvard, forthcoming).

27 "Diskursethik. Notizen zu einem Begründungsprogramm," in *Moralbewusstsein und kommunikatives Handeln* (Frankfurt: Suhrkamp, 1983), pp. 96–97. English translation in *The Communicative Ethics Controversy*.

28 "The Problem of Philosophical Fundamental Grounding in Light of a Transcendental Pragmatics of Language," in Kenneth Baynes, James Bohman, and Thomas McCarthy, eds. *After Philosophy* (Cambridge: MIT, 1987), p. 277.

29 "Rationality and Relativism. Habermas's Overcoming of Hermeneutics," in John Thompson and David Held, eds. *Habermas: Critical Debates* (Cambridge: MIT, 1982), p. 74.

30 The metastatus of such criticism—whether such social criticism needs to be philosophically grounded in some generally acceptable system of norms or whether it can be exercised immanently by internally appealing to, criticizing, or debunking the norms of a given culture, community, and group—is what sharply divides social theorists like Habermas and Walzer. Given also the large area of substantive agreement among them on the need for the radical-democratic reconstruction of late-capitalist societies, it is worth pursuing what status these metaphilosophical disagreements—immanent or transcendental, relativist or universalist—have. For Walzer, see *Interpretation and Social Criticism* (Cambridge: Harvard, 1987).

31 In "Discourse Ethics," in *The Communicative Ethics Controversy*.

32 *Ibid.*

33 See Barbara Herman's excellent discussion, "The Practice of Moral Judgment," in *Journal of Philosophy*, LXXXII, 8 (August 1985): 414-436.

34 "The Discourse Ethics of Habermas: Critique and Appraisal," in *Thesis Eleven*, X–XI (1984–85): 5-17, here p. 7; see also Wellmer, *Ethik und Dialog. Elemente des moralischen Urteils bei Kant und in der Diskursethik* (Frankfurt: Suhrkamp, 1986); and Höffe, "Kantian Skepticism Toward the Transcendental Ethics of Communication," in *The Communicative Ethics Controversy*.

35 *Ethik und Dialog*, p. 63 [my translation].

36 "The Discourse Ethics of Habermas," p. 8.

37 *Ethik und Dialog*, p. 64.

38 Wellmer also discusses this principle in *ibid.*, pp. 65 ff. His argument is that, since the universal

adherence to this norm would eliminate precisely those cases like the legitimate right to self-defense and justified punishment, the discourse ethics is obliging us to think of what is morally right only in relation to counterfactual ideal conditions and not real ones. Wellmer concludes that the conditions of action suggested by "U" can properly be thought of as those appropriate for a "kingdom of ends." But the fact that in actual life we must always make justified exceptions to such general moral rules has little to do with the question whether our moral theory is able to justify what we intuitively know to be a right moral principle, i.e., in this case, not to inflict unnecessary suffering.

39 Cf. Wellmer, *ibid.*, pp. 121–122; Heller, "The Discourse Ethics of Habermas," p. 9.

40 "Die Motive einer Verfahrensethik," in *Moralität und Sittlichkeit*, pp. 101ff.

41 See the "Introduction" in *Liberalism and Its Critics*, Michael J. Sandel, ed. (New York: University Press, 1984).

42 Part of the discussion which follows has appeared in my "Autonomy, Modernity and Community: An Exchange Between Communitarianism and Critical Social Theory," pp. 377-379.

43 *A Theory of Justice*, pp. 398ff.

44 "A Reply to My Critics," in *Habermas: Critical Debates*, p. 246.

45 "Ego Development and Moral Identity," in *Communication and the Evolution of Society*, Thomas McCarthy, trans. (Boston: Beacon, 1979), pp. 78ff.

46 Cambridge: Harvard, 1985.

47 *Philosophical Papers, vol. 2: Philosophy and the Human Sciences*, (New York: Cambridge, 1985), pp. 23-247.

48 Habermas, "Moralbewusstsein und kommunikatives Handeln," in *Moralbewusstsein und kommunikatives Handeln*, pp. 144ff.

49 *After Virtue*, p. 204.

50 "The Positivity of the Christian Religion," in *Early Theological Writings*, p. 154.

51 *The Philosophy of Right*, #270, Addition, pp. 168–169.

52 Cf. Robert Spaemann, "Die Utopie der Herrschaftsfreiheit," in *Merkur*, ccxcii (August 1972): 735-752; Niklas Luhmann and Habermas, *Theorie der Gesellschaft oder Sozialtechnologie. Was leistet die Systemforschung?* (Frankfurt: Suhrkamp, 1976).

53 Cf. Herman Lübbe's essay in *The Communicative Ethics Controversy*.

54 For a provocative consideration of the implications of discourse theory for a critical theory of new social movements in Western and soviet-type societies, see Andrew Arato and Jean Cohen, *Civil Society and Social Theory* (Cambridge: MIT, forthcoming).

55 I have dealt with the difficulties of the concept of the "suppressed generalizable interest" extensively in *Critique, Norm, and Utopia* (New York: Columbia, 1986), pp. 310ff.

56 "Toward a Discourse Ethic of Solidarity," *Praxis International*, v, 4 (January 1986), p. 425.

57 In *The Communicative Ethics Controversy*.

58 Cf. Rorty, "Community as the Context of Character," pt. four in *Mind in Action. Essays in the Philosophy of Mind* (Boston: Beacon, 1988), pp. 271-347; Nussbaum, *The Fragility of Goodness* (New York: Cambridge, 1986); Annette Baier, "What do Women Want in Moral Theory," *Nous*, xix (1985): 53-63, and "Hume: The Women's Moral Theorist?" in *Women and Moral Theory*, E. F. Kittay and Diana T. Meyers, eds. (New Jersey: Rowman & Littlefield, 1987), 37-56; Blum, *Friendship, Altruism and Morality* (Boston: Routledge & Kegan Paul, 1980); Wolff, *Das Problem des moralischen Sollens* (Berlin: de Gruyter, 1983); Virginia Held, "Feminism and Moral Theory," in *Women and Moral Theory;* Ruddick, *Maternal Thinking* (Boston: Beacon, 1989).

59 "Feminism and Moral Theory," pp. 114ff.

60 I have discussed the gender bias of modern conceptions of autonomy in "The Generalized and the Concrete Other: The Kohlberg-Gilligan Controversy and Moral Theory," in *Women and*

Moral Theory, pp. 154-178; reprinted in Benhabib and Drucilla Cornell, eds. *Feminism as Critique* (Minneapolis: Minnesota UP, 1987), pp. 77-96.

61 Cf. Rorty, "Virtues and the Vicissitudes," in *Mind in Action,* pp. 314ff.

62 See in particular Herbert Schnädelbach's reflections in "Remarks About Rationality and Language," in *The Communicative Ethics Controversy.*

63 For a recent statement of the hermeneutic critique of ethical theory from this point of view, cf. Ronald Beiner, "Do We Need a Philosophical Ethics? Theory, Prudence and the Primacy of Ethos?", *The Philosophical Forum,* xx, 3 (Spring 1989): 230-243.

64 Cf. Habermas, "Moralbewusstsein und kommunikatives Handeln," pp. 187ff, where the work of Norma Haan and Carol Gilligan is discussed; Apel, "Kann der postkantische Standpunkt der Moralität noch einmal in substantielle Sittlichkeit *aufgehoben* werden?", pp. 103ff.

65 "The Crisis in Culture," in *Between Past and Future. Six Exercises in Political Thought* (New York: Meridian, 1961), pp. 21-22.

66 For a more detailed presentation of the following argument, see Benhabib, "Judgment and the Moral Foundations of Politics in Hannah Arendt's Thought," pp. 34ff.

67 I have dealt with the types of responses to modernity among contemporary social theorists in "Autonomy, Modernity and Community. An Exchange Between Communitarianism and Critical Social Theory."

JUSTICE AND SOLIDARITY: ON THE DISCUSSION CONCERNING "STAGE 6"*

JÜRGEN HABERMAS

I. ARE THERE NATURAL MORAL STAGES ON THE POSTCONVENTIONAL LEVEL?

Lawrence Kohlberg has returned, albeit tentatively, to his earlier, temporarily suspended view that at the postconventional level there are two natural stages of moral development. His reason seems plausible enough: the construction of any stage hierarchy requires a normatively designated point of reference from which the developmental process in question can be described retrospectively as a learning process. Stage 5 moral judgment is not a suitable candidate for this reference point, however, since it fails to satisfy the criterion of stable, noncriticizable solutions. With Kohlberg (and in contrast to Bill Puka), I hold the view that cognitivist approaches in the tradition of Piaget necessarily require such a normatively determined end state for learning processes; in contrast to Kohlberg, however, I do not see why the highest moral stage would have to be conceived as a *natural* stage—that is, conceived in the same sense as Stages 1 through 4.

There are intrapsychic structures that correspond to the structural descriptions of natural stages. The same theoretical postulate has to hold for the description of the postconventional level of judgment: we have to assume a psychic representation of the capacity for principled moral judgment. Empirical evidence indicates that this competence manifests itself in a variety of typical strategies for resolving conflicts. These strategies bear a resemblance to familiar moral philosophies: roughly speaking, they resemble either utilitarian approaches, or counterfactual constructs of the Hobbesian type (based on rational egoism), or the deontological theories developed from Kant to John Rawls. Do these differences, which are variations in content, imply the existence of structural differences, and, if so, can the latter be interpreted as natural stages? Two considerations suggest otherwise.

(1) Differences in moral-philosophical orientation are not equivalent, prima

facie or necessarily, to psychologically relevant differences in the level at which systematic explanations are formulated, specifically, differences in the level of reflection of the moral justifications given by Kohlberg's subjects. Different stages of reflection can be demonstrated, for example, in the way concepts of rules are applied. To be sure, all those who judge on the postconventional level are characterized by taking a hypothetical attitude vis-à-vis institutions and maxims of action, as well as by judging and, if necessary, criticizing existing norms that are actually accepted in the light of abstract norms. But not all those on the postconventional level are able to distinguish such fundamental norms from simple rules on the basis that the former are principles. Not all those who in fact keep the logical roles of principles and rules separate[1] can order the variety of principles employed in a system in such a way that it is possible rationally to weigh principles from a still more abstract point of view—the "moral point of view." Not all those who adopt a moral point of view can distinguish their principle of morality from simple principles on the basis of its purely procedural character. And not all those who advance a procedural ethics of this sort adequately distinguish between applying the procedural principle monologically, in a merely virtual way, and conducting an intersubjectively organized test. If one disregards this last step in reflection (to which I shall return later), these stages of reflection do not permit any discrimination between different orientations in moral theory. All autonomous moralities, that is, those which are independent of metaphysical or religious background assumptions, can be expressed in terms of moral principles, and some of them can be understood as procedural ethics. On the other hand, there are also moral theories—such as the critiques of ethical formalism from Hegel to Scheler up to the neo-Aristotelianism of our time[2]—that dispute the notion that higher stages of reflection represent an advance in moral justifications. Puka's objections also tend in this direction.

As far as this discussion is concerned, I certainly do not subscribe to the view that "anything goes." In principle, I hold that it must be possible to decide on firm grounds which moral theory is best able to reconstruct the universal core of our moral intuitions, that is, to reconstruct a "moral point of view" that claims universal validity. Otherwise one would fail from the outset to capture the cognitive meaning of the 'ought' of normative propositions. But from the debate among the philosophers one can also learn that—at least up to this point—the competing approaches do not adequately discriminate between those forms of justification whose structural features might be of psychological relevance. The strategies through which interviewees and philosophers ground their statements may indeed be distinguishable in terms of stages of reflection, but the strategies used by philosophers do not have "hard" status: one could hardly claim for them the status of "natural," intrapsychically represented stages of development. The debate among the moral philosophers cannot be settled with the *psychological* assertion that Kantians have better, structurally privileged access to their moral intuitions than do rule utilitarians or social-contract theorists in the Hobbesian tradition. It was possible to read Kohlberg's original description of the two postconventional stages to mean something of that sort. The debate among cognitivist moral philosophers, however, is concerned with the questions of how and by what conceptual means the *same* intuition potential that becomes accessible to *everyone* with the transition to the postconventional level of autonomous morality can most adequately be explained. It is a question of a better explication of an intuitive knowing, which, at the postconventional level, has already taken on a reflective character and to that extent is from the beginning already oriented to rational reconstructions. This contest can be settled only on the field of philosophical argumentation, not on that of developmental psychology.[3]

(2) From the perspective of cognitive developmental psychology as well, there are several reasons to drop the postulate of natural moral stages at the postconventional level (which is itself presented as "natural"). It follows from the theoretical assumptions themselves that the relationship of psychologist to interviewee in the interview situation has to change as soon as the subject reaches the formal-operational or postconventional level of thought or moral judgment. For at this level the asymmetry that exists in preceding stages between the subject's prereflective efforts and the psychologist's attempt to grasp them reflectively disappears. And with this, the cognitive discrepancy that was originally built into the interview situation disappears. Principled moral judgments are described theoretically as no longer representing merely the prereflective expression or reproduction of an intuitively applied *know-how;* rather, they already represent the beginnings of an explication of this knowing, the rudiments, so to speak, of a moral theory. On the postconventional level, moral judgments are not possible without the first steps in the reconstruction of acquired moral intuitions, and thus they already have in essence the significance of moral-*theoretical* statements. At this level, learning processes can proceed only if the reflective abstraction previously operative as a learning mechanism is sublimated, as it were, into the procedure of rational reconstruction, however ad hoc and unmethodically that procedure may be pursued. The psychologist who proceeds reconstructively, who herself moves within the open horizon of a research process whose results cannot be predicted, can thus treat research subjects who are at the highest level of competence only as participants whose status in the work of scientific reconstruction is (in principle) equal to her own. All those who make moral judgments at the postconventional level, whether they be psychologists, research subjects, or philosophers, are participants in the *joint venture* of finding the most appropriate possible explanation of a core domain of moral intuitions to which they have access under fundamentally equal social-cognitive conditions. If that is so, however, the substantial variations in structure and content in postconven-

tional responses to moral dilemmas and in the various moral-philosophical approaches cannot be attributed to natural stages.[4]

The arguments given in (1) and (2) above do not in any way diminish the value of the new attempt by Kohlberg, Boyd, and Levine to expand and revise the criterion description of Stage 6, although they do place this attempt in a different light. I see their explanation as a stimulating and extraordinarily instructive contribution to a moral-philosophical discussion that, as Kohlberg also believes, will determine the choice of the correct moral theory and thereby decide on the correct description of the normatively designated end state of moral development.[5] I take the insights of Kohlberg the philosopher just as seriously as those of the psychological author of a theory of moral development which is accepted in its fundamentals.

I shall now first compare Kohlberg's explanation of the *moral point of view* with three other contemporary proposals (those of Rawls, T. M. Scanlon, and Karl-Otto Apel and myself), in order to begin by clarifying the strengths and weaknesses of *ideal role taking*. Then I shall discuss Puka's central objection to all the deontological approaches derived from Kant and trace it back to its basic (and correct) insight. What interests me most is Kohlberg's suggestion that one can meet this objection by including the two moral principles of *justice* and *benevolence* under the point of view of "equal respect for all." Finally, I shall try to show that this approach can be carried out more consistently—and thus also defended against further objections along the lines of Puka's—using the means provided by discourse ethics.

II. PROCEDURAL EXPLANATIONS OF THE "MORAL POINT OF VIEW"

Formalist ethics designate a rule or a procedure that establishes how a morally relevant action conflict can be judged impartially—that is, from a moral point of view. The prototype is Kant's categorical imperative, understood not as a maxim of action but as a principle of justification. The requirement that valid maxims of action must be able to serve as the basis for a "general legislation" brings to bear both the concept of autonomy (as the freedom to act in accordance with laws one gives oneself) and the correlative concept that the corresponding actions are capable of general consensus: the point of view of impartial judgment is assured through a universalization principle that designates as valid precisely those norms which *everyone* could *will*. The quantifier 'every' refers to everyone who could possibly be affected (that is, restricted in the scope of his or her action) if the norm in question were generally followed. The predicate 'will' is to be understood in accordance with the Kantian notion of the autonomous will; it means "accept as binding on myself on the basis of my own insight." The fundamental intuition is clear: under the moral point of view, one must be able to test whether a norm or a mode of action could be generally accepted by those affected by it, such that their acceptance would be rationally motivated and hence uncoerced. This intuition has been reformulated in various ways by contemporary philosophers, primarily in such a way, however, that the procedural character of the proposed testing emerges more clearly than it did in Kant. The most illuminating are the following four positions, which with varying accentuations are based on social-contract or role-taking models, that is, on models which construe the process of reaching agreement in counterfactual terms.

(1) The first position makes use of the central thought motif of social-contract theories (as it is commonly found in modern, rational, natural-law theory since Hobbes), namely, the motif, derived from civil law, of a contractual agreement between autonomous legal subjects. Both in terms of the history of philosophy and systematically, this represents a return to *pre*-Kantian concepts. In order to bring the contract motif up to the level of the Kantian intuition, certain conditions must be added. For this reason Rawls places his contracting partners—who are to enjoy equal freedom of choice, to make decisions in a purposively rational way, and to pursue only their own interests (that is, not to be interested in their *mutual* welfare)—in an original position. This original position is defined such that rational egoists must make their agreements under certain restrictions. The conditions that establish this framework, especially the "veil of ignorance" (ignorance of one's own status within the future social intercourse that is to be institutionally regulated), require that enlightened self-interest be reoriented toward the perspective of the universalizability of normatively regarded interests. The orientation that Kant built into practical reason through the moral law, and thereby into the motives of autonomously acting subjects themselves, now comes about only as the result of the interplay of rational egoism with the substantive normative conditions of the original position under which that egoism operates. At first, this seems to relieve the "theory of justice" from the presupposition-laden premises of Kantian moral philosophy. The parties making the contract need only act reasonably, rather than out of duty. To be sure, the theorist still has to check whether his construction of the original position and the principles agreed to in it actually accord with our moral intuitions. His assumptions, which are regulated only by the criterion of "reflective equilibrium," establish "the appropriate initial status quo which insures that the fundamental agreements reached in it are fair."[6] Only the procedure proposed in the theory guarantees the correctness of the results, and does so in such a way that "the parties have no occasion for negotiations in the usual sense."[7] For everyone who puts herself in the role of one of the contracting parties in the original position should be able deductively to reach the same conclusions that Rawls (with some obvious addi-

tional assumptions concerning life plans, primary goods, and so forth) develops in his theory. Like the categorical imperative, each person must be able to apply Rawls's model for testing on his own, *i.e.*, "in his imagination."

These advantages, however, have their reverse side. Rawls has by no means completely captured the fundamental intuition of Kantian ethics in his model of a contractual agreement supplemented by a framework of conditions. According to Kant, everyone can grasp the moral law by virtue of practical reason; the benefits derived from the moral law satisfy strictly *cognitive* demands. According to Rawls, however, in the role of a contracting party in the original position, only instrumental-rational decisions are required. Here the voluntarism of a contract model tailored to the understanding of private-legal subjects is readily apparent; from the point of view of those involved, the fictive agreement in the original position lacks any moment of insight that would point beyond the calculation of their own interests. Moral-practical knowledge is reserved for the theorist, who has to give a plausible explanation of why he constructed the original position in this way rather than another. If, however, the rationality of the rationally motivated acceptance of principles and rules is not guaranteed by the rational decision of the partners to the contract, but rather results only from an interplay, into which they have no subjective insight, with a framework of conditions that are established a priori, then the further question (raised by Ronald Dworkin) arises: How can Rawls motivate his audience to place themselves in the original position at all?[8]

(2) On these and similar grounds, Scanlon[9] proposes a revision that brings the social-contract model closer to Kantian notions. He drops the construct of an original position occupied by rational egoists shrouded with a veil of ignorance, and instead equips each of the contracting parties from the outset with the desire to justify her own practice to all who might possibly be affected, and to justify it so convincingly that the latter could not (whether or not they actually do so) refuse their assent to the universalization of this practice. Scanlon proposes the following test principle for the impartial judgment of moral questions: a mode of action is morally right if it is authorized by any system of universal rules for action which everyone concerned can rationally represent as being the result of an informed, uncoerced, and rational agreement of all concerned.[10] This formulation shifts the meaning of "agreement" from the decision in making a contract toward a rationally motivated understanding (judgmental harmony). With this emphasis on the element of insight or understanding in a process of will formation which is rational from the perspective of the participants themselves, Scanlon also hopes to resolve the question of moral motivation. The desire to justify one's own modes of action to others on the basis of norms that are acceptable or worthy of agreement already provides a motive for avoiding actions that are morally wrong because they cannot be justified.

Through his cognitivistic reinterpretation of the social-contract model, Scanlon revokes the distinction that Rawls undertook to make between the pre-established, transsubjective, justice-compelling perspective of the original position, on the one hand, and the perspective of the participants, limited to subjective rationality, on the other. The moral philosopher is thereby relieved of the task of justifying a priori the normative construction of the original position. At the same time, the parties themselves, with knowledge of all the circumstances, are required to determine what sort of action could not be rejected on good grounds as a general practice by anyone within the sphere of those concerned— given that all participants are interested in an uncoerced, rationally motivated agreement. This procedure can no longer be applied in a strictly monological manner, as could Rawls's. It is no longer enough for me, in the role of a party in the original position, to determine what admits of universal approval from the perspective of that role (thus, from my perspective); rather, the revised contract model requires me to examine what everyone would, from his own perspective, judge to be capable of universal approval if he were oriented to the goal of reaching an agreement. The additional burden on the subject making the moral judgment is shown by the fact that she must at least imagine, that is, perform virtually, the intersubjective execution of a procedure that cannot be applied monologically at all. According to Scanlon, principles and rules find *general* acceptance only when *all* can be convinced that *each* person could give his well-founded assent from his own perspective: "To believe that a principle is morally correct one must believe that it is one which all could reasonably agree to. . . . But my belief that this is the case may often be distorted by a tendency to take its advantage to me more seriously than its possible costs to others. For this reason, the idea of 'putting myself in another's place' is a useful corrective device."[11]

(3) It is no accident that at this point Scanlon has to borrow from another model. G. H. Mead's fundamental notion that one participant in a social interaction takes the perspective of the other is not a "useful corrective" to the social-contract model; it is rather the alternative that presents itself as soon as it becomes clear that a consistent attempt to reach the level of the fundamental intuition of Kantian ethics under post-Kantian premises (that is, having dispensed with the two-world doctrine) exceeds the capacity of the fundamental notions of the contract model. Thus, Kohlberg explains the moral point of view of impartially judging moral conflicts with the help of the concept of ideal role taking, which Mead (1934) had already used as the correlate of *universal discourse* in reformulating the fundamental idea of Kantian ethics within the framework of his theory of action.[12] Kohlberg develops this concept through a series of steps, beginning with simple interactions between at least two persons engaged in communicative action.

Ego must first fulfill the condition of sympathetic empathy with the situation of Alter; he must actually identify with her in order to be able to take the precise perspective from which Alter could bring her expectations, interests, value orientations, and so forth to bear in the case of a moral conflict. Then Ego must be able to assume that the project of perspective taking is not one-sided but reciprocal. Alter is expected to take Ego's perspective in the same way, so that the contested mode of action can be perceived and thematized in *mutual agreement,* taking into consideration the interests affected on both sides. In more complex circumstances, this dyadic relationship must be extended to an interlocking of perspectives among members of a particular group. Only under this social-cognitive presupposition can each person give equal weight to the interests of the others when it comes to judging whether a general practice could be accepted by each member on good grounds, in the same way that I have accepted it. Finally, Ego must satisfy the condition of universalizability of his reflections, which initially are internal to the group and refer to simple interactions: Ego must disregard the concrete circumstances of a particular interaction and examine abstractly whether a *general* practice could be accepted without constraint under comparable circumstances by each of those affected, from the perspective of her own interests. This requires a universal interchangeability of the perspectives of all concerned; Ego must be able to imagine how each person would put herself in the place of every other person.

What was sympathetic empathy and identification under the concrete initial conditions is sublimated at this level to accomplishments that are purely cognitive: on the one hand, *understanding* for the claims of others which result in each case from particular interest positions; on the other hand, *consciousness* of a prior solidarity of all concerned which is objectively grounded through socialization. At this level of abstraction, sensitivity to individual claims must be detached from contingent personal ties (and identities), just as the feeling of solidarity must be detached from contingent social ties (and collectivities).

All the same, the procedure of ideal role taking retains a strong emotivistic tinge from its origins in social psychology. Rawls made a procedure taken from the social-contract model the basis for judging the capacity of norms to achieve consensus; we have seen that the element of insight then became less significant in comparison to that of decision, specifically, that of calculated agreement among parties capable of deciding. If, instead, a procedure in accordance with the role-taking model is made the basis of this test, practical reason is relegated to a secondary position in a similar way—this time in comparison to empathy, that is, the intuitive understanding that parties capable of empathy bring to one another's situation. The discursive character of rational will formation, which can end in intersubjective recognition of criticizable validity claims only if attitudes are changed through arguments, is here neglected in favor of achievements of empathic understanding. The presentation by Kohlberg, Boyd, and Levine demonstrates a tendency (which is in any case suggested by the passages from the interview with Joan[13]) to view "dialogue" not as a form of argumentation but as a method from group dynamics for sharpening the capacity for empathy and strengthening social ties. Where this tendency becomes dominant, however, it is to the detriment of the purely cognitive meaning of ideal role taking as a procedure for the impartial judgment of moral states of affairs.

(4) To counter this emotivistic bias, one can, as Apel and I have suggested, interpret the role-taking model from the outset as a discourse model. There is already adequate support for this interpretation in Mead, who introduces ideal role taking as the quintessential social-cognitive presupposition of a universal discourse that extends beyond all purely local states of affairs and traditional arrangements.[14] Mead begins with the idea that what the categorical imperative was supposed to achieve can be accomplished through the projection of a process of will formation under the idealized conditions of a *universal discourse*. The subject making a moral judgment cannot test for himself alone whether a contested mode of action as a general practice would lie within the common interest; he can do so only socially, with all the rest of those concerned. When one recognizes (with Scanlon) that the goal of this sort of inclusive process of reaching understanding, namely, unconstrained agreement, can be attained only through the vehicle of good reasons, the reflective character of that universal discourse emerges more sharply than in Mead: discourse must be thought of not only as a net of communicative action which takes in all those potentially affected, but as a reflective form of communicative action—in fact, as argumentation.

With this, Mead's construction loses the status of a mere projection: in every argumentation that is actually carried out, *the participants themselves* cannot avoid making such a projection. In argumentation, the participants have to make the pragmatic presupposition that in principle all those affected participate as free and equal members in a cooperative search for truth in which only the force of the better argument may hold sway.[15] The principle of discourse ethics—that only those norms may claim validity which could find acceptance by all those concerned as participants in a practical discourse—is based on this universal-pragmatic state of affairs. It is those idealizing presuppositions, which everyone who engages seriously in argumentation must in fact make, which enable discourse to play the role of a procedure that explains the moral point of view. Practical discourse can be understood as a process of reaching agreement which, through its form, that is, solely on the basis of unavoidable general presuppositions of argumentation, constrains all participants at the same time to ideal role taking. It transforms ideal role taking, which in Kohlberg was something to be anticipated privately and in isolation, into a public event, something practiced, ideally, by all together.

Of course, when it is a question of examining norms with a genuinely universal domain of validity, that is, moral norms in the strict sense, this idea is purely regulative. By the standard of this idea, discourses conducted as advocacy, or internalized—set in the "inner life of the psyche"—can serve only as substitutes. Arguments played out in "the internal forum," however, are not equivalents for real discourses that have not been carried out; they are subject to the proviso of being merely virtual events that, in specific circumstances, can simulate a procedure that cannot be carried out. This reservation becomes more acceptable, however, given that discourses which are actually carried out also stand under limitations of time and space and social conditions that permit only an approximate fulfillment of the presuppositions, usually made counterfactually, of argumentation.[16]

III. IS THERE A PLACE FOR THE GOOD IN THE THEORY OF THE JUST?

From the beginning, deontological approaches in ethics have aroused the suspicion that they are on the wrong track in taking as their point of departure the question of the conditions of impartial moral judgment—and the question of the meaning of the moral point of view that assures impartiality. In particular, they arouse the suspicion that, under the compulsion to assimilate practical questions to scientific ones, they narrow the concept of morality to questions of justice and distort it by seeing it from the specifically modern perspective of bourgeois commerce carried on by subjects under civil law. There are several aspects to this critique. In part, it amounts to a defense of classical ethical theories that emphasize the primacy of questions of the good life, the successful conduct of one's individual life, and harmonious forms of social life—character and *ethos*. In part, it is concerned with defending motifs of modern utilitarianism, which aims at the welfare of all and subsumes the rights of individuals under the notion of distributable goods. In part, it has as its goal a defense of an ethics of compassion and love, which accord a privileged position to altruistic concern for the welfare of a fellow human being in need of help. It is always a question of welfare and concrete goods—whether of the community, the greatest number, or the weak individual; the appeal is to a dimension of happiness and suffering which does not seem to be touched at all by the deontological question of the intersubjectively accepted justification of norms and modes of action. Is it not the case that one simply passes over the question of morally right action and the good life when one focuses, as Kant did, on the phenomenon of the "ought," *i.e.*, on the obligatory character of commands—and thus on a question that is detached from all concrete life circumstances, all interpersonal relationships and identities, namely, the question of the grounds for the validity of maxims of action?

This philosophers' debate is currently being repeated on the field of a theory of moral development which shows its architect, Kohlberg, to be a student of Kant. The debate has been further dramatized by Carol Gilligan's proposal to oppose an ethics of care to the ethics of justice. Puka has already reduced this proposal to its proper proportions, but his own modifications of the theory point in the same direction. Kohlberg responds to this critique with an attempt to bring the two aspects of justice and concern for the welfare of the other together within the framework of his theory, which is set up deontologically as before. To evaluate the status of this interesting suggestion, which does in fact go beyond Kant, we will have to make clear in which controversies Kohlberg does *not* get involved—and in which he does not need to get involved.

(a) At first sight, Kohlberg's bringing together of justice and benevolence is reminiscent of Hegel's critique of Kant and of all the attempts to mediate between classical and modern approaches in ethics. Hegel already saw that the unity of the fundamental moral phenomenon is missed when one opposes the principle of justice to the principle of the general welfare, or to a concern for the welfare of one's fellow man—that is, when one keeps these two aspects separate. He grounds his concept of *Sittlichkeit* (ethical life) with a critique of two-sided conceptions that are mirror images of each other. On the one hand, he takes issue with the abstract universalism of justice as expressed in modern individualistic approaches, in rational natural law as well as in Kant's ethics of duty. On the other hand, he rejects just as firmly the particularism of concrete welfare, as expressed in Aristotle's ethics of the polis or in the Thomistic ethics of goods. Kohlberg takes up this fundamental intention of Hegel's. He does so, however, on the basis of the strictly postmetaphysical premise that evaluative questions concerning the good life must remain separate from normative questions concerning a just communal life—because, unlike the latter questions, the former are not capable of being formulated theoretically, that is, they are not accessible to rational discussion that claims to be universally binding. Kohlberg proposes to investigate whether limiting rationally decidable moral problems to questions of justice is too restrictive and might exclude elements that have nothing to do with the evaluation of concrete wholes, whether they be life histories and persons, or forms of life and collectivities.

(b) In another respect, Kohlberg's inclusion of benevolence is reminiscent of the debate between utilitarian and deontological approaches which is again current. Here too, however, Kohlberg does not take a mediating position. The procedure of ideal role taking goes beyond the boundaries of an ethics of conviction which excludes all orientation to consequences as inadmissible in moral justifications. Ideal role taking is intended, rather, to guarantee that a well-founded consensus is made dependent on consideration of the consequences that a contested general practice would have for the satisfaction of the interests of all concerned. This by no means signifies, however, a swing to a purely consequentialist view. As is evident in his treatment of the lifeboat dilemma, Kohlberg agrees with Dworkin and Rawls that the fundamental freedom and rights of individuals may not be restricted by considerations of overall utility. Thus, what Kohlberg has in mind is not limiting the principle of justice for the sake of the principle of utility, but rather the question whether the justice principle can be interpreted in the sense of equal respect for the integrity of each person, such that aspects of caring and concrete welfare are brought to light which only seem at first to be in competition with the aspect of justice.

(c) Finally, it may seem as though Kohlberg wants to extend a moral theory that was initially limited to questions of the right in such a way that the right can be mediated or integrated with morality—understood now in a broader sense, whether it be Aristotelian or utilitarian or Christian. Puka seems to be proceeding on this basis. Most of the examples he uses concern conflicts of rights in the narrower sense. At one point Puka speaks of rights as capable of being enforced. Even if we disregard this obvious confusion of moral rights with enforceable positive rights, the choice of examples suggests the implicit presupposition that questions of justice are identical to questions of rights. Puka is concerned with the boundaries of a moral theory that concentrates on questions of harmonizing and equally distributing subjective rights, thus with the question of how the autonomous will of each person can coexist with each person's freedom under universal laws. But this is precisely how the supreme principle of Kant's theory of law (*Rechtslehre*) reads, not his moral principle. If I am correct, this view is based on at least three misconceptions.

First of all, just principles and rules, that is, those which can be grounded through procedural ethics, can, especially when it is a question of the institutional regulation of "external life circumstances" in modern societies, naturally assume the form of negative freedoms and subjective rights as well—prototypically in the domain of basic rights and property rights. But justifications through procedural ethics apply just as naturally to principles of distributive justice, for instance, which are completely different from one another, depending on the structure of the action domain in need of regulation (the household, etc.); or to principles of care and aid to those in need of help; to conventions of self-restraint, consideration, truthfulness, the duty to enlighten others, and so on.

Secondly, one must understand that deontological approaches separate questions of justification from questions of application. The abstraction from contexts of the lifeworld, from the concrete circumstances of the individual case, that is complained about is in fact unavoidable in answering the question whether contested norms and modes of action are morally right and deserve the intersubjective approval of those concerned. In the impartial application of well-grounded principles and rules to the individual case, however, this abstraction must be reversed. It is in the light of concrete circumstances and particular constellations of interests that valid principles must be weighed against one another, and exceptions to accepted rules justified. There is no other way to satisfy the principle that like is to be treated in like manner and unlike in unlike manner.

Finally, however, moral commands can go beyond what is commanded by positive law, even, in fact, when legal relationships in turn are based on morally justified fundamental norms. This is due to the complementary relationship of positive law and morality, which I cannot discuss in more detail here. Cases such as Puka mentions, in which someone makes use of his subjective freedoms in a way that is legally incontrovertible but morally questionable (e.g., destroys his resources—burns his property, blows his brains out—without regard for what his resources could do for others), find a satisfactory resolution when one takes this complementary relationship into consideration, if resolution has not already been found from the perspective of equality of the rights involved.

There is one idea in the spectrum of objections raised by Puka that Kohlberg certainly has to take seriously. In modern doctrines of natural law and in Kantian ethics (according to one interpretation), the autonomous morality of the modern period has been conceived individualistically and in a one-sided manner. In this respect, deontological approaches have not been carried out radically enough. They are still caught up in the context of their origin and thus in bourgeois ideology, insofar as they begin with isolated, private, autonomous, self-possessing subjects who treat themselves like property—and not with relationships of mutual recognition in which subjects acquire and assert their freedom intersubjectively.

The concept of ideal role taking borrowed from Mead provides Kohlberg with a basis from which he can reach the level of Kant's fundamental intuition without possessive-individualistic abridgements. Mead himself already appropriated Kant in this way: "The universality of our judgments, upon which Kant places so much stress, is a universality that arises from the fact that we take the attitude of the entire community, of all rational beings." He then adds the characteristic thesis: "We are what we are through our relationship to others. Inevitably, then, our [morally justified] end must be a social end, both from the standpoint of its content and from the point of view of form. Sociality gives the universality of ethical judgments and lies back of the popular statement that the voice of all is the universal voice; that is, everyone who can rationally appreciate the situation agrees [to a morally justified end]."[17] Valid norms derive their obligatory character from the fact that they embody a universalizable interest, and the autonomy and welfare of individuals as well as the integration and welfare of the social collective are at stake in the maintenance of this interest. I gather that these thoughts lie behind Kohlberg's attempt to bring to bear the principle of concern for the welfare of the other in addition to the principle of justice. Viewed against the background of the contemporary discussion in moral philosophy, this program, which is not to be confused with the projects discussed under (a) to (c) above, is pioneering. I do not find the way the program is carried out, however, to be as convincing as its intention.

Kohlberg sets forth essentially three trains of thought. First, he relativizes the idea of justice derived from the moral point of view of impartial judgment of conflicts; this idea is downgraded to the status of a principle and supplemented by a second principle, the principle of benevolence. That principle, of doing good and avoiding doing harm, refers equally to individual and general welfare. On the level of attitude, this principle corresponds to concern for the welfare of the other, compassion, love of one's fellow man, and willingness to help in the broadest sense, but also to community spirit. The two principles stand in a relationship of tension to one another, but are nevertheless thought to be derivable from a common higher principle.

In a second step, Kohlberg grounds justice and benevolence in a further principle, one which since Kant has been considered the equivalent of the principle of equal treatment and thus of the justice principle. This is the principle of equal respect for the integrity or dignity of each person, which corresponds to the formula of the categorical imperative whereby each person is to be treated as an end in herself. Kohlberg establishes the connection to the principle of benevolence by an equivocation in the concept of the person. Equal respect for each person *in general* as a subject capable of autonomous action means equal treatment; however, equal respect for each person *as an individual* subject individuated through a life history can mean something rather different from equal treatment: instead of protection of the person as a self-determining being, it can mean support for the person as a self-realizing being. In this second variant the meaning of "respect" is quietly altered; strictly speaking, it does not follow from *respect* (*Achtung*) for the integrity of a vulnerable person that one *cares* for her well-being. Thus, Kohlberg cannot accommodate the principle of benevolence under the principle of equal respect for every person without an implicit shift in meaning. A further difficulty is more serious. The principle of equal respect, like the principle of equal treatment in general, refers only to individuals. A principle of benevolence "derived" from it might on that account be able to ground concern for the welfare of one's fellow man (or for one's own welfare), but it could not ground concern for the common welfare, and thus not the corresponding sense of community.

In a third step, Kohlberg has to show how both principles arise from the procedure of ideal role taking. Up to this point, the concepts of "the moral point of view'' and ''justice'' have had equivalent meanings. Thus, it was the meaning of justice which was explained with the help of ideal role taking. Now Kohlberg makes room for the meaning of benevolence by analyzing the concept of ideal role taking into three moments, as previously indicated. Perspective taking is linked to two further operations: on the one hand, to empathy or identification with the respective other, and, on the other hand, to universalization. Then sympathy can be brought into at least an associative connection with concern for the welfare of the other, and universalization into a similar connection with justice. This argument, too, which is only suggested, loses much of its power when one reflects that, with the transition to universalized, completely reversible perspective taking, not much more is left of a sympathy that is initially directed to concrete reference persons than a purely cognitive feat of understanding.[18]

IV. THE DISCOURSE-ETHICS ALTERNATIVE

Kohlberg formulates a correct intuition with the wrong concepts when he ascribes to the principle of equal respect for every person an expanded meaning that includes both equal treatment and benevolence. His intuition can be explicated through Mead's central insight that persons, as subjects capable of speech and action, can be individuated only via the route of socialization. They are formed as individuals only by growing into a speech community and thus into an intersubjectively shared lifeworld. In these formative processes, the identity of the individual and that of the collectivity to which she belongs arise and are maintained with equal primacy. The farther individuation progresses, the more the individual subject is caught up in an ever denser and at the same time ever more subtle network of reciprocal dependencies and explicit needs for protection. Thus, the person forms an inner center only to the extent to which she simultaneously externalizes herself in communicatively produced interpersonal relationships. This explains the danger to, and the chronic susceptibility of, a vulnerable identity. Furthermore, moralities are designed to shelter this vulnerable identity. Because moralities are supposed to compensate for the vulnerability of living creatures who through socialization are individuated in such a way that they can never assert their identity for themselves alone, the integrity of individuals cannot be preserved without the integrity of the lifeworld which makes possible their shared interpersonal relationships and relations of mutual recognition. Kohlberg is trying to develop this *double* aspect when he emphasizes the intersubjective conditions for the maintenance of individual integrity. Moral provisions for the protection of individual identity cannot safeguard the integrity of individual persons without at the same time safeguarding the vitally necessary web of relationships of mutual recognition in which individuals can stabilize their fragile identities only mutually and simultaneously with the identity of their group.

Kohlberg cannot do justice to this fundamental pragmatist insight, however, by *overextending* the concept of equal respect for the dignity of each person and then stopping halfway, *i.e.*, at a notion of benevolence toward one's fellow man (a direction in which Joan's partiality to the use of communicative means, with its overtones of group therapy, does point, albeit misleadingly). From the perspective of communication theory, there emerges instead a close connection between concern for the welfare of one's fellow man and interest in the general welfare: the identity of the group is reproduced through intact relationships of mutual recognition. Thus, the perspective complementing that of equal treatment of individuals is not benevolence but solidarity. This principle is rooted in the realization that each person must take responsibility for the other because as consociates all must have an interest in the integrity of their shared life context in the same way. Justice conceived deontologically requires solidarity as its reverse side. It is a question not so much of two moments that supplement each other as of two aspects of the same thing. Every autonomous morality has to serve two purposes at once: it brings to bear the inviolability of socialized individuals by requiring equal treatment and thereby equal respect for the dignity of each one; and it protects intersubjective relationships of mutual recognition requiring solidarity of individual members of a community, in which they have been socialized. *Justice* concerns the equal freedoms of unique and self-determining individuals, while *solidarity* concerns the welfare of consociates who are intimately linked in an intersubjectively shared form of life—and thus also to the maintenance of the integrity of this form of life itself. Moral norms cannot protect one without the other: they cannot protect the equal rights and freedoms of the individual without protecting the welfare of one's fellow man and of the community to which the individuals belong.

As a component of a universalistic morality, of course, solidarity loses its merely particular meaning, in which it is limited to the internal relationships of a collectivity that is ethnocentrically isolated from other groups—that character of forced willingness to sacrifice oneself for a collective system of self-assertion which is always present in premodern forms of solidarity. The formula, "Command us, Führer, we will follow you," goes perfectly with the formula, "All for one and one for all"—as we saw in the posters of Nazi Germany in my youth—because fellowship is entwined with followership in every traditionalist sense of solidarity. Justice conceived in postconventional terms can converge with solidarity as its reverse side only when solidarity has been transformed in the light of the idea of a general discursive will formation. To be sure, the fundamental notions of equal treatment, solidarity, and the general welfare, which are central to *all* moralities, are (even in premodern societies) built into the conditions of symmetry and the expectations of reciprocity characteristic of every ordinary communicative practice, and, indeed, in the form of universal and necessary pragmatic presuppositions of communicative action. Without these idealizing presuppositions, no one, no matter how repressive the social structures under which she lives, can act with an orientation to reaching understanding. The ideas of justice and solidarity are present above all in the mutual recognition of responsible subjects who orient their actions to validity claims. But *of themselves* these normative obligations do not extend beyond the boundaries of a concrete lifeworld of family, tribe, city, or nation. These limits can be broken through only in discourse, to the extent that the latter is institutionalized in modern societies. Arguments extend per se beyond particular lifeworlds, for in the pragmatic presuppositions of argumentation, the normative content of the presuppositions of communicative action is extended—in universalized, abstract form and without limitations—to an ideal communication community (as Apel, following C. S. Peirce, calls it) that includes all subjects capable of speech and action.

For this reason discourse ethics, which derives the contents of a universalistic morality from the general presuppositions of argumentation,[19] can also do justice to the common root of morality. Because discourses are a reflective form of understanding-oriented action that, so to speak, sit on top of the latter, their central perspective on moral compensation for the deepseated weakness of vulnerable individuals can be derived from the very medium of linguistically mediated interactions to which socialized individuals owe that vulnerability. The pragmatic features of discourse make possible a discerning will formation whereby the interests of each individual can be taken into account without destroying the social bonds that link each individual with all others. For as a participant in the practical discourses each person is on her own and yet joined in an association that is objectively universal. In this respect the role-taking model used in discourse is not equivalent to the social-contract model. Procedural ethics is one-sided as long as the idea of an agreement between subjects who are originally isolated is not replaced by the idea of a rational will formation taking place within a lifeworld of socialized subjects. Both in its argumentative methods and its communicative presuppositions, the procedure of discourse has reference to an existential pre-understanding among participants regarding the most universal structures of a lifeworld that has been shared intersubjectively from the beginning. Even this procedure of discursive will formation can seduce us into the one-sided interpretation that the universalizability of contested interests guarantees only the equal treatment of all concerned. That interpretation overlooks the fact that every requirement of universalization must remain powerless unless there also arises, from membership in an ideal communication community, a consciousness of irrevocable solidarity, the certainty of intimate relatedness in a shared life context.

Justice is inconceivable without at least an element of reconciliation. Even in the cosmopolitan ideas of the close of the eighteenth century, the archaic bonding energies of kinship were not extinguished but only refined into solidarity with everything wearing a human face. *"All* men become brothers," Schiller could say in his "Ode to Joy." This double aspect also characterizes the communicative form of practical discourse: the bonds of social integration remain intact despite the fact that the agreement required of all transcends the bounds of every natural community. On the one hand, every single participant in argumentation remains with her "yes" and "no" a court of final appeal; no one can replace her in her role of one who pronounces on criticizable claims to validity. On the other hand, even those interpretations in which the individual identifies needs that are most peculiarly her own are open to a revision process in which *all* participate; the social nature of that which is most individual shows itself here and in the mutuality of a consensus that adds the reciprocity of mutual recognition to the sum of individual voices. Both are accurate: without unrestricted individual freedom to take a position on normative validity claims, the agreement that is actually reached could not be truly universal; but without the empathy of each person in the situation for everyone else, which is derived from solidarity, no resolution capable of consensus could be found. Because argumentation merely extends, using reflective means, action that is oriented to reaching understanding, the consciousness that the egocentric perspective is not something primary, but rather something socially produced, does not disappear. Thus, the procedure of discursive will formation takes account of the inner connection of the two aspects: the autonomy of unique individuals and their prior embeddedness in intersubjectively shared forms of life.

This does not amount to a reconciliation of Kant with Aristotle. When it opposes one-sided individualistic conceptions and emphasizes solidarity as the reverse side of justice, discourse ethics draws only on the modern concept of justice. The structural aspects of the "good life," which from the perspective of communicative socialization in *general* are *universally* distinguishable from the concrete totalities of particular forms of life (and life histories), are included in its conception. Discourse ethics stands under the premises of postmetaphysical thought and cannot incorporate the full meaning of what classical ethical theories once conceived as cosmic justice or justice in terms of salvation. The solidarity on which discourse ethics builds remains within the bounds of earthly justice.

Kohlberg wants to dispense with metaphysics in this way—and yet, so it seems, he does not want to pay the full price for doing so. Joan's responses to the Korean dilemma (which has the same structure as the dilemma that arises in the lifeboat where only two of the three passengers have genuine chances of survival) provide Kohlberg with an opportunity to bring into play not only the principle of benevolence but also dialogue considered as a means whose end is concern for one's fellow man. It seems to me that this dilemma is better suited to clarifying the limits of discourse ethics. No one would deny that the leader of a commando group who had to send one of its men on a suicide mission in order to preserve some chance of survival for the rest finds himself in a moral dilemma. But the dilemma can be "resolved" only through a sacrifice that cannot be morally demanded of anyone—and thus could only be made voluntarily. Supererogatory actions—the term itself indicates as much—cannot be justified as moral obligations; and for this reason no discourse, insofar as it serves as a justification procedure, will be of any use. The only thing one can rationally justify is the refusal, on moral grounds, to admit a utilitarian resolution of the dilemma, which would adduce as its proof the sum total of utilities.

It becomes clear that supererogatory action alternatives that cannot be grounded morally are involved when one looks at the dilemma as a demand for principles and rules that could be applied in a case of this kind. In this regard there is no interest that could be universalized, and there is no corresponding norm to which everyone who could not exclude a priori the possibility of ever being in a comparable situation would have to assent.[20] Thus, this dilemma allows us to clarify something else as well. It is possible for the supererogatory character of the dilemma to remain hidden at first only if one understands the dilemma in a different way, namely, not as a heuristic stimulus to the grounding of norms but as an application problem, so that, in other words, presumably valid principles or rules are to be applied to a given cause. The postconventional level of moral judgment is distinguished, among other things, by the fact that here the two kinds of problems are strictly separate. Procedural ethical theories, in particular, first set themselves the task of indicating a procedure through which norms and modes of action can be *rationally grounded* or criticized, as the case may be. Because they must deal with this task separately, the impartial *application* of valid principles and rules arises only as a *subsequent problem*.[21]

On the conventional level, problems of justification and problems of application have not yet become separate, because here the substantive morality of a traditional milieu has not yet been called into question in a fundamental way; the conventional morality forms a horizon within which the various concrete duties and norms still refer to corresponding typical roles and situations. At this level, the case narrative of an action conflict that poses a dilemma is an appropriate instrument for data collection. Using the narrative of the individual case as a basis, the interviewee can feel her way forward in two directions: on the one side, to norms and duties; on the other, to typical situations of application, for the two still form an internal connection. This context of morality is disrupted by the postconventional shift in focus to a reflectively devalued social world that has been stripped of its naturalness. Interviewees who operate at the level of principled moral judgment have to analyze a dilemma like this from two different points of view: first, in the role of the legislator who examines impartially what mode of action, viewed as a general practice, deserves acceptance; second, in the role of the judge who must impartially apply valid principles and rules to a concrete case. In the requirement that the judgment be impartial, practical reason gets a hearing both times, but the moral point of view comes into play in a different way in each of the two functions—as, moreover, does solidarity. Solidarity with what is uniquely particular to the individual case is demanded of the judge, who must first find the criteria by which like things can be treated in like manner, and it is demanded of her to a higher degree than it is of the legislator, who may not ignore the "no" of suppressed needs.

Like the moral philosophers from whom he takes his orientation, Kohlberg's interest is directed primarily to problems of justification. For autonomous moralities, problems of application form a second, broader domain of questions for which developmental psychology might very well have to develop different instruments of data collection and analysis.

University of Frankfurt

translated by Shierry Weber Nicholsen

* This essay appears with the kind permission of MIT Press from *The Moral Domain*. Two essays to which Habermas refers in this article will appear in the same volume: Bill Puka, "The Majesty and Mystery of Stage 6," and Lawrence Kohlberg, Dwight Boyd, and Charles Levine, "Stage 6 Revisited."

NOTES

1 Following Ronald Dworkin, R. Alexy [*Theorie der Grundrechte* (Baden-Baden: Nomos, 1985), pp. 71-103] gives an illuminating analysis of the distinction between "principles" and "rules."

2 Cf. Michael Sandel, *Liberalism and the Limits of Justice* (New York: Cambridge, 1983).

3 The debate between ethical cognitivists and value skeptics is a different matter; it, too, has to be carried out on the field of philosophical arguments. Using a double coding, these opposing positions can be interpreted in terms of developmental psychology as well as philosophy; from this point of view, the value skeptics are trying to rationalize a moral consciousness that Kohlberg would ascribe to Stage 4½. Cf. my *Moralbewusstsein und kommunikatives Handeln* (Frankfurt: Suhrkamp, 1983), pp. 195ff [*Moral Consciousness and Communicative Action*, Shierry Weber Nicholsen and Christian Lenhardt, trans. (Cambridge: MIT, forthcoming)].

4 Following John C. Gibbs and Thomas McCarthy, I have developed this thesis more fully in *ibid.*, pp. 185ff.

5 From this point of view, it must also seem unproblematic that the discussion of Stages 5 and 6 is based on only two interview protocols in each case. The question of empirical demonstration of a "higher stage of reflection" does not become completely irrelevant, but it does lose its importance.

6 *A Theory of Justice* (Cambridge: Harvard, 1971), p. 17.

7 *Ibid.*

8 This is one of the reasons for later revisions; in his Dewey lectures, Rawls finds himself forced

to introduce a concept of the person that has normative content; "Kantian Constructivism in Moral Theory," in *Journal of Philosophy*, LXXVII, 9 (September 1980): 515-572.

9 "Contractualism and Utilitarianism," in Amartya Sen and Bernard Williams, eds., *Utilitarianism and Beyond* (New York: Cambridge, 1982), pp. 103-128.

10 *Ibid.*, p. 110.

11 *Ibid.*, p. 122.

12 Cf. my remarks in *The Theory of Communicative Action: Vol. II: Lifeworld and System: A Critique of Functionalist Reason*, Thomas McCarthy, trans. (Boston: Beacon, 1987), pp. 92ff.

13 Cf. the essay by Kohlberg, Boyd, and Levine cited in note*.

14 I have previously appropriated Kohlberg's theory on these premises; cf. my *Moralbewusstsein und kommunikatives Handeln*.

15 Cf. my excursus on the theory of argumentation in *The Theory of Communicative Action: Vol. I: Reason and the Rationalization of Society*, Thomas McCarthy, trans. (Boston: Beacon, 1984), pp. 22ff.

16 For this reason discourse ethics must assert the fallibility in principle of moral insights; nor can it proceed on the basis of the notion that conflicts in the social domain which are in need of regulation can be resolved through consensus within a set period of time. On account of these cognitive differences, if for no other reason, positive law must supplement morality to fill the need for functionally necessary regulation in socially sensitive domains of action.

17 *Mind, Self & Society from the Standpoint of a Social Behaviorist*, Charles W. Morris, ed. (Chicago: University Press, 1934), pp. 379-380.

18 Kohlberg's argument becomes completely problematic when he detaches ideal role taking from the communicative form of discourse to such an extent that he is able to assign "dialogue" to empathy with the other and the principle of concern for the other's welfare.

19 Cf. my notes on the grounding of discourse ethics in *Moralbewusstsein und kommunikatives Handeln*, pp. 53ff.

20 It may in fact be the case in an individual instance that those involved agree upon a lottery procedure; but this procedure would be universalizable only on the condition that it were voluntary, which would have to be determined ad hoc. I see no ground on which the *requirement* of a lottery procedure could be morally justified in a situation of this kind.

21 Cf. Klaus Günther, *Der Sinn für Angemessenheit* (Frankfurt: Suhrkamp, 1988).

THE CONTINGENT PERSON AND THE EXISTENTIAL CHOICE

AGNES HELLER

I

Moral philosophy cannot renounce the task of providing guidelines for all kinds of possible moral advice to any actor who formulates the question, "What is the right thing for me to do"? Nor can it renounce the simultaneous task of offering a general answer to the question, "How should I live"? Philosophers, who in a premodern fashion continue to address the members of one particular community, deriving authority from their membership, will perforce fail to offer this kind of general guideline. Their blueprint will be out of touch with the concerns of the members of another community or group whose moral customs, ideas, and values are of equal relevance. In addition, modern philosophers address men and women who simultaneously dwell amidst a great diversity of concrete norms. For example, they share professions and their professional ethics, but they do not share each other's family, religious, and civic ethics—or vice versa. As a result, the old-fashioned philosophical message only has one of two options. In the first place, it can make a case for granting unconditional priority in all our commitments and choices to one community as against all others. The fruit of such an approach in modernity is moral fundamentalism. Fundamentalist ethical theories behave as a religious morality, even if the substance of their moral precepts and goals are nonreligious in nature. Alternatively, philosophy can be departmentalized into branches like business ethics, family ethics, or sexual ethics. It can even go further by affixing adjectives to the branches and terming them 'liberal' (or 'conservative') business ethics, 'lay' (or 'religious') family ethics, 'gay' (or 'straight') sexual ethics, and the like. Thus, moral thinking that derives its authority from the membership of the speaker in a particular group may turn fundamentalist and thereby pose a threat to members of other communities. Or, in a best case scenario, it can present moral options, rules, and recommendations that have direct relevance to the lives of some people in certain walks of life, but not to others.

In universalistic ethics, the relation of authority to addressee is structurally quite similar. In fact, here, too, philosophers derive their authority from their membership in a community; and this is also how they address its members. To put the matter bluntly, however, the community which they both address and from which they derive their authority, namely, humankind, does not exist as an integration. As a result, humankind has not developed an *ethos,* not even in the form of a few common norms that would be binding for every member of the human race. By virtue of their authentic universalism, moral philosophies such as the Kantian (in all of its versions, including communicative ethics) in fact do provide guidelines for all possible types of moral advice to be given to any actor who might ask in any given situation, "what is the right thing for me to do?" insofar as they live up to the inherent norm of moral philosophy which has remained unfulfilled by particularistic quasi-moral philosophies, fundamentalist or departmentalized. Since the addressee of the universalistic philosophy (humankind) has not developed even the semblance of a common *ethos,* however, nor do its members share a single moral norm in common, the guideline provided by moral universalism must remain merely formal (lacking in any substance whatsoever). One cannot really address humankind, for it does not listen. One can, however, address "humankind" as manifested in every human person, in every human relation, in every human speech act. This kind of approach does not have to end up in mere formalism, although in fact it has so far. For "humankind" has always been identified with "reason" or with some versions of "reason." As a result, universalistic philosophy did not take into account the unique embodied in each individual. In the end, mere formalism leaves the initial task unaccomplished. The guideline provided by formalistic moral philosophies is not *the* guideline for all possible types of moral advice in all possible situations, as they must leave certain situations unrecognized. (This was the case with Kant concerning the conflict of duties, and with Jürgen Habermas in such instances where the fundamental principle of universalization does not apply.)

I have only briefly mentioned the two extreme solutions to the predicament of modern moral philosophy. One can also choose to address the members of a particular movement or of a particular class (the latter has been attempted in "socialist ethics" or in "proletarian ethics"). One can also choose one's own nation or ethnic group or race as the "special addressee." These kinds of attempts may flourish for a while only to disappear later. Or, alternatively, they may develop toward a powerful fundamentalist ideology. In either case, the basic pattern remains the same. The philosopher (the moralist, the moral advisor, or manipulator) claims authority on the grounds of her membership in a (particular or universal) community. She then goes on to address the members of the selected community with an authority based on her (and their) commonly shared, real or alleged, membership.

My recommendation, rather than to select one of the former solutions over another, is to leave the whole configuration behind. The model has been taken over from premodern philosophies, and made perfect sense in the premodern world where, in the main, moral norms, virtues, and ideas were divided along the lines of social stratification. This is why it worked then and there; this is also the reason why it no longer does. The shift of the model toward universalization has brought the message home even more forcefully.

In seeking new solutions, one cannot renounce the claim of moral philosophy to provide a guideline for all possible types of moral advice in all possible situations; nor can one rescind its specificity vis-à-vis religion (that it carries its own authority drawn from its addressee). Philosopher and addressee *must share something* that is morally relevant as well as something that may provide the foundation for the mutual understanding between philosopher and addressee. Yet this "something" need not be membership in an integration, whether it be a religious community, family, state, class, caste, nation, or even humankind. This "something" could perhaps also be nonmembership in all of them.

II

The philosophical metaphor that man is "thrown into the world" expresses the fundamental life experience of modern men and women. *The modern person is a contingent person.* In a broader sense, contingency is one of the main constituents of the human condition, for nothing in our genetic equipment predetermines us to be born in precisely such and such an age, in such and such a social condition, caste, class, and the like. Yet premodern men and women were rarely aware of this contingency. Blood ties, on the one hand, and domicile (the home), on the other, were normally perceived as determinants of a person's existence.

The modern person is "thrown into the world," because his condition is that of *dual* contingency. In addition to the initial, mostly unconscious, contingency of the person, a secondary one qua "form of existence" in modernity has been gaining momentum in the last two hundred years. The modern person does not receive the destination or telos of his life at the moment of birth as happened in premodern times when he had been born to do this and not that, to become this rather than that, to die as this and not as that, for better or for worse. The modern person is born as a cluster of possibilities without telos. Furthermore, this newborn bundle of possibilities without a socially patterned telos cannot make its choices within the framework of a socially determined destination: it must choose the framework for itself. The existentialist formula of "choosing ourselves" can also be read as a descriptive comment on the form of existence in modernity. The modern person must choose the framework, the telos of his life, that is, he is to choose himself. One can say with Kierkegaard that, if a person does not choose himself, others will choose for him. Those "others" do not convey the socially patterned telos as did "the others" in premodern times, for they are as contingent as the one instead of whom, for whom they choose, whose life they determine. If one does not choose one's own life, but lets others choose for one, no telos will appear at the horizon of one's life. The person will remain completely contingent throughout life. Born as a cluster of possibilities, he will not realize any of them in full. He will die without having lived. By contrast, the person who chooses his own telos, destiny, pattern of life, etc., thereby chooses himself, which is more than a figure of speech.

The modern condition of being born as a bundle of possibilities with no socially patterned telos to rely upon, as well as to be limited by, can also be experienced as "being thrown into freedom." This freedom, however, is empty, or in existentialist jargon: it is Nothing, Nothingness. It is "Nothing" in a triple sense. First, it indicates the mere absence of a socially patterned telos. There is no handrail to be grasped; one walks the tight rope over the abyss. Second, if one fails to choose oneself, but instead lets others choose for one, life becomes a kind of lingering toward death. One lives only in order to die, to become Nothing. Finally, this freedom is Nothing in the Hegelian sense. Out of the dialectic of Being and Nothing, Becoming emerges as the mediator. One is born, one *Is Nothing* in order to *Become*. The choice of oneself is to become what you are. Here "Nothing" is freedom in a positive sense. The statement, 'One can become everything', whether true or false, is irrelevant. Yet the other statement, 'One can become oneself', is both true and relevant. We need only to look around to see people who have indeed become themselves: there are plenty.

To be contingent in the dual sense of the word is both a blessing and a curse. Whatever our choices, one never chooses to be born, and, in particular, one does not choose to be born as a dually contingent person. Freedom as Nothingness becomes freedom as blessing if, and only if, the choice of self is successful. In becoming oneself while choosing oneself, the contingent person becomes as free as a person, qua person, can be. One becomes free as a person if one transforms one's contingency into one's destiny. A person transforms his contingency into destiny if he freely chooses what he did not choose in the first place: to be born precisely in this world, in this time as a dually contingent person, if he understands his self-created path as his destiny and dearest property.

The contingent person is not the abstract man or woman; no one is thrown into the world as such. Concrete human beings are born, each of them is singular, all of them have different clusters of talents, unique childhood experiences. They can be possessed of a merry constitution or a melancholic disposition. Yet all of them are contingent persons, and equally so, irrespective of whether they were born rich or poor, children of loving or uncaring parents, in war or peace, in democracy or dictatorship, predisposed to merriment or sadness. The situation into which one is thrown at birth conditions the "likelihood" of, or the "objective chances" for, one or another course of life. Yet it does not provide the newborn with a socially prepatterned telos for such a course of life.

Modern men and women share something in common: they are all contingent; they share a fundamental life experience and they are all in the same predicament: either they choose themselves or they let others choose for them. There are many things in each other's lives that they do not understand. One cannot expect them to agree with one another on issues that spring from their concrete life conditions, experiences, ideas, or goals. Yet because contingency is shared, modern men and women can understand each other on this *universal ground*. It is on the basis of this shared life experience and predicament that modern moral philosophy can be grounded.

A contingent person can communicate with all other contingent persons in addressing what they all share: contingency. Every contingent person has the authority to discuss the predicaments of contingency because he is also contingent, as are those with whom he is communicating. The relationship between the speaker and the addressee is one of *symmetric reciprocity*.

In what follows, I shall not address "humankind as such" nor shall I address humankind as it dwells in reason or in the reasoned speech of everyone. I shall rather address concrete persons who feel, enjoy, suffer, choose, reason, and speak. I shall not turn to any specific human group, class, party, profession, ethnicity, race, or citizenry. I shall not address any cluster in particular with the authority of being a member of the same cluster. I shall address the contingent person, to whatever concrete institution, profession, party, country, group, or class he belongs. I shall address contingent persons of both sexes, although I myself belong to the female gender and I do not claim honorary membership in the male gender. Perhaps I do therefore address humankind. Yet, if this is so, it will not be humankind "in us," but humankind that *is us* which will be addressed; each of us, all of us. Not the general will but the will of all.

III

To be contingent does not amount to being rootless. Among modern individuals there are "hotel dwellers," but there are also men and women who feel at home in a particular habitat. Moreover, finding a home, achieving the feeling of "being at home" may result from having transformed one's contingency into one's destiny. The person who chooses herself, and thus her life's telos, her destiny, "settles in" on the earth in general, in our time and world in particular, and perhaps also in her environment, relationships, and attachments, as well as the institutions with which she is affiliated. Modern moral philosophy appeals to all contingent persons, to those who "feel at home," as well as to those who "settle in the world." But premodern, noncontingent persons are not addressed directly by a moral philosophy of this kind. And yet we inhabit the world with human groups and cultures that are still characterized by the division of moral customs along lines of social stratification in which people, at the moment of their birth, are slotted into their social telos and destiny. Moral philosophy does not have a prophetic power; one cannot foretell whether in the future all cultures will become modern. Therefore, one cannot foretell whether the addressee of modern philosophy will ever be coextensive with "every human being."

The decision to address the contingent person in her "personhood" at the initial stage of a moral philosophy, instead of arguing for the validity of certain rules and norms for a start, has neither an ontological nor an epistemological status. One can make this decision and go through with it, irrespective of whether or not one subscribes to the paradigm of language, communication, action, consciousness, collective consciousness, work, etc., or from the standpoint of any metaphysics or of any antimetaphysics. One can provide different answers to questions concerning the formation of the human person, the source of her knowledge and self-knowledge, concerning the (subjective or intersubjective) constitution of the world, and yet still agree with others that persons qua persons simply exist, that one can communicate with them (as they can communicate with us), that one can address them (as they can address us) qua persons. Yet to address the contingent person in her "personhood" at the initial stage of a moral philosophy is certainly a matter of *decision*, precisely because this kind of gesture "does not follow" from the metaphysical, ontological, sociological, epistemological, or historical system or creed of any particular philosophy.

At this point, the suspicion might arise that "choosing onself" is simply a fancy term which stands for "making oneself," and that, therefore, the gesture of addressing the contingent person in his personhood at the initial stage of this moral philosophy has in fact been derived from the paradigm of work, and that it follows from that paradigm. But, in reality, "choosing oneself" is the modern equivalent of "knowing oneself" and not of "making oneself." The metaphor of "making oneself" carries with it associations with self-creation. One perceives the self as indeterminate, as raw material. At the same time, one also perceives the same self (or a particular aspect of it) as the creator, the worker, the artist molding the raw material into a predesigned shape according to a goal set by the actor himself. Once the creative, artistic dimensions of the metaphor are dismissed, one easily arrives at the positivist image of a mere goal-oriented general actor who has a life strategy and who chooses every step he takes rationally, fitting it into a preconceived "goal." The other metaphor, "choosing oneself," generates altogether different associations.

58

One cannot know oneself by mere introspection. If "choosing oneself" is the modern version of "knowing oneself," the interplay between the selves (at least between two "selves") is presupposed. Yet a modern knowledge of the self is not derived from the others' perception, from their regard alone. We cannot know ourselves, nor can others know what we "really" are *before we became what we are.* (If we fail to become what we are, we behave like characters in Erving Goffman's puppet theatre.)

The premodern interplay between action and character was accurately depicted by Aristotle, and since then by many others. The person's character is formed by action, and the more it becomes formed, the more the character determines every further action. Yet the kinds of action one was later supposed to perform were, so to speak, "on display" for the person at a very early stage. There was the father; the youngster was introduced into a circle of citizens; he knew exactly what he could become if he acted in such and such a way. Specific actions were affiliated with typical ideals (the ideals of the accomplished gentleman citizen). These circumstances in which modern men and women are unaware of what they are, unless they become what they are, do not modify the interplay between character and action, rather they change the framework within which this kind of interplay takes place. The dictum of Browning's hero, "I go to prove my soul," summarizes the story with poetic brevity. Since the actions that form the character are not predesigned for the person at the time of birth, because the person's course of life is not set by social expectations, ideals, and determinations, he has to "reach out" in order to find the kind of actions that are fitting to his character. Yet since it is actions that form the character, how can one know in advance what kind of actions one should seek? One could try to prove one's soul and to engage in all kinds of action in the wrong way, by which I mean, in a way through which one does not become what one is. The soul that has never proved itself is the lost soul who will never know what "it" is. Yet if "choosing yourself" is the modern equivalent of "knowing thyself," but if one knows oneself only when one becomes what one is, how can one choose oneself at all? It is assumed, on the one hand, that, once one chooses oneself, one becomes what one is, while, on the other, it is also assumed that one does not really know what one "is" prior to the choice. Yet we are only seemingly moving in circles. Choice of oneself is the choice of destiny; more precisely, choosing oneself is tantamount to knowing oneself as a person of a particular destiny. One does not "have" a self whose knowledge predates choice. Existence and the consciousness of existence are indivisible. The choice of self is an *existential choice,* for it is the choice of existence. Existential choice is, by definition, irreversible and irrevocable. One cannot choose one's destiny in a reversible way, for a reversible choice is not the choice of destiny, by definition not the existential choice.

Since the existential choice is irrevocable, it generates the telos of the person's life (it "restores" what was absent at birth from the modern person's life). Life now has a destination because the person has a destiny. The interplay between character and action is restored insofar as the existential choice preempts the possibility of acting in any way other than that predestined by the choice itself. As Kierkegaard once remarked, after having made the existential choice, one continues to choose all the time. Yet these consecutive choices occur within a framework that was already predestined by our choice of ourselves.

The inherent telos of a self-chosen life must not be confused with life strategies and goals that are devised in terms of rational-choice theories. Existential choice is our choice of ourselves, and not the choice of a concrete goal, not even "the" goal of life. No means can be applied in order to realize the goals of an existential choice. The end inherent in the existential choice is truly an "end in itself." To quote Aristotle, it is "the activity of the soul throughout the whole of our lives." Whatever one chooses existentially in choosing oneself is *energeia*. It is the activity, and not the end result, that men and women choose existentially, the "activity-toward-something," the "activity-that-we-are," the "activity-that-we-become-since-we-are." Whatever one chooses, this will invariably be the case. One can (existentially) choose oneself as an activist of a movement (a party), as a member of a religious community, as a man of science, and as so much else. Georg Lukács did not choose the victory of communism ("the" goal); rather, he chose himself as a communist. Max Weber, as he so movingly confessed in his "Science as a Vocation," did not choose "the progress of sciences," but rather himself as a social scientist, as a person of this particular, and no other, calling. Whatever one chooses existentially is irrevocable (as a choice). Once you revoke it, you lose yourself, your own personality, your own destiny, to relapse into contingency.

It is only in the existential choice, in choosing oneself, that modern men and women can transform their contingency into destiny. If they fail to do so, others will choose for them. All of their choices will then become revocable and, in due course, they will reverse all of them. They will then endlessly ponder what would have happened had they chosen otherwise, what they could have become had they done this and not something else, had they married another man or woman, had they emigrated instead of staying where they were born, had they taken this particular course and not another one, and so on *ad infinitum*. They will be busy with making a living, with choosing means for the realization of goals, and, once having realized them, they will feel weariness instead of satisfaction. They will always be dissatisfied with "life," with themselves, with the people around them. They will regret whatever they have done, and equally regret whatever they failed to do. They will run to the analyst who will not ease their neuroses. For, ultimately, an analyst is a person who creates the conditions for another person to choose herself. And if the person does not choose, the analyst has reached the limits of his power and can do no more.

If one chooses oneself as the "woman-of-this-particular-cause" or, as Weber put it, the "man-of-this-particular-calling," one chooses oneself as *difference*. The choice is irrevocable, and this is why it is existential. It is through the choice that one becomes what one is. She will never regret it, for if she does, she will lose herself. For her the choice is unambiguous, because it is herself who she had chosen. For others the same choice may appear ambiguous, however, for what she has chosen is the difference. It might even occur that, in other people's eyes, to revoke her choice, and thus lose herself, would be a morally better decision than to stick to her destiny; especially if this destiny is vested in a cause. This kind of existential choice ultimately separates us from, rather than unites us with, the rest.

A person who chooses herself existentially under the category of difference thus exposes herself to external powers, the bearers of blessing or curse, of good luck or bad luck. Such powers are external to the individual's existence, to her existential choice. They do not threaten a person's well-being, position or happiness alone, they can even poison one's choice of oneself. Or, alternatively, they can make the choice seem so much better than the one who had chosen could possibly dream. Whether one has chosen oneself as a woman of a particular cause or of a particular calling, as the friend (or lover) of a particular person or anything else in particular, she stands under the category of difference, and everything in her life will depend on blessing or curse. If the choice does not come off, there will be a discrepancy between the person's self-perception and her perception in the eyes of others. Other people will regard her as irrational, whereas she would continue to regard herself as rational.

Irrespective of the outcome of the choice made under the category of difference, however, the person who had chosen herself has transformed her contingency into her destiny. At this point, however, we might come to the conclusion that there is very little a moral philosophy could possibly do with the gesture of the existential choice. Modern moral philosophy turns to the contingent person— so far so good. The choice of the self as a woman of a particular cause, or a woman of a particular calling, is of little moral relevance unless the virtue of constancy is made an absolute, or unless it is proved that the person who has transformed her contingency into her destiny is morally better than the rest of us. But there is nothing to indicate that the latter is the case. On the other hand, moral philosophy can do very little with people who have never even attempted to make an existential choice, those who never choose themselves but let others choose for them, who therefore can hardly be approached as responsible moral agents. Only people of character can be people of good character.

Yet there is a way out of the impasse. Instead of considering further the kinds of existential choices that can be made under the category of difference, we may instead pose the following question: Is there an existential choice that can be made under the category of the *universal,* an existential choice of a kind that does not separate the person who chooses from the rest of us, but rather unites the person with us? Kierkegaard was not the first thinker to present such an existential choice, yet he was certainly the one who made the strongest case for it. Weber made a new, and to my mind theoretically problematic, attempt at the issue in his swan-song lecture on politics as a vocation. Since twentieth-century existentialism, in particular Jean-Paul Sartre, offered a strongly subjectivist version of the original idea, I would rather fall back on Kierkegaard in order to introduce my modifications toward a less subjectivistic direction.

IV

Choosing ourselves under the category of the universal is tantamount to choosing ourselves as *good persons.* This is *the* moral choice because this is the choice of morals.

In Kierkegaard's formulation, to choose ourselves ethically means to choose ourselves as persons who make the choice between good and evil. But, he adds, if one chooses oneself as a person who makes the choice between good and evil, he has by definition chosen the good. This does not mean that in the future he cannot choose an evil course of action. Rather, it means that he will not choose an action because it is evil. The person who has chosen himself ethically will do good for good's sake, but never evil for evil's sake. As a consequence, making the choice between good and evil means, by definition, choosing the good.

I recommend a slight modification of the Kierkegaardian rendering of the ethical choice of ourselves. The modification deradicalizes the idea to a point which makes it acceptable for thinkers of a different philosophical background, and which makes it more empirical, and thus more palatable, for everyone. "Choosing ourselves" means *to destine* ourselves to become *what we are. Choosing ourselves ethically means to destine ourselves to become the good persons who we are.* Let me briefly elaborate on this. We are children of particular parents, we had a particular childhood, we suffer from particular neuroses, we were born into a particular milieu, rich or poor, educated or uneducated—this is what we are. In choosing ourselves, we choose all these determinations, circumstances, talents, assets, infirmities: we choose our ill-fate and our good faith, in short, everything that we are. Therefore, we also choose ourselves as good persons *that we are* and precisely *as we are.* We choose all our determinations and thus we make ourselves free. With the same gesture or, as

Kierkegaard put it, in the same instant, we choose ourselves as persons who choose between good and evil and who thus choose the good, as well as choose ourselves as persons to be destined to be good. I shall be a decent person as I am for I, as I am, destine myself to be a decent person. This is a very simple idea. Whoever chooses to become what he is, that is, a decent, good person, chooses all his determinations with the same gesture. For only if he does precisely this can he destine himself to be good. Suppose that I do not choose myself completely; rather, I make a selection. I choose my talents but not my infirmities, I choose my tribe but not my parents; I do not rechoose the sufferings of my childhood, nor my disappointments. If I selectively choose in this manner, I cannot destine myself, because I am not free: that which I have left unchosen will, at least partially, *determine* my life and my fortune. A person who has chosen himself completely, cannot make excuses—such as "I did it because I had such an unhappy childhood," or "I could not help doing it, for I had to make up for the disappointments of my tender age"—rather, he had chosen all this. In choosing ourselves existentially-ethically, there will be no "alien" power, no compulsion built into our singular character. We will not have any excuses because we will not need any.

The existential choice of the ethical was said to be the choice of the self under the category of the universal. This sounds strange because, in this kind of choice, the person chooses precisely what he is, as he is—all his singular determinations. Yet since everyone can choose himself ethically to the same extent, the choice of our singularity, as the gesture of freedom, falls under the category of the universal: "every human being." This statement may appear unconvincing at first glance. Every person, as a singular, has his determinations. Not all of them can equally serve as a trampoline for an existential choice, however; for some, the choice may be easy, while for others it may be difficult. But this counter-argument is irrelevant. Whether it is easier or more difficult, the existential choice of goodness is the same, and equally possible for all human persons. In this respect, the existential choice shares the propensities of all universals, more-over, of all norms. "You should not murder" is an equally valid norm for those who cannot harm a fly as well as for those who have strong inclinations for physical violence. It is possible for both of them, and to the same extent, not to murder their fellow creatures.

The existential choice of the ethical falls under the category of universality. It is possible for everyone to choose freely all of his determinations and to decide whether to become the decent and good person that he is, as he is. The existential choice under the category of difference, however, implies in its concept that not everyone can make the same choice. Everyone could choose a particular calling, but not the same one; still less can everyone pursue this calling on the same level of quality. Everyone can choose a cause, but not everyone the same (even less one pursue the same cause with the same attachment)—yet everyone can destine himself to be a good, decent person.

The existential choice made under the category of difference can play a dirty trick on the person who has chosen, whereas the existential choice under the category of the universal cannot. This is not to say that the decent person is happier than the other person who has chosen himself as a man of a calling. A successful outcome of our choice of ourselves as difference may sometimes fill the soul of the person who has chosen with the triumphant feeling of infinite happiness. Yet although an existential choice cannot, on the pain of losing our "personhood," be revoked, once the source of choice becomes polluted, one often wishes the choice had not been made at all. Since the source of choice that has been made under the category of the universal cannot get polluted by any consecutive event, whether it be good luck or bad fate, no one could wish a choice like this had never been made. Put another way, a person who has chosen himself under the category of the universal destines himself to authenticity. Becoming what he is (a good person) accompanies the series of actions, attitudes, and gestures that are all authentic. An authentic person cannot desire to become an inauthentic one, although he can certainly complain about the ill-fate of goodness in the world, past or present.

The existential choice (under the category of universality) is the fundamental moral choice: it is the choice of morals. Undoubtedly, neither a discourse held in moral terms nor the distinguishing (in certain situations) of good from evil presupposes a moral choice. Furthermore, one need not speak the moral language in order to understand it. Hutcheson found the simplest and most convincing argument to support his thesis of "minima moralia." He remarked that even those who mock morals cry out "injustice" if they are the ones who are wronged. One could add that cynics who hold the view that moral terms are empty, mere fancies void of meaning and relevance, would take serious offense were they called "dishonest," "cowardly," or even "illiberal." Taking offense makes sense if the categories make sense and under no other circumstances. Interestingly enough, the same person who takes offense if termed dishonest would not take offense if someone remarked that he had not acted efficiently enough in protecting his interests, or that he had not sought his pleasures fully.

"Distinguishing" and "choosing" between good and evil are not coterminous. It need not be demonstrated, however, that choices between good and evil can, and are actually, made by everyone irrespective of whether the persons had chosen themselves existentially as moral agents. People in general choose between good and evil if it so happens that they must choose, if they cannot avoid or sidestep it, and if they care to know the moral implications of their choice.

Whoever has chosen himself existentially as a good person wills to choose between good and evil, for he wills to choose the good (to become what he is: a good person). He cannot and will not wait until told that a choice implies the choice between good and evil. Any time he embarks upon an action, or during the course of an action, he will raise the question (to himself) of whether the action implies the choice between good and evil. He will scrutinize all possible actions under the guidance of the categories ''right'' and ''wrong.'' One does not have to be morally rigorous to behave like this. Placing all of our actions under scrutiny from the perspective of ''right'' and ''wrong'' by no means implies the conclusion that all choices are between good and evil. Scrutiny can also result in finding the choice adiaphoretic, even if one is told that it is not. Yet once certain alternative courses of action present the choice between good and evil, the choice of the good takes absolute preference over all other kinds of possible choices, as well as over all other reasons for making other choices, such as goals, interests, passions, benefits (private or public), and any values whatsoever (excepting moral values where a conflict like this does not arise). Needless to say, if one chooses oneself existentially under the category of difference, one gives priority to those actions which are inherent in one's particular destiny; these actions will by no means be the morally best possible ones.

There is nothing paradoxical in the Kierkegaardian assumption that the person who has chosen himself existentially as a good person also chooses the evil, for there would be no choice at all if he could only choose the good. The issue at stake, however, is not merely whether the choice between good and evil includes the possible choice of evil as a category (which determines the character of an action); rather, the issue is whether a choice includes the *actual* choice of evil. Commonplace wisdom that holds that good persons do wrong things sometimes is in this context less trivial than it seems. Since in modern times, where morals are more reflexive, where theoretical reasoning must, more than ever, lend support to practical reason for the latter to find the right decision (with the proviso that theoretical reason can be in error), the person who makes the choice can be mistaken about the moral character of his choice. Thus, he can choose evil without knowing that it is evil. Furthermore, since one is sometimes presented with a choice where both (or more than two) courses of action are equally good while both (or more than two) include moral transgression of a kind, the person making the choice ''cannot help'' but choose evil knowingly. The person, having chosen himself existentially, chooses freely. Therefore, he cannot plead innocent with reference to the idea that he ''could not help'' but choose. To sum up, if one chooses oneself under the category of the universal, one chooses oneself ethically. One chooses oneself ethically, if one chooses to become what one is and as one is. He who chooses all his determinations, makes himself free to be a good person, a person who is self-destined to be good. He who chooses himself to become a good (honest) person, chooses the choice between good and evil.

One need not subscribe to Kierkegaard's assumption that men and women never choose evil for evil's sake in order to regard this problem as irrelevant to our present discussion. I trust Shakespeare more than Kierkegaard when it comes to knowledge of human nature. There can be (there have always been) people who choose evil for evil's sake. Radical evil may exist, yet it is certainly untypical and uncharacteristic of our human race in general. Thus, even if there are people who choose evil for evil's sake, they are the exception rather than the rule, while choosing good for good's sake is, if not the rule, at least the ideal norm. It is the ideal norm not because people generally do good for good's sake, but rather because, in general, people highly esteem those who do so.

V

Existential choice is inherent in the modern form of existence. Premodern societies neither provided conditions for such choices nor necessitated them. As long as, and to the degree that, a particular preset way of life was *socially* allotted to persons at the moment of their birth, these persons could not choose themselves. For what has been allotted, may be—peacefully, gaily, dutifully, modestly, humbly, or even proudly—accepted or enthusiastically embraced; but it cannot be *chosen*. One can choose something only if one can also *not* choose the same thing.

In principle as well as in practice, a person can make an existential choice under the category of the universal without (earlier, later, or simultaneously) making an existential choice under the category of difference and vice versa. To avoid misunderstanding, it should be noted that choosing ourselves as good persons without choosing ourselves as being destined toward a particular cause *is not tantamount* to remaining without a calling, cause, concrete goal, value commitment, and the like. The person who has chosen herself ethically is (or may be) involved with causes, people, institutions, family, friends, neighbors, developing talents, collecting and enjoying things of beauty. Yet she has not chosen herself as a person who becomes what she is through one particular kind of calling, cause, or something similar. Since her choices of a cause or calling are not existential ones, the choices can be revoked any time she wants. Moreover, even if she switches her choices, no matter how frequently, she will not expose herself to the danger of losing herself: the continuity of her character has been established by the (existential) moral choice. This person would lose herself and fall apart, however, if she failed to make a choice between good and evil, if she embarked on choosing activities or causes irrespective of their moral qualities.

Although a person can make an existential choice under the category of the universal without (earlier, later, or simultaneously) making an existential choice under the category of difference, it is entirely possible to choose oneself as a good person (under the category of the universal) *and* choose oneself existentially (earlier, later, or simultaneously) as a person of a particular calling or cause, that is, under the category of difference. A radical conception of existential choice rules out such a possibility whereby it reintroduces moral absolutism, if not exactly of the Kantian brand, at least one which represents a more recent version of the old theory and which is equally unfit for mediation. In my mind, philosophy has to pay its due to our incompleteness, and it can do so by foregoing the claim to absolutes and by becoming incomplete itself. There are thus decent persons who have only made the existential choice of the ethical, while there are others who make two existential choices. Even if moral philosophy models itself on the image of the good (decent) person, it is not authorized to exclude one kind of decent person from that image because she does not fit into the system.

Absolute choice and fundamental choice are distinguishable in precisely this context. If a person chooses herself both under the category of the universal and under the category of difference, there must be a hierarchy of choices, even if both are irrevocable. Since conflicts, and thus priorities between goodness and calling, cannot be eliminated, "irrevocability" must have a meaning that is different in the case of the super- and subordinated choices, respectively, when there is conflict as well as need for hierarchy between the priorities. The first is our *absolute* and the second is our *fundamental* choice.

If the ethical choice is the absolute choice, and the choice under the category of difference is the fundamental choice, one will give the absolute and incontestable priority to moral considerations in action, judgment, and so much else, if a conflict arises between the two existential choices. Even in this case, however, the original choice under the category of difference never needs to be revoked. Precisely because one's absolute choice is superior to one's fundamental choice, one will never come to regret (and in this sense revoke) one's fundamental choice. "Irrevocability" of the fundamental choice then simply has the following meaning: one does not "take back" the fundamental choice, for this is what has made one what one is (what one has become), and this has been built in one's character. All this does not mean, however, that one would choose again the *object* of one's choice.

The existential choice of the ethical may or may not permit the *free perseverance* in the object (objective) of fundamental choice in case of collisions. It does not permit it if, and only if, one would lose oneself in persevering in the object (objective) of the fundamental choice. It is painful, indeed tragic, to disavow the object (objective) of a fundamental choice in such a way, but it is not tantamount to the full reversal of that choice. It cannot be emphasized enough that the fundamental choice is a kind (in this case, a subordinate kind) of the existential choice and, as such, is irrevocable. If I give myself a law and later, led by moral integrity, I change this law, this gesture has no retroactive effect. But it must be stressed that the *ethical* choice of self has no *object or objective* other than the subject itself. There are no dual aspects of this choice. This makes us wonder whether the relationship of the absolute and the fundamental choice can possibly be reversed. Can the existential choice under the category of difference be the absolute one, while the existential choice under the category of the universal simply plays second fiddle to the fundamental choice? Can the universal be subjected to the difference as a result of the gesture of self-determination (of choosing our destiny)?

Forceful external powers hold sway over the person who has chosen herself under the category of difference. The choice can either come off or not. The existential choice of goodness is sheltered, however: it can never be contaminated by the interference of external forces. In the first combination (i.e., the universal is the absolute, the difference is the fundamental), the ethical choice cannot protect the person from being exposed to the whims of external powers to whom she has exposed herself in the act of choosing herself under the category of difference. Yet it can prevent the source of fundamental choice from becoming contaminated. This happens every time someone in a moral conflict disavows the objective of her fundamental choice (without revoking the choice itself). It is exactly the disavowal of the objective (object) which prevents the source from being contaminated. I have mentioned a "tragic" conflict, which is to be understood in the most traditional meaning of the term: cathartic, purifying, as well as simultaneously annihilating and elevating.

In the second combination (i.e., where the difference is the absolute and the universal is the fundamental), one will give an absolute, incontestable authority to those actions which will guide us toward our self-given destiny (a cause, a calling, a relationship, and much else) as against moral considerations, in the case of conflicting loyalties, duties, passions, wishes, and the like. One should not forget, however, that here we are dealing with a person who has also chosen herself as a good person, who risks her own integrity, the unity of her personality, and her own autonomy, if she did something in which her choice of good would indeed be revoked. She walks a tightrope above an abyss, and is therefore in need of a good sense of balance, good reflexes, tremendous luck, and the greatest among them: a network of friends who can hold her hand. "Tightrope dancing" means here giving priority to "what-one-has-destined-oneself-to-become," without losing one's identity under the category of the ethical. Choosing oneself under the category of the difference absolutely, while choosing oneself also under the category of the universal, is the *absolute risk,* for obvious reasons. A person who has chosen herself under the category of difference alone may not even notice that her choice did not come off. While cutting a comic figure in the eyes of others, she will not even be unhappy, but will instead live and die in the conviction that she had been good at the thing she had chosen (cause, calling, or a particular person) while the others were just fools. But if someone also chooses oneself under the category of the universal, she cannot seek and then find consolation in self-deception. She may even resign her absolute choice and thus cease to be "the-person-destined-to-become-this-and-that," and thereby become infinitely unhappy. To be good (decent) will be no consolation for her. People in this kind of predicament are the likely candidates for suicide.

Everyone who has chosen herself under the category of the universal as a good person intends, by definition, to make a moral choice every time a situation, an alternative, or an issue so requires. Viewed from this perspective, it is of no (or very little) relevance whether the person made an existential choice under the category of the universal alone, or whether she made a dual choice (both under the category of the universal and that of difference) and whether, in the second case, the ethical choice was the absolute or the fundamental one. Such a person will invariably ask the question, "What is the right thing for me to do?," whereby she will express the intention, moreover, the *resolution* to do the right thing or, at least, never to do the wrong thing. This kind of person is the natural addressee of a moral philosophy that provides guidelines for all possible moral advice to be given to actors who ask in any given situation, "What is the right thing for me to do?"

Graduate Faculty, New School for Social Research

MACINTYRE, HABERMAS, AND PHILOSOPHICAL ETHICS

MICHAEL KELLY

When Alasdair MacIntyre discusses the notion of tradition in *After Virtue,*[1] he claims that we inherit a variety of debts, rightful expectations, and obligations from our families, cities, and nations, and that these inheritances constitute the moral particularity of our lives, which he refers to as our ''moral starting point.'' Moreover, he claims that this same particularity also constitutes the starting point for philosophical ethics:

> . . . a philosophical theory of the virtues is a theory whose subject-matter is that pre-philosophical theory already implicit in and presupposed by the best contemporary practice of virtues . . . philosophy necessarily has a sociological, or as Aristotle would have said, political starting-point (AV, 139).

MacIntyre is quick to add, however, that this

> of course does not entail that practice, and the pre-philosophical theory implicit in practice are normative for philosophy and thereby exempt from philosophical criticism . . . (AV, 139).

He thus maintains that, although philosophical ethics has a sociological/political or, in short, historical starting point in the sense that it is bound to a certain tradition along with the practices on which it reflects, it can still be critical. The challenge MacIntyre addresses in his more recent *Whose Justice? Which Rationality?*[2] is how such a tradition-bound philosophical ethics can be rationally defended.

Jürgen Habermas argues in *The Philosophical Discourse of Modernity* that a distinctive feature of modernity, meaning roughly the historical period from the Enlightenment to the present, is that it *''has to create its normativity out of itself.''*[3] This does not mean that its principles or theories are self-evident; rather, it means that they are to be rationally justified independently of any particular cosmology or religion or any mode of argumentation not rooted in modernity proper. In the case of modern ethical theory, best represented by Kant, the implication is that morality must be grounded in the mode of rational argumentation developed in modernity. The task of philosophical ethics, as it is interpreted by Habermas, is to analyze the presuppositions of rational argumentation and thus clarify and justify the modern ''moral point of view.''

Does this creation of normativity out of itself also mean, in effect, that modernity has a historical starting point and that it justifies itself in terms of its own tradition? Habermas would not refer to modernity as a tradition, for while invoking the distinction between traditional and modern societies,[4] he understands modernity as having broken with all dependence on tradition for the justification and legitimation of social, political, and moral norms. At the same time, and for him this is the distinctive characteristic of modernity, ''Modernity sees itself cast back upon itself without any possibility of escape.''[5] What else could 'itself' mean, however, if not that modernity is cast back upon a tradition, upon itself qua tradition? I shall argue that, while it is true that modernity breaks from other appeals to tradition, it constitutes a new tradition from which it has no possibility of escape; modernity is a tradition, and is in this sense tradition-bound. What I shall analyze here are the restraints this tradition-boundedness places on philosophical ethics in particular. MacIntyre's *Whose Justice? Which Rationality?* will prove crucial to my argument, because he offers there an account of how liberalism has constituted itself as a tradition precisely by creating its own normativity out of itself.[6]

In section I, I shall explain MacIntyre's notion of tradition-bound moral-practical rationality and his defense in *Whose Justice? Which Rationality?* of the following thesis: that all conceptions of justice and practical rationality are tradition-bound. This discussion will lead to a comparison between MacIntyre's ethics and Habermas's ''universal proceduralism,'' which will, in turn, be followed in section II by my interpretation of what MacIntyre's critique of Habermas would be. I shall then argue in section III that, although MacIntyre's ethical theory seems incompatible with Habermas's, because one is thoroughly tradition-bound and the other claims not to be, they can in fact be rendered compatible, at least on a methodological level. This ''methodological convergence''[7] depends, however, on the rejection, which I advocate, of a *strong* universalism in philosophical ethics, by which I mean the position that the ground of ethical theory is universal in the sense that it transcends the very tradition from which it emerges and on which it is dependent for its articulation, intelligibility, and application.

In section IV, I shall analyze MacIntyre's account of how a tradition develops its rationality by resolving its moral crises, and then discuss some consequences of his general argument for a philosophical ethics that has abandoned strong universalism. My principal purpose overall will be to demonstrate that both MacIntyre and Habermas make important contributions to the conception of a philosophical ethics which, like hermeneutic ethics, is tradition-bound, but which is, at the same time, rational and critical, like Kantian ethics.

I. MORAL-PRACTICAL RATIONALITY IN MACINTYRE AND HABERMAS

Both at the end of *After Virtue* (AV, 242) and at the beginning of the more recent *Whose Justice? Which Rationality?*, MacIntyre acknowledges that he needs to explain "what rationality is, in the light of which rival and incompatible evaluations of the arguments of *After Virtue* could be adequately accounted for" (WJWR, ix).[8] A main purpose of *Whose Justice? Which Rationality?* is to defend a concept of rationality which allows him to show that, despite its starting point in practices, unities of life, and tradition, a philosophical ethics can indeed be coherent, intelligible, rational, and critical. This concept of rationality is introduced and defended in terms of the larger, more central thesis that a particular conception of justice (as one type of virtue) is always tied to a particular conception of practical rationality, and that both conceptions are determined by the same historical tradition. Their shared historicity—the fact that they are tradition-bound—is what makes them inextricably linked to one another for their intelligibility and, MacIntyre argues, for their rational justification.

MacIntyre cites a number of examples from the history of moral philosophy to illustrate his thesis. As is well-known, Plato, Aristotle, Augustine, Aquinas, Hume, and Kant had competing conceptions of justice *and* of practical rationality, and their conceptions of justice and practical rationality supported one another. According to MacIntyre, it was not a coincidence that these conceptions were intertwined throughout the history of philosophy; his illustrations are thus intended to have more than a descriptive function. They are offered as evidence to support the claim that the two conceptions are possible not only despite, but in fact because of, their mutual conceptual dependency and shared historicity; each concept is unintelligible and unjustifiable without the other.[9]

What does it mean to claim that, because justice and practical rationality are both tradition-bound, they are conceptually interrelated or else unintelligible and unjustifiable? Two major implications are that the validity of any conception of practical rationality used to defend particular principles of justice cannot transcend the tradition to which the principles it defends are also bound, and that the principles cannot be articulated in the first place unless the conception of practical rationality bound to the tradition from which the principles have emerged is explicitly introduced.

To understand what MacIntyre is arguing here, I would like to contrast three different views about the status of, and interrelationship between, practical rationality and moral principles:[10] (1) there are universal moral principles which are applicable to all societies under the guidance of a universal practical rationality; (2) there are tradition-dependent moral principles which are nonetheless justified by discourse ethics so that they are able to transcend their tradition; and (3) there are tradition-dependent moral principles which are defended only by tradition-bound, practical rationality. Kant would be a good example of the first alternative, Habermas of the second, and MacIntyre of the third. In the context of the current debates in political and moral philosophy, wherein the strong Kantian position is not often, if ever, defended, the relevant difference is between Habermas's and MacIntyre's alternatives.

Habermas agrees that specific moral principles (e.g., about justice) are historically determined in the sense of stemming from concrete lifeworlds; he thus concedes that moral principles are at least tradition-dependent. At the same time, Habermas argues that the validity of these principles can be justified independently of the tradition from which they emerged.[11] He claims that universal, structural features of communication provide a procedure for identifying and grounding the universal validity of certain moral principles.[12] On the basis of such a procedure, what is universal is the validity of the moral principles that are initially tradition-dependent; this is why Habermas would say that the normative principles are dependent on, but not bound to, tradition. So the conflict between MacIntyre and Habermas, and thus the real difference between alternatives (2) and (3), concerns the possibility of such a procedure for making it possible for the validity of moral principles to transcend tradition.

Habermas himself even acknowledges the historical embeddedness of moral-practical rationality, but he then carefully distinguishes two positions:

> One insists on the context-boundedness of the faculty of moral judgement and contests the view that a universalistic ethic is at all possible. The other asserts that the independent logic of moral-practical rationality can be developed only by way of ethical universalism. . . .[13]

The first position is skepticism, which clearly offers no hope of establishing a philosophical ethics and which Habermas falsely associates with MacIntyre and Gadamer.[14] The second is his own position, which takes up "the universalistic line of questioning of transcendental philosophy, while at the same time detranscendentalising the mode of procedure."[15] The new, nontranscendental method, which he claims to be compatible with the hermeneutic, ontological claim of the basic historicity of moral-practical rationality, is called "rational reconstruction," an empirical research strategy directed at universals: "the reconstructive sciences explain the presumably universal bases of rational experience and judgment.''[16]

The task of the method of rational reconstruction is to reconstruct the universal competence to validate norms discursively which, Habermas claims, is always already operative (as a "know-how") in everyday communicative action (understanding-oriented action), but which is made explicit (as a "know-that") only on the level of theory.[17] When normative validity claims—truth, authenticity, rightness, and comprehensiveness—are challenged, they can then be validated only under the universal conditions of rational speech—symmetry and reciprocity—which constitute the procedural universalism referred to as the "ideal speech situation."

Habermas offers two different arguments to defend his claim to have rationally reconstructed *universal* procedural criteria for the justification of moral norms.[18] The first strategy is to argue that the universal conditions of rational speech are conditions of communicative action as such. Individuals engaging in communicative action are willing and able, if called upon, to justify whatever normative claims they advance in the course of such action. Although they may at first justify their actions by appealing to some norms uncritically derived from the lifeworld in which they are acting, they must be able, in principle, to provide a justification of these norms themselves. Such justification is possible, according to Habermas, only on the basis of the universal criteria that define the ideal speech situation. This means that the commitment to be able and willing to justify norms discursively and universally is said to follow, in principle, from our engagement in communicative action. The goal of rational reconstruction is to make this implicit commitment explicit.

The second strategy is to argue that procedural universalism or discourse ethics is integral to the form(s) of argumentation particular to modernity, which is defined, at the same time, by the set of conditions of rational speech outlined above. Although these conditions, as well as the competence to employ them, are particularly modern in the sense that they first emerged in the Enlightenment, their validity is not restricted to this period; they are universal. To defend their universality, Habermas introduces a Hegelian dimension into his argument: "The release of a potential for reason embedded in communicative action is a world-historical process. . . ."[19] The "supposition of reciprocal accountability" which is characteristic of modernity is the result of a historical process, but one which is not to be understood in terms of a concrete historical development confined to modernity.[20] To explain these points, Habermas introduces a distinction between the logic and dynamics of (moral) development: the logic is universal and concerns the structures of social evolution, while the dynamics are empirical and refer to the actual history of particular societies and individuals. What he rationally reconstructs is only the logic of moral development, i.e., the universal competence to validate normative claims on the basis of universal procedural criteria.[21] Habermas's basic contention is thus that the validity of the claims and principles of moral-practical rationality are not tradition-bound, because the modern "moral point of view" is the outcome of a developmental process with universal significance.

If MacIntyre is to challenge Habermas's procedural universalism, at least the strong version of it, he must show that the modern moral point of view is tradition-bound and that its claims and principles do not have universal validity, despite the conditions of communicative action as such or the conditions of the modern form of communicative action. He must show that the *validity* of moral norms is restricted to the very same tradition in which they and practical rationality are historically situated.

II. MACINTYRE'S CRITIQUE OF HABERMAS

(A) MacIntyre's challenge is made easier by the problems immanent within each of Habermas's strategies for defending his procedural universalism. The problem with the first strategy is that Habermas has not been successful in defending the *necessity* of the supposition of reciprocal accountability within communicative action.[22] He argues that those who deny the supposition are trapped in a "performative contradiction," because they must presuppose the supposition to justify their denial of it. But this argument carries less force than Habermas would like it to. First of all, he associates the supposition with a principle of universalization: participants in discourse must not only be willing to justify their norms, they must agree that a norm is valid only if it is universalizable. Yet the appeal to the threat of a performative contradiction is not enough to defend these strong ties between accountability, justification, and the principle of universalization. As Albrecht Wellmer has argued, even if the conditions of rational speech were tied to communicative action, they are not enough to generate the principle of universalization.[23] Habermas's account of the ethics of discourse does not necessarily imply, without further assumptions which Habermas may be aware of but which he does not explicitly defend, the language of ethics proper. It simply does not follow that, whenever we engage in communicative action, even as Habermas has defined it, we are necessarily bound to the universalization principle that he defends. This principle and the moral point of view itself must be defended by more than just the definitions of communicative action and discourse.[24]

Another problem with Habermas's first strategy is that it may have the unintended consequence of not allowing the conditions of rational speech to be subject to rational dialogue; that is, by claiming that they are unavoidable presuppositions, Habermas seems to present the conditions as being simply *given* in discourse instead of advocating them as the most rational outcomes of dialogue. Since these same conditions are the basis of ethical theory for Habermas, he would thereby, in effect, close the dialogue about the conditions of ethical theory as well. As Michael Walzer and others have noted, Habermas's own notion of the ideal speech situation, in which all participants are free to introduce whatever topic they want, must allow the conditions of rational speech themselves to be subject to dialogue; they can only be the result of consensus, not the presuppositions thereof.[25] If they are the result of a particular dialogue, however, as Habermas himself sometimes seems to suggest, they cannot be the presuppositions of all dialogue and discourse, but those only of a certain kind, namely, of the discourse of modernity. Such a discourse is subject to conflicting interpretations and constant revision which may, in turn, change the conditions of rational dialogue itself.

The problem with the second strategy is that Habermas must be able to show that his interpretation of the discourse of modernity (not to mention the proposals for a discourse of postmodernism[26]) is superior to other interpretations of it, that it is not confined to the "tradition" of modernity, and that it is universal. He is convinced that he can support these claims in two ways; first, by appealing to the notion of a performative contradiction again and, second, by using his rational reconstructive method. The performative contradiction here is that the conditions of rational discourse are simply the presuppositions of communicative action which define us as moderns; we are free to reject these conditions, but, according to Habermas, only by denying that we are modernists. Such a denial would result in another performative contradiction; for we have to give reasons for rejecting modernity, and any reasons we give will presuppose the same modernist point of view (based on rational argumentation) which we claim to deny. We are undeniably moderns and are thus irrevocably committed to the discourse of modernity. The difficulty with this strategy is that it seems to imply that there is but one discourse of modernity.[27] One way of understanding the so-called postmodernism debate is to see it as a debate about what modernity is, and about those parts of it we want to perpetuate and those we want to discard. In the context of such a debate, Habermas can make (and has made) a strong case for his interpretation of the discourse of modernity, but he cannot claim that it is the only interpretation.

The problem with the other angle of this second strategy—the use of the method of rational reconstruction—is the following: Does it provide inductive evidence to support a hypothesis about the universality of communicative competence, or does it provide a proof of this universality in a stronger sense? As Seyla Benhabib has convincingly argued, Habermas's method of rational reconstruction cannot sustain strong universalistic claims, because such claims require transcendental arguments unavailable to rational reconstruction as science.[28] The results of the rational reconstruction have a provisional status like any other scientific claims, which means that they are open to refutation and revision as additional empirical evidence is gathered. At best, Habermas's rational reconstructions of the competence underlying communicative action (either as such or in modernity) are provisionally universal. At times, he acknowledges this:

> Philosophy today is no longer in possession of metaphysical truths. It is involved, almost to the same extent as the sciences, in the fallibilism of a research process which takes place on the shaky ground of argumentation which is never immune to revision.[29]

But he rejects the conclusion that Benhabib has drawn from this acknowledgement, namely,

> To say that the structures of communicative rationality are irrevocable can mean only the following: this legacy contains a potential which we would like to see realized, and for which we are ready to engage ourselves.[30]

Although Habermas may object to Benhabib's formulation, he ultimately has to accept something very like it, because he does not contest the principle behind it—that rational reconstruction, being subject to fallibilism, cannot support a strong universalism (e.g., that communicative competence is universal and discourse is necessary). Habermas may still draw universalistic conclusions, but only so long as it is clear that they are provisional (inductive, empirical—or simply, hypotheses, as Habermas sometimes calls them[31]) rather than strong (universal and necessary).

Yet Habermas has good reason to resist Benhabib's conclusion, because it touches on what is perhaps the most distinctive dimension of his moral philosophy. He argues that there is a core of moral intuitions which are articulated in different ways by diverse societies and cultures, but which are, at the same time, universal and can be articulated in the form of the universalization principle.[32] Habermas's strong universalism comes in, neither because of the universal core of intuitions nor the universalization principle, but because of the attempt to justify this principle through a rational reconstruction of the universal structures of communication.[33] This attempt is Habermas's distinctive step;[34] for many contemporary philosophers, such as John Rawls, Thomas Scanlon, and others,[35] share Habermas's "moral point of view," which might be best summarized as an impartial point of view concerning moral matters, but they do not provide a philosophical justification of this point of view other than by appealing to an "overlapping consensus" or some such basis of shared assumptions. But if the results of the method of rational reconstruction are, by definition, provisional and hypothetical, what is the force of the claim that the universalization principle is universally grounded? It, too, can only be provisional; it cannot be universal in the strong sense, nor can it be irrevocable. As a result, Habermas's ethics has the same status as the ethical theories (of MacIntyre, Rawls, and others) that he criticizes.

(B) I would now like to return to MacIntyre's notion of tradition-bound moral-practical rationality both to understand why Habermas's ethics has this status and to begin discussing what becomes of philosophical ethics when this is the case. We have seen that, according to Habermas, the ground of the justification of moral norms must transcend the historical, tradition-bound context in which the norms themselves first emerged; the problem of the justification (of the validity) of norms is separate from the problem of the emergence of the norms so justified. Habermas even argues that the moral philosopher's task is completed when the problem of justification has been solved. He recognizes the other problems (emergence, application, motivation) but, qua philosopher, is not troubled by them; for he thinks they can best be solved by participants in moral action, by actual moral dialogue, or by social theory.[36]

MacIntyre argues, on the contrary, that the problems of emergence and justification are solved together or not at all. For even the competence to justify norms discursively according to procedural criteria—Habermas's "ground"—does not transcend the historical tradition from which it and the norms themselves have emerged; the logic and dynamics of this competence cannot be separated. Discourse ethics, like any moral theory or conception of practical reason, is itself intelligible and justifiable only in relation to its own historical tradition:

> . . . the present is intelligible only as a commentary upon and response to the past in which the past, if necessary and if possible, is corrected and transcended, yet corrected and transcended in a way that leaves the present open to being in turn corrected and transcended by some yet more adequate future point of view . . . each particular theory or set of moral or scientific beliefs is intelligible and justifiable—insofar as it is justifiable—only as a member of an historical series (AV, 137).

Any present moral theory cannot be independent of its historicity without becoming unintelligible. So, if discourse ethics insists on its independence from its own tradition, it becomes unintelligible (to the very people who are universally expected to practice it). Moreover, since Habermas's procedural universalism can hardly be justified if it is unintelligible even to itself, its intelligibility is a necessary condition for its own justification.

MacIntyre's point is that Habermas's discourse ethics is unintelligible without, and only justifiable within, its conscious links to its tradition. What, then, is the tradition that renders discourse ethics intelligible and thus a candidate for justification? Its philosophical tradition is clear; for Habermas self-consciously adopts discourse ethics from the Kantian moral tradition. Take the "fundamental principle of universalization" (*Universalisierungsgrundsatz* or "U"), for example, which has become the conceptual core of discourse ethics:

> Every valid norm must satisfy the condition that the consequences and side-effects which foreseeably follow from its general compliance can, for the satisfaction of the interests of every individual, be accepted without force by all those affected.[37]

This principle is unintelligible unless it is seen in the light of the general Kantian moral tradition (which includes the responses to Hegelian and other critiques of Kantian formalism) within which it offered as a modified, dialogical version of the categorical imperative.[38] To see the principle "in the light of" means that it is not intelligible outside its relationship to certain other Kantian claims about morality, such as those concerning the reasons why moral theory must be procedural rather than substantive, why moral laws must be universal, why moral conflicts must and can be resolved discursively, etc. This principle is unintelligible unless these other claims are brought into the picture. Furthermore, the principle is justified only on the basis of the other moral concepts that make up the Kantian moral tradition, thus illustrating the sense in which modernist moral philosophy must create its normativity out of itself, that is, out of its own tradition.

Habermas would concede that the principle of universalization is unintelligible unless its conceptual links to the Kantian moral tradition are clear; but he would object that it does not follow from this concession that the principle itself cannot be justified independently of this same tradition. He would insist on a separation between the issues of intelligibility and justification, and argue, again, that the universalization principle is universal on the basis of the universal structures of communicative competence. It is this basis which is independent of tradition.

What does 'independent' mean here? The task of practical rationality is to establish the conditions under which moral principles—for example, about justice—can be chosen impartially and then used to resolve conflicts—again, about justice—impartially. 'Independent' means, in short, "impartial."[39] According to Habermas, in order for it to be impartial in this respect, we cannot appeal to tradition as a final arbiter; practical reason must be procedural on the basis of the conditions of rational speech. But Habermas's insistence on this interpretation of impartiality brings us right back to the problem that his claim about the "unavoidability" or "irrevocability" of the presuppositions of discourse can be defended only by empirical, tradition-bound arguments that can yield only provisional, if universal, results.[40] The proceduralism—and hence the independence and impartiality—would likewise be provisional.

Even if Habermas were able to defend the independence of the core of moral intuition from its moral tradition, his problems would not be over; for the principle of universalization is not just dependent on the general Kantian moral tradition. It is also dependent on the social-political tradition of liberalism and its well-entrenched principles of freedom, equality, and justice. As Hegel originally pointed out in his critique of Kant, and Benhabib recently pointed out in her critique of Habermas, the principle of universalization presupposes a social-political development which is then embodied in what Hegel referred to as "ethical life." Habermas tries to incorporate this point in discourse ethics by conceiving of the logic of historical development underlying the project of the Enlightenment as a learning process which culminates in the conditions of reciprocity and symmetry and on which we cannot willingly turn our backs. But the appeal to a learning process alone does not capture enough of the historical depth presupposed by the principle of universalization, because Habermas reduces the complex learning process to the competence to utilize the universalization principle or, in Benhabib's words, to the ability to engage in the ideal role taking that results in the "generalized other." In effect, he reduces the learning process to a principle which presupposes the learning process (perhaps this is what he means by saying that modernity "cast itself back on itself"). Benhabib argues convincingly, however, that the "concrete other" cannot be excluded or abstracted out of this process.[41] To clarify what including the concrete other means is to spell out the concrete, historical dynamics that determine the identity of the selves who undergo this learning process and who are then expected to recognize and apply the universalization principle. By excluding these dynamics, Habermas has inadvertently excluded the generalized other as well; for there cannot be a generalized other unless there is, at the same time, a concrete other. It is with a concrete other that we engage in the role taking that is supposed to culminate in the "criteria of reversibility and universalizability said to be constituents of the moral point of view."[42] Benhabib thus argues, in effect, that the dialectic between the concrete and generalized other must be understood as part of the tradition that renders the principles of universalization intelligible and justifiable.

MacIntyre's claim that the principle of universalization is unintelligible when abstracted from its tradition is another way to say that the understanding of our moral-political-social tradition is a condition for our critical self-reflection which, in turn, is a necessary component of philosophical ethics. Ethics cannot be philosophical unless it is critical; that much seems obvious to both Habermas and MacIntyre. They would also agree that philosophical ethics cannot be critical unless it understands its historical origins. Such understanding or intelligibility is thus a precondition for philosophical-critical ethics; it is what MacIntyre has called its "moral starting point." We need to know who we are who have come to the point historically where we defend the universalization principle as the basis of our ethical theory and our conception of justice. *How* did we come to this point historically? What practices and institutions are required for us to be able to live under the concrete conditions that this principle expresses? How are the needs and goods that define who we are related to this principle, its history, and its realization? The answers to these questions establish the conditions for the intelligibility of the principle of universalization, an intelligibility which, as a component of philosophical ethics, is a necessary condition for the principle's justification. The problem with Habermas's discourse ethics is that, although he is aware of the importance of these issues, he excludes them from the structure of ethical theory.

MacIntyre's argument, as I have construed it, about the conditions for the intelligibility and justification of the principle of universalization helps to clarify a number of objections that critics have raised against Habermas's ethical theory. We have already seen how it fits with one of Benhabib's objections, i.e., that the principle of universalization requires a notion of the concrete other. It also fits with Wellmer's criticism, which Benhabib shares, that the conditions of rational speech do not necessarily entail the principle of universalization; for other as-sumptions about the "semantic content" of these conditions have to be clarified first in order for any specific principles to follow from them. Explaining the semantic content is not a problem for the philosophy of language, however; as Habermas himself recognizes, it requires an understanding of the historical con-ditions that influence the options for this semantic content and for the principles that are then said to follow from it. Third, MacIntyre's argument also helps to explain McCarthy's objection that, even if Habermas's appeal to Kohlberg's theory of the stages of moral development clarifies his principle of universal-ization, this appeal alone is not enough; for several ethical theories other than Habermas's could satisfy the conditions of the highest level of postconventional morality.[43] To make a choice between the various theories at this level, we have to introduce other assumptions, ones which again Habermas recognizes and which involve an understanding of who we are, what our historical origins are, what our needs are, etc. We must understand all these issues before we can understand our options and thus before we can choose from among the possible postconventional ethical theories. A fourth objection—that Habermas's accep-tance of the priority of the right over the good as a necessary and irrevocable feature of modernity[44] ought to be reconsidered—can also be explained from the perspective of MacIntyre's critique. For all notions of the good are clearly tied to tradition both for their intelligibility and justification. As Benhabib and others have argued,[45] however, such reconsideration of the relationship between the right and the good does not mean that we must reverse the modernist preference or reject the right for the good; rather, it means we must understand their interrelationship, perhaps in the way that Rawls has done recently.[46] Finally, MacIntyre's analysis also illuminates the issues of application and motivation which, in general, concern what happens once we have settled on our ethical theory and our principles. Clearly, the universalization principle alone is not sufficient to provide the conditions which will encourage people to abide by the principle and which will motivate them to concretize it in social-political institutions. Habermas, of course, recognizes that the moral point of view is incomplete without these conditions, that is, unless and until it is exercised and concretized; but he argues that it is the role of social theory, not philosophy, to provide them. Although the concrete historical conditions from which the universalization principle has been abstracted are now necessary to complete the principle itself, that is, to make it have concrete practical efficacy in individual lives and society at large, such "completion" is not a philosophical problem. But it is a philosophical and moral problem, as are all the problems that are raised by the other four objections just mentioned. None of these problems would be as difficult if we expanded Habermas's minimalist ethics, that is, if we did not abstract from our historical conditions in the first place, if we conceptualized ethical theory from the beginning as being broader than the task of justification. Although MacIntyre's argument about the conditions for the intelligibility and justification of ethical theory may not actually resolve all these problems, it does, I think, open the way to a philosophical understanding of what may make their resolution possible.

III. A METHODOLOGICAL CONVERGENCE BETWEEN MACINTYRE AND HABERMAS?

Habermas recognizes that he is "defending an outrageously strong claim [about the universality of intuitions which form the core of the moral point of view] in the present context of philosophical discussion."[47] Because he continues to have great difficulty defending it, one wants to ask whether it is necessary in order to support a cognitivist, procedural ethics. Rawls, to take another philosopher "in the present context of philosophical discussion," defends a procedural theory which is in many respects similar to Habermas's, but which is historical and empirical, while also being philosophical.[48] That is, relative to the three options offered earlier, Rawls would agree with MacIntyre that conceptions of both justice and practical rationality are tradition-bound. Habermas thinks, however, that Rawls's position is weaker than it could be, precisely because he gives up the possibility of providing a strong universalist justification of his principles of justice.[49] But this is the possibility I have argued Habermas does not have and, I would also want to argue (but not here), that he (rather, we) do not need.

If all that is at stake with the issue of the independence of the moral point of view is impartiality secured by proceduralism, then it does seem that Habermas insists on too strong a claim. He could defend a form of proceduralism, even a procedural universalism, so long as he does not violate the empiricism of his method of rational reconstruction. To take Rawls as an example again, he defends a proceduralism that does not require the strong claim about the justification of, in his case, the principles of justice. Rawls even has virtually the same intuitions—about the conditions of symmetry and reciprocal recognition—in his conception of the "original position" as Habermas has in his discourse ethics. But Rawls is content to ground them in a particular tradition, while leaving open the (in his eyes, metaphysical) question of whether they are universal;[50] to this extent, his position is not incompatible with MacIntyre's, at least not on a methodological level. If this is true, and Rawls's and Habermas's proceduralisms are indeed methodologically similar, then why do MacIntyre's and Habermas's ethical theories continue to seem incommensurable?

There would be a general methodological convergence between MacIntyre and Habermas as well, if they were to agree that practical rationality, as well as particular moral principles, are tradition-bound (option three above). Procedural universalism need not be methodologically opposed to MacIntyre's conception of tradition-bound practical rationality, so long as it is from the start and remains tradition-bound itself; that is, if it abandons the attempt to discover the tradition-transcendent ground of moral principles. MacIntyre, for his part, need not reject proceduralism, at least so long as it is tradition-bound; nor need he exclude universal claims or even the universalization principle, so long as they are presented as empirical, revisable claims. This does not mean that the principle of universalization is untenable; for the universalization principle need not be universal (in the strong sense); it need not be universally grounded in order to be widely and perhaps universally applicable. The universalization principle and its application need only be grounded in the only way a principle, scientific or moral, can be grounded: in tradition. Agreement between MacIntyre and Habermas on this point would make it clear that the real issue between them is not whether there is some strongly universal conception of practical rationality, but what dependent conception can be most rationally defended.

Where would this methodological convergence between MacIntyre and Habermas leave us?

The conclusion to which the argument so far has led is not only that it is out of the debates, conflicts, and enquiry of socially embodied, historically contingent traditions that contentions regarding practical rationality and justice are advanced, modified, abandoned, or replaced, but that there is no other way to engage in the formulation, elaboration, rational justification, and criticism of accounts or practical rationality and justice except from within some one particular tradition in conversation, cooperation, and conflict with those who inhabit the same tradition (WJWR, 350).

If and when methodological convergence is attained on the point that justice *and* practical rationality are inescapably tradition-bound, and there is also an agreement about what this tradition-boundedness entails, a debate between MacIntyre (the Thomist) and Habermas (the liberal Marxist) about *substantive* conceptions of justice, practical rationality, and modernity could begin.

IV. MACINTYRE AND THE RESOLUTION OF MORAL CRISES

Habermas might be more willing to acknowledge the tradition-boundedness of procedural universalism, if he could be convinced that a universalism with such a status could be justified in a rational manner. He insists on the universality of discourse ethics for fear that the "moral point of view" will otherwise lapse into relativism. MacIntyre believes that it is possible, and in fact only possible, to articulate and justify an ethical theory if it is understood as being tradition-bound. Moreover, he believes he can provide a tradition-bound conception of practical rationality which is nevertheless nonrelative in the sense that it is not (in principle) incommensurable with alternative conceptions from other traditions. How is this possible?

MacIntyre argues that the rationality of a tradition develops in three stages.[51] The first stage is that "in which the relevant beliefs, texts, and authorities [of a tradition] have not yet been put in question" (WJWR, 355), and they are thus able to provide a "structure of normality" to which individual agents within the tradition can turn for guidance when they act. This structure serves as the focus of the individual's rationality in the sense that it is "an arena of systematic activity" in which "goods are unambiguously ordered and within which individuals occupy and move between well-defined roles" (WJWR, 141). This means that, in this stage, an individual can answer the question "What am I to do?" only by turning to the structure of normality which provides the basic framework for understanding and engaging in action within that tradition (WJWR, 123).

The second stage is that "in which inadequacies of various types have been identified, but not yet remedied" (WJWR, 355). The inadequacies result from unresolved normative conflicts, newly revealed incoherences in the established system of beliefs, confrontations by new situations that the structure is unable to handle, the coming together of two previously separate communities that have different, perhaps incompatible belief systems, etc. One of these events, or maybe a combination of them, renders the structure of normality questionable or incoherent, and thus inadequate as a normative guide until it can justify itself in the face of its present conflicts. Thus, practical rationality, which in general is possible only within a tradition, is first consciously exercised when an agent begins to challenge the normative structure of that same tradition (WJWR, 54).

When this challenge occurs, the tradition moves to the third stage, "in which response to those inadequacies has resulted in a set of reformulations, reevaluations, and new formulations and evaluations, designed to remedy inadequacies and overcome limitations" (WJWR, 355). In this new stage,

> . . . rationality then requires of such a person . . . that he or she confirm or disconfirm over time this initial view of his or her relationship to this particular tradition or enquiry by engaging, to whatever degree is appropriate, both in the ongoing arguments within that tradition and in the argumentative debates and conflicts of that tradition of enquiry with one or more of its rivals (WJWR, 393-394).

That is, although an individual in a tradition first answers the question "What shall I do?" by unreflectively seeking guidance from the structure of normality constitutive of his particular tradition, he must also be willing at times to question these norms whenever a conflict about them arises. This does not mean that the individual must reject the norms by which he had once abided; rather, it means that he must justify them to himself and others because of the conflict that has arisen. The problem of justification first arises in this stage because of the conflicts. What rationality requires, according to MacIntyre, is that the individual, and by extension all the individuals of a tradition, engage in this activity of justification until the verdict about its structure of normality (as well as the system of beliefs from which this structure stems) is clear.

Every tradition has the possibility to take advantage of the "reformulations and reevaluations" and thereby to solve the moral crises that challenge it; but the realization of this possibility depends on whether it is open to other traditions.[52] The openness that is required by reason takes the concrete form of a dialectical inquiry of norms.

> What such an individual [or tradition] has to learn is how to test dialectically the theses proposed to him or her by each competing tradition, while also drawing upon these same theses in order to test dialectically those convictions and responses which he or she has brought to the encounter (WJWR, 398).

The individuals of a tradition must therefore conduct a dialectical inquiry of the conflicts with which they are confronted and engage in a dialogue about them with other traditions.[53] This inquiry and dialogue reflect "a kind of self-knowledge" (WJWR, 398), which itself is a sign of a tradition's rationality and which has at least the possibility of culminating in the enhancement of its rationality. This possibility—of the development of rationality—is what motivates the people of a tradition to be open to the "other," as this openness is a necessary, though not sufficient, condition for the development of their rationality qua tradition.

MacIntyre's principal claim here is thus that the rationality of a tradition is determined by its ability to resolve its moral crises. As Habermas might very well object, however, there is an epistemological problem here: Has MacIntyre provided an adequate account of how these crises can be resolved *rationally?* For it is very possible for traditions to be open to other traditions, even to engage in a dialectical inquiry of norms, but then to resolve their crisis in a nonrational manner. Such resolutions could hardly be said to contribute to the development of the tradition's rationality. MacIntyre's point about the historicity or tradition-boundedness of all rational inquiry raises, but so far has not answered, this epistemological question.

MacIntyre himself is aware of this problem, and, to address it, he introduces procedural criteria that must be satisfied if a tradition is to arrive at a *rational* resolution of any of its moral crises. The criteria are introduced in terms of the notion of "epistemological crisis," which is the philosophical concept underlying MacIntyre's account of the productive role of conflict in the stages of the development of a tradition's rationality (WJWR, 361).[54] As we just saw, a crisis erupts within a tradition because of problems or conflicts within it which cannot be resolved by its present resources—beliefs, principles, norms, methods, etc. If these problems persist, the tradition will eventually lose confidence in itself; there will be a general dissolution of the certitudes that characterized the first stage of its development. The epistemological problem is to explain how this certitude can be restored rationally; this means that both the process of restoration itself and the result—certitude—must be rational.

MacIntyre argues that a resolution of a crisis, if there is to be one at all, occurs in the third stage of a tradition's development and according to the following three requirements:

> First, this in some ways radically new and conceptually enriched scheme . . . must furnish a solution to the problems which had previously proved intractable. . . . Second, it must also provide an explanation of just what it was which rendered the tradition . . . sterile or incoherent. . . . And third, these first two tasks must be carried out in a way which exhibits some fundamental

continuity of the new conceptual and theoretical structures with the shared beliefs in terms of which the tradition of enquiry had been defined up to this point (WJWR, 362).

A tradition resolves its (internal or external) crisis when it adopts the "conceptually enriched scheme" of another tradition; the new scheme must also help to explain why the first tradition could not resolve its crisis on its own; finally, in addition to providing the solution and explanation, this scheme must allow there to be a certain continuity between the two stages of the first tradition before and after it underwent the crisis, plus a continuity between the two traditions that at first seemed incommensurable. There is a productive exchange between the traditions, because an otherwise intractable crisis has been resolved without undermining the tradition that suffered from it.[55]

But are these requirements, and thus MacIntyre's account of how moral crises are rationally resolved, descriptive or normative? This question is important to Habermas, for he insists at this point that these requirements themselves must be justified. MacIntyre repeatedly uses the words 'demand', 'require', and 'must', both in this account and especially in the earlier discussion about openness, which suggests that he intends his account to be normative. And throughout *Whose Justice? Which Rationality?* he offers explanations of the conditions that have made possible the resolution of moral crises in the history of philosophy.[56] These explanations are presumably intended to serve as a normative guide in future attempts to resolve moral crises. Yet there is a limit to the normative force of MacIntyre's account of the three requirements for the rational resolution of crises. Although a tradition must be open to other traditions in order to be in a position to solve its moral crises, clearly a tradition does not *have* to be open to other traditions or to engage in the dialectical inquiry of norms described earlier. Similarly, even though a tradition may know what its most reasonable course of action would be in response to an inevitable moral crisis, there is no guarantee that it will act that way, i.e., reasonably. Moreover, it does not *have* to resolve its moral crises at all, even if it were to agree that the conditions MacIntyre introduces are necessary; that is, it might agree that MacIntyre's conditions are necessary in order for a tradition to be rational, but then insist that it is not necessary for a tradition to be rational. But these are limits (which may imply a certain voluntarism about being rational) that no ethical theory alone, Habermas's discourse ethics included, can overcome; for they are part of the problematics either of the motivation for being moral or rational, or of the application of ethical theory to moral action and practice.

Does this mean that MacIntyre's criteria for resolving moral crisis are unjustified? It does not mean that, but it does indicate the kind of justification which is available to him. Given the limits of the normative force of his theory, what

MacIntyre says, in effect, is the following: every tradition, like every segment and individual within it, encounters moral problems that it cannot resolve; thus, every tradition, segment, and individual can expect to fall into states of moral crisis, confronting it with two basic options: (1) it can ignore the crisis, and perhaps stubbornly insist on its superiority over its competitors, while hoping that the crisis will not dissolve it at its seams; or (2) it can make an effort to acknowledge that it has a crisis and that the others may be able to help resolve it. The second option is the most rational, according to MacIntyre, because it is the only one that offers a solution to the crisis which, because of the third requirement, will at the same time preserve at least some part(s) of what the tradition, segment, or individual formerly believed (WJWR, 388). The criteria explain how, if a tradition chooses, it can resolve its crises rationally and thereby enhance its rationality; if and when its crises are resolved, it is, at least in part, because of the requirements MacIntyre has introduced. These criteria are bound to a specific tradition, as is practical rationality itself, although they may be applicable beyond a single tradition if they prove useful, from the standpoint of other traditions, in resolving crises in those other traditions.

Habermas would not agree with MacIntyre's account of how moral crises can be rationally resolved; for he would argue that MacIntyre cannot defend his criteria of rationality without presupposing principles of modernity which he has otherwise rejected. Of course, MacIntyre has to provide some defense of these criteria, especially since he claims they are tradition-bound but not relativistic; and this means he will undoubtedly have to spell out the presuppositions to which he is committed.[57] This does not mean, however, that MacIntyre is engaged in a form of performative contradiction in Habermas's sense of the term, because MacIntyre's three criteria need not presuppose Habermas's account of the discourse of modernity. But clearly MacIntyre has to say more on this issue.[58]

V. CONCLUSION

MacIntyre's tradition-bound, dialectical-ethical inquiry and Habermas's discourse ethics are best understood as two alternative procedures that parties (individuals, parts of a single tradition, or whole traditions) may utilize in order to resolve their substantive moral crises and disagreements. Which is the best or most rational? This question remains open to further philosophical debate; but at least it is clear that the answer does not depend on which alternative is universal in the strong sense, for none is.

The principal intention here has been to determine the moral starting point of a philosophical ethics and to explain the conditions of intelligibility and justification of ethical theory. Even without claiming that MacIntyre has necessarily won any concessions from Habermas leading to a methodological convergence, I hope to have shown that MacIntyre's arguments about the status of moral-practical rationality and Habermas's defense of universalism have advanced the dialogue about justice and practical rationality by clarifying the intimate and intricate relationships between justice, practical rationality, and tradition. They both continue to make serious philosophical contributions to a profound dialogue, one on which both agree the very possibility of a philosophical ethics depends.

Columbia University

NOTES

1 Notre Dame: University Press, 1981 [hereafter AV].

2 Notre Dame: University Press, 1988 [hereafter WJWR].

3 *The Philosophical Discourse of Modernity: Twelve Lectures,* Frederick G. Lawrence, trans. (Cambridge: MIT, 1987), p. 7 [hereafter PDM]. Elsewhere Habermas offers a succinct description of modernity: ". . . in the modern period it [the potential for reason] leads to a rationalization of life-worlds, to the differentiation of their symbolic structures, which is expressed above in the increasing reflexivity of cultural traditions, in processes of individuation, in the generalization of values, in the increasing prevalence of more abstract and more universal norms, and so on" [in *Habermas: Autonomy and Solidarity,* Peter Dews, ed. (London: Verso, 1986), p. 184].

4 In "Philosophy as Stand-In and Interpreter" [in *After Philosophy: End or Transformation?,* Kenneth Baynes, James Bohman, and Thomas McCarthy, eds. (Cambridge: MIT, 1986), pp. 296-315], Habermas uses the term 'posttraditional ethics'.

5 PDM, p. 7.

6 Liberalism and modernity are not the same thing; perhaps liberalism is best understood in this context as one part or direction within the larger "project" of modernity. MacIntyre defines liberalism as the claim that justice and practical rationality are grounded universally.

7 Georgia Warnke argues that there is a similar "methodological convergence" between John Rawls and Michael Walzer and, to a lesser extent, between Habermas and Walzer; cf. her "Rawls, Habermas, and Real Talk: A Reply to Walzer," in this volume.

    While focusing on the methodological level of the differences between MacIntyre and Habermas, I shall suspend judgment on their substantive differences. For this reason, 'liberalism' will be understood here on this same methodological level. It should be noted, however, that MacIntyre's rejection of "methodological liberalism" does not necessarily entail a rejection of "moral-political" liberalism, even though MacIntyre himself seems to reject both. Cf. Roger Paden's application of Nancy Fraser's distinctions concerning Michel Foucault's anti-humanism to MacIntyre's anti-humanism/anti-liberalism; "Post-structuralism and Neo-romanticism or Is MacIntyre a Young Conservative," in *Philosophy and Social Criticism,* XIII, 2 (1987): 125-143. Fraser's distinctions are introduced in her "Michel Foucault: A Young Conservative?" in *Ethics,* XLIX (1985).

8 Marx Wartofsky was one of the few to recognize that the problematic of rationality was crucial in *After Virtue* and would require a more substantial treatment in its own right (which has become

MICHAEL KELLY

Whose Justice? Which Rationality?); cf. "Virtue Lost or Understanding MacIntyre," in *Inquiry,* xxvii, 2 (1985): 235-250, esp. p. 238.

9 MacIntyre could be criticized for stacking the deck when he offers examples from the history of moral philosophy to illustrate and defend this claim about the tradition-boundedness of justice and practical rationality; for he discusses philosophers who would never have accepted this claim. At the same time, the more theoretical arguments that he provides to defend his claim do not seem convincing without some examples. Cf. WJWR, p. 10, where MacIntyre argues that the claim can be defended only with and through examples; and p. 252, where he acknowledges that the philosophers he discusses were not aware of their historicity. Cf. also, "Moral Rationality, Tradition, and Aristotle: A Reply to Onora O'Neill, Raimond Gaita, and Stephen R. L. Clark," in *Inquiry,* xxvi, 4 (1984): 447-466, esp. p. 452, where he discusses some of the objections raised against his general historicist epistemology. But I am not concerned here about the accuracy of MacIntyre's claims about figures in the history of moral philosophy; I am concerned only about the status of contemporary ethical theory.

10 I shall focus on moral principles, in general, rather than on justice in particular, because it will make it easier to relate MacIntyre's position to Habermas's.

11 He argues that normative claims are tradition-dependent but their validity can, at the same time, transcend any local context because of their "moment of unconditionality." Cf. PDM, pp. 322-323; and Dews, ed., p. 206.

12 Cf. Dews, ed., pp. 160, 170, 207.

13 *Habermas: Critical Debates,* John Thompson and David Held, eds. (Cambridge: MIT, 1982), p. 251.

14 Cf. my "The Habermas/Gadamer Debate Revisited: The Question of Ethics," in *Philosophy and Social Criticism,* xiv, 3-4 (Fall 1989), where I defend Gadamer against Habermas.

15 Thompson and Held, eds., p. 239; cf. also, p. 58, and pp. 58-59.

16 In "Philosophy as Stand-In and Interpreter," p. 310, Habermas defines philosophy in terms of this rational reconstructive method.

17 On the relation between communicative action and discourse, see *The Theory of Communicative Action: Vol. I, Reason and the Rationalization of Society,* Thomas McCarthy, trans. (Boston: Beacon, 1984), pp. 19, 42, 94-101. An example of this know-how and know-that distinction would be a theory of meaning that reconstructs the intuitive know-how of speakers of a language.

18 Habermas introduces three possible strategies in *The Theory of Communicative Action, Vol. I* to support the universality of communicative action: one is "the formal-pragmatic development of the concept of communicative action"; the second is "to assess the empirical usefulness of formal pragmatic insights"; and the third, which he chose to pursue, is a theory of societal rationalization (cf. pp 138-139). Cf. also Seyla Benhabib's discussion of Habermas's strategies in *Critique, Norm, and Utopia: A Study of the Foundations of Critical Theory* (New York: Columbia, 1986), ch. 8.

19 Dews, ed., p. 184.

20 Cf. Thompson and Held, eds., pp. 254-255. Cf. Stephen K. White, *The Recent Work of Jürgen Habermas: Reason, Justice and Modernity* (New York: Cambridge, 1988), pp. 50-55.

21 Habermas appeals to Lawrence Kohlberg's theory of the stages of moral development to ground his claim about the logic of moral development culminating in the ideal speech situation. In PDM, he relates this logic to the general structures of modernity as a whole.

22 For a clarification of this sense of "necessity," cf. Dews, ed., p. 51, and White, p. 52.

23 Cf. Albrecht Wellmer, *Ethik und Dialog: Elemente des moralischen Urteils bei Kant und in der Diskursethik* (Frankfurt: Suhrkamp, 1986); cf. also White, p. 23.

24 Part of Habermas's argument in *The Theory of Communicative Action* is that communicative action has a certain logical priority over its alternative—strategic or instrumental action; the latter is said to be parasitic on the former. To defend this claim he uses his method of rational

reconstruction, proposing to reconstruct the universal competence for communicative action and thereby establish its priority. But, as we shall see below, the status of the claims based on this method is more tenuous than Habermas realizes.

25 Cf. his critique of Habermas in his article in this volume. Cf. also Carol Gould's argument that Habermas's justification of moral norms by a discursive, consensual procedure ends up being circular, because the procedure itself is justified in moral terms. "Therefore, I would argue that the normative ground that violates any consensual judgment must lie outside the consensual procedure itself in some wider context of human activity [self-development]." Cf. *Rethinking Democracy: Freedom and Social Cooperation in Politics, Economy, and Society* (New York: Cambridge, 1988), p. 127; cf. also pp. 119-127 and 299-306, where she compares Habermas and Rawls.

26 Cf. the work of Jacques Derrida, Michel Foucault, and others, who are criticized by Habermas in his PDM.

27 Cf. PDM, where Habermas seems to be arguing, as the title alone suggests, that there is but one discourse of modernity; and cf. "Philosophy as Stand-In and Interpreter," where he explicitly claims that there is only one criterion by which opinions in science or morality can be judged valid—that they are based on agreement reached by argumentation (p. 309)—and this is a criterion distinctive of modernity.

28 Cf. *Critique, Norm, and Utopia*, p. 267. Cf. also White, pp. 129-136, where he discusses some of the same problems with the method of rational reconstruction, but then defends it.

29 Dews, ed., pp. 131-132. Cf. also Habermas's comments in *Habermas and Modernity*, Richard Bernstein, ed. (Cambridge: MIT, 1985), p. 196: ". . . philosophy shares with the sciences a fallibilistic consciousness, in that its strong universalistic suppositions require confirmation in an interplay with empirical theories of competence"; and "Interpretive Social Science vs. Hermeneuticism," in *Social Science as Moral Inquiry*, N. Haan, R. N. Bellah, P. Rabinow, and W. M. Sullivan, eds. (New York: Columbia, 1983), p. 261: "It is important to see that rational reconstructions . . . have only a hypothetical status. . . . [as input in empirical theories] They are in need of further corroboration."

30 *Critique, Norm, and Utopia*, p. 277. Cf. also Thompson and Held, eds., p. 253, where Habermas rejects Benhabib's tendency to give ethical life priority over abstract morality. Cf. also Wellmer's critique (in *Ethik und Dialog*) of Habermas from a similar perspective.

31 Cf. "Philosophy as Stand-In and Interpreter," p. 310, where Habermas refers to "reconstructive hypotheses."

32 PDM, pp. 322-323.

33 The principle of universalization captures a "a universal core of moral intuition in all times and in all societies" which stems "from the conditions of symmetry and reciprocal recognition which are unavoidable presuppositions of communicative action." Cf. Dews, ed., pp. 206-207; also, cf. p. 205.

34 White formulates it so: "The sort of cognitivist position which Habermas wants to defend is one which follows the Kantian tradition in arguing, first, that valid norms are ones which have the quality of fairness or impartiality; secondly, that this quality can be expressed by some version of the principle of universalization; and finally, that this principle itself can be justified" (p. 48).

35 Cf. Habermas's discussion of Rawls and Scanlon in his article in this issue.

36 Cf. Bernstein, ed., pp. 209-210.

37 "Über Moralität und Sittlichkeit—Was macht eine Lebensform 'rational'," in *Rationalität: Philosophische Beiträge*, Hans Schnädelbach, hrsg. (Frankfurt: Suhrkamp, 1984), pp. 218-235, p. 219; and "Diskursethik—Notizen zu einem Begründungsprogramm" and "Moralbewusstsein und kommunikatives Handeln," in *Moralbewusstsein und kommunikatives Handeln* (Frankfurt: Suhrkamp, 1983), pp. 53-125 and pp. 127-206; here, pp. 75, 103.
  This principle, in turn, assumes the form of a "fundamental principle" (*Grundsatz* or "G"):

"Every valid norm must be able to be accepted by all affected" (cf. "Über Moralität und Sittlichkeit—Was macht eine Lebensform 'rational'," p. 219). These two principles form Habermas's minimal ethics, cf. Dews, ed., pp. 170-171; also, cf. pp. 160, 207.

38 This principle is clearly a reformulation of Kant's categorical imperative, but, as McCarthy makes clear, with the important shift of emphasis "from what each can will without contradiction to be a general law, to what all can will in agreement to be a universal norm" [*The Critical Theory of Jürgen Habermas* (Cambridge: MIT, 1978), p. 326].

39 Cf. Thompson and Held, eds., pp. 256-257, where Habermas also refers to G. H. Mead's notion of "ideal role taking."

40 Habermas continues to flirt with the quasi-transcendental performative contradiction strategy which Karl-Otto Apel and others (e.g., Wolfgang Kuhlmann, Victorio Hösle) have continued to pursue. Although Habermas is often ambivalent on this issue, he seems to be watching Apel and the others from a cautious distance, still hoping that this stronger type of argument will prove to be viable. Cf., for example, the recent "Law and Morality," in *The Tanner Lectures on Human Values, Vol. VIII,* Sterling M. McMurrin, ed. (Salt Lake City: Utah UP. 1988), p. 244. But compare "Interpretive Social Sciences vs. Hermeneuticism," p. 261, where he says he is not seduced by the search for ultimate foundations.

41 Cf. *Critique, Norm, and Utopia,* pp. 340-342; and "The Generalized and Concrete Other: The Kohlberg-Gilligan Controversy and Feminist Theory," in *Feminism and Critique,* Drucilla Cornell and Seyla Benhabib, eds. (Minneapolis: Minnesota UP, 1987), pp. 77-95; whereas she uses these terms in relation to individuals, I am using them to refer also to cultural traditions.

42 "The Generalized and Concrete Other: The Kohlberg-Gilligan Controversy and Feminist Theory," p. 90.

43 Cf. "Rationality and Relativism: Habermas's 'Overcoming' of Hermeneutics," in *Habermas: Critical Debates,* pp. 57-78.

44 "Cognitivist moral theories disgorge issues of the good life, focusing instead strictly on deontological, generalizable aspects of ethics, so that all that remains of 'the good' is the just" [in *After Virtue,* p. 312].

45 Benhabib introduces a relationship between the community of solidarity and needs and the community of rights and entitlements; cf. *Critique, Norm, and Utopia,* p. 339. If Adi Ophir is right, once we reconsider the "good," we must also rethink the notion of "evil" in the sense discussed in his article in this volume.

46 Cf. Rawls, "The Priority of Right and Ideas of the Good," *Philosophy and Public Affairs,* XVII, 4 (1988): 251-276.

47 Dews, ed., p. 206.

48 Because of the role of the "veil of ignorance" in Rawls's conception of the "original position," he is commonly interpreted as offering an ahistorical moral-political theory of justice. In his most recent writings, however, Rawls has made a conscious effort to distance himself from this interpretation. I shall not venture to resolve the debate about whether he has changed his position since *A Theory of Justice* or whether he is just trying to set the record straight.

49 Cf. Habermas's criticisms of Rawls's interpretation of the "moral point of view" in "Justice and Solidarity," in this volume. And cf. also Benhabib's comparison of Habermas and Rawls in *Critique, Norm, and Utopia,* pp. 288-290; and in "The Methodological Illusions of Modern Political Theory," in *Neue Hefte für Philosophie,* XXI (Spring 1982): 47-74.

50 Cf. "Kantian Constructivism in Moral Theory: The Dewey Lectures 1980," *Journal of Philosophy,* LXXVII, 9 (September 1980): 515-572.

51 An individual's moral rationality also develops in three stages: (1) he acts according to implicit norms derived from his family, society, and other segments of tradition that constitute his "structure of morality"; (2) his actions are challenged by himself or another individual (most likely one acting according to a different structure), and he makes his formerly implicit norms

explicit and defends them according to some part of the tradition—e.g., by referring to certain customs, a sacred text, or the like; at this stage, he is still acting uncritically, although his reflection is emerging; (3) at this stage, the norms used to defend his actions are now questioned, and even the tradition itself from which these norms were derived is subject to critical inquiry; this is the level of real critical reflection. The philosophical problem is how this critical reflection can be conducted—according to what principles and criteria?

52 This openness between traditions depends, in turn, on whether they are able to learn one another's languages (WJWR, 387-388); it thus involves translation. The result of this learning ability is not only a linguistic achievement or an increase in understanding, however; it is what makes it possible for the rationality of a tradition to progress. Cf. Habermas's discussion of "learning processes" in his account of the stages of moral development.

53 In my "The Dialectical/Dialogical Structure of Ethical Reflection," *Philosophy and Rhetoric,* XXII, 3 (1989): 174-193, I make similar points about how the practice of ethical reflection is structured according to a dialectical inquiry that itself has the structure of a dialogue between individuals or traditions who hold conflicting ethical beliefs and principles.

54 Cf. also "Epistemological Crises, Dramatic Narrative and the Philosophy of Science," *The Monist,* LXIX, 4 (1977); and "Moral Rationality, Tradition, and Aristotle: A Reply to Onora O'Neill, Raimond Gaita, and Stephen R. L. Clark," pp. 452-453. An objection could be raised about the appropriateness of the notion of epistemological crisis, since it was originally developed in the context of the philosophy of science. Can it be transferred to the realm of ethical-political theory? I agree with MacIntyre that it can be, because the notion concerns the relationship between rational inquiry and tradition and that is the same problem being discussed here in ethics. That is, the similarity of the problem that the notion treats is more important than the differences in the modes of rational inquiry in which it is treated. Cf. MacIntyre's "Bernstein's Distorting Mirrors: A Rejoinder," in *Soundings,* LXVII (Spring 1984), p. 32, where he argues that philosophy and science share the same type of rationality, one which develops through crisis resolution. Thus, as I have been doing all along, I shall talk about "moral" rather than "epistemological" crises.

55 Only the crises resolved according to the three requirements contribute to the development of a tradition's rationality. Other crises either are not resolved at all, or else are concluded when one tradition is forced to acknowledge the superiority of another. This last option would not be a solution to the crisis in MacIntyre's terms, however, because the third requirement would not have been met. What has happened in such a case is that the tradition itself has been *dis*solved. The difference between a crisis which can be solved and which can thereby enhance a tradition and one that results in a total dissolution of a tradition is thus one of continuity.

56 Cf. esp. chs. VI, X, and XVII.

57 Cf. Kenneth Baynes's critique of MacIntyre in his article in this volume; Richard Bernstein's objection that, in MacIntyre's critique of the Enlightenment in *After Virtue,* he appropriates principles inherent in this very project—*Soundings,* LXVII (Spring 1984): 6-29; and see MacIntyre's response in the same issue, p. 40. Finally, see Charles Larmore's review of WJWR in *Journal of Philosophy,* LXXXVI, 8 (August 1989): 437-442, where he makes a similar objection to MacIntyre's critique of modernity.

58 In the context of the continuing dialogue and debate between MacIntyre and Habermas, it could turn out that a modified version of Habermas's discourse ethics could be chosen as the most rational ethical theory from among the alternatives, MacIntyre's own included, within the general type of ethical theory which MacIntyre himself has argued is the only type available to us as the tradition-bound beings that we are. This would mean that MacIntyre would have scored a key *hermeneutic* point against Habermas, for he would have explained what happens behind the back of Habermas's procedural universalism. But it would also mean that Habermas would be better at MacIntyre's own game of tradition-bound rational inquiry. This remains to be seen.

BEYOND GOOD—EVIL: A PLEA FOR A HERMENEUTIC ETHICS

ADI OPHIR

I

Evil is no less widespread than money and no less dangerous than the worse things money can buy, yet it is noted, predicted, and accounted for like changes in the weather, and it is no more thought about, and even less understood.

Recently, thinking about evil has played a certain role in the growing body of literature and research related to the Holocaust, with some illuminating results. That the systematic extermination of Jews and Gypsies is an archetype of evil is self-evident. Even the worst revisionist historian can dare no more than deny the facts or compare them with other forms of horror, e.g., the Gulag. In its less wicked face, revisionist historiography forces us at least to ask how absolute or unique the Holocaust was, and what made it possible as the terrible and unique form of evil it was.[1] Others who study the Holocaust and encounter its survivors are no less preoccupied with personal and collective ways to cope with memories of the horrors: How much, and how, ought one to remember, tell, and retell? But the presence of evil in Nazi Germany is so overwhelming that it hardly allows any attempt to problematize evil and contemplate its nature in the context of recent European history. On the contrary, people tend to measure the forms of evil in other contexts against the unquestionable presence of evil under the Nazi regime, which has been conceived as the form of absolute evil. This comparison often forces distorting analogies that only mask or block any genuine attempt to think evil as such, and to think it in different historical contexts and in less extreme situations,[2] and less extreme situations are terrible and numerous enough.

Modern political philosophy, however, has paid little attention to the notion of evil.[3] Its tendency to shy away from any serious attempt to contemplate evil has deep roots. Ever since Plato, and more so after Plotinus and Augustine, evil has been defined as the privation of the good,[4] and its account has usually been mediated through the concept of the good. In the metaphysical tradition, evil is the negative sign of an ever absent presence, the good;[5] in the utilitarian tradition, it is a sign of a contrary good, always interchangeable with it: "What may be predicated of each may, by an appropriate change in the context, be with equal truth and propriety predicated of the other," for "whatever be the shape in which it is possible for evil to show itself, the exclusion or removal of it is a correspondent good," and vice versa.[6]

There have been a few exceptions. In Hegel, the contemplation of evil resulted in a metaphysical *Aufhebung* that explains evil away.[7] Schopenhauer[8] makes evil primordially omnipresent, a cosmological first element deprived of any particular political significance, which thus allows him to end up in a vain gesture of "pessimistic" political escapism. Nietzsche's genealogy of evil is inseparable from that of the good, and it leads toward a too easy (and dangerous) identification of evil with the mob, the "Plebian," or, in general, with that which is "all too human" to be desired by a "free spirit."[9] Perhaps the most noteworthy exception was Montaigne, who "put cruelty first"[10] and seriously considered different forms of evil independently of the state of their positive elimination. Montaigne placed the infliction of bodily pain on top of all other vices, and was therefore capable of contemplating evil with no recourse to the notion of the good or to a Christian God who provides it. He could articulate different conceptions of evil relative to changing moral sensibilities, whose psychological, cultural, and historical-context dependence he so well understood, yet without relativizing his basic moral stand: uncompromising condemnation of cruelty as the vain infliction of excessive pain upon another. It is from him that we may learn most when trying to rethink evil in its modern context.[11]

As it has paid little attention to the notion of evil, modern political philosophy has not been very interested in the notion of the good either. Kant rehabilitated a suspiciously transcendent "highest good" (*Summum Bonum*)[12] only after establishing the proper boundaries of critical moral discourse and grounding its guiding formal principles. His contemporary heirs, like John Rawls and Jürgen Habermas, give up the second half of his second Critique with its ramifications in the third and in the lesser writings. They rather set out to develop procedures for rational competitions among rival conceptions of the good life, of the goods in life, and of who deserves to take more of their share. The emphasis put on the concepts of justice and justification in contemporary moral discourse is due, in part at least, to that inherent suspicion toward any theoretical position that claims to represent the good itself. Thus, Rawls's theory of justice gives the good a marginal position and a secondary role. The good is shown to be "congruent" with justice, but it cannot ground a theory of justice (as it does, e.g., in Plato's *Republic*), or even serve as its regulative idea, the horizon toward which all procedural arrangements aim (as may be suggested by Hans-Georg Gadamer's notion of *die Sache*),[13] since there is not, and need not be, any agreed upon concept of the good but only multiple, conflicting conceptions of the good, hence too many horizons at which to aim.[14]

If this is the place of the good, why should a theory of justice bother about evil? Apparently it should not, if it only pretends to be a theory about the just distribution of goods; but in fact it should, at least as long as it claims to be a theory of distributive justice, for the simple fact that society distributes evils as well as goods. No theory of justice takes account of this fact, I believe. An argument about the independent existence of mechanisms for the distribution of evils lies at the core of my attempt to revise and limit the scope of both reconstructivist and communitarian ethical conceptions of justice. The distribution of evils, as well as its political structures and social mechanisms, I shall argue, are neither transparent nor self-evident for most social agents. This places hermeneutic ethics at the center of moral argumentation, presenting it not as a necessary supplement, but as a discursive framework and a regulative idea. At the same time, the conflict between tradition and universalization is transcended without being resolved, as both attempts to appeal to a shared tradition of values or to universal principles are situated in the context of concrete ethico-political struggles.

In order to argue this point further, let me take as my point of departure the general framework of an existing theory of distribution, Michael Walzer's theory of complex equality and pluralistic, "multidimensional" justice, as developed in his *Spheres of Justice*.[15] Walzer's theory may serve as a good starting point, (a) because his basic picture of a multidimensional society seems to me more adequate to modern social reality than other models presupposed by rival theories of justice, Rawls included; and (b) because it is, at the same time, all the more lacking, precisely because it disregards sophisticated mechanisms for the distribution of evils. Walzer is right in his attempt to represent society as a multiple system of distributive spheres, in which goods are conceived, evaluated, created, and exchanged according to a more or less autonomous logic of relations which prevails in each of the distinct, yet interrelated spheres.[16] In what follows, I presuppose this picture of social reality without arguing it further, trying, however, to show the particular sense in which I think it to be a deficient picture.

II

"Human society is a distributing community" (SJ, 3), says Walzer, and "distribution is what social conflict is all about" (SJ, 11). Distributive principles are supposed to control, constrain, and direct the movements of goods people conceive and create, as well as the means needed for, and the social positions involved in, the conception, creation, acquisition, and exchange of these goods.

Naturally, means and positions are also goods of a sort; they are exchanged, distributed, acquired, and lost through civil or violent conflicts. Walzer's original contribution is, as mentioned above, his conception of society as a cluster of relatively autonomous distributive spheres (of, e.g., economic goods, political power, membership, knowledge, honor, etc.), among which there are rules of conversion and exchange. Goods are exchanged within some spheres according to more or less defined exchange values. Goods are convertible across spheres, if possession of enough goods in one sphere can provide easy access to the acquisition of goods in another sphere while bypassing the second sphere's rules and relations of exchange. For example, when the prince enjoys the right of the first night, political power is converted into sexual pleasure; when students are exempted from military duty, cultural capital is converted into release from danger and effort, and gain in free time. Tyranny is defined as a social system in which the possession of a dominant good (e.g., political power) is convertible across the spheres (e.g., to money, love, honor, etc.) (SJ, 19, 315–316). A pluralist democracy, on the other hand, maintains the autonomy of the spheres, allows one to acquire or lose goods in one sphere independently of one's situation in the other spheres. A theory of justice, according to Walzer, must not only account for just distribution, but also for the different spheres where distribution takes place and for the just interrelations among them. This is not a small task; it takes no less than the systematic attempt "to map out the entire social world" (SJ, 26).

But the entire social world includes regions of "evils," not only spheres of goods. It is not enough to describe the "central process" to which a distributive theory applies as one in which "people conceive and create goods, which they then distribute among themselves" (SJ, 6). For people also conceive and create "evils," which they then distribute among themselves, especially among others; and they sometimes also distribute evils not conceived of before, which they then conceptualize, recreate (or rather reproduce), and distribute. Much like goods, the production, distribution, and reproduction of evils are done in more or less regular patterns within more or less regulated fields of socio-politico-cultural interaction.[17]

Equipped with Ockham's razor, quick readers would certainly tend to get rid of the new cluster of vaguely defined "regions" added to an already crowded multiple system of social "spheres." The following example may demonstrate the apparent redundancy. When a government allocates money, say, for transportation infrastructure, when it allocates only this amount and invests it only in those districts and kinds of traffic, it certainly distributes hazards of car or airplane accidents among its subjects. A government may even be blamed for letting a predictable number of members of a specific group, say, Harlem's pedestrians, die by not investing enough in their safety. But this is done by the same system that distributes the goods one may call "transportation safety," and it is utterly useless to double that system by a ghostly one that distributes, say, "transportation mortality."

But who says which is the ghostly system here and which is the "real" one? At the very least, it can be argued that even the mere inversion of perspectives—which allows one to look at the same social mechanism from the point of view of the evils rather than of the goods it produces and distributes—is worthy of serious consideration. In some contexts, shifting perspectives is at least a matter of convenience. Walzer himself finds it more appropriate to deal with certain distributive spheres in terms of the "negative goods" distributed there. Military duty or grueling work in a communal kitchen in an Israeli kibbutz are examples discussed at some length in terms of "negative goods" (SJ, 165 ff.), stressing the burden or suffering which has to be shared in justice, without trying to resort to their privation (exemption from military service or the number of days a year a kibbutz member is free of "kitchen duty"). But is it not a matter of sheer convenience? For after all, within the same distributive sphere, goods and their negatives are perfectly convertible, by definition.[18] And if this is the case, a theory of distributive justice need not bother with "evils," let aone with the dubious notion of Evil.

III

But this is not the case. Despite a certain overlapping, some "spheres of evils" are as autonomous as some of the spheres of goods; they are conducted according to their proper logic of interrelations, and exchange and distributive positions, and cannot be described in terms only of the allocation of "negative goods" or the systematic deprivation of positive goods. It is not that the removal of single evils cannot be described as negative goods; rather, those evils are not privations of negative goods regularly distributed in a sphere of their own (like membership, authority, or material goods). The symmetrical relation between good and evil may work only when an object is abstracted from the context of its production and distribution. The symmetry does not hold for the entire sphere. When an entire sphere is concerned and accounted for, it is impossible to conceive one (a sphere of evils) as the privation of another (a sphere of goods). In the "negative" sphere, the regular distribution is a distribution of evils; goods are the exception and they are conceived of as privation of evils. The removal of evils may be described as negative goods, but the presence of evils is not dependent on the systematic distribution of a particular type of goods that are now absent. Evils are experienced by individuals as objects with a presence of their own. They may remain invisible when their distributive sphere is looked upon from good's point of view. But the asymmetry goes much further: evils may be produced and distributed across several, more recognized spheres (of goods); within their proper sphere, their economy may be based on principles entirely different from those which guide other spheres (of goods); and they may be at stake in distinct social conflicts, different from those which characterize the competition over (positive) goods. In order to argue this point fully, we need a developed "discourse of evil"; a few examples may at least illustrate where the argument goes.

(1) The modern prison is one case in point. It is a sophisticated mechanism for the distribution of one form of punishment, i.e., denial of civic liberty according to strict rules. But, unlike other burdens the state distributes among its citizens, whether universally (like taxes) or particularly (like fines), a variety of other evils besides the deprivation of liberty is being distributed in the modern prison system. This happens not because the people who run our prisons are especially wicked. It happens because the mechanisms of power relations within prisons are so constituted that they create positions from which power can be exercised, and bodies and souls can be disciplined and manipulated, "shaped" and reshaped, sometimes tortured, according to rules and regulations, but not according to the law and the system of distribution which it dictates. Distributing the denial of freedom, the law determines only the term of imprisonment, or at most it may state the type of prison; all the rest belongs to a different distributive sphere, animated by wholly different distributive mechanisms. In this respect, at least, Michel Foucault was right when he said that prisons resemble factories, schools, barracks, and hospitals, which, in turn, all resemble prisons.[19]

All the disciplines that Foucault describes are well-structured and specifically located distributive mechanisms that work alongside and behind the larger and more visible, recognized spheres of power, law, and the distribution of goods. They distribute "things" which cannot be articulated, conceived, or acquired in the visible spheres, yet without which those spheres cannot function. The "things" distributed are not necessarily evils. They are first and foremost positions from which power is legitimately exercised in various ways, and which, purposefully or not, allow individuals to acquire goods and inflict evils. The orders of power in and around the "disciplines" have to be brought to light and accounted for as an essential stage of any attempt "to map the social world."

The distribution of evils that these orders of power allow and foster must be deciphered and analyzed in terms specific to the system of social interaction involved, and to that which is produced and exchanged within it. In prison, that which is produced and exchanged are means and forms of suffering and modes of behaviors, as well as means and forms of pleasure and modes of knowledge, all of which are peculiar to the system of power and enclosed within its walls. A form of suffering, e.g., the crowdedness of one's cell, is no less an object of discourse and action within the prison than a form of pleasure, e.g., the length of time one is allowed to go for a walk outside one's cell. Isolated and taken out of context, crowdedness may be accounted for in terms of deprivation of privacy; time outside one's cell may be accounted for in terms of time inside. But what really matters here, and can be grasped only within the context of prison as an entire system of power relations, is the manipulation of space, time, and bodies which creates spare space and outside time as positive objects, and crowded space and inside time as negative objects, both to be distributed among the inmates. Here both goods and evils are distinct objects, spoken of, perceived, and acted upon by all social agents involved as separate objects, each with its own presence, positive and negative attributes, without the redundant, distorting translation of evils into negative goods. Both goods and evils are produced in order to control and manipulate individuals, not in order to be consumed, enjoyed, or used by them for their own purposes. Looking at the system of power in the prison only from the point of view of the goods it creates and distributes means overlooking both its manipulative character, the techniques it uses, and the specificity of the objects it creates.

(2) In the autumn of 1988, dozens of Palestinian children living under Israeli occupation in the West Bank and Gaza were denied their on-going medical treatment in Israeli hospitals. The Israeli military government justified this unusual act by referring to the uncivil, sometimes rebellious behavior of adults and youngsters in those children's families; due to their unlawful behavior, the children of these families lost whatever right they had to receive the special medical care provided to the Palestinian population by the military government through Israeli hospitals. One may well reconstruct the distributive sphere of state provisions in the occupied territories and demonstrate how it accords with this or that theory of distributive justice. But to remove a five-year old child who suffers from severe kidney disease from a dialysis machine, or to deny a leukemia patient his chemotherapy (when there is no sudden shortage of medical equipment) is certainly evil. If conceived of as a simple privation of a good, this evil is deceivingly abstracted from the complex system of power which was established through the Israeli occupation and from the distribution of evils for which that system is responsible. The occupying regime may be justified in general— when the distribution of goods is concerned—but it produces and distributes evils nonetheless. It does so in quantities, ways, and forms that no account of the distributive spheres and their complex interrelations may exhaust, let alone justify.

Occupation,[20] not only or particularly the Israeli one, is a classic example of a multiple system of power which works across the spheres of distribution of goods while producing, distributing, and reproducing its own evils in more or less regular patterns. Most democracies today are involved with systems of power less conspicuous than a regime of occupation, but no less sophisticated in the ways they cross distributive spheres while distributing, often exporting, their own evils. But, like the prison, a state of occupation may be more conspicuous than, but not necessarily radically different from, other evil-producing systems of power. For Foucault, prison was a kind of metonymic figure through which he tried to think about his present social reality.[21] From an Israeli point of view, the occupation may play the same metonymic role.

(3) The homeless in New York are deprived of one particular kind of goods distributed, not very equally, among their fellow city dwellers. But the evil they suffer cannot be reduced to, or accounted for, by this particular lack alone. The social system that produces their homelessness is not simply the economic system which produces less apartments than families or which fixes their prices too high. Homelessness is an effect of the economic system (specifically, of the real estate market) but not of this system alone, and it affects one's position across the distributive spheres. Being homeless is being at once deprived of shelter, of a place to make love and raise children, of a place to recreate properly and socialize decently. The homeless are not merely poor citizens who enjoy and practice the rights for elementary education, equal voting, and free marriage, only they cannot afford to have access to one of those goods most other people have. Homelessness seems a unique social object; its modes of production and distribution and its peculiar presence at the heart of an affluent society call for an attempt to reconstruct its peculiar mechanisms of power and patterns of reproduction within the framework of a social grid different from the one that accounts for the distribution of goods or their privation. In order to reconstruct that grid, and perhaps before looking for the distribution of material goods, labor, and capital, one needs to look for open and blocked roots of exchange and conversion of goods, for certain needs that were cultivated among those more vulnerable to homelessness, and for others that were suppressed. To produce homelessness in such quantities in a rich, predominantly Christian society takes a certain coordination and cooperation of several distinct spheres: school and market, court and municipality. Unlike the prison or a state of occupation, it may be that, even from evil's point of view, no independent sphere of distribution may be reconstructed here. Yet the presence of evil cannot be reduced to the logic of any of the recognized spheres of goods; it presupposes a sui generis, complex social mechanism that transcends any of them. Also, much like understanding a state of occupation or what's really going on in and around prison, understanding homelessness necessitates an attempt to remap an entire social world. One needs to deconstruct the discourse of both participants and theorists, to suspend or question existing social categories (of socio-economic scales, desert and right, life expectancy, health situation, etc.) and look for a new totalizing point of view. Only then and from there would the production and distribution of evils appear in their own right, and would evils appear as proper objects of social and moral discourse.

What these three examples make clear is that evils are not merely the infliction of suffering or pain, no more than goods are the sheer means to achieve pleasure or joy. Evils have a presence of their own; this fact, at once social and moral, should be taken seriously into consideration in ethics and social theory alike. Theologians used to distinguish between social and natural evil; however, they often tried to develop a coherent theodicy, justifying a world that includes both. Natural evils—the death of an innocent child or a catastrophic earthquake, as far as they are unpreventable (precisely how far they should be thus conceived is a question which must remain open)—lie beyond the realm of the evils society distributes. Preventable suffering, on the other hand, is social and political through and through. Its distribution is what social conflict is mainly about (not entirely, for there are goods whose distribution bears very little on the prevention of suffering), and it always involves both goods and evils. Both goods and evils are social products lying at the core of political discourse and at stake in political conflicts, but they are at stake in distinct, if interrelated, ways. They belong to two distinct "positivities" of discourse.[22] For suffering is never simply the privation of pleasure, any more than evil is the privation of good or good of evil. The presence of evils serves me here as a basis for the next stage of my argument.

Like goods, evils are social products, socially endowed with meanings shared by a certain community. But here the analogy ends. Goods are possessed, acquired, searched, and fought for, because they are conceived of as beneficial or good for the one who possesses them, as enjoyable for themselves, or as useful for the sake of other things one values. Evils are inflicted and suffered for the advantage of another—Thrasymachus was not utterly wrong, after all—or for the advantage of no one in particular. The economy of evils is not necessarily an economy of rational investment and maximization of profit; evils may be by-products of otherwise rational investments, and those who enjoy these investments should not necessarily be aware of the suffering from which they benefit.

This is precisely what differentiates evils from the mere privation of goods and establishes them as sui generis social objects, which means eo ipso moral objects as well.[23] The mere privation of goods may be a source of suffering, but this suffering may be conceived of as necessary for the attainment of some goods that the bearer of suffering would finally possess. On the other hand, evils are sufferings or disadvantages[24] conceived of as beneficial for another or for nobody, but always excessive and superfluous from the point of view of the one who suffers them. From her point of view, evils consist in an utterly superfluous suffering, which she has never agreed to bear. If evil consists in superfluous suffering, it presupposes the possibility of voluntary agreement to suffering, and its denial. Let me postpone dealing with this component of the concept of evil, however, until a later stage in the argument.

Both goods and evils are at stake in all domains of social conflict. Goods are distributed through conflict, because there is always too little of them and they seem to be useful for the achievement of what seems to be good. The goods one possesses and seeks may partake in the good or they may not, one never knows, unless one knows the good. Evils are distributed through conflict, because there is always too much of them and they cause suffering that apparently could have been prevented at the cost of a lesser suffering. That they could have been prevented is always true, for they are social objects that come into being through and within certain orders of power which regulate, control, and institutionalize their production and distribution. It is always possible to conceive of a social map according to which the institutionalized diffusion of suffering in society will be conducted differently. More risky is the assumption that the prevention of superfluous suffering in one sphere would not cause an unbalanced increase of suffering in other spheres. One often errs about this, and one should always leave room for doubt. But one does not have to be a metaphysician on top of a Platonic divided line to speculate about the preventability of suffering, since it is always an empirical question.[25] It suffices that one is right about the preventability of evils—and for this one does not have to know "what is evil"—in order to establish that the evils at stake do partake in evil. For evil, not being the privation of a divine, transcendental good, does not lie in hell either. It is here on earth lying within the different distributive spheres and allocating mechanisms of human societies. It is present in their midst not as a *deus ex machina,* but simply as the relatively stable but often transformed order of the evils that social agents conceive, produce, distribute, and reproduce in more or less regular patterns.[26]

IV

Let me reiterate my proposed notion of (political) evil: socially distributed and politically legitimized suffering may be preventable at the cost of a lesser suffering; it is evil, if it is continuously inflicted for the advantage of another, or of no one, without the voluntary consent of the individual who suffers. Looking back at the homeless person, one may possibly argue that her suffering is socially preventable, that it is certainly preventable at the cost of a lesser suffering to the homeless person herself (though, perhaps, one may argue, not for society at large), and that, if anyone benefits from the system that deprives her of a home, it is certainly someone else. The homeless person suffers superfluously for the benefit of another, or of no one. From her point of view, at least, homelessness is evil. But what about her society? If her suffering is preventable at the cost of a lesser suffering both to herself and to the society in which she is a member, her society is unjust. If, on the other hand, her suffering is preventable at a cost which is favorable for her yet which her society cannot bear, she has less reason than others to be one of its members and more reason to look for alternatives. If being homeless seems unbearable to her, she would probably not have given her consent—had she been asked to do so—to a social contract that allocates people to homeless positions to begin with. In principle, it would be very hard to attribute political obligations to her, if she has never been asked, indeed, and never given her consent. Her dissent, in the form of political struggle, rebellion, or desertion, may be justified according to circumstances, given her share in other spheres of goods and evils, the price and prospects of each form of action to attain a positive change, etc. And she would better never try to look back at a hypothetical state of nature in order to understand the futility of breaking the rules that make her so much inferior to others. She would rather consider real, conceivable alternatives, not hypothetical ones. Some social contracts are more rational than a state of nature, especially a Hobbesian one, but right now she seems to be out of any contract. Instead of accepting the constraints imposed by a hypothetical contract, she would rather fight for a real one that may render her suffering worthwhile or obliterate it altogether. If she remains an obedient citizen, it is only because she is too weak, discouraged, or optimistic about the possibility to change her society "from within," or perhaps she is constrained by moral duties other than the usual political obligations of a free and equal citizen. It is not without reason that so often the poor, the unemployed, and the drug addicts have been considered "enemies of the society" by the society that has been their worst enemy.[27]

By way of some examples and an inversion of perspectives, we have come to recognize a necessary condition (no more than that) for the possibility of a just society: only a society in which no one suffers more than one's share may be really just. In other words, in a just society all socially preventable suffering is prevented, indeed the distribution of suffering eliminates excessive suffering created and reproduced through regular, institutionalized patterns of social interaction. An ideally just society is one in which suffering is distributed so as to eliminate entire distributive spheres responsible for the distribution of evils. But we have by no means come back to a theory of justice based on the distribution of goods only. The picture of distributive spheres in which goods alone are at stake does not belong to a model of real society to which a theory of distributive justice is applied as a corrective mechanism or a balancing principle. That picture belongs rather to the ideal horizon toward which moral politics necessarily aims. And moral politics could aim there only when recognizing its proper ground, the field for its discourse and action, the field where both goods and evils are constantly distributed.

Yet the picture is more complicated, and the inversion of perspectives may prove to be even more fertile. It should be remembered that evils are not distributed wholesale but according to one's positions in different distributive spheres. One could reasonably agree to suffer more than one's share in one sphere, if one were compensated in others. For example, a poor person may agree to suffer more than her share in the economic sphere, knowing—that is, accepting a dominant ideology which states—that she is paying a necessary price for economic stability (in the real estate market, at least) and that such stability is a necessary condition for her own and the whole community's economic well-being. Perhaps she will be willing to suffer for even less, say, for the honor of being a proud member of a community that is so worthy of pride. A theory of a just society must allow for the conversion of preventable suffering in one sphere for a desired good or reduction of suffering in another sphere. Inspired by Walzer's characterization of tyranny (SJ, 19 ff. and cf. above), we may make the following observation: in an unjust society, the conversion of suffering consistently replaces political attempts to eliminate preventable suffering; in an evil society, the very possibility to convert suffering among the spheres is severely restricted; radical evil is the systematic elimination of the convertibility of an ever growing amount of suffering. The situation of the Jews during the last few years of the Nazi regime would fit this characterization.[28] (This does not mean that other regimes would not fit, or that, if they would, they are "like" the Nazi regime). Thus, an important distinction between injustice and evil (which is no less important than that between justice and goodness, yet which cannot be drawn out of its inversion or negation) is kept and assumes new meaning. Injustice is not only congruent with evil; rather, evil can be seen as a special case of an unjust situation, its ultimate deterioration, whereas injustice always contains the grains of radical evil. Recognizing an unjust society means understanding the sense in which it is different from a radically evil society, and yet may deteriorate to become one.

V

The idea of the convertibility of suffering can be taken further to the heart of social coexistence. A person may suffer more than her share, not only for her own benefit in another sphere, but also, more importantly, for relieving her fellows of their own suffering. Suffering is convertible both across spheres and among individuals, and usually conversion is a mixture of the two dimensions. When suffering is thus converted, one may bear it voluntarily, notwithstanding the fact that it is preventable, out of moral duty, pity, sharing, or love. This reshuffling of preventable suffering is essential for the possibility of human community, the family first and foremost. Social beings share space and time, pain and hardship; the sharing of goods comes later. No political or metapolitical rule, however, no matter how strictly derived and from where, can determine to what extent one should agree to suffer more than one's share, and for whom precisely.[29] The conversion of suffering must always be open to negotiation, cultivation of moral sense, solidarity and friendship, and to new interpretations of the other's otherness, his humaneness or wickedness. But one crucial rule is clearly determinable: the conversion of the forms and modes of suffering must be based on voluntary agreement. Thus, I accept here, without arguing it any further, Habermas's universalization principle, which demands the consent of anyone affected by the consequences of the compliance of a norm in order for that norm to be valid.[30] When the universalization principle is mediated by the idea of the convertibility of suffering, the notion of a social contract may be reformulated as a model for an agreement regarding the forms and modes of conversion of socially organized and preventable suffering. A social contract is valid when all (rational) individuals who enter it agree to bear preventable suffering for the benefit of (1) specified and unspecified others, (2) in more or less specified circumstances, and (3) for specified purposes. It is a just contract, when the agreement is indeed directed toward a continuous reduction and gradual elimination of preventable suffering and does not stop at the agreed forms for its conversion. Not surprisingly, an ideal of moral progress is a necessary component of a just social contract.

From evil's point of view, a just society is based on a double confrontation between the real and the ideal. On the one hand, present mechanisms of conversion always fall short of, yet should aim at, an ideally rational agreement over actual forms of conversion. On the other hand, the future elimination of all preventable suffering is an unrealizable yet shared ideal that directs actual conflicts and negotiations over the redistribution of suffering; it is an ideal that is always already embodied in the various dimensions of moral politics. A just society is guided by an ideal of a hypothetical contract as far as the present is concerned: any rational agent would have agreed to these procedures for the distribution of evils and conversion of suffering at the present state of affairs. At the same time, a just society is guided by an actual agreement as far as the future is concerned: social agents rationally accept existing procedures that constrain political struggle and make the voluntary conversion of suffering a substitute for its elimination only while assuming that all parties to the struggle aim at the elimination of suffering, theirs included.

Within the framework of the contract, the political conflict is not about the ideal state of affairs—elimination of socially distributed suffering, for this ideal is what constrains social conflicts (i.e., constrains them as civil conflicts) in the first place. Rather, social conflicts are about the hypothetical agreement about the present procedures for the conversion of suffering. They constantly involve dispute and competition among social maps, grids for the articulation and representation of the distribution of goods and evils, as well as the evaluation of suffering, deciphering of its beneficiaries, and prediction of its preventability. The rationality of the hypothetical agreement depends on the interpretive description of social reality, not on the analytical construction of an image of an asocial reality, a state of nature. Instead of taking its reference point in a state in which no regular, socially institutionalized and guaranteed conversion of suffering is possible, this type of social-contract discourse constantly refers to another, all too political state: a state in which an established order of power severely restricts or almost eliminates the convertibility of suffering in socially regulated, institutionalized ways. This is the state I called above "radical evil." In the state of nature, conversion is possible, but radically unstable; in a state of radical evil, conversion is inherently impossible. It is the latter alternative, not the former, which social agents should have in mind, if they are to give their rational consent to the restrictions on the struggle for changing patterns of suffering conversion imposed by the existing order of power and justified by their hypothetical contract. The anarchy of an envisaged state of nature is less threatening than the suffering inflicted in a state of radical evil. Social contract should be directed more toward the prevention of the latter and less toward the possibility of the former. Rebellion is often less dangerous than obedient cooperation.

VI

The image of a state of radical evil underlies the social contract in yet another crucial respect. Suffering created by a system of power which systematically blocks ways for its possible conversion is also suffering which, when understood as such, should not be merely converted; no moral agent should be satisfied with its conversion, she must struggle to prevent it altogether. Because it should never be compromised, the attempt to prevent an unconvertible social suffering—that is, suffering whose nonconvertibility is a systematic attribute of the sociopolitical mechanism that produces and distributes it—is a categorical imperative. Unconvertible suffering is uncompromisable, because it is unjustifiable. A line should be drawn here between unjustified and unjustifiable suffering (or evils which follow from that). Socially unconvertible suffering, being that which constitutes the negative reference point of the social contract, cannot be justified within it; for the social contract is about how to institutionalize the distribution and conversion of suffering. By way of negation, unconvertible suffering constitutes the outer boundaries of a possible social contract. A consensus regarding this form of suffering is a condition for the contract's possibility (in all its various forms, from Hobbes to Rawls). For the relation may also be inverted, and in social life it often is: unjustifiable suffering is unconvertible—through legitimate social institutions—at least as far as an agreeable contract is concerned. Unjustifiable suffering is suffering, the conversion of which could never be legitimized; it must be prevented or else constantly delegitimized in whatever form it assumes. Social contract in both its hypothetical-present and actual-future moments presupposes a social consensus over what counts as unjustifiable evil, unconvertible suffering. This consensus is a necessary condition for the possibility of a moral community. It is usually articulated only when violated and interpreted on the basis of its violation. The articulation of this consensus in social theory and moral discourse is hardly argumentative; it is rather expressed as a basic, shared moral sensibility toward radical evil.

Recent communitarian approaches to ethics, such as Walzer's and Alasdair MacIntyre's, take this shared sensibility for granted. They propose moral "tradition" as the proper domain for moral and political debate; and traditions (of values, images of man and society, discursive practices), in so far as they are what the communitarians suppose they are, presuppose a shared sensibility toward radical evil.[31] This shared sensibility marks the outer boundaries of a possible agreement, and hence of a possible dialogue, while drawing a line where dialogue must end and a political struggle must assume other forms. But it does not mark the realm of possible moral interpretation. For in the same way that the homeless person may question the social contract and its obligations, she may question the moral sensibility that takes homelessness as unjustified, perhaps, but not unjustifiable, i.e., it takes this form of suffering to be convertible. The expected communitarian move at this point would be to reinterpret social reality in light of a rearticulated traditional sensibility. Tradition is reinterpreted, of course; this is its very nature, but only in order to remain the same. Society's immoral face will be illuminated from within a reinterpreted tradition in order to make it up in accordance with the rearticulated moral sensibility. What counts, in any case, are the good old values that presuppose this sensibility and make it enunciable, those values which help us to recognize, read, and correct evils.

But a victim of the social order, such as the homeless person, may remain unsatisfied with this move. She may rather try to switch perspectives here as well, taking as her point of departure the real presence of evils instead of the ideal presence of values. Starting from evils, she would decipher the margins of sensibility which tolerate them before interpreting the values that censor them. And a prevailing moral sensibility should not be reactivated through the values that presuppose it; they should rather be measured against those evils which a dominant tradition has allowed to be produced and distributed. The articulation of those evils and the criticism of a dominant tradition in their light do not require an Archimedean point from which alone a moral argument can be developed, or an alternative tradition in which such argument must be embedded. Different, dissenting moral sensibilities are first experienced and shown, and only later rationalized and justified in moral discourse.

By taking the position that homelessness should not be a convertible suffering, that it must be prevented altogether, the homeless person is already challenging the realm of the justifiable. She is violating a shared sensibility, forcing its adherents to try more radical (more aggressive, more deconstructive) reinterpretations of their tradition, or else to face an unavoidable social clash. And she may take this position through the mere decision to bear no more, or through whatever reason that would bring her to experience her suffering as unbearable. The same is true for the Palestinian youngsters or prison rebels. Indeed, the homeless may be too weak to enter a battle, and the prisoners too weak to win it; only the Palestinian boys seem to force upon Israeli society both a violent clash of forces and a reinterpretation of its shared sensibility toward evil. But this fact is contingent on my examples and does not touch the core of the argument. The core of the argument lies with the attempt to decipher, through interpretive analysis alluded to in the above three examples, patterns of evils distribution and to understand them as patterns of distribution of preventable suffering and the social contract as a double system of agreement over patterns of suffering conversion. The convertibility of suffering makes possible both sharing and coercion, and a whole spectrum of various modes of human coexistence. Humans inflict suffering systematically through regular patterns of social interaction. But human social coexistence cannot be reduced to patterns of powerful coercion, because suffering is systematically converted, not only inflicted, and it cannot be detached from a moral horizon, because suffering can be systematically prevented and partly eliminated as well. And whereas the good remains transcendent, perhaps divine if there is a God to deserve it, and goods are, or may be, that God's very dubious representations, evil is a constant, ever-changing formation of human coexistence. Social criticism must therefore begin as a deciphering and analysis of the distribution of evils; hermeneutic ethics must begin as the interpretation of evil.

VII

A just regime takes care to prevent superfluous, excessive suffering. Moral politics strives toward the elimination of preventable suffering, on the one hand, and toward redistribution of suffering according to the accepted patterns of conversion based on voluntary agreement, on the other. We are dealing therefore with the interpretation of evil, not with the construction of regulative models for a just society, or at least not only with these. The need to interpret systematically is implied by the conception of evils presented above. From a philosophical point of view, the interpretation of evil is not an emblematic appendix to the attempt to construct a regulative model of a just society; these two aspects of the philosophical discussion are inseparable and irreducible.

But the hermeneutic position may seem fragile. For in order to account for the distribution of evils (to be eliminated) and the conversion of suffering (to be transformed), too many debated issues must be settled first, and too many open questions must be answered. The meaning, harm, and durability of different forms of suffering, the advantages and disadvantages of alternative means to prevent it, the proper chain of conversion, the worthiness of individuals, groups, and institutions to bear or enjoy the suffering of others—all these must be agreed upon before a regime can claim itself just or a politics moral. But only a comprehensive understanding of social reality, a complete transparency of the most complex and hidden social mechanisms, can guarantee such an agreement. This idea is therefore no less utopian than the ideal of a total elimination of superfluous suffering which it serves. It requires a perfect map of the social world, which would be topographical, geological, and archeological at the same time, and a perfectly asocial, apolitical act of mapping. The social cartographer must sit on the moon, or else he must admit there is and always will be something his map hides, and also adds or helps to create. Maps of the social terrain are social products, and they are goods at stake in more than one distributive sphere.

It is precisely for this reason that neo-Kantian philosophers, like Habermas or Karl-Otto Apel, have turned from that which is at stake to the procedures of the arguments about it, and have transferred justice—and the entire moral discourse with it—to the sphere of communicative action. In this sphere, they claim, it is possible to extract a logic of exchange and distribution from the very nature of the things at stake, i.e., arguments, social maps, normative claims about the meaning and worth of suffering, etc. It is then possible to extract an argumentative model of exchange which would regulate exchange in all other distributive spheres. In Walzer's terms (SJ, 12), arguments have become the dominant goods which, without being monopolized, are convertible through all distributive spheres. In fact, the conversion of any kind of goods into arguments about one's desert or right to possess it is a necessary condition for determining its just distribution. Even if one establishes local "courts of dispute" in each of the spheres, one always presupposes and relies upon a certain metalanguage, a fundamental logic and pragmatics of argumentation, to which one resorts whenever dispute fails to yield an agreement.[32] The metalanguage would not solve the issue at stake, yet it would direct one how to go on arguing about it, and how to live with undecided arguments. In a free atmosphere of deliberation, when the proper procedures of argumentation are tightly guarded, each social agent would be able to offer for sale in the market of opinions her own social map. It is the map that purports to be best equipped to articulate superfluous suffering, determine wrong patterns of its conversion, and expose who benefits from that suffering and how. Social agents may discuss evils as they choose: instead of, alongside, or before discussing claims of right, desert, and need—it does not really matter. From the point of view of the theorist of procedural (argumentative) justice, the interpretation of social reality regarding both goods and evils is the predicament of every social agent; no particular agent specializing in interpretation is privileged, the hermeneuticist or the cartographer of evil included. It is the task of a social theory with practical intent and metatheoretical orientation, or of moral philosophy proper, to salvage the theory of justice from the war of interpretations and save it the time, blood, and sweat of those who muddle in the trenches.

I shall not confront here the theory of argumentative justice directly,[33] but rather sketch, with the help of a few examples, two distinct lines of argument that, without undermining the framework of the constructivist approach, severely limit its scope.

(A) Even if some theory of procedural justice, argumentative in our case, were valid, adequate, and applicable, still the philosophical task of hermeneutic ethics qua an interpretation of evil may be no less, perhaps even more, urgent than that of the constructivist.

(B) The procedural argument is limited by two crucial presuppositions: that a consensus is a positive end to be reached through argumentation; that a consensus regarding the procedure itself is to be respected and challenged only through argumentation. But moral discourse in general and the interpretation of evil in particular are most urgently needed precisely in situations when the very content and existence of a particular consensus and the forms of argumentation it authorizes are the objects of moral debate and political struggle. Such a debate calls for hermeneutic skill and tools, exegetical as well as deconstructive, for it is the language of morality itself which is at stake; and the political struggle involved in that debate is enmeshed in a politics of interpretation, for it is the very sense of a communal collective identity which is at stake. The construction of hypothetical contracts and extraction of regulative presuppositions would come much later, when both the boundaries of a community and the language through which it shares, cultivates, and transmits its values have been more or less stabilized.

VIII

(A) Social maps are usually drawn by members of a hegemonic culture;[34] at least this has been true for most maps upon which the modern discourse of justice is based. It is only natural that these maps represent social reality in terms of the goods which members of a hegemonic culture are more likely to possess or to which they are more likely to have access. The underprivileged are more likely to develop a discourse of evils. Their maps, however, are usually less marketable, perhaps also less valuable, because the underprivileged are likely to have less access to that type of good given by recognized skill and positions of authority in the intellectual-discursive sphere. That traditional moral discourse has been so pregnant with goods and so impoverished of evils may be explained in part by the fact that, from Plato through Bentham to Rawls and Walzer, this discourse has been usually produced by members of social elites and within hegemonic cultures. The maps they have used are naturally colored by the hues of the material goods, titles, and social positions that constitute the network of everyday life of an average member of the hegemonic culture. This is the network that shapes one's intellectual horizons, political aspirations, career expectations, life projects, good taste, and moral judgment. When the social map is portrayed according to the patterns of differentiation inscribed on the social terrain by actual mechanisms of distribution, the terms of social conflict would probably be determined by the social categories that privilege the already privileged. The closer a social map comes to the point of view of a social elite or hegemonic culture, the more corrective and less distributive, let alone less radical, would become the principles of distributive justice this map can support (in practice, at least, if not explicitly in theory).

In order to turn corrective principles back into distributive ones, the very patterns and mechanisms of distribution must be challenged.[35] A more radical Marxist critique would call for a transformation of the entire social system, a reorganization of all distributive spheres based upon a redistribution of control over, and access to, the means of production. Marxists can claim this transformation to be just only because they assume that the means of production are the dominant good, and that in capitalist society this good is monopolized by a recognizable social group (cf. Walzer, SJ, 11 ff.) But between the limited aspiration of liberal theories and the radical vision of some Marxists, a certain form of "radical liberalism" (or "local Marxism") may find its proper niche precisely by placing itself at the heart of a discourse of evil. This discourse neither would be satisfied with the corrective mechanisms of the liberal state nor would it challenge and try to transform its entire social system. The task of such a discourse would rather be to question the political and moral discourse of the hegemonic culture; it will not let that culture's social grid be unproblematically employed, and it will constantly call into question those social maps which give presence to dominant social positivities only, those goods of which dominant groups always have a better share.

The brief examples of the homeless, the prisoner, and the Palestinian should have indicated that evils have a "positivity" of their own. They could not have done more than indicate, for they, too, still rely on a dominant grid and on a social map that gives priority to the distribution of goods. The new type of positivity requires its own grid, which only a fully developed discourse of evil could supply. Even though he never mentions evil in his work, Foucault's studies of the history of madness, the clinic, and the prison supply us with excellent examples of such a discourse.[36] His "interpretive analytics" of power/knowledge in the restricted domain of modern "disciplines" gives presence and voice to so far little recognized, hardly speakable modalities of suffering produced through variegated mechanisms of power, technologies of pain, and regular manipulations of body and soul. Some critics have accused Foucault of moral nihilism or anarchism, because he never named what he described, never evaluated what he analyzed, and never launched an argument that would justify one form of power and determine its preference over others.[37] This seems to me to be no more than naming one for not naming others, and for not using the ready-made moral categories of the very system of morality one tries to undermine. Thinking of evils as the infliction of superfluous, involuntary suffering that individuals bear for the benefit of others or for no one's benefit, however, it is possible to re-read Foucault's studies of the disciplines as chapters in the history of modern (Western) evil.

Foucaultian genealogy and archaeology should be taken very seriously from our moral point of view, but it is certainly not the only form a discourse of evil may take. "Minority discourse" and its theory—in philosophy, social theory, psychology, but mainly in literature[38]—may play a similar role. Minority discourse uses and abuses the moral and ideological discourse of a hegemonic culture in order to expose and problematize its social grid, invert its scale of values, and make it ashamed of its own social differentiations. It articulates the distribution of evils through a violent dissolution of dominant forms of discourse. The dominant discourse is attacked precisely at those points where it shifts one's attention away from the evils distributed in one's society (with one's more or less conscious cooperation) and precisely due to those mechanisms which allow it to focus attention on the goods to which one has rights, but also better chances to possess or enjoy.

A hegemonic culture, however, need not necessarily be monolithic; it is probably impossible to account for a hegemonic culture only from the point of view of its relation to prevalent modes and relations of production; the "oppressed" should not consist in one class, political group, or subculture; and minorities are certainly not the only ones who suffer. Evils are distributed across the social system, differentiating it and creating groups within it, in ways that sometimes do and sometimes do not overlap with the differentiation formed by and through the distribution of goods. In any case, evils create and allow for forms of experience which no theory of goods distribution can capture. Hermeneutic ethics must therefore relate first and foremost to those types of discourse which do capture what the hegemonic moral discourse usually misses. Its reading consists in radical social theory and minority literature, but also journalism and graffiti, poetry and folk songs, in short, every form of expression in discourse and in art which gives presence to evils. The hermeneutic discourse does not posit itself above these forms, as their (ever-redundant) metatheory that comes to criticize and pass judgment, or to regulate and guide; it rather relates to them as its closest informants and conversants. Its task is to relate those various representations of the experience of evil (both the more theoretical ones produced "from without" and the first-hand accounts produced "from within") to the dominant forms of moral and political discourse. Hermeneutic ethics should use its resources in order to challenge a dominant social map and undermine a dominant social grid, but also to force those captive of such a map or grid to listen to the voices that come from "below," from behind these or those bars, from across this or that boundary. Relying on the social theorist as well as the criminal, the poet as well as the journalist and pamphleteer, hermeneutic ethics should articulate evil in order to expose its conditions of possibility, as well as its regularities and techniques; it should deconstruct conceptual schemes that make one deaf to the outcry, and posit or reconstruct new schemes that would let one see the horrors, how close to home they are, and how awfully one is responsible for them.

It must be noted, however, that the hermeneuticist's discourse most probably emerges from within a dominant group and is still a part of its hegemonic culture. Too often, perhaps always, hermeneutic discourse belongs neither to those who suffer nor to their "authentic representatives"; it is not written from their point of view, nor does it use their proper language. The positivities to which it gives presence need not be those which the underprivileged experience subjectively, in the form of pain, threat, limited possibilities, etc. Hermeneutic ethics would be no less interested in the boundaries of such experience, understood from without, from the point of view of a privileged theorist, philosopher, or writer.[39] Yet whatever form it assumes, wherever the position from which it is announced, the discourse of evil must find its way into the quiet halls where distributive, procedural justice is calmly deliberated. Procedural justice claims to guarantee that, once enunciated, the discourse of evil will not be silenced. The task of hermeneutic ethics qua an interpretation of evil is to guarantee that the voice will be heard in the first place.

IX

(B) Beyond Rawls's "veil of ignorance" or within Habermas's "ideal speech situation" there can be no enemies. Rational speakers who deliberate their and others' interests never experience hatred or animosity, only polite differences of opinions. The moral debate, hypothetical or utopian, is conducted among disembodied individuals (or within different voices within one's own rational self) in an atmosphere free of social divisions and cultural differences. Imagine yourself without your particular self, says Rawls, try to generalize your particular interests, says Habermas, and see what that abstract self would really prefer, whether those particular interests are really "generalizable." Some troubles may arise, however, when one leaves rationality's castle and returns to the cave of

114

social reality. Suppose that even in the midst of struggle one still recognizes one's abstract self and is still capable of making the distinction between particular and generalizable interests. But what about one's fellows? If your fellow citizens refuse abstraction and generalization, try to face them with their own sense of justice, try to show them that their insistence on certain particular interests, inherited social advantages, and the like, contradicts values that they actually share with you and do in fact want to preserve. In other words, interpret for them your common tradition, that from which your shared sense of justice is drawn, and show them how it fits the rational yardstick for justice you claim to represent. Interpret for them their own social conduct and show them how it contradicts that yardstick. In short, put hermeneutic ethics to work in the service of moral constructivism.

But what if one's fellow citizens refuse to listen? What if they are suspicious of moral generalizations and abstractions and insist on very particularistic moral arguments? What if they ground their morality on very particular features of their particular selves and take some of their particular interests to be morally justified precisely because these interests belong to a special group of ungeneralizable interests? How should the argument for justice proceed from there? Should one still respect the actual procedures of the ongoing political debate? Should one consider those procedures justified because they formally presuppose an ideal speech situation? Should one still respect the consensus these procedures presuppose, use, and cultivate, because agreement is said to lie at the intentional horizon of moral debate (Habermas) or to be its hypothetical end (Rawls)? Or should one abandon moral discourse altogether?

These questions are not hypothetical. Those stubborn particularists are not imaginary figures, they are my own fellow citizens. Allow me a short digression on this point. Israeli society, being more cohesive today than some of its observers realize, is yet deeply divided among different communities that do not share basic moral sensibilities. One of the presently dominant communities in Israel grounds its morality on a modern, particularistic interpretation of Jewish nationalism. Refusing to generalize over certain interests, forms of suffering, and patterns of injustice, it is not very sensitive to evils as long as they are distributed to "the other," the gentile, the Palestinian. It has a threshold of intolerable evil very different from the one characterizing its rival community, which, in principle at least, insists on universalization in moral discourse.

The debate between these two communities[40]—for the purpose of this discussion, let me call them chauvinists and liberals—has gone on in Israel ever since the Six-day War in June 1967. One of the more conspicuous features of this always democratic debate has been the stalemate into which it has apparently led the Israeli political system, which seems unable to decide whether to swallow or get rid of the occupied territories. This stalemate, which may have other, more substantial reasons, has not been without political significance: over the last twenty years, it has helped to solidify a status quo that actually means an undeclared, de facto, and until recently deepening Israeli annexation of the territories.[41] It is true that, since the beginning of the Palestinian uprising in December 1987, there have been some changes. One does not speak about actual annexation with such confidence any longer; but the consensus that allows the Israeli government to deal with the (mostly civil) disobedience of the Palestinian population as if the annexation were a fait accompli has not been weakened much. The occupation itself has remained intact. In the last twenty years, it has become a power order that shapes Israeli, not only Palestinian, life. The occupation has structured and constrained Israeli society in its entirety, the above-mentioned debate included. For the debate has been conducted between seemingly incommensurable moral sensibilities, yet within the framework of a shared political system based on a procedural consensus. This framework and that consensus have long been legitimizing the on-going occupation, no matter how oppressive it has become, allowing "the liberals" to take safe positions of protest and condemnation within the embracing, totalizing framework itself.

For "radical liberals," and for radical moral discourse, it is the consensus itself that is finally at stake. The common ground presupposed by theories of procedural justice has been lost, temporarily at least, and in any case the concepts of justice and human rights have been constantly abused by the juridical system (both military and civil), which is never tired of legalizing new techniques for the distribution of evils. It is this distribution of evils which moral discourse must articulate now. Such a discourse interprets the occupation as a multisystem that, from evil's point of view, constitutes one distributive sphere. The "conventional," impassed political and moral debate is understood as one part of that system's face and its language is deconstructed accordingly. Consequently, radical discourse should develop its own moral language, based on an improved "grid of evils," and from there draw new boundaries between friend and foe, "us" and "them," dialogue and struggle, "their" sensibility and "ours."

This type of radical moral discourse has only recently made its appearance in Israel—although it was needed long ago—partly as a response to the Palestinian uprising and the consequent worsening of Israeli repression. No wonder it sometimes resonates with the young Palestinian stone throwers, on the one hand, and a handful of Israeli (reserve) soldiers who refuse military orders to serve in the occupied territories, on the other. For these two types of political "activists," very different in temper and intensity and wholly unequal in political significance, share nevertheless one particular discursive role. They let the evils of the occupation be visible, and the system that distributes them be recognizable and articulable; they force each citizen to take sides, to choose between two rival moral sensibilities, and to face the consequences. Together with some engaged intellectuals, poets, and journalists they mark a line, draw a boundary on the slope: "Here I stand, I can go no further; here you stand, dare not go any further."

This digression may seem beside the point. It deals with an extreme situation, one may argue, with a divided society and with people in a war of liberation; it mixes external struggle (Israelis/Palestinians) with an internal one (chauvinists/ liberals); and it leaves the issue of argumentative justice well behind. But is this extreme situation really so unique? Was it "extreme" before the Palestinian uprising? Was it philosophically different then and now? Was it so remote from the question of justice then? Was it then so different from many other, more or less local struggles, political crises, and civil strifes? Is the difference between "external" and "internal" so clear? Is it not the case that many distributive spheres (of goods and evils alike) are open systems that often cross local boundaries of communities and states, that evils are exported and imported in various, more or less "respectful," legal ways, and that the systems exporting evils deserve our moral attention no less urgently than those distributing goods inside our societies? Is it not the case that often the orders of power which produce and distribute evils have no recognizable, ideological, national, ethnic, or religious face? In fact, they sometimes have no face at all, and it is the task of hermeneutic ethics qua interpretation of evil to give them one, to let those who share relevant moral sensibilities recognize them for what they are, call them into question, and target them in discourse as well as in other forms of political struggle. It is the task of hermeneutic ethics to problematize social categories and distinctions, like "us" and "them," internal and external, crisis and everyday life, which let a discourse of justice prosper among those who hardly need it, and deafen their ears to the discourse of evil. Not that a discourse of justice is necessarily unjustified or redundant; its ideological significance is after all presented here as a challenge more than as an unproblematic affirmation. But it is usually less urgent. And urgency—a notion so foreign to the philosophical game which was and is born at leisure and seems mute when leisure has gone—belongs nevertheless to the heart of moral discourse. For if suffering is preventable and one knows, even vaguely, how, it is immoral to stand by; and if thinking and discourse are capable of making suffering appear and be conceived of as preventable and unbearable when not prevented, the philosopher has an urgent task. He is morally obliged to practice hermeneutic ethics qua interpretation of evil.

Tel Aviv University

NOTES

1 From a philosophical point of view, most prominent in this context is the work of Emil Fackenheim; see, e.g., *God's Presence in History* (New York: Harper & Row, 1972); *The Jewish Return to History: Reflections in the Age of Auschwitz and a New Jerusalem* (New York: Schocken, 1978). See also the special issue on the Holocaust in this JOURNAL, XVI, 1–2 (1984–85).

2 Not surprisingly, perhaps, political discourse in Israel is inflated with such analogies and their criticism. See, for example, my essay "On Sanctifying the Holocaust: An Anti-Theological Treatise," *Tikkun*, II, 1 (1987): 61-66.

3 The reader may find a classic survey of the problem of evil in theology, philosophy, and literature in Radoslav A. Tsanoff, *The Nature of Evil* (New York: Macmillan, 1931). For a modern theological discussion see, for example, Kenneth Surin, *Theology and the Problem of Evil* (New York: Blackwell, 1986). Paul Ricoeur's seminal work on *The Symbolism of Evil,* Emerson Buchanan, trans. (Boston: Beacon, 1969) is a phenomenology of religious images and conceptions of evil. For a recent psychoanalytic discussion see "Le Mal," a special issue of the *Nouvelle Revue de Psychoanalyse,* XXXVIII (Automne 1988).

4 For Plato see, e.g., *Lysis* 220-221, *Theaetetus* 176a; for Plotinus, see, e.g., *Enneades* I, 8; and for Augustine, see, e.g., *The City of God,* bk. xi, chs. 9, 16, 22; bk. xii, chs. 1-7.

5 The paradigmatic case is, no doubt, Leibniz's *Theodicy* (La Salle, IL: Open Court, 1985). In fact, we may paraphrase Jacques Derrida here and claim that, throughout the history of Western metaphysics and of the moral discourse it has generated, the absence of the good is the precondition of moral discourse, of the identity of its object, and of the interpretive effort required to retrieve that object out of the plurality of its false, distorted traces, signs, or representations. On the absence of the good in Plato, see Derrida, "Plato's Pharmacy," in *Dissemination* (Chicago: University Press, 1981), pp. 167-169.

6 Jeremy Bentham, *Economic Writings,* W. Stark, ed. (London: 1952), v. iii, p. 438; and cf. v. i. p. 103.

7 For Hegel, evil is a form of "subjectivism." In *The Phenomenology of Spirit,* it is discussed under the heading "Conscience" with regard to "the beautiful soul" (IV, C, c); in the *Philosophy of Right,* it is addressed in the section on morality (139-140). In a strict sense, evil does not belong to ethical life (*Sittlichkeit*), to the realm of the communal and the political.

8 *The World as Will and Representation,* E. F. J. Payne, trans. (New York: Dover, 1969), esp. vol. II, supplements to bk 4. Schopenhauer, however, is important in our context, for he breaks the symmetry between good and evil, pleasure and suffering: "evil can never be wiped off, and consequently can never be balanced, by the good that exists along with or after it" (*ibid.,* p. 576). And, quoting Petrarch, he adds: "*Mille piacer non vagliono un tormento.*"

9 Cf. *The Genealogy of Morals,* I. Nietzsche's etymological and psycho-historical inquiry into the origin of good and evil does differentiate the two concepts, but not in any way informative for our discussion.

10 This is the name of a chapter dedicated to Montaigne in Judith N. Shklar's *Ordinary Vices* (Cambridge: Harvard, 1984). This philosophical essay, quite unique in its form and subject matter, is, to the best of my knowledge, the one that comes closest to an analysis of evil in a modern political context.

11 For Montaigne on evil, see *The Essays on Montaigne,* bk. I, 14, 18; bk. II, 11, 12, 23, 27; bk. III, 5, 6, 9. My paper is in no way an attempt to interpret Montaigne, but it is in part a result of thinking with his *Essays.*

12 For the place of the highest good in Kant's political philosophy and philosophy of history, see Yirmyahu Yovel, *Kant and the Philosophy of History* (Princeton: University Press, 1980), ch. 1.

13 For more on Gadamer's concept of *die Sache,* see *Truth and Method* (New York: Seabury, 1975), pt. III; and for a discussion of Gadamer's ethics, cf. Michael Kelly, "Gadamer's Philosophical Ethics," *Man & World,* XXI (1988): 327-346.

14 John Rawls, *A Theory of Justice* (Cambridge: Harvard, 1971), pt. III, esp. pp. 60, 68, 86. It is a sense of goodness confirmed by Rawls's "thin theory of the good," but not a conception of the good as such, which should serve a moral being "as regulative of his plan of life" (*ibid.,* pp. 569-570).

15 New York: Basic, 1985 [hereafter SJ].

16 Walzer's multidimensional picture of society is congruent with that of contemporary sociologists like Pierre Bourdieu and Anthony Giddens. See, for example, Bourdieu, *Distinction: A Social Critique of the Judgement of Taste* (Cambridge: Harvard, 1984), pt. II, and "The Social Space and the Genesis of the Group," *Theory and Society,* XIV (1985); and Giddens, *The Construction of Society* (London: Polity, 1984).

17 In this work, I am not interested in haphazard, individual outbursts of evil-inflicting behavior that cannot be related to, and accounted for, in the framework of regular social practices. I believe that most occurrences of evil, and certainly the most outrageous among them, can be thus related and accounted for, but this is a claim which must be addressed separately. Its implication, however, marks the domain of my whole discussion below: evils are discussed in so far as they are social and political objects.

18 This is precisely what Bentham means when he formulates the distinction: "Good may accordingly be divided and distinguished into positive and negative. . . . Negative good is good consisting in the exclusion or removal of evils" (*op. cit.,* v. 1, p. 103).

19 Michel Foucault, *Discipline and Punish: The Birth of the Prison,* Alan Sheridan, trans. (New York: Vintage, 1979), p. 228.

20 A state of occupation may seem abnormal, but it is strictly relevant to our discussion. A continuous military occupation is a paradigm of a double system in which the distribution of goods and evils do not overlap. A cluster of distributive spheres (of goods) exist in a state of apparent normalcy alongside a powerful apparatus in which evil-inflicting mechanisms constitute a sphere or spheres of evils distribution. The lack of overlapping between the two systems is not a by-product of the state of occupation but a necessary condition for its stable reproduction. But a state of occupation only shows more conspicuously, perhaps more dramatically, what is true for many "normal" social systems, whose cohesion and stability depend on their ability to separate the two types of distribution, while maintaining an apparent overlapping. And see note 27 below.

21 Cf. *Discipline and Punish,* p. 228; "La societé punitive" (Resume du cours, annee 1973), in *Annuaire de College de France* (Paris: College de France, 1973): 255-267; and "Prison Talk" and "The Eye of Power," in *Power/Knowledge: Selected Interviews and Other Writings 1972-1977,* Colin Gordon, trans. & ed. (New York: Pantheon, 1980), pp. 37-54, 146-165.

22 I am using the word in Foucault's sense as developed in *The Archeology of Knowledge,* A. M. Sheridan Smith, trans. (New York: Pantheon, 1972), esp. pp. 126-128, 171-181.

23 An obvious implication of this is the systematic blurring of the demarcation between fact and value.

24 A continuum must be drawn here between sheer cruelty that causes suffering, on the one hand, and relatively innocent manipulation that limits one's field of action, on the other. In the strict sense, to the extent that the mere existence of a person in the presence of another exerts power and limits the latter's field of action, co-presence is a potential source of disadvantage, hence of evils. In the vein of Schopenhauer and Nietzsche, Martin Buber insisted that "life, in that it is life, necessarily entails injustice . . . there can be no life without the destruction of life." But, he adds, life is "truly human when [a person] pictures to himself the results of his actions and, accordingly, attempts to encroach upon other creatures as little as is necessary"; cf. *A Land of*

119

Two People: Martin Buber on Jews and Arabs, Paul R. Mendes-Flohr, ed. (New York: Oxford, 1984). From this point of view, it is a contextualized, situated self-restraint that makes moral action possible. Evils come first; their minimalization constitutes the properly human, that is, the ethical.

25 In principle, evils are always preventable, by definition, for they are products of a socially organized and politically regulated distributive sphere. The question is a question of the price. Usually it is a very complicated question, yet in the extreme cases precision is not very important and the evaluation of suffering is not controversial. The more excessive suffering tends to be, the easier it becomes to demonstrate its preventability at the cost of a lesser suffering.

26 It is the order of evils which renders the isolated infliction of evil a political matter. And it is interpretive political discourse that would introduce order into the aggregate of evil inflicting actions. Example: a six-year old child played with his father's gun and killed a man passing by. The child may be no less innocent than the dead man and suffering may seem utterly accidental, a pure case of bad luck, until one considers the way a government licenses guns and controls their use and toy companies design and market their products.

27 The other two examples would have led to a somewhat different formulation: the Palestinian does not really belong to the society that oppresses him and the prisoner lives on the very margins of the society that excludes him. But, in fact, there is a continuum between the homeless person, the prisoner, and the Palestinian, as these three positions mark three possibilities of being "a client" of a distributive system (or more than one) without really being part of the society at large. The three are not real subjects of the societies that determine their fate, they are "types" that represent a problem to be dealt with. From this perspective, the difference is just a matter of degree. Hence the emblematic role of the state of occupation, which underlines trends and intensifies social mechanisms already in existence in a "normal" society. And see note 21 above.

28 Primo Levi recounts the possibilities of exchange in the concentration camp: in the first day of spring, when the cold is no more the worst enemy, hunger becomes unbearable. Conversion is possible only within the individual, between different forms of suffering. See *Survival in Auschwitz: The Nazi Assault on Humanity* (New York: Macmillan, 1961).

29 Justice cannot be a predicate of love or compassion, which seem to be important determinants in this context.

30 Cf. *Moralbewusstsein und kommunikatives Handeln* (Frankfurt: Suhrkamp, 1983).

31 Walzer, *Spheres of Justice; Exodus and Revolution* (New York: Basic Books, 1985); *Interpretation and Social Criticism* (Cambridge: Harvard, 1987); *In the Company of Critics: Social Criticism and Political Commitment in the Twentieth Century* (New York: Basic Books, 1988); Alasdair MacIntyre, *Whose Justice? Which Rationality?* (Notre Dame: University Press, 1988).

32 For Habermas's theory of argumentation, see his *The Theory of Communicative Action, Vol. 1,* Thomas McCarthy, trans. (Boston: Beacon, 1984), pp. 8-42; for Karl-Otto Apel, see *Towards a Transformation of Philosophy,* G. Adey and D. Frisby, trans. (Boston: Routledge & Kegan Paul, 1980), chs. 4, 5, 7.

33 I have done it elsewhere: "Against the Very Idea of an Ideal Speech Situation," in Yrmyahu Yovel, ed., *Kant's Practical Philosophy Reconsidered* (Dordrecht: Kluwer, 1989).

34 For the notion of hegemony in culture from a "soft" Marxist perspective, see Robert Bocock, *Hegemony* (Essex: Open UP, 1986). A different sociological framework for dealing with cultural hegemony is offered by the work of Bourdieu; see especially his *Distinction,* and *Reproduction in Education, Society and Culture* (with Jean-Claude Passeron) (London: Sage, 1977). The concept as applied above is open to both approaches, to the one inspired by Lukacs and Gramsci, and to the semiotic sociology of the other.

35 Rawls's theory of justice, for example, may be seen as a construction of a mechanism of correction applied to an existing social order. Redistributions are restricted by the principles of

the theory, but within their limits there is no incentive to question the very division of society into distinct distributive spheres, their conditions of possibility, or the relation of conversion, exchange, or interdependence among them.

36 Besides the above mentioned *Discipline and Punish,* cf. *Madness and Civilization,* Richard Howard (New York: Random House, 1965); *The Birth of the Clinic,* A. M. Sheridan Smith, trans. (New York: Vintage, 1975); and *Power/Knowledge.*

37 Most noteworthy is Habermas's critique in *The Philosophical Discourse of Modernity: Twelve Lectures,* Frederick Lawrence, trans. (Cambridge: MIT, 1988). See also Michael Walzer, "The Lonely Politics of Michel Foucault," in *The Company of Critics;* and Charles Taylor, "Foucault on Freedom and Truth," *Political Theory,* XII (1984).

38 For a general theory of minority literature, see Gille Deleuze and Felix Guattari, *Kafka: Toward Minor Literature* (Minneapolis: Minnesota UP, 1986); Abdul R. Janmahamed, "Humanism and Minority Literature: Toward a Definition of Counter-Hegemonic Discourse," *Boundary,* II (Spring/Fall 1984): xii:3/xiii:1; David Lloyd, *Nationalism and Minor Literature: James Clarence Mangan and the Emergence of Irish Cultural Nationalism* (Berkeley: California UP, 1987); *Cultural Critique,* VII (Fall 1987) (special issue: "The Nature and Context of Minority Discourse"), with a special reference to Israeli culture in Hannan Hever's "Hebrew in an Israeli Arab Hand: Six Miniatures on Anton Shammas's *Arabesques.*"

39 The field of reading of the hermeneuticist (moral) philosopher is therefore wide open, and it goes from poetry to history, and from journalism to sociology. But this spectrum is not only hermeneutics' field of reading, but the field in which it is situated itself. All these genres of writing and practices of discourse, philosophical hermeneutics included, give presence to evil, and the important difference is a matter of explicitness and reflexivity, on the one hand, and of sensitivity toward the yet unarticulated, on the other.

40 I do not pretend to capture the essence of the debate or its many different aspects, only that aspect in it which is morally relevant in the context of the present discussion.

41 This claim is best documented by the 1987 report of Meron Benvenisti, "The West Bank Data Project: Demographic, Economic, Legal, Social and Political Development in the West Bank," *The Jerusalem Post,* Jerusalem 1987.

RATIONAL RECONSTRUCTION AND SOCIAL CRITICISM: HABERMAS'S MODEL OF INTERPRETIVE SOCIAL SCIENCE

KENNETH BAYNES

For more than a quarter-century, Jürgen Habermas has elaborated and defended a model of interpretive social science which would, in turn, contribute to the larger project of a critical social theory. From the point of view of social scientific method, that model can be viewed as an attempt to meet two related challenges: first, it takes seriously the social construction of reality (and our knowledge of it), without succumbing to relativism or the view that there is no type of objectivity in the social sciences; second, it ties the conditions and criteria for social criticism to the internal perspective of the participant or social actor, without thereby ascribing incorrigibility to that perspective or relinquishing the possibility of developing a general theory about social structures and the systemic causes of social pathologies.[1] Habermas's attempt to address both of these challenges helps to explain why he is critical of naturalist or positivist approaches that deny the existence of any unique methodological requirements for the social sciences, while at the same time distancing himself from more radical hermeneutic approaches.[2]

In *On the Logic of the Social Sciences* (1967),[3] Habermas described his own approach as a ''hermeneutically enlightened and historically oriented functionalism'' that combined interpretive and causal analyses.[4] Grounded in a theory of language, its aim was to provide a normative reconstruction of the end states for the formative learning processes of a society in light of which systemic hindrances or disturbances to those processes could be identified. More recently, in *The Theory of Communicative Action* (1981),[5] he continues to present his model as a unique combination of action and systems theory.[6]

My guiding idea is that, on the one hand, the dynamics of development are steered by [systemic] imperatives issuing from problems of self-maintenance, that is, problems of materially reproducing the lifeworld; but that, on the other hand, this societal development draws upon structural *possibilities* and is subject to structural *limitations* that, with the rationalization of the lifeworld, undergo systematic change in dependence upon corresponding learning processes (II, 148).

Since Habermas chose to present his views within the context of a quasi-systematic reading of the history of social theory—a "history of theory with systematic intent"—the underlying assumptions and basic features of this model are, however, not easily discerned. This essay attempts to clarify some of these assumptions and features and to set out some of the arguments for them. I shall begin with an analysis of Habermas's model of the rational explanation of action by contrasting it with a comparable project undertaken in analytic action theory by Donald Davidson. In the second section, as an alternative to Alasdair MacIntyre's notion of the rationality of traditions, I shall relate Habermas's model of rational explanation to his discussion of the "rationalization of the lifeworld." This notion is introduced in connection with his own "communication-theoretical" appropriation of Alfred Schutz and Thomas Luckmann's analysis of the general structures of the lifeworld. Finally, in the last section, I shall suggest even more briefly and tentatively how his project of rational reconstruction, when combined with a functionalist or "systems-theoretical" perspective, completes the project of critical social theory.

I. INTERPRETIVE SOCIAL SCIENCE AND THE RATIONAL EXPLANATION OF ACTION

Habermas defends a broadly interpretive approach within the social sciences, since, according to him, the primary field of inquiry or object domain is the "symbolically pre-structured reality"—the socio-cultural lifeworld—constituted by the meaningful behavior (or action) of its members.[7] Such an approach gives rise to the problem of *Verstehen* (or interpretive understanding), since the interpreter must not only learn the rules and practices of the community of inquirers to which she belongs, but must also become familiar with the rules and practices that define the lifeworld (or segment of it) that she is interpreting. Following Peter Winch,[8] Anthony Giddens[9] refers to this interpretive requirement as the "double hermeneutic"; according to Habermas, it provides the principal basis for the methodological distinction between the natural and social sciences.

The problem of *Verstehen* is of methodological importance in the humanities and social sciences primarily because the scientist cannot gain access to a symbolically prestructured reality through *observation* alone, and because *understanding meaning [Sinnverstehen]* cannot be methodically brought under control in the same way as can observation in the course of experimentation. The social scientist basically has no other access to the lifeworld than the social-scientific layman does. He must already belong in a certain way to the lifeworld whose elements he wishes to describe. In order to describe them, he must understand them; in order to understand them, he must be able in principle to participate in their production; and participation presupposes that one belongs (I, 108).

The requirement of *Verstehen* arises because the objects that the social sciences study are embedded in "complexes of meaning" (*Sinnzusammenhänge*) constituted by the social actors themselves, and because the inquirer can understand these meaning complexes only by systematically relating them to his or her own pretheoretical knowledge as a member of the lifeworld (I, 110, 132-133). Without such an interpretation of the meaning that social agents connect with their action, the objects of social-scientific inquiry cannot even be brought into view.[10]

Habermas further contends that a recognition of the fuller implications of an interpretive approach yields "methodologically shocking consequences" (I, 111). In particular, it gives rise to the "disquieting thesis" that the interpretation of action cannot be separated from the interpreter's taking a position on the validity of the claims explicitly or implicitly connected with the action (I, 107). The interpretation of action (as well as its products) requires making clear the reasons that actors would give for their action (or could possibly give within their social and historical setting); but,

[O]ne can understand reasons only to the extent that one understands *why* they are or are not sound, or why in a given case a decision as to whether reasons are good or bad is not (yet) possible. An interpreter cannot, therefore, interpret expressions connected through criticizable validity claims with a potential of reasons (and thus represent knowledge) without taking a position on them (I, 116).

The interpretation of action draws the inquirer into the process of identifying the agent's reasons for the action, but reasons can appear as reasons (as opposed to local causal determinants) only to the extent that one adopts the performative attitude of a communicative participant.[11] Understanding the reasons for action requires taking a position on the validity or warrantedness of those reasons according to our own lights, and that means (at least initially) setting aside an external or "third person" perspective in favor of an internal or "first person" perspective in which both actor and interpreter belong to the same "universe of discourse."

Now the interesting point is that reasons are of a special nature. They can always be expanded into arguments which we then understand only when we *recapitulate* (*nachvollziehen*) them in the light of some standards of rationality. This "recapitulation" requires a reconstructive activity in which we bring into play our own standards of rationality, at least intuitively. From the perspective of a participant, however, one's own rationality standards must always claim general validity; this claim to general validity can be restricted only subsequently, from the perspective of a third person. In short, the interpretive reconstruction of reasons makes it necessary for us to place "their" standards in relation to "ours," so that in the case of a contradiction we either revise our preconceptions or relativize "their" standards of rationality against "ours."[12]

It would seem that this strong formulation of the implications of an interpretive approach would preclude the possibility of acquiring any objective knowledge in the social sciences or of developing a general social theory. Yet Habermas criticizes hermeneutic approaches like Hans-Georg Gadamer's precisely for having abandoned such goals for social science, and he poses his own project in terms of the following question: "How can the *objectivity of understanding* be reconciled with the performative attitude of one who participates in a process of reaching understanding?" (I, 112).[13] At the same time, however, Habermas also rejects the solution offered by Schutz (and adopted by some ethnomethodologists), whereby the objectivity of interpretation is assured by the social inquirer adopting a "theoretical attitude" detached from the practical interests of the everyday actor (I, 122).[14] Habermas's own alternative is to claim that the conditions for the objectivity of interpretation (and even the formation of law-like generalizations) can already be found within the "general structures of the processes of reaching understanding" which the interpreter shares with the actors in the object domain (I, 123). At times, this claim appears to be an exercise in intellectual gymnastics, as when Habermas is compelled to distinguish the objective knowledge available from within a performative attitude from "objectivating" knowledge, and to argue that the performative attitude adopted by the social inquirer makes possible objective interpretations—"*subject to the withdrawal, as it were, of his qualities as an actor*" (I, 114, 116).[15] The intent of his position, however, is fairly clear: the acceptance of an interpretive approach does not mean that the inquirer relinquishes all forms of "reflective self-control." Rather, the criteria for such reflective self-control are derived from standards of rationality which are immanent within the most general structures of communication, and "[i]t is this potential for critique built into communicative action itself that the social scientist, by entering into the contexts of everyday action as a virtual participant, can systematically exploit and bring into play outside these contexts and against their particularity'' (I, 121). I shall return, in my discussion of his notion of reconstructive science below, to a consideration of what Habermas means by this "sort of objective and theoretical knowledge" and its potential for critique.

Without calling into question the "methodologically shocking consequences" of his approach (nor denying some of the paradoxes to which it leads), I would like to argue that Habermas's model of interpretive social science is more plausible than some of his critics have supposed. As a first step in defending this claim, I shall argue that Habermas's model of a "rational interpretation" of action can, in fact, be construed as a modification of the type of action explanation offered by Davidson.[16] Like Habermas, Davidson argues that the explanation of action is a normative (or evaluative) enterprise, and requires that the interpreter make use of the same standards of rationality she would employ in providing an account of her own action. As I shall argue, however, Davidson's interpretive strategy is limited by its adherence to a model of instrumental or economic rationality—Bayesian decision theory—and, contrary to his own claims, is thus unable to take into account the social character of rationality.

According to Davidson, an interpreter has explained an action when she has identified the combination of the agent's beliefs and desires (or "pro-attitudes") that caused or produced that action.[17] Such an explanation of the action will generally include a principle of the form:

If A wants ϕ and believes x-ing is a way to bring about ϕ and that there is no better way to bring about ϕ, and A has no overriding want, and knows how to x, and is able to x, then A x's.[18]

Such explanations are distinguished from (and irreducible to) explanations in the natural sciences, since they are both intentional in structure and normative in character. Action explanations are intentional, because propositional attitudes (beliefs and pro-attitudes) are included as part of the explanans. They are normative, not only in the sense that such explanations apply norms or standards to the phenomena to be explained, but (more importantly) in the sense that the interpreter attributes her own norms of action to the agent in the process of identifying the agent's reasons for the action.

The point is . . . that in explaining action we are identifying the phenomena to be explained, and the phenomena that do the explaining, as directly answering to our own norms; reason explanations make others intelligible to us only to the extent that we can recognize something like our own reasoning powers at work.[19]

The most fundamental of these norms for Davidson is the norm of rationality: the interpreter assumes that the agent is both attitudinally and behaviorally rational. That is, the interpreter assumes that the beliefs that form part of the agent's reason for the action are reasonable and consistent with other beliefs the agent holds (attitudinal rationality), and the action is treated as a reasonable consequence of beliefs and desires held by the agent (behavioral rationality).[20]

According to Davidson, this norm of rationality requires that the interpreter employ a "Principle of Charity" in the interpretation of an agent's beliefs and intentional acts.[21] Unless the interpreter initially assumes that a large number of the beliefs an agent holds true are, in fact, true (by the interpreter's lights), it will not be possible to interpret a particular belief (the one that produced the action in question) as reasonable and the aim of rational explanation will be thwarted. Understood in a weak sense, the principle states that, if a combination of beliefs and desires which the agent possesses is to be identified as the reason for an action, then those beliefs and desires must be intelligible to us.[22] They cannot appear as reasons, if they do not cohere with a wider set of beliefs which the agent holds true *and* which is intelligible to us, but this wider set of beliefs would be unintelligible to us if, by our own lights, we judged it to be largely false.

As I have construed it, Davidson's model of a reason explanation is analogous to Max Weber's model of "rational interpretation." According to Weber,[23] a "rational interpretation" of a teleological (or purposive-rational) action need not remain confined to the "subjective" point of view of the actor. Rather, once the interpreter has ideal-typically reconstructed the intentions of the actor, it is possible to assess *from the interpreter's standpoint* whether the beliefs were rational in light of other beliefs held by the actor, whether the means chosen were the most efficient for realizing the intended goal, and whether the means produced consequences other than those intended. In summarizing Weber's view, Habermas writes,

> In advancing what Weber calls a rational interpretation, the interpreter himself takes a position on the claim with which purposive-rational actions appear; he relinquishes the attitude of a third person for the performative attitude of a participant who is examining a problematic validity claim and, if need be, criticizing it. Rational interpretations are undertaken in a performative attitude, since the interpreter presupposes a basis for judgment that is shared by all parties, including the actors (I, 103).

If my analogy to Weber is appropriate, then Davidson's model of action explanation also assumes a connection between meaning and validity, at least with respect to claims about the truth of beliefs and the efficacy of action.[24] Interpretation can proceed only if we attribute our standards of rationality to the agent whose action we are interpreting; but, in attributing our standards of rationality to the agent, we cannot avoid evaluating the rationality of their beliefs and actions in light of those shared standards. At the same time, however, Habermas's model of interpretive social science would require modifying Davidson's project in at least three respects.

First, the formulation of the method of rational interpretation in the preceding paragraph is obviously too strong. In developing such interpretations, we do not simply attribute our standards of rationality to actors in the object domain. That would be to commit the most extreme form of the "ethnocentric fallacy." Rather, as we have seen, what is necessary is that the explication of the agent's reasons for acting be placed in relation to "our" standards of rationality within the framework of one, hypothetically reconstructed "universe of discourse."[25]

Furthermore, Habermas argues that "rational interpretations" in Weber's sense need not be limited to judgments about the truth of the agent's belief or the efficacy of his action in obtaining the desired goal. It is also possible to develop rational interpretations about the appropriateness of the beliefs and actions with respect to existing social norms and about the sincerity of the agent's intentions. In these cases, it is not a claim to truth or efficacy which is being judged by the inquirer, but a claim to normative rightness and sincerity (or authenticity), respectively. Just as in the case of a rational interpretation of the truth of a belief or efficacy of an action, however, rational interpretations in these two further cases require that the interpreter make use of her own norms of rationality in assessing the agent's action, and thus that the interpreter move beyond the standpoint of the "subjective" rationality of the actor to a judgment about the "objective" rationality of the action.

Habermas has clarified this expanded schema of rational interpretations in connection with his own theory of communicative action. For purposes of our own discussion, this type of action can briefly be described as a form of social interaction in which actors coordinate their actions on the basis of mutually shared definitions of their situation. In acting communicatively, individuals more or less naively accept as valid the various claims raised with their utterances or actions, and mutually suppose that they each stand ready to provide reasons for them should the validity of those claims be questioned. It is because of this intimate connection between validity, reasons, and action that communicative action must initially be approached from the internal perspective of the participant. Communicative action is connected to domains of validity which can only be understood "from the inside," that is, by those who as (virtual) participants are able to give and assess the reasons for an action. In a slightly more technical sense, and one that is tied more specifically to modern structures of rationality, Habermas states that individuals who act communicatively self-reflectively aim at reaching understanding about something in the world by relating their interpretations to three general types of validity claims connected with three basic types of speech acts: a claim of truth raised in constative speech acts, a claim to normative rightness raised in regulative speech acts, and a claim to authenticity raised in expressive speech acts (I, 319f.).

Rational interpretations of normatively-regulated and dramaturgical (or self-expressive) action, like the interpretations of purposive action, thus make use of standards of validity which are already operative in the general structures of communicative action. Habermas speaks of these standards as "suppositions of commonality" which the interpreter shares with the social actor (I, 104). He also refers to this interpretive process as one in which the interpreter "equips" the actors with the same formal world concepts of an objective, social, and subjective world as those employed by the interpreter in communicative action (I, 118-119). This schema of concepts provides a "reference system" or "categorial scaffolding" to which the interpreter can appeal in developing rational interpretations. If, for example, the interpretation involves reference to a culture other than our own, it may be possible to make an action intelligible only by observing a failure to make use of such differentiated world concepts (I, 63f.).[26]

Finally, such a modification of Davidson's model of action explanation would also require that the interpreter attend more closely to social institutions, rules, and practices than Davidson seems to think necessary. For the rational explanation of an action, it is not sufficient merely to cite the agent's beliefs and desires that produced the action. It is also necessary to locate those beliefs and desires within the context of specific social institutions and practices if they are to be recognized as reasons. MacIntyre vividly illustrates this point with the following anecdote:

> I am being shown by my fellow-scientists the first and so far the only specimen of a new hybrid fruit developed because of its possible ease of cultivation and food-value for peoples in some particularly barren and starvation-prone part of the world. I snatch them from the hands of the scientist who is preparing to analyse them and gobble them down. When asked 'Why on earth did you do that?' I reply 'I just felt hungry. I like fruit.' It is important to notice that this answer renders my behavior more rather than less unintelligible than it was before. For in the context of this kind of scientific practice eating something just because one felt hungry is not an intelligible way of behaving. The practice imposes norms which constrain and limit the expression of immediate desire in the institutionalized social settings informed by the practice.[27]

Citing the relevant belief and desire rationalizes the action only if it presents a good reason within the context of specific social practices and institutions. Although Davidson states that "rationality is a social trait, only communicators have it,"[28] he does not seem to grant that what counts as rational might depend crucially on the social contexts of action. Although an interpreter needs to be familiar with the social contexts of action to determine whether an action is rational, the rationality Davidson connects with an action is not itself socially determined and is not modified in the process of social evolution.

The distinction I have attempted to draw in the preceding sentence can perhaps be more clearly seen by contrasting Davidson's notion of a "pro-attitude" to Taylor's notion of the "desirability characterization" of an action. Davidson introduces this neologism to cover, not only the desires and wants of an agent, but also "a great variety of moral views, aesthetic principles, economic prejudices, social conventions, and public and private goals and values in so far as these can be interpreted as attitudes of an agent directed toward actions of a certain kind."[29] The fact that a pro-attitude is asked to perform such "yeoman service" (Davidson) suggests, however, that these different stances toward an action are, in the last analysis, not particularly relevant for an assessment of its rationality. What is crucial is simply that the agent's belief be accompanied by some desire (or pro-attitude). For Taylor, by contrast, making an action intelligible (and thus assessing its rationality) requires being able to apply the "desirability characterizations" that are constitutive for the agent and his world:

> I come to understand someone when I understand his emotions, his aspirations, what he finds admirable and contemptible, in himself and others, what he yearns for, what he loathes, etc. Being able to formulate this understanding is being able to apply correctly the desirability characterizations which he applies in the way that he applies them. . . . My claim is that the explicit formulation of what I understand when I understand you requires my grasping the desirability characterizations that you self-clairvoyantly use, or else those which you would use if you had arrived at a more reflective formulation of your loves, hates, aspirations, admirabilia, etc.[30]

Desirability characterizations are not simply desires or preferences to which the agent (and his reasoning processes) are contingently related; they "are portrayals (or imply portrayals) of how things are with us" and thus entail ontological commitments.[31] We can understand others only when we are able to make clear the ontological commitments implicit in the agent's desirability characterizations, but this requires becoming familiar with the social rules and practices in which those characterizations operate.

Of course, the claim that reason explanations require familiarity with the social context of action should not be pushed to the point of insisting that it is social convention rather than the agent's intention which rationalizes the action. The claim is rather that it is only possible to identify the agent's intention (in this case his possible reason for the action) by reference to the social (and linguistic) conventions in connection with which intentions of that kind are standardly displayed.[32] Nor should the claim about the relevance of social practices and institutions be taken to imply that the agent is always conscious of the conventions that render his action intelligible. In many cases, the institutionalized social setting that makes the action intelligible is one provided by "whatever the established routines are which in a particular group constitute the structure of the normal day."[33] These routines are for the most part performed habitually and thus, though they render action intelligible, they are not among the reasons for which an agent acts (if, indeed, the agent acts for a reason at all). What is claimed, however, is that reference to social practices and institutions will be incorporated into the account the agent would provide, were he asked to give the reasons for his action. That is, an understanding of these practices and institutions form a large part of the cultural stock of knowledge to which the agent has access and which he implicitly knows as a result of having been educated or socialized into them.

The claim that rational interpretations of action can only be provided by locating the action within the context of specific social institutions and practices inevitably raises the spectre of relativism. Winch's *Idea of a Social Science* has often been understood to entail relativism, and MacIntyre and Taylor (as well as Habermas) have each sought hard to distinguish their own interpretive models from that position.[34] They both argue that a recognition of the tradition-bound character of standards of rationality does not preclude the possibility of making judgments about the rational superiority of one tradition over another. Since this claim has obvious implications for the development of rational interpretations of action in the social sciences, I shall briefly consider MacIntyre's argument for it.

In *Whose Justice? Which Rationality?*[35] MacIntyre defends the position that standards of rationality and rational inquiry are always embodied within a particular tradition of argument. The principal antagonists in his account are those adherents of the "Enlightenment project" who maintain that rationality consists in independence from all tradition. Nevertheless, MacIntyre also defends his historicism against the "relativist challenge" that debates between rival traditions cannot be rationally resolved or that judgments about rational superiority can never be made. What both Enlightenment thinkers and their relativist "inverted mirror-image" fail to see is "the kind of rationality possessed by traditions" which makes possible such rational resolutions and judgments.[36] MacIntyre goes on to list three "highly exacting requirements" of this form of rationality in connection with the way a tradition confronts epistemological or moral crises:

The solution of a genuine epistemological crisis requires the invention or discovery of new concepts and the framing of some new type or types of theory which meet three highly exacting requirements. First, this in some ways radically new and conceptually enriched scheme, if it is to put an end to epistemological crisis, must furnish a solution to the problems which had previously proved intractable in a systematic and coherent way. Second, it must also provide an explanation of just what it was which rendered the tradition, before it had acquired these new resources, sterile or incoherent or both. And third, these first two tasks must be carried out in a way which exhibits some fundamental continuity of the new conceptual and theoretical structures with the shared beliefs in terms of which the tradition of enquiry had been defined up to this point.[37]

For an "adequate response" or rational resolution of a crisis, the newly invented or discovered mode of reasoning should provide a solution in terms that make it clear why the crisis seemed intractable and do so in a way that exhibits a "fundamental continuity" with the previous mode of reasoning. Traditions that resolve crises in this way are considered rationally superior to those which do not, and (presumably) traditions that, in keeping with these requirements, are able to absorb other traditions plagued by crises will emerge as rationally superior to those which are absorbed. Judgments of rational superiority thus rest on a claim about the greater conceptual adequacy of one tradition or mode of reasoning over another.

There are, I believe, at least two difficulties presented by MacIntyre's notion of the rationality of traditions—one related to his notion of rationality, the other to his notion of a tradition. First, although it is reminiscent of Hegelian dialectics or conceptual *Aufhebungen,* now "fallibilistically" conceived (p. 360), unlike Hegel, MacIntyre's "highly exacting requirements" do not provide any specific principles or criteria for determining whether a resolution is rational. Rather, either the requirements remain hopelessly vague or they will most likely invoke some of the very Enlightenment ideals that MacIntyre elsewhere criticizes. For example, a resurgence of religious fundamentalism could resolve many of our moral crises by claiming that certain rights were, in fact, "legal fictions" imposed by an activist court, it could explain their appearance as the result of moral promiscuity or the lack of moral resolve characteristic of a materialistic and consumer-oriented society, and it is certainly not obvious that such an argument would fail to exhibit a "fundamental continuity" with the past. But even should such a resolution be achieved through existing democratic processes, MacIntyre would not necessarily consider it rational.[38] When MacIntyre elsewhere makes these "highly exacting requirements" more specific, however, the standards of rationality begin to sound like the very principles voiced in the Enlightenment project:

> For the reasoning that vindicates itself on those occasions when the issue *is* resolved by reasoning rather than by the use of power in some arbitrary way or by violence or by social fatigue is the reasoning that commends itself as *the best piece of reasoning on this issue advanced so far.*[39]

This stipulation of the absence of arbitrary power, coercion, and social fatigue (*sic*) points to the counterfactual ideal of an open debate among free and equal persons in which no force but that of the better argument prevails. Of course, MacIntyre is correct in claiming that the "best piece of reasoning" will always appear as such relative to a particular tradition of argument, and thus that what we assert with warrant to be true or right now may prove to be mistaken in the future. But, as MacIntyre notes, the recognition of human fallibility and the historical conditionedness of our reasoning does not deprive that reasoning of its own claim to universality (e.g., truth or normative rightness).[40]

Second, the notion of a tradition which MacIntyre employs is ambiguous and ill-defined. In *Whose Justice? Which Rationality?* he identifies four traditions in Western societies (Aristotelianism, Augustinianism—in both an "earlier" and "Thomistic version," the Scottish Enlightenment, and liberalism), but it is not clear how these are demarcated from one another or what determines the emergence of a new tradition (as opposed to a conceptually enriched version of the same). Is liberal Protestantism a separate tradition from Fundamentalism, or are they both part of the larger tradition of Christianity—Augustinianism in still more recent versions? Do liberal Christianity, liberal Judaism, and liberal Islam, together with liberal secularism, form one tradition opposed to more orthodox variants of these religions, or is each a liberal version of a separate tradition? MacIntyre's description of a living tradition as "an historically extended, socially embodied argument, and an argument precisely in part about the goods which constitute that tradition,"[41] offers little guidance for settling such questions. Yet answers to those questions are relevant for an assessment of the rationality of a tradition. Moreover, without making clear the connection between the two sorts of uses, MacIntyre employs the concept of a tradition both normatively (or prescriptively) and descriptively. He speaks, for example, of features a tradition *must* possess and of how it *should* behave it if is properly to be called a tradition (see pp. 354f.). Finally, I would like to suggest, the concept of a tradition is not well-suited for characterizing the differences between the structures of rationality in premodern and modern societies. What is central to this distinction is not the emergence of a new tradition—e.g., "the tradition of modernity"—but a process of societal differentiation which affects the structures of rationality both at the level of social institutions and individual competencies.[42] It is for social-theoretic considerations such as this that Habermas prefers to speak of the "rationalization of lifeworld" rather than the rationality of traditions.

II. INTERPRETIVE SOCIAL SCIENCE AND THE CONCEPT OF THE LIFEWORLD

Habermas describes the lifeworld as "the culturally transmitted and linguistically organized stock of interpretive patterns" which forms the symbolic core of a society, and introduces it as a correlate to the concept of communicative action.

> Subjects acting communicatively always come to an understanding in the horizon of a lifeworld. Their lifeworld is formed from more or less diffuse, always unproblematic, background convictions. This lifeworld background serves as a source of situation definitions that are presupposed by participants as unproblematic (I, 70).

His treatment of the lifeworld is greatly indebted to the phenomenological analysis of Schutz and Luckmann which emphasizes its fundamentally implicit or taken-for-granted character, its holistic structure, and the fact that it does not stand at the conscious disposition of actors but remains in the background as a preinterpreted horizon (II, 126ff.).[43] So understood, the lifeworld forms a "vast and incalculable web of presuppositions" against which particular actions and utterances acquire their meaning. Furthermore, in a manner analogous to MacIntyre's characterization of a tradition, the lifeworld as such cannot become problematic or the subject of controversy, according to Habermas; at most, it can fall apart (II, 131).

In contrast to MacIntyre's description of a tradition (which remains more or less restricted to the idea of the transmission of cultural knowledge), however, the concept of the lifeworld is broad enough to include reference to processes of social integration and socialization as well. More specifically, Habermas describes the basic symbolic structures of the lifeworld in connection with the general institutional components of societies singled out by Talcott Parsons (e.g., culture, society, and personality):

> I call *culture* the store of knowledge from which those engaged in communicative action draw interpretations susceptible of consensus as they come to an understanding about something in the world. I call *society* (in the narrower sense of a component of the lifeworld) the legitimate orders from which those engaged in communicative action gather a solidarity, based on belonging to groups, as they enter into interpersonal relationships with one another. *Personality* serves as a term of art for acquired competences that render a subject capable of speech and action and hence able to participate in processes of mutual understanding in a given context and to maintain his own identity in the shifting contexts of interaction.[44]

Social actors draw upon the lifeworld as a resource in the form of cultural knowledge, legitimate social orders, and acquired individual competencies; at the same time, the symbolic reproduction of the lifeworld depends on the interpretive accomplishments of its members in each of these institutional domains. A thorough description of an agent's reasons for an action would ultimately require an elaboration of the relevant features and structural components of the lifeworld in which the action occurs and to which it refers.

By correlating the concept of the lifeworld with the concept of communicative action, Habermas is able to highlight a distinction that is only implicit in phenomenological analyses. On the one hand, as a *resource* that is drawn upon in communicative action, the lifeworld remains in the background as implicit knowledge. On the other hand, as a *topic* about which communicative actors seek to reach agreement, segments of the lifeworld are selectively thematized as problems (I, 82).[45] In communicative action, social actors draw upon resources of the lifeworld, but they also make use of the reference system of formal world concepts in their efforts to reach agreement about something in the world. Habermas frequently distinguishes these two dimensions of the lifeworld by means of a contrast between lifeworld (resource) and world (topic) and in connection with a spatial metaphor:

> While the segment of the lifeworld relevant to the situation encounters the actor as a problem which he has to solve as something standing as it were in front of him, he is supported in the rear by the background of his lifeworld. Coping with situations is a circular process in which the actor is two things at the same time: the *initiator* of actions that can be attributed to him and the *product* of traditions in which he stands as well as of group solidarities to which he belongs and processes of socialization and learning to which he is subjected.[46]

In *The Philosophical Discourse of Modernity*, Habermas warns that this description of a circular process should be accepted with caution: actors are not products of the lifeworld in the sense that the latter can be viewed as a self-generating process that has a life of its own. Rather, individuals (and groups) reproduce the lifeworld through their communicative action and with reference to the formal world concepts, and the lifeworld as resource is "saddled *on*" the interpretive accomplishments of its members.[47] Thus, although Habermas rejects conceptualizing the lifeworld as the noematic correlate of an act of (transcendental) consciousness (a possibility Schutz and Luckmann apparently always held out), he also resists reifying it in ways that obscure its roots in the interpretive accomplishments of concrete individuals and groups.

This brief summary of the general structures of the lifeworld also permits us to see how Habermas is able to speak of a "rationalization of the lifeworld." What is central to this notion is not, as for Weber, the expansion of formal or instrumental reason to more and more dimensions of social life, but an opening up of the processes of symbolic reproduction to consensual agreement among autonomous individuals in light of criticizable validity claims. He describes the rationalization of the lifeworld in terms of three related processes: (1) the structural differentiation of its basic components (culture, society, and personality); (2) the separation of form and content; and (3) the increasing reflexivity of symbolic reproduction (II, 145-146).

(1) The structural differentiation between culture *and* society consists in "the gradual uncoupling of the institutional system from worldviews"; between society *and* personality, in "the extension of the scope of contingency for establishing interpersonal relationships"; and between culture *and* personality, in "the fact that the renewal of traditions depends more and more on individuals' readiness to criticize and their ability to innovate" (II, 146). In the wake of such societal differentiation, the components of the lifeworld become less concretely homogeneous and "interpenetrate" (Parsons) one another in more general and abstract ways.[48]

(2) Second, a separation of form and content accompanies this differentiation of the structural components of the lifeworld:

> *On the cultural level,* the core, identity-securing traditions separate off from the concrete contents with which they are still tightly interwoven in mythical worldviews. They shrink to formal elements such as world-concepts, communication presuppositions, argumentation procedures, abstract values, and the like. *At the level of society,* general principles and procedures crystallize out of the particular contexts to which they are tied in primitive societies. In modern societies, principles of legal order and morality are established which are less and less tailored to concrete forms of life. *On the level of the personality system,* the cognitive structures acquired in the socialization process are increasingly detached from the content of cultural knowledge with which they were at first integrated in "concrete thinking" (II, 146).

In short, the symbolic reproduction of society through the interpretive accomplishments of its members increasingly depends upon abstract cultural norms and values, formal principles and institutionalized procedures of social order, and decentered forms of intellectual, social, and moral cognition. It also becomes possible to criticize and revise these interpretive accomplishments in light of norms, principles, and individual competencies that are embodied in the differentiated institutional complexes.

(3) Finally, the processes of symbolic reproduction—cultural transmission,

social integration, and socialization—associated with each of the structural components of the lifeworld become increasingly reflective and are in many cases also given over to treatment by professionals. This occurs not only, as Weber observed, in connection with the transmission of culture (in the differentiated spheres of science and technology, law and morality, and art and art criticism), but also with respect to social integration (through democratic forms of collective political will formation) and socialization (with the development of formal systems of education and pedagogical sciences) (II, 147).

According to Habermas, the rationalization of the lifeworld along these lines proceeds only to the extent that symbolic reproduction comes to rely more upon the interpretive accomplishments of participants who reciprocally raise and redeem the formal validity claims inherent in their communicative practices than upon a pre-existing "normatively *ascribed* agreement" (I, 340). For this reason, while such differentiation "signals a release of the rationality potential inherent in communicative action" (II, 146), it also brings about a situation in which symbolic reproduction is increasingly fragile and risk-filled (I, 340).[49]

To summarize the argument of this section, a model of interpretive social science which is concerned with constructing rational interpretations in Weber's sense and which takes seriously the social dimensions of rationality cannot rest content with an interpretation of the beliefs and action of an individual agent, but must place those interpretations in relation to the social practices and institutions in which the action occurs and, finally, clarify it in connection with the rational potential contained within the general structures of the particular socio-cultural lifeworld as a whole. Habermas also attempts to avert the threat of relativism (as well as ethnocentricism), however, by developing those interpretations in connection with principles and criteria derived from an internal reconstruction of the development of individual and collective learning processes—what he refers to as the "rationalization of the lifeworld."

III. RATIONAL RECONSTRUCTION AND CRITICAL SOCIAL THEORY

As I suggested in my introduction, Habermas's model of interpretive social science forms only a part of the larger project of critical social theory. In order to be rendered more fully serviceable for the purpose of social criticism, rational interpretations also need to be (1) supplemented with insights from the reconstructive sciences and (2) complemented by a functionalist or "systems-theoretic" approach to society. In the final section, I can at most sketch out the general contours of these two additional aspects to the project of critical social theory. These remarks on the overall methodological form of a critical theory are also offered even more tentatively than my discussion of his model of interpretive social science.

(1) In connection with his notion of rational interpretations, Habermas has introduced a unique category of "reconstructive science." Although distinct from the "objectivating" or nomological sciences, he claims these sciences nevertheless generate "some sort of objective and theoretical knowledge" that provides a "critical stance" toward individual action and social institutions.[50] As examples of reconstructive sciences, Habermas cites the disciplines of logic and metamathematics, formal pragmatics and theories of meaning, epistemology and philosophy of science, theories of rationality and argumentation, and ethics and theories of action. What each of these disciplines share is the attempt to explicate the intuitive know-how that speakers and actors possess about conditions of validity for various classes of expressions and performances. For just this reason, in each case the theorist must work with a performative attitude and take up the internal perspective of the participant, since these disciplines assume that the subject is intuitively able to produce and identify valid expressions and performances.[51] Nevertheless, the goal of reconstruction is to provide a theoretical explication of this intuitive knowledge: "To the extent that rational reconstructions succeed in their search for very general conditions of validity, they can claim to identify universals and thus to produce a type of *theoretical* knowledge."[52] Moreover, such reconstructions are not limited to individual competencies but can also treat "the collective knowledge of traditions" (II, 399). Their object then becomes "collective learning processes," and the theorist aims at reconstructing "the emergence and the internal history of those modern complexes of knowledge that have been differentiated out, each under a different single aspect of validity—truth, normative rightness, or authenticity" (II, 398). Habermas seems to have in mind something like the Lakatosian notion of reconstructing the internal history of scientific disciplines, although this Popperian "third-world history" is now broadened to include moral/practical and aesthetic reasoning as well as more strictly cognitive reasoning.[53]

Furthermore, because they deal with validity claims initially accessible only in connection with a performative attitude, reconstructive sciences involve a claim to universality that preserves a "transcendental flavor" and stands in need of philosophical argument and clarification. That is, they attempt to describe the pretheoretical knowledge of rule systems for different performances in such a way that a possible alternative description is shown to be derivative or "to utilize portions of the very hypothesis it seeks to supplant."[54] At the same time, however, they renounce the search for "ultimate foundations" characteristic of stronger forms of transcendental argument, since the claims possess a hypothetical status and can be submitted to forms of "indirect" testing in connection with empirical theories.[55] Habermas again seems to have in mind something like the Lakatosian notion of disconfirming scientific research programs (which cannot generally be falsified on the basis of a single crucial experiment).[56]

Finally, when they are used in connection with rational interpretations, reconstructions of individual competencies acquire a critical dimension and can help identify deviant cases of belief and action (e.g., instances of fallacious arguments, inadequate explanations, infelicitous speech acts, inappropriate evaluations, etc.). At the level of collective learning processes, such reconstructions can be used to identify more general "processes of unlearning."

> Processes of unlearning can be gotten at through a critique of deformations that are rooted in the selective exploitation of a potential for rationality and mutual understanding that was once available but is now buried over (II, 400).

In either case, the idea is that such deformations can only be identified by means of a theoretical reconstruction of the goals or end states of highly abstract learning processes that are embodied in the structures of the lifeworld and reflected in individual competencies. The reconstructions enable the social inquirer to discern "systematic distortions to communication" and one-sided or unbalanced processes of societal rationalization—phenomena generally referred to in the tradition of Western Marxism as false consciousness and social reification.[57]

(2) Finally, the project of a critical theory of society is not limited to the task of identifying processes of unlearning or other disturbances to the communicative infrastructure of the lifeworld. It also seeks to uncover the possible systemic causes of such distortions. In a renewed synthesis of Weber and Marx, Habermas locates these causes in a one-sided rationalization process spurred on by capital accumulation (I, 342-343). The process of societal rationalization which sets in with the differentiation of the structural components of the lifeworld (culture, society, and personality) also brings about conditions for the relative autonomy of the subsystems of the economy and political administration vis-à-vis traditional normative structures (II, 153ff.). These "purposive-rational" subsystems of action depend less upon the mutually shared interpretations of social actors for their maintenance and reproduction than upon the functional interconnections of action consequences via highly generalized media of exchange, e.g., money and power (II, 173, 183). According to Habermas, this "second order" process, which is more or less inevitable with increased societal complexity, does not produce social crises and pathologies within the lifeworld per se (II, 318).[58] Rather, the individual and collective pathologies associated with modernity— e.g., the loss of freedom and meaning—occur only when "mediatization" disturbs or displaces the communicative infrastructure of the lifeworld," that is, only when symbolic reproduction becomes subordinated to the systemic imperatives of material reproduction (II, 305). In a reworking of Marx's notion of commodity fetishism and the process of "real abstraction," Habermas refers to

such systemically-induced disturbances to the communicative infrastructure of the lifeworld as the "internal colonization of the lifeworld" (II, 322, 332ff.).

I do not have space here to consider the problems associated with Habermas's conceptualization of society as "system" and "lifeworld."[59] I mention it only to indicate why Habermas maintains that the project of a critical social theory must not rest content with an exclusively hermeneutic approach to society, but must combine it with a functionalist or systems theoretic perspective.[60] A critical theory of society requires that the critical theorist be able to move back and forth between an internal and external perspective.

On the one hand, working solely from within the internal perspective of the participant—and thus treating action and their products as tied to the domain of reasons—the social inquirer is unable to perceive distortions to the structures of communication as such.

> A *verstehende* sociology that allows society to be wholly absorbed into the lifeworld ties itself to the perspective of self-interpretation of the culture under investigation; this internal perspective screens out everything that inconspicuously affects a sociocultural lifeworld from the outside (II, 150).

In particular, the inquirer will be unable to perceive phenomena such as mediatization, since "[t]he mediatization of the lifeworld takes effect on and with the structures of the lifeworld; it is not one of those processes that are available as themes *within* the lifeworld, and thus it cannot be read off from the intuitive knowledge of members" (II, 186).

On the other hand, systemic disturbances to the communicative infrastructure of the lifeworld cannot be identified from an exclusively external or observer's perspective, since, as we have seen, the structures of the lifeworld (and the forms of collective learning processes corresponding to them) are only accessible through a reconstructive analysis that begins with the members' intuitive knowledge (II, 151, 186). Thus, if communicative distortions and their systemic causes are to be identified, the critical theorist must be able to work simultaneously with both an internal (participant's) and an external (observer's) perspective, that is, with an analytic perspective on society as lifeworld and system. (The extent to which the lifeworld is actually given over to systemic imperatives via the media of money and power is, however, an empirical question.)

So conceived, the project of a critical social theory certainly implies a more modest conception of the relation between theory and practice than that found in traditional Marxism or earlier critical theory. On the one hand, theory is both more fallible and stands in a more indirect relation to social practice. This is especially evident in Habermas's notion of a reconstructive science. On the other hand, it also remains more dependent on concrete situations of social action which arise from within the lifeworld. Although it might be illuminated with the aid of a developmental logic, history does not contain an inevitable telos. Whether or not a more balanced process of societal rationalization will come about in the future depends on the nature of the social conflicts (and their resolution) that, on this model, arise on the boundary between "system" and "lifeworld." As Habermas indicates in the final section of *The Theory of Communicative Action,* the critical theorist can perhaps contribute to the clarification of what is more or less progressive within new social movements and forms of social protest. But the realization of a more "rational society"—e.g., a more communicatively balanced and rationalized lifeworld—ultimately depends upon the collective learning and practice of the social actors themselves.

State University of New York/Stony Brook

NOTES

1 Both of these challenges are more or less directly posed in "Some Difficulties in the Attempt to Link Theory and Praxis," in *Theory and Practice,* John Viertel, trans. (Boston: Beacon, 1973), pp. 1-40; more recently, see the brief remarks in "Questions and Counterquestions," in *Habermas and Modernity,* Richard Bernstein, ed. (Cambridge: MIT, 1985), pp. 204-205.

2 Habermas has recently characterized his own position as "hermeneutic reconstructionism" in contrast to both "hermeneutic objectivism" (e.g., Abel and Rudner) and "radical hermeneuticism" (e.g., Winch, Rorty, and Gadamer); see "Interpretive Social Science vs. Hermeneuticism," in *Social Science as Moral Inquiry,* Norma Haan, Robert Bellah, Paul Rabinow, and William Sullivan, eds. (Berkeley: California UP, 1983) [hereafter, ISS], p. 258.

3 Shierry Weber Nicholsen and Jerry Stark, trans. (Cambridge: MIT, 1988).

4 *Ibid.,* p. 187.

5 *The Theory of Communicative Action,* Vols. I and II, Thomas McCarthy, trans. (Boston: Beacon, 1984, 1987) (page references within the body of the text are to this work; in the notes, it will be referred to as TCA).

6 For a survey of other recent attempts to combine action and systems theory, see *The Micro-Macro Link,* Jeffrey C. Alexander, et al., eds. (Berkeley: California UP, 1987).

7 "The object domain of the social sciences encompasses everything that falls under the description 'element of a lifeworld'. What this expression means can be clarified intuitively by reference to those symbolic objects that we produce in speaking and acting, beginning with immediate expressions (such as speech acts, purposive activities, and cooperative actions), through the sedimentations of these expressions (such as texts, traditions, documents, works of art, theories, objects of material culture, goods, techniques and so on), to the indirectly generated configurations that are self-stabilizing and susceptible of organization (such as institutions, social systems, and personality structures)" (TCA, I, 108).

8 *The Idea of A Social Science* (London: RKP, 1958), pp. 86-87; and TCA, I, 110.

9 *New Rules of Sociological Method* (New York: Basic, 1976), p. 158.

10 Charles Taylor also defends this version of the *Verstehen* thesis in "Interpretation and the Sciences of Man," reprinted in his *Philosophical Papers,* vol. 2 (New York: Cambridge, 1985), pp. 15-57; and "Understanding and Explanation in the *Geisteswissenschaften,*" in *Wittgenstein:*

To Follow A Rule, S. Holtzman and C. Leich, eds. (Boston: Routledge, 1981), pp. 191-210. Mark Okrent ["Hermeneutics, Transcendental Philosophy, and Social Science," *Inquiry,* XXVII (1984): 23-49] and Joseph Rouse [*Knowledge and Power* (Ithaca: Cornell, 1987), ch. 6] misconstrue this formulation of the "double hermeneutic" and, hence, of the methodological distinction between the natural and social sciences: Taylor (and Habermas) do not claim that the thesis requires that agents be understood *as* self-interpreting agents (thus leading to the paradox or "paralogism" of man as a transcendental/empirical double), but that the inquirer initially seeks to understand their action in terms of the meaning it has for them.

11 This is not to deny that reasons can be causes, only that they must first be identified as reasons. In this respect, despite my comparison below, Habermas differs significantly from Davidson, since, for Davidson, reasons *qua* reasons cannot be causes [see Frederick Stoutland, "Oblique Causation and Reasons for Action," *Synthese,* XLIII (1980): 35-67]. This constraint on the identification of reasons would also provide the basis for a Habermasian critique of the "strong program" in the sociology of knowledge which denies any asymmetry in the treatment of reasons and causes of action; see Barry Barnes and David Bloor, "Relativism, Rationalism and the Sociology of Knowledge," in *Rationality and Relativism,* Martin Hollis and Steven Lukes, eds. (Cambridge: MIT, 1982), pp. 21-47.

12 "Questions and Counterquestions," in *Habermas and Modernity,* p. 204.

13 For Habermas's critique of philosophical hermeneutics and particularly its denigration of general theory, see his early review of *Truth and Method,* in *On the Logic of the Social Sciences,* esp. pp. 166-170; more recently, see TCA, II, 148 and ISS.

14 See Schutz, "Concept and Theory Formation in the Social Sciences," in *Collected Papers,* vol. I, M. Natanson, ed. (The Hague: Nijhoff, 1962), p. 63; for a more extensive comparison of Schutz and Habermas, see my "Crisis and Lifeworld in Husserl and Habermas," in *Crises in Continental Philosophy,* Charles Scott and Arlene Dallery, eds. (Albany: SUNY, forthcoming).

15 See also his distinction between "objectivating attitude^1" (observer) and "objectivating attitude^2" (performer), and remarks on the importance of recognizing a "hierarchy of attitudes" in "Reply to Skjei," *Inquiry,* XXVIII (1985), p. 109.

16 For an extended comparison of Habermas and Davidson which arrives, however, at quite different conclusions from my own, see Theodore Schatzki, "The Rationalization of Meaning and Understanding: Davidson and Habermas," *Synthese,* LXIX (1986): 51-79.

17 "Actions, Reasons and Causes," in *Essays on Actions and Events* (New York: Oxford, 1980), pp. 3-19. It should be noted, however, that Davidson does not maintain that reasons qua reasons cause action, but rather that such a causal connection exists only under a different description of the two events (namely, one that would be formulated in terms of a physical science, e.g., neurophysiology). Davidson describes his position as "anomalous monism," and it has been subject to sharp criticism by Stoutland, MacIntyre, and others. Habermas's model of action explanation would not reject the possibility of reasons qua reasons being the cause of action, where causal generalizations are understood in a non-Humean way—see MacIntyre, "The Intelligibility of Action," in *Rationality, Relativism and the Human Sciences,* Joseph Margolis, Michael Krausz, Richard M. Burian, eds. (Dordrecht: Nijhoff, 1986), p. 68.

18 This formulation of the "logical character of action explanations" is taken from "Freedom to Act," in *Essays on Actions and Events,* p. 77. It is a simplification of a schema provided by Paul Churchland in "The Logical Character of Action Explanations," *Philosophical Review,* LXXIX (1970): 214-236.

19 "Problems in the Explanation of Action," in *Metaphysics and Morality,* P. Pettit, R. Sylvan, and J. Norman, eds. (New York: Blackwell, 1987), p. 47; this aspect of the normative character of rational explanations is discussed in Michael Root, "Davidson and Social Science," in *Inquiries into Truth and Interpretation* (New York: Blackwell, 1986), pp. 281-283.

20 Philip Pettit and Graham MacDonald discuss these two aspects of rationality in their application

of the Davidsonian program to the social sciences; see *Semantics and Social Science* (Boston: Routledge, 1981), ch. 2.

21 "Belief and the Basis of Meaning," in *Essays on Actions and Events*, p. 152; and "Introduction" to *Inquiries into Truth and Interpretation*, p. xvii.

22 This "weak" sense of the principle of charity is close to what some have called a "Principle of Humanity," in contrast to a "strong" reading of the principle of charity as the requirement that the interpretee's beliefs must be held true even when it would seem more reasonable to regard them as in error (see MacDonald and Pettit, *Semantics and Social Science*, pp. 26-31; and Lukes, "Relativism in Its Place," in *Rationality and Relativism*, pp. 263-264). That Davidson does not hold to the "strong" interpretation of the principle seems clear from his remarks in the "Introduction" to *Inquiries into Truth and Interpretation*, p. xvii; and in "Reply to Quine and Lewis," in *Synthese*, xxvii (1974), p. 346: "The improved principle of charity, in so far as it says there are cases where you make exceptions right from the beginning, is what I espouse" (cited in Lukes, p. 264, fn. 6).

23 *Roscher and Knies*, Guy Oakes, trans. (New York: Free Press, 1981), p. 188; and *Economy and Society*, vol. I, G. Roth and C. Wittich, eds. (Berkeley: California UP, 1968), pp. 5-6; see also TCA, I, 103f.

24 This depends on how one understands the status of Davidson's truth-conditional semantics. If truth is merely a device for describing "semantic ascent," detached from any pragmatic notion of justification or warranted assertibility, then Davidson's model of action explanation begins to look quite different from Weber's (and Habermas's). This seems to be the view adopted by Schatzki in his article referred to above (n. 13); see pp. 76-77. For a critique of this interpretation of truth-conditional semantics, see Hilary Putnam, "Why Reason Can't Be Naturalized," in *After Philosophy: End or Transformation?*, Kenneth Baynes, James Bohman, and Thomas A. McCarthy, eds. (Cambridge: MIT, 1987), pp. 240-241.

25 On this point, Habermas's model is thus closer to Taylor's notion of the "language of perspicuous contrast," and Hans-Georg Gadamer's notion of the "fusion of horizons"; see Taylor, "Understanding and Ethnocentricity," in *Philosophical Papers*, vol. 2, pp. 125f.

26 See also Taylor, "Rationality," in *Rationality and Relativism*, p. 97.

27 "The Intelligibility of Action," p. 73.

28 "Rational Animals," *Dialectica*, xxxvi (1982), p. 327.

29 "Actions, Reasons and Causes," p. 4.

30 Taylor, "Understanding and Explanation in the *Geisteswissenschaften*," p. 192.

31 *Ibid.*, p. 200.

32 This is similar to the point that Peter Strawson makes in a different context with particular reference to speech acts; cf. "Intention and Convention in Speech Acts," in *Logico-Philosophical Papers* (London: Methuen, 1971), pp. 149-169.

33 MacIntyre, "The Intelligibility of Action," p. 66.

34 Taylor, "Explanation and Understanding in the *Geisteswissenschaften*"; and MacIntyre, "The Idea of a Social Science" and "Is Understanding Compatible With Believing," in *Rationality*, Bryan Wilson, ed. (New York: Blackwell, 1970).

35 Notre Dame: University Press, 1988 [hereafter WJWR].

36 WJWR, p. 353.

37 WJWR, p. 362; see also MacIntyre's (slightly different) formulation of these requirements in "Moral Rationality, Tradition and Aristotle: A Reply to Onora O'Neill, Raimond Gaita, and Stephen R. L. Clark," *Inquiry*, xxvi (1984), p. 451; and the discussion by Michael Kelly, "MacIntyre, Habermas, and Philosophical Ethics," in this volume.

38 MacIntyre in fact expresses a certain amount of contempt for the "dominant social order of modernity": "I do not see any prospects of overthrowing the dominant social order. But perhaps it can be outlived; and even if it cannot be overthrown, it ought to be rejected. The grounds for

hope lie in that from the premodern past which has survived the worst that the dominant social order of modernity has been able to visit upon it'' ["*After Virtue* and Marxism: A Response to Wartofsky," *Inquiry,* xxvii (1985), p. 252]. Curiously, this remark echoes Herbert Marcuse's call for a "great refusal" which MacIntyre once sharply criticized; see his *Herbert Marcuse: An Exposition and a Polemic* (New York: Viking, 1970).

39 *Inquiry,* p. 451; also, *After Virtue* (Notre Dame: University Press, 1981), p. 269; Bernstein develops a criticism similar to my own in his review of *After Virtue,* "Nietzsche or Aristotle?" *Soundings,* lxvii (1984): 6-29.

40 See WJWR, pp. 363–364, and "Epistemological Crises, Dramatic Narrative and the Philosophy of Science," *The Monist,* lx (1977), pp. 469-471. It is in a similar vein that Putnam speaks of reason as being both immanent and transcendent; see his *Reason, Truth and History* (New York: Cambridge, 1982), pp. 54–55; and my introduction to Putnam's "Why Reason Can't Be Naturalized," in *After Philosophy,* pp. 217-220.

41 *After Virtue,* p. 222.

42 For a general overview and discussion of this process of social differentiation which has been central in sociological studies since Parsons, see Reinhard Bendix, "Tradition and Modernity Revisited," in *Embattled Reason: Essays on Social Knowledge* (New York: Oxford, 1970); and Niklas Luhmann, "The Differentiation of Society," in *The Differentiation of Society* (New York: Columbia, 1982).

43 See Schutz and Luckmann, *The Structures of the Lifeworld,* R. Zaner and H. T. Engelhardt, Jr., trans. (Evanston: Northwestern, 1973).

44 *The Philosophical Discourse of Modernity,* Frederick Lawrence, trans. (Cambridge: MIT, 1987), p. 343; see also TCA, II, 138.

45 Habermas suggests that the aspect of the lifeworld as a resource is emphasized by the phenomenological approach of Edmund Husserl and Schutz, while the aspect of the lifeworld as that about which actors negotiate is emphasized in ethnomethodological approaches; see "Remarks on the Concept of Communicative Action," in *Social Action,* G. Seebass and R. Tuomela, eds. (Boston: Reidel, 1985), p. 160.

46 "Remarks," p. 167; TCA, II, 135.

47 *The Philosophical Discourse of Modernity,* p. 342; also TCA, II, 145.

48 For a discussion of these general modes of interpenetration, see Richard Münch, *Theory of Action: Towards A New Synthesis Going Beyond Parsons* (Boston: Routledge, 1987), pp. 35ff.

49 Cf. *The Philosophical Discourse of Modernity,* p. 350.

50 ISS, p. 261; and "Questions and Counterquestions," p. 205. The notion of rational reconstruction is discussed in "A Postscript to *Knowledge and Human Interests,*" *Philosophy of Social science,* iii (1973), pp. 182-185; and "What Is Universal Pragmatics," in *Communication and the Evolution of Society* (Boston: Beacon, 1979), pp. 8-15. See also "Reply to My Critics," in *Habermas: Critical Debates,* John Thompson and David Held, eds. (Cambridge: MIT, 1982), pp. 229ff.; TCA, II, 396-403; and "Philosophy as Stand-In and Interpreter," in *After Philosophy,* pp. 309-312.

51 In his critical discussion ["Is Habermas's Reconstructive Science Really Science?" *Theory and Society,* xiv (1985): 421-440] C. Fred Alford misses this important feature of a reconstructive science. Habermas's argument for the uniqueness of the reconstructive sciences is in this regard comparable to Putnam's argument against a naturalized epistemology in "Why Reason Can't Be Naturalized," in *After Philosophy,* p. 241: "But if all notions of rightness, both epistemic and (metaphysically) realist, are eliminated, then what are our statements but noise-makings? . . . The elimination of the normative is attempted mental suicide." For Habermas, the dimension of normativity—reasons and their assessment—is inextricably tied to the internal perspective of a participant.

52 ISS, p. 260.

53 Cf. Imre Lakatos, "History of Science and Its Rational Reconstruction," in *Scientific Revolutions*, Ian Hacking, ed. (New York: Oxford, 1981), pp. 107-127; compare TCA, I, 3, 66–67; II, 326; and Habermas's remarks on Popper's "third world," I, 83f.; Hacking refers to Lakatos's concept of internal history as a "third-world history" in "Lakatos's Philosophy of Science," in *Scientific Revolutions*, p. 138.

54 "Philosophy as Stand-In and Interpreter," in *After Philosophy*, p. 301. Habermas compares this "more modest" form of a transcendental argument to Strawson's version (see TCA, I, 138, note 58).

55 ISS, p. 261.

56 Lakatos, "Falsification and the Methodology of Scientific Research Programmes," in *Criticism and the Growth of Knowledge*, Lakatos and Musgrave, eds. (New York: Cambridge, 1970), pp. 91-196.

57 For an interesting application of Habermas's theory to the critique of ideology, see James Bohman, "Formal Pragmatics and Social Criticism: The Philosophy of Language and the Critique of Ideology in Habermas's Theory of Communicative Action," *Philosophy and Social Criticism*, x (1985): 331-353.

58 Cf. "Entgegnung," *Kommunikatives Handeln: Beiträge zur Theorie des Kommunikativen Handelns*, Axel Honneth and Hans Joas, eds. (Frankfurt: Suhrkamp, 1986), p. 391.

59 For criticisms of Habermas's two-level concept of society, see Honneth, *Kritik der Macht* (Frankfurt: Suhrkamp, 1985), pp. 328-334; McCarthy, "Complexity and Democracy, or The Seducements of Systems Theory," *New German Critique*, xxxv (1985): 27-53; and Hugh Baxter, "System and Lifeworld in Habermas's 'Theory of Communicative Action'," *Theory and Society*, xvi (1987): 39-86. Habermas replies to some of these criticisms in "Entgegnung."

60 By insisting on this dual perspective on society, Habermas is in keeping with the approach advocated earlier by Theodor Adorno: "Society is full of contradictions, yet determinable; rational and irrational in one, a system yet fragmented: blind nature yet mediated by consciousness. The sociological mode of procedure must bow to this"; "On The Logic of the Social Sciences," in *The Positivist Dispute in German Sociology*, T. Adorno et al., eds. (New York: Harper & Row, 1976), p. 106; see also "Society," *Salmagundi*, x–xi (1969/70): 144-153.

THE POLITICS OF THE INEFFABLE:
DERRIDA'S DECONSTRUCTIONISM*

THOMAS MCCARTHY

In an interview conducted in 1981,[1] Jacques Derrida acknowledged that he had "never succeeded in directly relating deconstruction to existing political codes and programs," and complained that "the available codes for taking a political stance are not at all adequate to the radicality of deconstruction."[2] He went on to note that this "absence of an adequate political code to translate or incorporate the radical implications of deconstruction has given many the impression that deconstruction is opposed to politics or is at best apolitical."[3] "But this impression only prevails," he explained, "because all our political codes and terminologies still remain fundamentally metaphysical, regardless of whether they originate from the right or the left."[4] This is an admirably concise statement of the much discussed problem of the politics of deconstruction. On the one hand, Derrida has repeatedly insisted on the political character of deconstructionist practice: "it is not neutral," he assures us, "it intervenes."[5] On the other hand, he has been rather evasive about just which politics, or approach to politics, it involves. His politically "codable" stands—on neocolonialism, women's liberation, and apartheid, for instance—have shown him to be generally on the "progressive" side; but they have been backed by little historical or institutional analysis, and not much more explicit normative critique. As a result, his readers can and do disagree widely about just which general political standpoint the particular stands reflect. They cannot turn to Derrida's political "theory" to settle the issue, for he has not offered one, and indeed regards the whole genre as eminently deconstructible. As to other means of conveying his general point of view, he has bemoaned, as we just heard, the absence of any political code "adequate to deconstruction."

Thus, the debate concerning deconstructionist politics stems in no small measure from Derrida's unwillingness or inability to "decide" it by word or example. "The Politics of Friendship" is important in this context because it addresses itself specifically to political philosophy. Unfortunately, after reading it, we are left with much the same questions and doubts as before. I want to argue that this is no accident, that the "radicality of deconstruction," as Derrida conceives it, inexorably carries it in the direction of the ineffable, and that, while this may be harmless enough when dealing with metaphysics, it is seriously disabling where morals and politics are concerned. To make this argument, it will first be necessary (in part I) to review, very broadly, Derrida's conception of deconstruction and its political implications. This is no routine exercise, as he has self-consciously built into his own texts the "undecidability" he attributes to meaning in general. One can, in short, find passages on the other side(s) of any interpretation. Thus, it is no surprise that the standard response to Derrida's critics has been that they have misunderstood him. I cannot hope to avoid this, but I shall rely heavily on citations to indicate just which texts I am misreading. In part II, I shall turn to criticisms of Derrida's approach to politics, both in general and in his paper on the politics of friendship.

I

Derrida has written of the politics of deconstruction in a number of different tones. Toward the end of the 1960s, the tone was at times apocalyptic, if not revolutionary. In "The Ends of Man,"[6] a paper first read in 1968, he spoke of the "total trembling" (or shaking: *ébranlement*) of the Man-Being coappurtenance that "inhabits, and is inhabited by, the language of the West."[7] This "radical trembling," he told us, is being "played out in the violent relationship of the whole of the West to its other, whether a 'linguistic relationship' . . . or ethnological, economic, political, military relationships, etc."[8] During the same period and subsequently, the tone was often one of patient resistance to the ultimately unslayable Hydra of Western logocentrism. Thus, in an interview with Julia Kristeva,[9] Derrida professed his disbelief in "decisive ruptures": "Breaks are always, and fatally, reinscribed in an old cloth that must continually, interminably be undone."[10] Deconstruction, then, cannot aim to rid us, once and for all, of the concepts fundamental to Western rationalism, but only, again and again, "to transform [them], to displace them, to turn them against their presuppositions, to reinscribe them in other chains, and little by little to modify the terrain of our work and thereby to produce new configurations."[11] By these means, it "organizes a structure of resistance" to the dominant conceptuality.[12]

In the 1980s, the tone becomes explicitly anti-apocalyptic, at least insofar as the latter is linked to eschatalogy. Deconstruction is not prophetic or visionary; it does not announce an imminent end or a new dawning.[13] Indeed, Derrida even characterizes it at times as new form of *Aufklärung*.[14] In that intonation, deconstruction is not a matter of renouncing "the principle of reason," but of interrogating "its meaning, its origin, its goal, its limits," that is, of inquiring after "the grounding of the ground itself."[15] It does not oppose classical logic, but calls for another discourse that "accounts for this logic and its possibility" and for the impossibility of concluding a 'general theory' [of language and meaning]."[16] Indeed, this tone can sound surprisingly like Kant's—at some remove, to be sure, for "the type of 'enlightenment' granted our time" has to be based on a recognition of "the unclarity of the good old *Aufklärung*."[17]

Throughout these changes in tone, however, Derrida's account of deconstruction has remained constant in central respects.[18] To begin with, it involves a radical decentering of the subject in relation to language. As signification is always a function of largely unconscious differential relations (among signifiers, speakers, hearers, situations, contexts, etc.), and as these relations unfold in social spaces and historical times, we are never completely masters of what we say: "The subject, and first of all the conscious and speaking subject, depends upon the system of differences and the movement of *différance*."[19] The process of signification, as Derrida puts it, is a "play of differences," such that "no element can function as a sign without referring to other elements" that are not themselves present, and every element is "constituted on the basis of the trace within it of the other elements of the chain."[20] Because the tissue of relations and differences inevitably leaves its trace in any signifier, we can never achieve simple univocity of meaning. Beyond any present meaning lies the absent, unspoken, unthought, indeed largely uncomprehended network of conditions, presuppositions, and mediations on which it depends. As a result, our meaning always escapes any unitary conscious grasp we may have of it, for language, as "writing," inevitably harbors the possibility of an endless "dissemination" of sense, an indefinite multiplicity of recontextualizations and reinterpretations.

Philosophy is a kind of writing which is essentially predicated on denying all of this, which attempts to uproot meaning from the "relational and differential tissue" in which it is always enmeshed.[21] Throughout its history, it has tried one device after another to freeze the play of *différance:* ideal univocal meanings (Forms), an ultimate referent or "transcendental signified" (Being), clear and distinct ideas in self-conscious and self-transparent minds, absolute knowledge, the logical essence of language, and so on—all calculated to call a halt to the dissemination of meaning at the borders of this or that closed system of truth. But such closure is impossible; philosophy cannot transcend its medium. The claim to have done so always relies on ignoring, excluding, marginalizing, or assimilating whatever escapes the grids of intelligibility it imposes on the movement of *différance*. And this repression of what does not fit inevitably has its effects, in the forms of the paradoxes, internal contradictions, and systematic incoherencies, which it is the task of deconstructive analysis to bring to light. Its aim in doing so is not to produce a new and improved unified theory of the whole, but ceaselessly to undermine the pretense to theoretical mastery, the illusion of a "pure" reason that could gain control over its own conditions, and the dream of a definitive grasp of basic meanings and truths. In short: "It inaugurates the destruction, not the demolition but the de-sedimentation, the deconstruction, of all the significations that have their source in that of the logos. Particularly the signification of *truth*."[22]

This kind of totalized critique of reason has to deal with the paradoxes of self-referentiality which inevitably follow in its wake. How does one deconstruct "all the significations that have their source in the logos," including that of "truth," without at the same time relying on them, at least tacitly? Derrida's response to this dilemma is his well-known "double gesture," combining, roughly, elements of internal and external critique. As his use of this strategy will figure in my remarks about deconstructionist political analysis, it will be worthwhile to get clearer here about what it involves. In "The Ends of Man," Derrida writes of "weaving and interlacing" two tactics: the first does not "change terrain" but turns "what is implicit in the founding concepts and the original problematic" against those very concepts and problematic; the second involves a "discontinuous" change of terrain, "placing oneself outside" of, and "affirming an absolute break" with, those concepts and problematic.[23] When the "terrain" in question is Western logocentrism, the idea of an absolute break is an illusion, for "the simple practice of language ceaselessly reinstates the new terrain on the oldest ground."[24] On the other hand, the first tactic, that of internal critique, has been that of the philosophical tradition, in which each generation of thinkers uncovers and criticizes the presuppositions of the previous generation. "Here, one risks ceaselessly confirming, consolidating, relifting [*relever:* the word Derrida uses to translate Hegel's *Aufhebung*], at an always more certain depth, that which one allegedly deconstructs."[25] Hence the appropriate strategy is a "double writing" which combines both internalist and externalist tactics.

If deconstruction is to get a critical purchase on the system it targets, it cannot simply "junk" the concepts basic to the latter but has to "transform" or "displace" them. The danger in this is that any use of a concept "necessarily assumes, in a non-critical way, at least some of the implications inscribed in its system."[26] The trick, then, is to "overturn" established conceptual oppositions and hierarchies through patient analysis, while *simultaneously* releasing new concepts "that can no longer be and never could be included in the previous regime," thereby "disorganizing the entire inherited order and invading the entire field."[27] I am not interested here in deciding whether this strategy succeeds vis-à-vis the philosophical tradition as a whole,[28] but only in weighing its advantages and disadvantages as an approach to politics. For that purpose, however, we have to understand why Derrida is convinced that deconstructing philosophical concepts and problematics is of decisive political importance. In what sense is deconstruction itself political intervention?

Despite his own qualifications and the heated denials of his defenders, there can be no doubt that Derrida considers philosophy to be, in Richard Rorty's words, "at the heart of Western culture."[29] In passage after passage, he treats it as co-constitutive of Western science and scholarship, language and literature, politics and society, ethnocentrism and imperialism. Thus, for example, he writes that the "metaphysics of phonetic writing," which "always assigned the origin of truth in general to the logos," is "nothing but the most original and powerful ethnocentrism, in the process of imposing itself on the world."[30] The concept of science "has always been a philosophical concept";[31] and there is an "a priori link" between "the essence of the philosophical and the essence of the political."[32] Deconstruction, as a "simultaneously faithful and violent circulation between the inside and the outside of philosophy—*that is of the West*," enables us "to read philosophemes—and *consequently all the texts of our culture*—as kinds of symptoms."[33] He is not referring here only to philosophy's permeation of high culture. Everyday language is also "the language of Western metaphysics," bearing within it "presuppositions inseparable from metaphysics," which are "knotted into a system."[34] It is just this system which is trembling today, and "this trembling is played out in the violent relationship of the whole West to its other," where military and economic violence is "in structural solidarity with 'linguistic' violence."[35]

It is not surprising, given this view, that "what has seemed necessary and urgent to [Derrida], in the historical situation which is our own, is a general determination of the conditions for the emergence and limits of philosophy, of metaphysics, of everything that carries it on and that it carries on."[36] Nor is it surprising that critics should find this estimation of the importance of metaphysics in our culture an overestimation—influenced, perhaps, by Martin Heidegger's similar view of the modern world. Of course, Heidegger did not develop it in *explicitly* political terms.[37] But the wholesale rejection of Western rationalism was given a sociopolitical articulation by Max Horkheimer and Theodor Adorno[38] at about the same time. As the dreams of bourgeois culture turned into the nightmare of National Socialism, it was difficult for them to resist Nietzsche's judgment that "nihilism represents the ultimate logical conclusion of our great values and ideas." Western reason, they came to agree, had been from the start keyed to mastery and control. This was true of "enlightened" reason as well; the "dialectic of enlightenment" consumed even the "critical" reason developed from Kant through Marx. In his later philosophy, Adorno elaborated this skeptical view of reason into a "negative dialectics" that repeatedly displayed the coercion and distortion at the heart of what passes for reason, the nonidentical in every claimed identity, without offering any positive account of his own: to do so would only be to encourage further the illusion that the truth can be found in theory.

There are more than superficial affinities between Adorno's negative dialectics and Derrida's deconstruction.[39] Like Adorno, Derrida has been characterized as a "post-Holocaust philosopher."[40] And in an interview published in 1983, he does indicate that his youthful experience of Fascism profoundly affected his view of the world.[41] But my topic here is not how Derrida came to his *Weltanschauung,* nor whether his (or Adorno's) life experience gives him (or Adorno) more of a "right" to it than, say, Heidegger. What is at issue is its translation into a philosophico-political program. The broad outlines of that program seem clear enough. It can be summed up, very roughly, in the following points, which we might tendentiously refer to as Derrida's "Theses on Heidegger."

1. "Logocentrism in its developed philosophical sense is inextricably linked to the Greek and European tradition"; it is a "specifically Western response to a much larger necessity" (the structural lure of phonocentrism) that exists in other cultures as well, but did not develop into a systematic, logocentric metaphysics in any non-European culture.[42]

2. The dominance of "the principle of reason" which marks the modern West is rooted in that original metaphysical response: "Not only does that principle constitute the verbal formulation of a requirement present since the dawn of Western science and philosophy, it provides the impetus for a new era of purportedly 'modern' reason, metaphysics, and technoscience."[43]

3. The form this takes is an "interpretation of the essence of beings as objects . . . placed and positioned before a subject . . . who says 'I', an ego certain of itself, [who] thus ensures his own technical mastery over the totality of what is" (9-10).

4. Progress in the natural and social sciences cannot deliver us from metaphysics, for "philosophy, as logocentrism, is present in every scientific discipline."[44] In particular, the post-Marxian idea of radicalizing the critique of reason by drawing upon the historical and human sciences makes no sense, for these disciplines themselves are "founded on a logocentric philosophical discourse and remain inseparable from it."[45] Consequently, "they never touch upon that which, in themselves, continues to be based on the principle of reason" (16).

5. The general "informatization" of knowledge in the present age, which is the culmination of the "original intermingling of the metaphysical and the technical," makes the principle of reason a principle of "integral calculability" (14). It is this total subjection to the "informative and instrumental value of language" which lies behind the "finalization" or "ends-orientation" of scientific and scholarly research in all advanced industrial societies: "We know better than ever what must have been true for all time . . . . One can no longer distinguish between technology, on the one

hand, and theory, science, and rationality, on the other. The term techno-science has to be accepted . . ." (12).

6. The ends-orientation built into research in all disciplines—from psychology, biology, and telecommunications, to linguistics, hermeneutics, and literature—ultimately serves the interests of the "defensive and offensive security establishment," the military, the state, and the economy (13-14). The logocentric metaphysics underlying that technoscience also structures our political codes themselves. Its core assumptions are "common to the axiomatics of numerous (perhaps even all) politics in the West, whether of the right or of the left."[46] It is thus internally connected to the violence and repression that mark the history of the West.

7. These same factors shape the relations of the West to the non-Western world. Thus, for example, one can view South Africa as a giant screen onto which "Europe, in the enigmatic process of its globalization and of its paradoxical disappearance," projects "the silhouette of its internal war, the bottom line of its profits and loses, the double-bind logic of its national and multinational interests."[47]

8. The only way to counter this fateful dispensation is to "think" ourselves beyond the principle of reason. This thought would "unmask—an infinite task—all the ruses of ends-orienting reason," including those of philosophy as it is conventionally practiced (16). It would "raise questions at the level of the foundation or non-foundation of the foundation," not merely by posing "questions that one formulates while submitting oneself . . . to the principle of reason," but also by "preparing oneself thereby to transform the modes of writing (17). It would, in short, deploy the deconstructionist double gesture: " 'Thought' requires both the principle of reason and what is beyond the principle of reason"; between the two "only the enactment of this 'thought' can decide" (19).

9. Interrogating the principle of reason, questioning "its meaning, its origin, its possibility, its goal, its limits," leaves us "suspended above a most peculiar void," for a principle of grounding cannot ground itself (9). Thus, the practice of deconstruction is risky; "it always risks the worst" (19), but this is "the risk of the future itself" (17). In taking it, one is "playing off one risk against another," the abyss against the barrier (17). The "decision" to do so "exceeds the calculable program that would destroy all responsibility by transforming it into a programmable effect"; it is a "trial and a passage by way of the undecidable," a "response" to a "call," a "new way of taking responsibility."[48]

10. The politics of deconstruction is rooted in this response to the call of the other which has been repressed and denied by Western logocentrism: "The rapport of self-identity is itself always a rapport of violence with the

other," so that "the notions . . . central to logocentric metaphysics are essentially dependent on an opposition with otherness."[49] More precisely, deconstruction counteracts the "politics of language" which conceals practices of exclusion, repression, marginalization, and assimilation behind the apparent neutrality of "purely theoretical" discourses. Its effects, however, are not confined to language, but "touch all the social institutions. . . . More generally, it touches everything, quite simply everything."[50] Striving to weaken the hegemony of logocentrism for the sake of a future it can neither define nor predict, it is a kind of "responsibility anarchy" which serves as "a political ferment or anxiety, a subversion of fixed assumptions and a privileging of disorder."[51]

11. The philosophers have only *interpreted* the logos in various ways, the point, however, is to *deconstruct* it.

In the second part of this paper, I want to examine in more detail the types of political theory and practice which result from Derrida's interrogation of the reason of reason. Are the methods he developed for dealing with questions of language and meaning adequate to moral, social, and political questions? Is it, for instance, merely by accident that his writings contain little analysis of political institutions and arrangements, historical circumstances and tendencies, or social groups and social movements, and no constructions of right and good, justice and fairness, legitimacy and legality? Is it the case, as Nancy Fraser[52] has put it, that the politics of deconstruction amounts to little more than the deconstruction of politics?

II

Derrida's deconstructionism is generally perceived to be a critical, even skeptical enterprise—a perception nurtured, no doubt, by his characterizations of it. To deconstruct, he has told us, is to "desediment," "destabilize," "uproot," and "overturn" inherited concepts and schemes, "to turn them against their own presuppositions," to "loosen," "undo," "decompose," and "dismantle" them. Questions can be raised about the self-sufficiency of any wholesale attack on "logocentrism." These questions become all the more pressing in the domains of ethics and politics, for social life cannot be organized solely on the basis of a prohibition of graven images. Deconstructive activities seem here to be necessarily complementary to activities of building, repairing, and improving the norms, principles, laws, and institutions by which we live. Thus, the more Derrida has insisted on the practical-political import of deconstruction, the more he has had to face the objection that it is essentially parasitic on construction and reconstruction, and that he has had very little to offer in the way of positive ethico-political proposals. His standard responses to this objection have not been convincing.[53] If we allow ourselves to be guided by his own dictum that deconstruction " 'is' only what it does and what is done with it,"[54] rather than by the many different, often conflicting characterizations he gives of it, we can scarcely avoid the conclusion that it is primarily iconoclastic.

The "ethico-political impulse" behind this practice has been interpreted as a commitment to bear witness to the other of Western rationalism: to what has been subordinated in hierarchical orderings, excluded in the drawing of boundaries, marginalized in identifying what is central, homogenized or colonized in the name of the universal.[55] On this reading, deconstruction constantly reminds us that rationalism's constitutive assumption of the fundamental intelligibility of experience and reality has underwritten a history of repression in theory and practice—the repression of the other in nature, in ourselves, in other persons and other peoples. As the bad conscience of an imperialistic logocentrism, deconstruction speaks on behalf of what does not fit into our schemes and patiently advocates letting the other be in its otherness. There is undoubtedly something to this reading, but even so, deconstruction can hardly *give voice to* the excluded other. The wholesale character of its critique of logocentrism deprives it of any language in which to do so. Nonetheless, Derrida apparently wants to have it both ways: to undermine all logocentric concepts and yet to continue to use them for his own purposes. The tactic of using them "under erasure" strikes me as less like being "suspended over an abyss" than like trying to be on both sides of a fence.

We can see how this works in the domain of ethico-political analysis by looking at "The Laws of Reflection: Nelson Mandela, in Admiration."[56] All of the analytical and critical work is done via "logocentric" concepts and norms, from which Derrida is at the same time obliged to distance himself. Despite his repeated cautions to the reader, one cannot help but notice that he has no other means of conveying the power of Mandela's witness than those same concepts and norms. Mandela is said to have turned "the very logic of the law" against those who wrongfully and scornfully usurped it, to have revealed something in the law which they concealed behind legality, to have brought its true force to bear against them. Derrida is aware that these types of critique are not discontinuous with but dependent upon enlightenment conceptions. He brings undecidability into the picture *post festum,* as it were, when he raises, without answering, the question whether Mandela has "let himself be captured . . . in the view of the West," or rather bears a "promise of what has not yet ever been seen or heard."[57] The "promise" is itself identified, however, in terms of a traditional notion of "conscience": it arises from placing "respect for the law which speaks immediately to conscience" above "submission to positive law."[58] The residual undecidability amounts, it seems, to nothing more than our inability to say today how Mandela will be understood in the future.[59] But we do not need the apparatus of deconstruction to make us aware of that.

Consider now a somewhat different case. When Anne McClintock and Rob Nixon[60] criticized Derrida's analysis of apartheid in "Racism's Last Word," his response was laced with appeals to just the sorts of concepts, norms, and standards that he has elsewhere undercut. Presented with this apparent inconsistency, Derrida has responded that it was never his intention to put such concepts as truth, reference, and the stability of interpretive contexts radically into question: rather, he wanted to explore the conditions of their possibility and to show that they are never guaranteed absolutely, but only in "pragmatically determined situations."[61] It was, he tells us, only because he considered the context of the apartheid discussion to be pragmatically stable in that sense, that he felt free to appeal to demonstrable ties between words and things and to the difference between true and false. Indeed, he asserts that no research is possible without some "minimal consensus" (146), and that "norms of minimal intelligibility" belong to the requirements of all culture (147). In particular, all "conceptual production," including his own, inevitably involves certain idealizations (117), and this "structural idealism" underlies classical logic and scientific truth (120). The deconstructionist point is only that whatever has been constructed is deconstructible (147), every contextualization is open to recontextualization (136). There are, he allows, cultural and institutional contexts that exhibit great stability, so great as to appear natural and immutable; but such stabilization is always relative: "The norms of minimal intelligibility are not absolute and ahistorical, but merely more stable than others. They depend upon socio-institutional conditions, hence upon non-natural relations of power that by essence are mobile and founded upon complex conventional structures that in principle may be analyzed, deconstructed, and transformed" (147). The values of "objectivity" and "truth," for instance, "impose" themselves "within a context which is extremely vast, old, powerfully established, stabilized or rooted in a network of conventions (for instance, those of language), and yet still remains a context" (136).

With these remarks, Derrida heads in the direction of a pragmatist account of language. The big divide, it seems to me, comes with the negative slant he gives to his recognition of the pragmatic presuppositions of meaning: whatever has been constructed can be deconstructed, destabilized, recontextualized, and so on. True enough, but by the same token it can also be reconstructed, improved, restabilized, and so forth. Derrida rarely mentions this side of the ledger. His fixation on metaphysics, and the pressing need he sees to battle its ideal essences at every turn divert his attention and energies from the real task of postmetaphysical thought. The insight that "one cannot do anything, least of all speak, without determining (in a manner that is not only theoretical, but practical and performative) a context" (i.e., defining a situation), and that this entails "a certain type of non-natural relationship to others" (i.e., social relations),[62] is hardly new, nor is the idea that this signals the end of a certain type of metaphysical thinking. But rather than meditate at the edge of the abyss, pragmatically inclined thinkers have tried to reconstruct the notions of reason, truth, objectivity, and the like in nonfoundationalist terms. The recognition of the social-practical basis of language and meaning has seemed to them, too, to point toward an ethico-political thematization of what were traditionally regarded as "purely theoretical" questions. But that project has a positive, constructive side as well as a negative, critical side. Some of the "vast, old" contexts Derrida remarks on are as old as the human race; others arose historically, but in such a manner as to render alternatives less and less desirable or even possible; others are determined by cultural consensuses which are indeed contingent and particular, but which there is good reason to defend; and, of course, many others are based on relations of force which are disguised by talk of reason, truth, objectivity, and the like—but why suppose all are?

It seems to be an axiom of Derrida's deconstructionism that "norms of minimal intelligibility" always depend upon "non-natural relations of power" (147), and that any determination of context involves "force or irreducible violence" (137). But to use "power," "force," and "violence" in this way—to cover everything from mutual agreement and negotiated compromise to false consciousness and open repression—is to go into the night in which all cows are black, that is, to go back behind all of the differentiations so crucial to social and political theory. It is also to abandon entirely *the participant's point of view* for that of the observer as critic. As participants in social life, we cannot avoid meeting what Derrida refers to as "the minimal requirements of culture." We have to undertake certain idealizations, share certain presuppositions, follow certain rules, be bound by certain norms, and so on. We can and, of course, should interrogate the limits of these undertakings, but not exclusively, at least not without ceasing to be participants: even irony has its limits. As reflective participants, we can also seek to expand the cooperative bases of our lives together and to reduce the violence and coercion that critical discourse (of many different types) brings to light. To this constructive ethico-political task, deconstruction has little to contribute. It does not produce pragmatic conceptualizations "for all practical purposes," but constant reminders of the groundlessness of all our basic schemes. This is the reaction, it seems to me, of a disappointed metaphysician still under the sway of its arch-opposition: all or nothing. The same can be said of Derrida's tendency to hypostatize this lack of ultimate foundations into a *différance* prior not only to subject and object, but to all of the oppositions basic to logocentrism—prior even to the distinctions between identity and nonidentity, sameness and difference.[63]

Be that as it may, the deconstruction of our logocentric culture leaves Derrida with nothing substantive to say—at least not without an ironic reminder that he could not possibly have meant it. In regard specifically to politics, it places him in the awkward position described in the lines quoted at the start of this essay. Because "all of our political codes and terminologies still remain fundamentally metaphysical" on his account, if he wants to express himself politically at all, he has to do so in codes that are "incommensurate with [his] intellectual project." Whenever he does so, however, he must at the same time mark his "distance and suspicion" with regard to them. The effects of this strategy—wholesale subversion, with no suggestion of remedies or alternatives, combined with a measure of ironic use—are, all assurances to the contrary notwithstanding, largely skeptical. To play the skeptic in ethical-political matters is, of course, to adopt an ethico-political stance. The warrant for this in Derrida's case seems to be the same sort of pessimistic diagnosis of the modern world that one finds in Heidegger. If reason is in the end nothing more than subjectification and objectification in the service of domination, then some form of *Abbau* or deconstruction seems a more appropriate response than any form of *Umbau* or reconstruction. But this argument supposes that a particular interpretation—and a rather global and undifferentiated one at that—of Western history, culture, society, politics, technology, etc., is the correct one, or at least that it is superior to competing interpretations—such as those of Marx, Weber, Durkheim, and Jürgen Habermas, for example—that stress the ambivalence of rationalization processes, their amalgamation of undeniable achievements and palpable distortions, growing emancipation and expanded domination. I shall argue below that Derrida has in effect deprived himself of the means he needs to enter into that debate. Here I want to note that the political stakes between the competing interpretations are quite high. In their various cultural and institutional forms, expectations of reason and truth may also play a moderating role in the conduct of social life. Drawing boundaries and setting limits may often be what is needed to achieve a common purpose.[64] And while it is necessary to interrogate and revise received notions of liberty, equality, justice, rights, and the like, to disassemble without reassembling them may be to rob excluded, marginalized, and oppressed groups of an important recourse. In short, undercutting the appeal to reason, truth, and justice as presently "coded," without offering alternatives, may harbor not so much the "promise" of a better world as the "danger" of some "monstrous mutation."[65]

Derrida holds the view that an author or signatory must accept responsibility for the effects of his or her text.[66] Thus, it is fair to ask him what effects he anticipates for his own texts, or, since the effects of a critical practice will be different in different historical situations, what analysis of our contemporary situation lies behind his own estimation of the effects of deconstructionist practice? And what is the evaluative perspective from which he judges those effects to be good? Given his devaluation of empirical and normative social analysis, we are unlikely to get from him anything more than broad hints regarding our present ills and their possible remedies. But a general reminder of the myriad forms of violence that have accompanied the march of the universal through history is not a sufficient basis for restructuring politics and society. It is sheer romanticism to suppose that uprooting and destabilizing universalist structures will of itself lead to letting the other be in respect and freedom rather than to intolerant and aggressive particularism, a war of all against all in which the fittest survive and the most powerful dominate. Enlarging the social space in which otherness can be, establishing and maintaining a multifarious and spacious pluralism, seem, on the contrary, to require that we inculcate universalistic principles of tolerance and respect, and stabilize institutions that secure rights and impose limits. Otherwise, how is the tolerance of difference to be combined with the requirements of living *together* under *common* norms? And, in justifying such norms, is there any alternative superior to free and open discussion of matters of public interest? Repeated attacks on the metaphysics of presence, incessant reminders of our finitude, do not at all obviate these familiar questions from political theory. Having placed himself beyond all existing codes, however, Derrida is in no position to answer them.

This is the critical point. As I noted in part I, Derrida considers all specialized modes of inquiry to be permeated with metaphysics. And it is this "logocentrism present in every scientific discipline" which, in his view, accounts for the complicity of science in the history of Western domination. Given this more or less Heideggerian *Zeitdiagnose,* it is perfectly comprehensible that what seems "necessary and urgent to [him], in the historical situation which is our own," is a general deconstruction of philosophy. This diagnosis and the strategy it dictates rest on some rather questionable assumptions. It is, writes Habermas, "as if we were living in the shadow of the 'last' philosophers, as were the first generation of Hegelian disciples," so that we must still battle "against the 'strong' concepts of theory, truth, and system," which have actually "belonged to the past for over a century and a half," for "the fallibilist consciousness of science caught up with philosophy, too, a long time ago."[67]

Derrida has all along insisted on the secondary, derivative status of "scientificity," "objectivity," and "historicity" in relation to *différance* or arche-writing: "The very idea of science was born in a certain epoch of writing"; writing is "the condition of possibility of ideal objects and therefore of scientific objectivity"; historicity, too, is "tied to the possibility of writing," which "opens the field of history." Consequently "the science of writing should look for its object at the roots of scientificity. The history of writing should turn back toward the origin of historicity."[68] Peter Dews has traced how Derrida adopted from Edmund Husserl the priority of phenomenological over empirical inquiry, detranscendentalized it, and made it central to his intellectual project.[69] Like Husserl, he rejected the penetration of the human sciences into the foundational domain reserved to philosophy. When he distanced himself from Husserl's subjectivism, he did so not by moving "downstream towards an account of subjectivity as emerging from and entwined with the natural and historical world," as Maurice Merleau-Ponty and Adorno did, but by moving further "upstream in a quest for the ground of transcendental consciousness itself."[70] The result was to withdraw philosophical thought from the sorts of interdependence with empirical research which it has entered into since Hegel. Deconstruction "cannot learn from its objects, but occupies a position of superior insight. . . . In this way the successor to philosophy continues to evade the exposure of thought to the contingency of interpretation and the revisability of empirical knowledge. But this then raises the question of whether it might not be possible to think the end of metaphysics in a different way—precisely in terms of this exposure."[71]

Derrida continues to pose the issue in terms of a choice between deconstruction and naive objectivism.[72] What gets left out of this binary opposition are all the nonobjectivistic—e.g., hermeneutical, critical, interpretive, and reconstructive—forms of historical, social, and cultural inquiry which developed alongside of and against positivism and have enjoyed something of a renaissance in recent years. The inadequacy of this oppositional scheme has been registered even within central domains of philosophical inquiry. We have, for example, abandoned the idea of constructing a "logic" of science before and independently of the history and sociology of science. The idea of "deducing" the "essence of the political" before and independently of substantive historical studies is even less plausible. Fraser has shown how the attempt of French Derridians to do that—to interrogate philosophically the "constitution and institution of the political (*le politique*) in Western culture," in a way that was prior yet relevant to politics (*la politique*)—inevitably came apart from its own inner tensions. Their hope that metapolitical, philosophical reflection could itself produce relevant political insights, thus obviating a need for entering into empirical, normative, and critical debates at the level of politics, landed them on the horns of a dilemma: "Either they will try to maintain the rigorous exclusion of politics, and especially of empirical and normative considerations—in which case the political import of their philosophical work will diminish. Or they will cross the line and enter upon concrete political reflection—in which case their work will become increasingly *contested*."[73]

Derrida's "The Politics of Friendship," a text devoted to interrogating *le politique*, shows him to be caught in the same dilemma. It is no accident that he singles out from Carl Schmitt's work the latter's discussion of "the concept of the political" and ignores Schmitt's substantive (and rather unfortunate) views on political institutions, arrangements, and tendencies.[74] It is a commonplace of Schmitt scholarship that his *politics* had a decisive influence on his concept of *the political*. The shift from his early, more or less neo-Kantian, outlook to his later, rather Hobbesian, views of human nature and the state, for example, seems to have been influenced by his views on the history and future of the nation state and his diagnosis of the post-World-War-I situation in Germany. A parallel case could be made concerning Heidegger's reflections on the essence of the political;[75] and, as I have suggested in part I, concerning Derrida's as well. Large-scale sociopolitical views and analyses of our present situation are not the special province of philosophical insight. They have to be entered into discursive competition with other accounts—which often have the virtue of laying their empirical, theoretical, and normative cards on the table for everyone to see and challenge.

The methodological ill effects of Derrida's withdrawal from the specificity of politics and of empirical social research are evident in ''The Politics of Friendship.'' His derivation of ''the political itself'' via a ''thinking of *différance*'' centers around a ''grammar of the response'' which, while based on French usage, is, he conjectures, ''translatable into the set of European languages,'' though not perhaps into every language.[76] This, he suggests, will provide a key to ''our concept of responsibility.''[77] In the same spirit, he tells us that Aristotle's whole discourse on friendship is a discourse on language, on the word *philia,* its uses, contexts, etc.[78] But Aristotle could draw upon his reflective participant's understanding of Greek culture and society in fashioning his discourse. If we want now to understand *philia,* we have not just to read Aristotle's texts, but to become students of that culture and society, its patterns of interpretation and interaction, its traditions and institutions, its class, race, and gender divisions, and so on. But then we will discover that many of the uses and contexts of key Greek moral and political terms are foreign to us precisely because we no longer live in the world of the polis. This awareness may well lead us to wonder whether our own grammar of responsibility is similarly interwoven with the fabric of our culture and society; and we may then become interested in historical studies that throw light on the circumstances in which that grammar arose, developed, and was stabilized, or in comparative studies, based on ethnographic materials, that could throw light on the advantages and disadvantages of our own understandings by presenting us with alternatives from other cultures. We might do this partly in the hermeneutic spirit of participating in the conversation of humankind, and partly in the critical spirit of unmasking the play of power and interest in and around our received notions of responsibility. The point here is simply that the notion of a ''grammar'' of responsibility is at best an airy abstraction from the historical, comparative, and critical inquiries relevant to comprehending and assessing the structures of social practice in which that grammar is embedded. It is those inquiries and not that grammar which should serve as the basis of our social and political theorizing. Fraser quotes Gayatri Spivak as calling for a decentering of deconstruction that would open it up to ethical-political contingency.[79] I would add only that this entails an opening to all the modes of inquiry developed to study these contingencies, and hence to the procedures of evidence, argument, criticism, and the like they involve.

This is not what we find in Derrida's deduction of the political via the thinking of *différance*. In a manner reminiscent of Heidegger's "essential thinking," his approach devaluates the usual procedures of empirical and normative inquiry as being, one and all, shot through with the metaphysics of presence. Their place is taken by the deconstructive reading of selected texts, in this case "the great philosophical and canonical discourses on friendship."[80] To be sure, Derrida at the same time distances himself from the notion of a "canon," but it performs its usual functions. One might well ask why a reading of Aristotle, Montaigne, Nietzsche, Schmitt, Heidegger, and Maurice Blanchot on friendship should serve as the basis for "thinking the essence of the political," or even of friendship. Why not some other selection of classical texts? Why not discourses that never achieved classical status for a variety of reasons? Why not suppressed or marginalized discourses? Why confine oneself to analyzing discourse in the first place? To the charge of "textual idealism," Derrida's standard response has been that his infamous dictum, "there is nothing outside the text," does not refer to books and the like, but to "con-texts," to "the entire 'real-history-of-the-world'"; it does not, then, "suspend reference to history, to the world, to reality, to being."[81] The question at this point is whether he draws the appropriate *methodological* conclusions from this. If attending to con-text is compatible with approaching political theory via a deconstructive reading of selected classical texts, it is difficult to see how it constitutes a response to the charge of "textualism."[82] The only effective response would be to make "the real history of the world," in the form of the vast array of materials generated in studying it, figure prominently in one's thinking about politics.

The normative implications of Derrida's approach are no less problematic than the methodological. "No politics without *différance*," he declares.[83] One might as well say, "No politics without language." But it is obvious that the latter declaration points us in no *particular* direction, whereas Derrida asserts that *différance* points us in the direction of democracy. He hastens to add, however, that this is a "democracy to come" and "not the one we think we know." It is, rather, a democracy beyond "formality" and "calculable relations." I think it is fair to ask for more specificity before setting our sights beyond any known ethico-political horizon in this way. What sorts of social, political, legal, economic institutions of democracy does he see superseding those we have experienced or imagined? What replacements does he envision for received notions of rights, justice, tolerance, respect, and other such "edifying humanist" conceptions? Derrida does not attempt to satisfy us on such matters, nor is he likely to do so. As we have seen, deconstruction aims at "a language and a political practice that can no longer be comprehended, judged, deciphered by [existing] codes." Given this ambition, in what terms could he possibly discuss the new order of things? Although he explicitly eschews any idea of a radical break, the politics of friendship gestures toward a transformation so radical that we can say nothing (positive) about what lies beyond it. I have found nothing in Derrida's writings to persuade me that his quasi-apocalyptic, near-prophetic mode of discourse about politics should displace the more prosaic modes available or constructible in our tradition.[84] Even if his heart is in the right place, and even if his "anarchy" is "responsible," we know from experience that the devaluation of these modes opens a space, or rather creates a vacuum that can be filled in quite different ways—for instance, by a call for submission to some indeterminate authority.

Derrida's discourse, it seems to me, lives from the enormous elasticity, not to say vagueness and ambiguity, of his key terms.[85] In the case at hand, much of what he says about "minimal friendship," the "friendship prior to friendship," makes sense only if friendship is roughly equivalent to social interaction, viewed from a perspective that highlights allocution and response.[86] On the other hand, his quasi-normative deployment of it in relation to politics—for example, in the idea that the democracy to come should, as he put it, no longer be an insult to friendship, but should rather be a respectful test of it—makes sense only if "friendship" signifies some yet to be specified ideal of true friendship, which, as he uses it, has to be higher than any "political friendship" or concord.[87] If the "allocution" involved in minimal friendship, as minimal community, refers to modes of address and response constitutive of "being together" socially at all, it is doubtful that it can bear the freight of the apostrophe "oh my friends" as set forth earlier in the paper.[88] Rather, the structure of what Derrida calls "waiting, promise, or commitment" seems to have been imported into the ontology from a normative perspective, which is then said to be founded upon it. The figures of recall and appeal, memory and waiting, community and commitment, are of course familiar from our religious tradition, especially when they are connected, as they are by Derrida, to "infinite heterogeneity" and "infinite alterity."[89] At one point he asks: "And what politics could one found upon this friendship which exceeds the measure of man, without becoming a theologem?" To that question, I can find no answer in his work.

Northwestern University

NOTES

* This is a revised and expanded version of comments on Jacques Derrida's paper, "The Politics of Friendship," read at the 85th annual meeting of the American Philosophical Association, Eastern Division, in December 1988. An abbreviated version of Derrida's paper appeared in the *Journal of Philosophy*, LXXXV, 12 (1988):632-645, together with my initial comments, "On the Margins of Politics," *ibid.*, pp. 645-648. As the full text on which Derrida based his APA talk has not yet been published, I shall refer at times to his oral presentation.

1 "Deconstruction and the Other," an interview with Richard Kearney, in Richard Kearney, *Dialogues with Contemporary Continental Thinkers* (Manchester: University Press, 1984), pp. 107-126.

2 *Ibid.*, p. 119.

3 *Ibid.*, pp. 119–120.

4 *Ibid.*, p. 120.

5 *Positions*, Alan Bass, trans. (Chicago: University Press, 1981), p. 93.

6 In Derrida, *Margins of Philosophy*, Alan Bass, trans. (Chicago: University Press, 1982), pp. 109-136. Cf. the opening "Exergue" in Derrida, *Of Grammatology*, Gayatri Chakravorty Spivak, trans. (Baltimore: Johns Hopkins UP, 1976), pp. 3-5, where he writes of the "closure" of a "historico-metaphysical epoch," and characterizes grammatology as "a way of thinking that is faithful and attentive to the ineluctable world of the future which proclaims itself at present," a future that "can only be anticipated in the form of an absolute danger," as it "breaks absolutely with constituted normality." This was published in 1967; sometime later, in a paper read in 1980, "Of an Apocalyptic Tone Recently Adopted in Philosophy" [*Semeia*, XXIII (1982):63-97], Derrida claimed that his adoption of an apocalyptic tone had always been qualified, distanced, ironic (p. 90).

7 *Ibid.*, p. 133.

8 *Ibid.*, pp. 134–135.

9 "Semiology and Grammatology," an interview with Julia Kristeva, in *Positions*, pp. 15-36.

10 *Ibid.*, p. 24.

11 *Ibid.*

12 "Positions," an interview with Jean-Louis Houdebine and Guy Scarpetta, in *Positions*, pp. 37-96, here p. 69.

13 Cf. "Of an Apocalyptic Tone," esp. p. 94.

14 Derrida uses the German term for enlightenment in a number of places; see for example "Of an Apocalyptic Tone, p. 87; "The Principle of Reason: The University in the Eyes of its Pupils," *Diacritics*, XIX (1983):3-20, here pp. 5,19; and "Afterword: Toward an Ethic of Discussion," in *Limited Inc*, Samuel Weber, trans. (Evanston: Northwestern UP, 1988), pp. 111-160, here, p. 141.

15 "The Principle of Reason," pp. 9-10.

16 *Limited Inc*, p. 117.

17 *Ibid.*, p. 119.

18 In *The Tain of the Mirror: Derrida and the Philosophy of Reflection* (Cambridge: Harvard, 1986), Rodolphe Gasché presents Derrida's project as an inquiry into the conditions of possibility and impossibility of philosophical discourse. On this account, the motifs of Derrida's "more philosophically discursive texts" also inform his "more literarily playful texts," which make essentially the same points in "a nondiscursive manner" (p. 4). In *Contingency, Irony, and Solidarity* (New York: Cambridge, 1989), Richard Rorty contests this interpretation, arguing instead for a

distinction between an earlier and later Derrida (pp. 122-137). Focusing chiefly on *The Post Card: From Socrates to Freud and Beyond* [Alan Bass, trans. (Chicago: University Press, 1987)], with supporting references to *Glas* [John P. Leavey and Richard Rand, trans. (Lincoln: Nebraska UP, 1987)], he takes Derrida to have gone beyond, finally, the dream of philosophy, not by deploying new methods or techniques but by experimenting with new styles. According to Rorty, in Derrida's later work the writing becomes "more eccentric, personal, and original" (p. 123). It relies on private "fantasies," "idiosyncrasies," and "associations" rather than on public "generalities" and "arguments." Because some of Derrida's most vivid fantasies concern past philosophers, however, "only people who habitually read philosophy could possibly enjoy it" (p. 136). Christopher Norris sides, more or less, with Gasché, distinguishing two categories (rather than periods) of Derrida's writing, in which the same points are made in very different ways ["Deconstruction, Postmodernism and Philosophy: Habermas on Derrida," *Praxis International*, VIII (1989):426-446]. My view is closer to that of Gasché and Norris. The two-periods approach has a hard time accounting for some of the latest material—for instance, the fifty-page "Afterword" to *Limited Inc*, in which Derrida is on his best post-Kantian behavior. It has an even harder time explaining Derrida's continued insistence on the political relevance of his work. One has difficulty imagining the small band of philosophically schooled and literarily sensitive readers who can appreciate Derrida's "private fantasies" as the vanguard of the revolution, or even as the midwives of the "ineluctable world of the future."

19 *Positions*, p. 29.

20 *Ibid.*, p. 26.

21 *Ibid.*, p. 32. On the same page, he writes that "metaphysics has always consisted in attempting to uproot the presence of meaning, in whatever guise, from *différance;* and every time that a region or layer of pure meaning or a pure signified is allegedly rigorously delineated or isolated this gesture is repeated."

22 *Of Grammatology*, p. 10.

23 "The Ends of Man," p. 135.

24 *Ibid.* Cf. "Structure, Sign and Play in the Discourse of the Human Sciences," in *Writing and Difference*, Alan Bass, trans. (Chicago: University Press 1978), pp. 280–281: ". . . we can pronounce not a single deconstructive proposition which has not already had to slip into the form, the logic, and the implicit postulations of precisely what it seeks to contest."

25 *Ibid.*, p. 135.

26 *Positions*, p. 19.

27 *Ibid.*, p. 42.

28 Rorty has argued in "Deconstruction and Circumvention," in *Critical Inquiry*, XI (1984):2-23, that it cannot succeed in escaping the orbit of Western philosophy, for, notwithstanding the differences in terminology and style, it appears to be just what philosophers have been up to all along, if not always so self-consciously; see pp. 12ff.

29 "Deconstruction and Circumvention." See the response by Henry Staten, "Rorty's Circumvention of Derrida," in *Critical Inquiry*, XII (1986):453-461. Derrida's qualifications still give philosophy a privileged place as "the most powerful *discursive* formation of our 'culture' " (*Positions*, p. 102, n. 21).

30 *Of Grammatology*, p. 3.

31 *Ibid.*

32 "The Ends of Man," p. 111.

33 "Implications," an interview with Henry Ronse, in *Positions*, pp. 1-14, here pp. 6–7 [my emphases].

34 *Positions*, p. 19. Derrida apparently holds that there are certain "effects of *différance,*" built into the use of language, which persistently and inescapably produce the kinds of illusions that lead

THE POLITICS OF THE INEFFABLE

to logocentrism. For instance, the conception of language as "expressive representation, a translation on the outside of what was constituted inside"—a conception basic to Western logocentrism—is, he tells us, "not an accidental prejudice, but rather a kind of structural lure, what Kant would have called a transcendental illusion. The latter is modified according to the language, the era, the culture." Western metaphysics is a "powerful systematization of this illusion" (*Positions*, p. 33). Elsewhere he seems to suggest that the fulfillment or "plenitude" toward which intentionality inevitably tends (*Limited Inc*, p. 129), truth (*Positions*, p. 105), the classical logic of binary opposition (*Limited Inc*, p. 117), and the idealization intrinsic to conceptualization (*ibid.*) are "transcendental illusions" of this sort. Thus, he seems to hold, like Kant, that the "ideas of reason" built into thought (language) inevitably give rise to illusions which we can, with difficulty, detect, but never dispel. It is these illusions which, enhanced and systematized, comprise Western metaphysics: "Logocentric philosophy is a specifically Western response to a much larger necessity which also occurs in the Far East and other cultures . . ." ("Deconstruction and the Other," p. 115). As these are some of the same "idealizing presuppositions of communication" which Habermas makes central to his "postmetaphysical" conception of rationality (Habermas, *Nachmetaphysiches Denken* (Frankfurt: Suhrkamp, 1988), the Derrida-Habermas debate could, I think, be fruitfully continued around the question: Are the idealizations built into language more adequately conceived as pragmatic presuppositions of communicative interaction or as a kind of structural lure that has ceaselessly to be resisted? (Or perhaps as both?)

35 "The Ends of Man," p. 135.

36 *Positions*, p. 51.

37 He did, unfortunately, give it political expression during the period of his participation in National Socialism. For a recent discussion, see the Symposium on "Heidegger and Nazism" in *Critical Inquiry*, xv (1989):407-490.

38 *Dialectic of Enlightenment*, John Cumming, trans. (New York: Continuum, 1972).

39 See the brief comparisons in Peter Dews, *Logics of Disintegration* (London: Verso, 1987); and Habermas, *The Philosophical Discourse of Modernity: Twelve Lectures*, Frederick Lawrence, trans. (Cambridge: MIT, 1987); and the extended discussion in Christoph Menke-Egger's *Die Souveränität der Kunst* (Frankfurt: Suhrkamp, 1988).

40 Allan Megill, *Prophets of Extremity* (Berkeley: California UP, 1985), reads him in this way; see esp. pp. 303-320.

41 Of course, in his case the experiences were of French Fascism under the Vichy Government: "I came to France when I was nineteen. Before then, I had never been much past El-Biar [a suburb of Algiers]. The war came to Algeria in 1940, and with it, already then, the first concealed rumblings of the Algerian War. As a child, I had the instinctive feeling that the end of the world was at hand, a feeling which at the same time was most natural, and, in my case, the only one I ever knew. Even for a child incapable of analyzing things, it was clear that all this would end in fire and blood. . . . Then, in 1940, the singular experience of the Algerian Jews, incomparable to that of European Jews, the persecutions were nevertheless unleashed in the absence of any German occupier. . . . It is an experience which leaves nothing intact, something you can never again cease to feel. . . . Then the Allies land, and . . . racial laws were maintained for a period of almost six months, under a 'free' French government. . . . From that moment—how can I say it—I felt as displaced in a Jewish community, closed unto itself, as I would in the other. . . . From all of which comes a feeling on non-belonging that I have doubtless transposed." "An Interview with Derrida," in David Wood and Robert Bernasconi, eds., *Derrida and Différance* (Evanston: Northwestern, 1988), pp. 71-82, here pp. 74–75. Elsewhere Derrida mentions the ensuing horror of France's wars in Algeria and Indochina (cf. "The Principle of Reason," p. 13).

There is nothing like the "belatedness" of German history to explain how the "most civilized" of Western nations disposed of its Enlightenment heritage.

42 "Deconstruction and the Other," pp. 115-116. Cf. note 27, above.

43 "The Principle of Reason," p. 8. The numbers in parentheses in the following theses refer to this piece.

44 "Deconstruction and the Other," p. 114.

45 *Ibid.*, p. 115.

46 *Limited Inc,* p. 139.

47 Derrida, "Racism's Last Word," in *Critical Inquiry,* xII (1985):290-299, here p. 298.

48 *Limited Inc,* p. 116; and "The Politics of Friendship," passim. The language of call and response appears repeatedly in Derrida's writings. In the "Afterword" to *Limited Inc,* he plays this as a variation on a Kantian theme: the "injunction that prescribes deconstruction," he writes, "arouse[s] in me a respect which, whatever the cost, I neither can nor will compromise" (p. 153). But this is Kant at the limits of his thought, where he comes closest to Kierkegaard, whom Derrida mentions in a similar context in "The Principle of Reason," p. 20. The allusion to Kierkegaard seems to me to capture better what is involved here, though Derrida's "decision" is apparently located "in the order of ethico-political responsibility" (*Limited Inc,* p. 116) rather than in that of religious faith.

49 "Deconstruction and the Other," p. 117. On pp. 116-117, Derrida mentions several sources of the fissures in Western culture that serve as points of incision for deconstruction: the impact of non-European cultures on the West and the always incomplete attempts to absorb them; the heterogeneous elements of Judaism and Christianity that were never completely assimilated or eradicated; traces of alterity within Greek culture that philosophy could not completely domesticate.

50 *Limited Inc,* p. 136.

51 "Deconstruction and the Other," p. 120.

52 "The French Derrideans: Politicizing Deconstruction or Deconstructing Politics," *New German Critique,* xxxiii (1984):127-154.

53 For instance, he reminds critics that deconstruction is not simply demolition but always operates within the context of established conceptualities. When the "double gesture" was introduced, however, the "positive" relation to receive concepts and schemes was explained as a tactical move to ensure that deconstruction has a critical purchase on what is to be deconstructed—it lodges itself within the old conceptuality so as all the more effectively to dismantle it, thus avoiding a simple "change of terrain" which would reinstate the old beneath the new. Another type of response has been to present deconstruction as an attempt to understand how an "ensemble" is constituted (cf. for instance his "Letter to a Japanese Friend," in *Derrida and Différance,* pp. 1-5, here p. 3). This knowledge might then be used to restore or reconstruct the ensemble as well as to destabilize or dismantle it. In the abstract, there may be something to this. But if we look at what Derrida actually does with deconstruction, the reconstructive moment is not in evidence. A third sort of response is, as we have seen, to represent deconstruction as "motivated by some sort of affirmation," as a "positive responsive to an alterity which calls it" ("Deconstruction and the Other," p. 118). But what is at issue is not whether deconstruction is a positive response, but whether that response is positive—that is, the nature of the activity engaged in as a result of the "decision" to respond affirmatively. If the proof of the pudding is in the practice, the call is apparently one to incessant subversion of dominant conceptual regimes. Finally, there are frequent mentions of deconstruction as a kind of memory that preserves tradition (cf. for instance, *Limited Inc,* p. 141 and "The Principle of Reason," pp. 16, 20). But, in practice, it seems, the chief way in which deconstruction "keeps alive the memory of a tradition" is by deconstructing its texts, and that merely brings our question full circle.

54 *Limited Inc*, p. 141.

55 Recently and very effectively by Richard Bernstein, "Serious Play: The Ethical-Political Horizon of Jacques Derrida," unpublished.

56 In Derrida and Mustapha Tlili, eds., *For Nelson Mandela* (New York: 1987), pp. 13-42.

57 *Ibid.*, p. 38.

58 *Ibid.*, pp. 38–39.

59 *Ibid.*, p. 41. The same combination of using existing schemes, while simultaneously devaluating them and gesturing toward something wholly other, which is as yet ineffable, marks Derrida's discussion of women's studies in "Women in the Beehive," in Alice Jardine and Paul Smith, eds., *Men in Feminism* (New York: Methuen, 1987), pp. 189-203. There he acknowledges the "positive research" of feminist scholars, while noting their failure adequately to "put back into question the structural principles" of "university law" and "of social law in general" (p. 191). The more feminist research "proves its positivity," the more it risks "repressing the fundamental question we must pose," and becoming "just another cell in the university beehive" (*ibid.*). The same can be said of the struggle for equal rights for women: it remains "caught in the logic of phallogocentrism" and thus rebuilds "the empire of the law" (p. 193). The analytic and strategic advantages of depreciating "calculable" results by comparison to the "unprogrammable" project of deconstructing structural principles and philosophical frameworks are never identified— apart from one curious reference to joint appointments (*ibid.*).

60 Their critique, "No Names Apart: The Separation of Word and History in Derrida's 'Le Dernier Mot du Racisme'," appeared in *Critical Inquiry*, XIII (1986):140-154; Derrida's response, "But Beyond. . . ," appeared in the same issue, pp. 155-170. Cf. the analysis of this exchange by Alexander Argyros, "Prescriptive Deconstruction," in *Critical Texts*, VI (1989):1-16.

61 "Afterword" to *Limited Inc*, pp. 150–151. The numbers in parentheses in the text refer to this afterword.

62 *Ibid.*, p. 136. The brackets contain my glosses in sociological terms; for more of the same, see my comment, "On the Margins of Politics."

63 In *Logics of Disintegration*, Dews has argued that this line of thought, rigorously pursued, leads to a kind of Schellingian absolute (pp. 19-31). Whether one then characterizes the "non-originary origin" of identity and difference in terms of absolute identity, as Schelling did, or absolute difference, as Derrida does, becomes a matter of rhetorical strategy.

64 This is one of Habermas's points in *The Philosophical Discourse of Modernity*, pp. 204-210, where he distinguishes the "poetic, world-disclosive" function of language from its "inner-worldly, problem-solving" functions. Derrida seems to accept this point in the "Afterword" to *Limited Inc* (cf. pp. 132-138), but he simply takes all such social constructions for granted and zeroes in on deficiencies, delusions, and dangers. He does not, and in the deconstructive mode, cannot tell us what we should look for in reconstructing them, nor how to orient ourselves in judging sociopolitical arrangements as better or worse. Critical interrogation of limits is surely essential in the ethico-political sphere; and it is certainly open to Derrida to choose to do only or chiefly this. As I shall argue below, the problem arises when he claims that this is the only philosophically legitimate intellectual activity in this sphere, since substantive empirical and normative inquiries are all blinded by the metaphysics of presence.

65 These are Derrida's own terms in *Of Grammatology*, p. 5, and in "Deconstruction and the Other," p. 123.

66 See, for example, his discussion of Nietzsche in *The Ear of the Other*, Christie V. McDonald, ed. (New York: Schocken, 1985), esp. pp. 23ff.

67 *The Philosophical Discourse of Modernity*, p. 408, n. 28. On this point, see also Rorty, "Deconstruction and Circumvention," passim.

68 *Of Grammatology*, p. 27.

69 *Logics of Disintegration*, pp. 5ff., 15ff., and 36ff.

70 *Ibid.*, p. 19.

71 *Ibid.*, pp. 37–38.

72 Most recently in *Limited Inc*, p. 118. See also *Positions*, p. 102, n. 21, where the alternative to deconstruction's philosophical orientation is characterized as "empiricist improvisation."

73 "The French Derrideans," p. 149.

74 I am referring here to Derrida's oral presentation at the APA, where he discussed at some length Schmitt's *The Concept of the Political* (New Brunswick: Rutgers UP, 1976). Even then, he selected from the diverse topics Schmitt dealt with in that work only the quasi-ontological themes.

75 Cf. Habermas's contribution to the Symposium on "Heidegger and Nazism" cited in note 30 above, "Work and *Weltanschauung*," pp. 431-456.

76 "The Politics of Friendship," p. 638.

77 *Ibid.*

78 In his oral presentation.

79 "The French Derrideans," p. 130.

80 "The Politics of Friendship," p. 641.

81 *Limited Inc*, pp. 136–137.

82 I am not, of course, arguing that one should not study these texts. The issue is whether deconstructing texts *suffices* as an approach to political theory.

83 In his oral presentation. The remarks on democracy referred to in the following paragraphs also come from the version delivered at the APA.

84 Cf. "Of an Apocalyptic Tone," p. 94: "Now here, precisely, is announced—as promise or threat—an apocalypse without apocalypse, an apocalypse without vision, without truth, without revelation . . . an apocalypse beyond good and evil. . . . Our apocalypse now: that there is no longer any place for the apocalypse as the collection of evil and good"; and "Deconstruction and the Other," p. 119: "Unfortunately I do not feel inspired by any sort of hope which would permit me to presume that my work of deconstruction has a prophetic function. But I concede that the style of my questions . . . might produce certain prophetic resonances. It is possible to see deconstruction as being produced in a space where the prophets are not far away."

85 As well as from the assumption of a broad normative consensus with his readers, which, because it is presumably shared, need not be spelled out or defended.

86 For the details of this argument, see my published comment, "On the Margins of Politics."

87 Cf. "The Politics of Friendship," pp. 633-636; the relation to democracy was drawn in the oral presentation.

88 *Ibid.*, p. 635–636.

89 In the oral version, as was the question posed in the next sentence.

KANT AND THE INTERPRETATION OF NATURE AND HISTORY

RUDOLF A. MAKKREEL

The purpose of this paper is to examine Kant's views on interpreting nature and history and to attempt to see them as coherent by relating them to his theory of reflective judgment. On the basis of this reconstruction of a Kantian conception of interpretation it will then be possible to shed some new light on Kant's approach to political history.

I shall propose that reflective judgments as defined in the *Critique of Judgment* should be conceived first of all as interpretive and only derivatively as either aesthetic or teleological. This way of approaching reflective judgments will allow us to create a spectrum of them ranging from the noncognitive to the cognitive and from the aesthetic to the practical. By means of this enlarged conception of reflective judgment, it becomes possible to overcome the overly aesthetical analysis of political judgment provided by Hannah Arendt, while still preserving the fruitfulness of the Kantian approach to political theory and history. In conjunction with this, I shall show that Kant's moral response to the French Revolution must be explicated in teleological as well as aesthetic terms.

Whereas determinant judgments are defined by Kant as proceeding from given universals to particulars, reflective judgments find universals for given particulars. A determinant judgment is directly determined by concepts of the understanding; a reflective judgment is not. In the latter, judgment is left to its own devices, and can at best appeal to certain indirect guidelines provided by ideas of reason in the effort to interpret experience as a formally purposive system.

Kant did not develop an explicit theory of interpretation in the *Critique of Judgment,* yet much in that work has a hermeneutical import. After first briefly reviewing what Kant says elsewhere about the understanding and interpretation of nature, we can then develop some of the concepts in the *Critique of Judgment* that contribute to the theory of interpretation in general.[1]

I. THEORETICAL INTERPRETATIONS OF NATURE AND THE PROBLEM
OF THEODICY

In the *Critique of Pure Reason* and the *Prolegomena to Any Future Metaphysics,* Kant indicates that the task of understanding is to give a reading of nature. Pure concepts of the understanding have no objective meaning if they are thought to go beyond experience. To acquire such meaning they must be applied to the manifold of sense. In Kant's words, concepts of the understanding "serve, as it were, only to spell out appearances, that we may be able to read them as experience."[2] We can elaborate Kant's reading metaphor by distinguishing four phases of textual construal: spelling (*buchstabieren*), deciphering (*entziffern*), reading (*lesen*), and interpreting (*auslegen*). Normally, one reads a series of letters as a word having meaning; but if the letters are illegible or scrambled, one must attempt to decipher them one by one. Only if there is a problem on the level of the meaning of words or sentences must one appeal to interpretation.

If the material to be construed is what Kant calls the book of nature, the task of deciphering is to discover the basic mathematical patterns (*Urbilder*) that run through what is intuited. Those patterns which recur can be derived from mathematical schemata. In an essay published in 1764, Kant specifically speaks of deciphering in relation to mathematics. It should be noted, too, that the German word for algebra used by Kant is *Buchstabenrechnung* (calculation by means of letters). Mathematical letters or ciphers become independent of their original reference and can then be manipulated without thinking of their object. Yet what is learned through the manipulation of the ciphers also applies to the objects.[3] The mathematical cipher becomes an intuitive replacement of the object (it is called a "sign *in concreto*"), whereas philosophical language is restricted to words that can at best represent their objects abstractly (Ak II, 278–279).

To explicate what is involved in reading and interpreting nature as a text, we must first examine the section on "Ideas in General" in the Transcendental Dialectic of the *Critique of Pure Reason*. The opening discussion of ideas contains some interesting reflections on meaning and interpretation as Kant seeks to define his own use of the term 'idea' through an interpretation of its past usage in the history of philosophy. After warning that "to coin new words is to advance a claim to legislation in language that seldom succeeds,"[4] he proposes a critical appropriation of Plato's theory of ideas. This is the context in which Kant makes the much-noted claim—subsequently associated with the hermeneutics of F. D. E. Schleiermacher and Wilhelm Dilthey—that it is possible to understand an author "better than he has understood himself" (C1, A314/B370). Applying this hermeneutic maxim to his own understanding of past philosophers, Kant claims that Plato was wrong to conceive of ideas or forms as the archetypes (*Urbilder*) of things themselves. Yet Kant goes on to say that Plato "realised that our faculty of knowledge feels a much higher need than merely *to spell out* appearances according to a synthetic unity, in order to be able *to read* them as experience. He knew that our reason naturally exalts itself to modes of knowledge which . . . transcend the bounds of experience" (C1, A314/B370-371; emphases added). In this passage, Kant's language suggests a way to reformulate the differing goals of the understanding and reason as the difference between reading and interpreting. The goal of the understanding is to "read" as experience what is spelled out in the manifold of appearances. But reason seeks more. It seeks to interpret these experiences in terms of an idea of a whole. If concepts of the understanding provide the *rules for reading* the manifold of sense in order to produce knowledge of objects in nature, then ideas of reason can be said to provide the *rules for interpreting* these objects in order to form a coherent and complete system of nature.

A relation between the ideas of reason and an interpretation of the system of nature is actually suggested in the *Reflexionen zur Metaphysik* where Kant warns that ideas of reason may not be used dogmatically to explain nature by means of causes that transcend nature. Such ideas of reason can only be used regulatively, "for nature is our task, the text of our interpretations (*Auslegungen*)" (R 5637; Ak XVIII, 274; 1780-1783). The notion of interpreting nature is more fully explored in the *Opus postumum* where Kant discusses the systematization of fundamental forces and of the laws of nature. He distinguishes two kinds of "interpretation (*Auslegung*) of nature" (Ak XXII, 173). The first kind is a "doctrinal (*doktrinal*)" interpretation that he retrospectively attributes to the *Metaphysical Foundations of Natural Science* (Ak XXII, 173): in that work Kant interpreted substance as matter that is movable in space and subject to motion in time (Ak XXII, 189). The second kind of interpretation is called "authentic (*authentisch*)" and will be provided by the science of physics when it works out the actual laws of nature (Ak XXII, 173).

Kant makes the distinction between doctrinal and authentic interpretations without explicitly defining it. He merely calls the doctrinal interpretation of the *Metaphysical Foundations of Natural Science* "a scholastic system (*Lehrsystem*)" (Ak XXII, 189), in contrast to the "experiential system (*Erfahrungssystem*)" of physics (Ak XXII, 173). In the Canon of Pure Reason of the first *Critique*, Kant applies the term 'doctrinal' to belief rather than to interpretation. He places doctrinal beliefs between contingent pragmatic beliefs and absolute moral beliefs (C1, A825/B853-A828/B856). A doctrinal belief is strongly held as "hypothetically necessary" (C1, A823/B851) for the attainment of some theoretical end. It falls short of a moral belief, which is characterized as "absolutely necessary" (C1, A828/B856). This suggests that the doctrinal interpretation or scholastic system of the *Metaphysical Foundations of Natural Science* provides a systematization of nature which is still hypothetical or speculative. The authentic interpretation of nature aimed at by physics will provide a nonspeculative system by going back to the original sources of experience and by being purely law-derived.

The distinction between doctrinal and authentic interpretation was first used by Kant in the essay, "On the Failure of All Attempted Philosophical Theodicies" (1791). The task of theodicy differs from that of interpreting nature as a scientific system. The problem is not just one of organizing our theoretical knowledge of nature, but of finding a moral or practical meaning of the telos of nature. Kant writes: "All theodicy must be an interpretation (*Auslegung*) of nature and must show how God manifests the intention (*Absicht*) of his will through it."[5] In relation to the broader aims of a moral or teleological interpretation, nature also encompasses human history and is no longer considered the open book that it was for the theoretical point of view. According to Kant, nature is "a closed book when we want to read the *final* intention (*Endabsicht*) of God (which is always a moral one) from a world which is only an object of experience" (FPT, 291; Ak VIII, 264).

Traditional theodicies have been doctrinal in speculating about the final moral end that God intends nature to have. Whereas doctrinal interpretations of the theoretical system are hypothetical, doctrinal interpretations of the practical goal of nature can merely be "sophistical (*vernünftelnd*)" (Ak VIII, 264). Their claim is not only to systematize the theoretical *meaning* of experience, but also to know what God *meant* nature to accomplish. They presume to be able to read God's intention into the course of human experience so that events seemingly "contrary to purpose (*zweckwidrig*)" (FPT, 283; Ak VIII, 255) are reinterpreted to disclose a deeper divine purpose. Such doctrinal interpretations are beyond our capacity.

Although traditional doctrinal theodicies must by their very nature fail, a more modest but authentic form of theodicy is possible for Kant. An authentic interpretation of the moral meaning of nature cannot appeal to experience and the laws of physics, but appeals to the laws of morality within us that precede all experience. Without speculation on how God acts in relation to nature, it affirms the postulate of practical reason that He must somehow relate nature to the highest good for the sake of morality. Such an authentic, moral interpretation does not give a complete explanation of God's plan for nature, but by means of it at least "the letters (*Buchstaben*) of His creation can be given a sense (*einen Sinn*)" (FPT, 291; Ak VII, 264).

Kant cites the story of Job as an allegorical model of an authentic theodicy. Job's friends give a doctrinal interpretation of his suffering when they assume that God has punished him for unknown past sins. Job, however, declares that his suffering is inscrutable to him and rejects their advice to plead for God's forgiveness. While acknowledging his human frailty and the sovereignty of God's will, he insists upon being guided by his own conscience, which does not condemn him. According to Kant, Job's rejection of doctrinal explanations is ultimately vindicated by God, who shows him "an ordering of the whole which manifests a wise Creator, although His ways remain inscrutable for us" (FPT, 292–293). What counts is "only the uprightness of the heart, not the merit of one's insights, the sincere and undisguised confession of one's doubts, and the avoidance of feigned convictions which one does not really feel" (FPT, 293). Thus, an authentic theodicy makes no speculative theoretical claims. It is rooted in practical reason and appeals to genuine moral feeling as its guide. Kant's later discussions of authentic interpretations of religious texts place less emphasis on the sincerity of feeling.[6] Reference to feeling is a factor, however, in all interpretations that go beyond the objective meaning sought in a strictly scientific interpretation of nature.

II. AESTHETIC CONTINGENCY AND REFLECTIVE INTERPRETATION

In so far as interpretations of the world and of our place in it as human beings are evaluative, they require reflective judgments in which feeling plays an integral role. Here feeling is not understood in a mere private or emotive sense. In the *Critique of Judgment,* aesthetic pleasure is defined as a disinterested, formal feeling arising from a harmony of the cognitive faculties. This aesthetic pleasure is also conceived as the enhancement of a general feeling of life (see C3, §1). Kant uses this furtherance of life as an aesthetic criterion, but it can also be seen to accompany our reflections on the meaning of experience and to authenticate our interpretations of the world.

Interpretations that are evaluative cannot be objectively demonstrated, but they can approximate the intersubjectivity that Kant claims for aesthetic judgments. The intersubjective validity of aesthetic judgments is grounded in what Kant calls a *sensus communis* or a sense common to all. A reflective judgment based on the *sensus communis* "takes account (a priori) of the mode of representation of all other men in thought, in order, as it were, to compare its judgment with the collective reason of humanity, and thus to escape the illusion arising from the private conditions that could be so easily taken for objective."[7] This a priori sense shows how feeling can escape the narrowness so often associated with it. The aim of the *sensus communis* is most clearly formulated in Kant's maxim of enlarged thought, which requires us to compare our judgment "with the possible rather than the actual judgment of others" (C3, 136). This maxim is applicable to judgment in interpretation, where a text is to be regarded not so much for the actual meaning intended by the author, as for the possible meanings that lie implicit in it as a human or cultural product. The author's intention can serve at best as a model for reflection on the common meaning of a text.

As first discussed in the "Critique of Aesthetic Judgment," the idea of common sense is a presupposition for the universal communicability of feeling. Because of its identification with aesthetic feeling, the broader implications of Kant's theory of common sense have not been adequately recognized. According to Hans-Georg Gadamer, Kant's theory of common sense represents an unfortunate dissipation of the humanist common-sense tradition. This tradition, going back to Cicero, Vico, and Shaftesbury, regards common sense as a mode of knowledge rooted in the moral and civic community. It is this sense of tradition as a mode of knowing which Gadamer reappropriates as the framework of his philosophical hermeneutics. In his view, Kant's common sense is an aesthetic, noncognitive alternative to traditional common sense which led nineteenth-century hermeneutics into a subjective *cul-de-sac*.[8] It is precisely through common sense, however, that the aesthetic judgment can be intersubjective as well as subjective. According to Kant, common sense makes it possible to represent the "subjective necessity" of the judgment of taste as "objective" (C3, §22, 76) in the sense of claiming universal assent. More importantly, however, Kant goes on to make the broader claim that common sense is a presupposition of the communicability of *knowledge*. He asserts that "common sense is assumed . . . as the necessary condition of the universal communicability of our knowledge, which is presupposed in every logic and in every principle of knowledge that is not sceptical" (C3, §21, 76). This cognitive dimension of Kant's theory of common sense means that it cannot be simply restricted to agreement about taste, as Gadamer assumes, but applies to reflective judgment in general.

Although it is true that Kant defines the pure aesthetic judgment as a singular, nonconceptual judgment, it would be misleading to characterize it as noncognitive. The aesthetic pleasure that is predicated of the beautiful object involves a harmony of the cognitive faculties which is at the same time a condition for *all* cognition. Kant's claim that pure aesthetic judgments do not use concepts proves, upon analysis, to mean only that they do not use *empirical* concepts.[9] These judgments are never divorced from the categorial structure of the understanding. To the extent that aesthetic judgments are also said to contribute to knowledge *in general* they suggest a possible systematization of experience which can be accounted for only on the basis of aesthetic ideas. Like a rational idea, an aesthetic idea can serve as a rule of interpretation which transcends experience. Yet, unlike a rational idea, it does not create the illusion that we can directly intuit anything beyond the bounds of experience. The object produced by the imagination in aesthetic ideas is an indirect object based on analogies between actual experience and rational ideas.

Although Kant introduces aesthetic ideas rather late in his account of aesthetic judgments, the two can be seen to be essentially related. Already in the introduction of the *Critique of Judgment,* the reflective judgment is defined as finding a universal for a particular by applying a principle whose "function is to establish the unity of all empirical principles under higher ones" (C3, Intro, iv, 16). Reflective judgment is not just an inductive judgment, but according to Kant's *Logic* it can be said to appeal to a "principle of specification."[10] What is being specified in a reflective judgment about a particular object is the *idea* of systematic order. The specification involved in a reflective judgment is interpretive, because it *coordinates* the order apprehended in a particular object with a more general idea of systematic order in nature. In a determinant judgment, the particular is *subsumed* under or *subordinated* to a universal. The singularity of the particular is ignored in the determinant judgment, but is preserved in the reflective judgment. Although it is true that in reflective judgments we " 'meet the phenomena head-on,' that is, as *singular*,"[11] these phenomena are not isolated from our cognitive framework. It is precisely the way a reflective judgment coordinates a particular form with an idea of an overall sense of order which makes it an interpretive mode of cognitive judgment.

Whereas judgments that appeal to aesthetic ideas may be only implicitly cognitive, judgments appealing to teleological ideas involve explicit cognitive claims. Both kinds of reflective judgment are interpretive in that they use ideas to discern order and meaning in those aspects of experience left contingent by the laws of the understanding. What distinguishes a reflective interpretation of the particulars of experience from purely theoretical explanations using concepts and from dialectical reconstructions on the basis of rational ideas is that such an interpretation will "never analyze the structure of its object to the point of eliminating all contingency."[12] Reflective interpretation is hermeneutical because, to paraphrase Jürgen Habermas, it apprehends *meaning* relations as relations of *fact*.[13] It might seem anachronistic to relate Kant's analysis of reflective judgment to language used by Habermas to characterize the hermeneutics of facticity of Dilthey and Martin Heidegger, whose common concern is to understand the individuality and historicity of the particulars of experience.[14] But, as I shall attempt to show, it is precisely this coordination of particularity and universality which makes a historical event like the French Revolution worthy of interpretation for Kant. A contingent historical fact can intimate a necessary human goal.

The coordination of contingency and necessity is found in all reflective judgments concerning purposiveness. I have called the kind of interpretation involved here *reflective* to distinguish it from the purely theoretical interpretation of nature discussed earlier. Because Kant's interpretation of the system of nature on the basis of the first *Critique* was merely an extrapolation of reason from the reading of experience, it remained a one-directional, abstract process removed from the contingency of experience. The ideas of reason used to project the systematic unity of experience merely strove for the maximum integration of the rules of the understanding. Reason directed "the understanding to a certain goal upon which the routes marked out by all its rules converge, as upon their point of intersection. This point was indeed a mere idea, a *focus imaginarius* . . . quite outside the bounds of experience" (C1, A644/B672). In projecting the *focus imaginarius,* reason employed the imagination to extend the lines determined by the rules of the understanding, rather than to mediate between it and sense.

The power of imagination is used more concretely when nature is interpreted in accordance with aesthetic ideas. Not only does the aesthetic imagination emulate "the play of reason in its quest after a maximum," but it also attempts to "present [rational ideas] to sense with a completeness of which there is no example in nature" (C3, §49, 158). When we consider nature aesthetically, Kant asserts that its forms "have no meaning (*bedeuten nichts*), depend on no definite concepts, and yet they please" (C3, §4, 41; Ak V, 207). Because beautiful forms in nature carry with them no determinate meaning, Kant calls them "ciphers (*Chiffreschrift*) through which nature speaks to us figuratively" and whose "true interpretation (*Auslegung*)" will show aesthetic feeling to be "akin to the moral feeling" (C3, §42, 143; Ak V, 301). To decipher the significance of beauty in nature is to read between the lines of the ordinary experiential reading of objects and to find a hint or "trace (*Spur*)" (C3, §42, 143; Ak V, 300) that nature is in general agreement with a principle of purposiveness. This trace of a larger systematic order is pleasurable precisely because it is experienced "as if it were a lucky chance favoring our design" (C3, Intro, v, 20). The harmony of the cognitive faculties which is felt when we apprehend a beautiful object is pleasurable at least partly because it is unexpected. Reflective judgment is always looking for the systematic organization of our experience, but whenever it succeeds in finding a specific instance of such integral order it is regarded "as merely contingent" (C3, Intro, vi, 24). Aesthetic harmony and order can only be felt as a purposiveness without a definitely conceived purpose. Such indeterminate purposiveness is interpretive, for, as Kant writes, "the important point is not what nature is, or even, as a purpose, is in relation to us, but *how we take it*" (C3, §58, 195; emphasis added).

The contingency or facticity of the beautiful form could be called a "fact of a priori feeling," just as Kant calls our consciousness of the fundamental moral law a "fact of reason" in the *Critique of Practical Reason*.[15] This fact of reason cannot itself be rationally derived nor can it be given in an intuition. It has a paradoxical status, because it is a datum that cannot be intuited either empirically or purely. If it were available to empirical intuition, it could not be a fact of *reason.* Nor can it be given through pure intuition, because the sole kind of pure intuition available to humans is that which provides the source of mathematics. Since we are not capable of having an intellectual intuition of a moral fact of reason, it seems appropriate to conceive our access to it through the only other mode of receptivity available to us, namely, feeling. Indeed, at a later point in the *Critique of Practical Reason,* Kant interprets our consciousness of the moral law through our feeling of respect for it—a feeling which is not pathological or empirical, but purely the effect of an intellectual idea. This interpretation of the "sole fact of pure reason" (C2, 31) as a felt fact accessible through the "singular" (C2, 82) feeling of respect should be kept in mind when we consider the relation of teleological and practical judgments.

III. TELEOLOGY AND THE INTERPRETATION OF HISTORY AND POLITICS

In the "Critique of Teleological Judgment," Kant specifies the purposiveness of nature by showing that certain natural processes can be fully understood only if, in addition to being explained by mechanical causation, they are described in terms of purposes. Through the teleological idea of a natural purpose, determinant explanations of organisms on the basis of theoretical reason are supplemented with reflective judgments concerning their ends.

Human beings embody a natural purpose like all organized beings, but they also represent a moral purpose from the standpoint of practical reason. These two perspectives on human beings can be brought together through the idea of culture. According to Kant, the ultimate purpose of nature considered as a teleological system is culture, that is, the production of our human capacity to set our own purposes and make ourselves moral beings independent of nature. Kant also claims that, for the maximum development of our human capacities, the ultimate purpose of nature requires the ordering of all civil states into a cosmopolitan whole wherein they will be unified in a morally grounded system.

This cosmopolitan idea was first set forth in the essay, "Idea for a Universal History from a Cosmopolitan Point of View" (1784), where human history was regarded as a teleological extension of natural history. Kant speculates that history will realize nature's plan to bring forth a "universal civic society" and "a league of nations" in which all states on earth will coexist in peaceful harmony.[16] Kant admitted that this historical projection of a cosmopolitan society could strike critics as "only a romance,"[17] but he nevertheless defended it as philosophically pragmatic. In terms of our analysis of the third *Critique,* this idea of a cosmopolitan society is more appropriately reconceived as a teleological idea subject to the limits of reflective judgment. It serves as the counterpart in the historical realm of the abstract rational idea of a kingdom of ends. The hermeneutical implications of this cosmopolitan idea can be further specified by examining Kant's interpretation of the meaning of a particular historical event like the French Revolution.

For this we must turn to the essay, "An Old Question Raised Again: Is the Human Race Constantly Progressing?" (1798). What I shall characterize as a reflective interpretation of history can be related to Kant's own distinction between three kinds of predictive (*vorhersagende*) history. The first kind, to which Kant does not give a special name, attempts to predict on the basis of known laws of nature. A second kind, which he calls prophetic or *weissagende* history, attempts to supplement prediction by making a determinant use of supernatural signs, and is for that reason uncritical. A third kind, called divinatory or *wahrsagende* history, also goes beyond the known laws of nature, but does so by using natural rather than supernatural signs. Its claims concerning moral progress in history must be based on some experience in the human race—an actual event that can be considered a "historical sign . . . demonstrating the tendency of the human race viewed in its entirety."[18]

It is clear that the first kind of predictive history aims at a determinant explanation of the future. Were it possible to establish historical laws equivalent to the laws of physics, this kind of history would be authentic in the same sense that the scientific interpretation of nature discussed earlier was authentic. But the only example Kant gives of this kind of history appeals to eclipses of the sun and moon. This suggests that Kant does not take it very seriously. For its part, prophetic history using supernatural signs is a religious interpretation of history based on doctrinal speculations. Knowing how critical Kant was of doctrinal interpretations, we can also dismiss this kind of history. The divinatory or *wahrsagende* history adopted by Kant[19] establishes an intermediate philosophical position between supposed scientific explanations and religious interpretations of history. It can be shown to be both reflective in its use of teleology and authentic in its appeal to a principle in which "there must be something moral" (CF, 157).

In his lectures on anthropology, Kant calls *wahrsagen* or divining the truth "a natural skill."[20] *Wahrsagende* history thus involves a reflective art of interpreting historical events rather than a determinant science of explaining them. Kant looks to the French Revolution as an actual event that could be interpreted as a sign of possible historical progress toward the perfect civil constitution, which is defined as "republican" in *Perpetual Peace*. But he focuses neither on the causal consequences of the revolution nor the particular actions or interests of its direct participants. The reason for this is that some of the actual results of the French Revolution did not spell moral progress. For example, in *The Metaphysical Elements of Justice* of 1797 he expresses a moral "horror"[21] at the perversion of justice involved in the formal execution of Louis XVI. Nevertheless, Kant finds a sign of historical progress in the experience of those like himself who had witnessed the French Revolution from a distance and sympathized with its republican ideals. Just as in the interpretation of a text the author's actual intention is not decisive, the actual intention of historical agents are not central to *wahrsagende* history, which is concerned with the moral tendency of the human race as a whole. What is significant is the fact that even at a distance the

French Revolution aroused in its spectators a "universal yet unselfish participation (*uneigennützige Teilnehmung*) of players on one side against those on the other, even at the risk that their partisanship could become very disadvantageous for them if discovered" (CF, 153; Ak VII, 85). The favorable response of these spectators makes it possible to interpret the revolution as a hopeful sign of progress, for as Kant writes, their "well-wishing participation . . . can have no other cause than a moral predisposition in the human race" (CF, 153; Ak VII, 85).

There has been considerable disagreement about the best way to characterize this response to the French Revolution. To the extent that Kant speaks of unselfish spectators, the response seems to be aesthetic.[22] This impression is reinforced by the English translation of *uneigennützige Teilnehmung* as "disinterested sympathy" (a term used in the *Critique of Judgment*) rather than as "unselfish participation." Such an aesthetical interpretation fits with Arendt's conception of the political as the public realm "constituted by the critics and the spectators, not by the actors or the makers."[23] Arendt claims that the spectator is "impartial by definition."[24] This may be true for the disinterested spectator of the aesthetic judgment, but the spectators that Kant refers to here are clearly not impartial. They display a "partisanship" for the republican cause bordering on "enthusiasm," which according to Kant involves a "passionate participation in the Good" (CF, 154). Because the spectator's response to the French Revolution is at the same time aesthetic, teleological, and moral, it is possible to compare it with Kant's account of the sublime. The spectacle of this revolution is marked by a certain "grandeur" (CF, 154), and like the sublime it involves a transgression of limits. Both require a shift of perspective to transform what at first glance may be fearsome into something uplifting. Just as our representations of the starry heavens and the ocean are sublime only if we abstract from their actual content, so the French Revolution is sublime only if we abstract from its direct participants and the violence they may have committed. There is also an important difference, however. The sublime is terrifying if we judge it purely naturalistically as a phenomenon that overpowers our own physical and empirical capacities. It is by shifting to the moral perspective that we transform pathological fear into sublime wonder. In Kant's response to the French Revolution, it is the legal perspective that produces a sense of moral horror at those direct participants who used the semblance of a "formal execution" (MEJ, 88n) to subvert the basis of political institutions. It is by focusing on the response of the indirect participants that it becomes possible to replace a moral condemnation of revolution with reflection about the moral incentives that inspire revolutionary enthusiasm.

Whatever value the comparison of Kant's account of the sublime and his response to the French Revolution may have, it is crucial to understand the latter as part of an attempt to delineate a mode of philosophical or *wahrsagende* (literally truth-telling) history in which reflective teleological and determinant practical judgments intersect. Only in this way can interpretation relate the contingency of historical fact to the search for the essential meaning and purposiveness of human life. *Wahrsagende* history uses a particular historical event as a sign that not only intimates a better future for the human race, but also confirms a moral predisposition that can help to bring it about. We can see here the movement of reflective judgment from particular to universal, with the French Revolution serving as a historical intimation of the universal confederation of republican states projected by the teleological idea of a cosmopolitan society. Such a reflective interpretation is authenticated by a universal moral tendency disclosed in the historical experience of the spectator participant.

Instead of leaving us with three distinct Kantian perspectives on political history—the aesthetic, the teleological, and the moral—the idea of reflective interpretation allows us to relate them. Practical reason must ultimately authenticate the interpretation of history, but no simple determinant judgment based on reason alone can grasp the historical meaning of particular events. The idea of a Kantian reflective interpretation of history requires that moral purposes be related to the reflective framework established by aesthetic harmony and the teleological idea of a cosmopolitan society. It must be possible for reflective judgment to apply reason to the interpretation of what Thomas Seebohm has called "anthropological facts,"[25] without, however, diluting the validity of the determinant laws of morality. What is needed for the interpretation of history is the perspectival *intersection* of determinant and reflective judgments, not an *integration* that would dissolve their differences. To keep interpretation critical we must preserve a sense of the difference between the reason that authenticates norms and the reflection that brings them to bear on the actual world. Accordingly, any reflective judgment about political history is merely an indirect appropriation of the moral insights of reason and will also have to rely on aesthetic symbols of hope and experiential intimations of progress to discern meaning in history.

Emory University

NOTES

1 For a fuller treatment of Kant's views on interpretation, cf. my *Imagination and Interpretation in Kant: The Hermeneutical Import of the Critique of Judgment* (Chicago: University Press, forthcoming). An earlier, and somewhat different, version of this paper was presented at the 1988 Meeting of the International Association for Philosophy and Literature at the University of Notre Dame. This earlier version, entitled "The Hermeneutical Relevance of Kant's Third Critique,"

will appear in *Politics/Hermeneutics/Aesthetics,* Gerald Bruns and Stephen Watson, eds. (Albany: SUNY, forthcoming).

2 *Prolegomena to Any Future Metaphysics,* G. Carus and L. W. Beck, trans. (Indianapolis: Library of Liberal Arts, 1950), p. 60. Here and throughout the paper the German reference is given whenever I have revised the translation. *Kants gesammelte Schriften* (hereafter Ak), herausgegeben von der Preussischen Akademie der Wissenschaften zu Berlin (Berlin: de Gruyter, 1902-1983), 29 vols.; IV 312.

3 See *Untersuchung über die Deutlichkeit der Grundsätze der natürlichen Theologie und der Moral,* Ak II, 278.

4 *Critique of Pure Reason* (hereafter C1), Norman Kemp Smith, trans. (New York: St. Martin's, 1965), A312/B369.

5 "On the Failure of All Attempted Theodicies" (hereafter FPT), Michel Despland, trans., in his *Kant on History and Religion* (Montreal: McGill-Queen's UP, 1973), 291; Ak VIII, 264.

6 This will be dealt with in ch. 7 of *Imagination and Interpretation in Kant.*

7 *Critique of Judgment* (hereafter C3), J. H. Bernard, trans. (New York: Hafner, 1974), p. 136; Ak v, 293.

8 Gadamer, *Wahrheit und Methode,* 2nd ed. (Tübingen: J. C. B. Mohr, 1965), pp. 28-39.

9 See Lewis White Beck, *Essays on Kant and Hume* (New Haven: Yale, 1978), p. 56.

10 *Logic: A Manual for Lecturers,* Robert S. Hartman and Wolfgang Schwartz, trans. (Indianapolis: Bobbs-Merrill, 1974), p. 136.

11 Cf. Reiner Schürmann, ed., *The Public Realm: Essays on Discursive Types in Political Philosophy* (Albany: SUNY, 1989), p. 5.

12 Habermas, *Knowledge and Human Interests,* Jeremy Shapiro, trans. (Boston: Beacon, 1971), p. 161.

13 See *ibid.,* p. 162.

14 The term 'Faktizität' occurs in both the writings of Dilthey and Heidegger. In 1923 Heidegger subtitled his lectures on ontology "Hermeneutik der Faktizität."

15 *Critique of Practical Reason* (hereafter C2), Lewis White Beck, trans. (Indianapolis: Bobbs-Merrill, 1956), p. 31.

16 "Idea for a Universal History from the Cosmopolitan Point of View," in Immanuel Kant, *On History,* Lewis White Beck, ed. & trans. (Indianapolis: Library of Liberal Arts, 1963), pp. 16, 19. For the relation between nature as a system of phenomenal objects and nature as used in this essay, see Beck's introduction, pp. xxi-xxii.

17 *Ibid.,* p. 24.

18 *Conflict of the Faculties* (hereafter CF), Mary J. Gregor, trans. (New York: Abaris, 1979), p. 151.

19 Unfortunately, the term 'wahrsagende' is not consistently translated. At first it is translated as "divinatory" (see CF, 141), but at crucial points in Kant's later discussion it is rendered incorrectly as "prophetic" (see CF, 151, 157).

20 *Anthropology from a Pragmatic Point of View,* Mary J. Gregor, trans. (The Hague: Nijhoff, 1974), p. 61.

21 *Metaphysical Elements of Justice* (hereafter MEJ), John Ladd, trans. (Indianapolis: Library of Liberal Arts, 1965), p. 87n.

22 This is what I emphasized in my book, *Dilthey, Philosopher of the Human Studies* (Princeton: University Press, 1975), pp. 19-20, in order to explore the idea of an aesthetic of history in Kant and Dilthey.

23 Arendt, *Lectures on Kant's Political Philosophy,* Ronald Beiner, ed. (Chicago: University Press, 1982), p. 63.

24 *Ibid.,* p. 55.

25 Thomas Seebohm, "Kant's Theory of Revolution," in *The Public Realm,* p. 77.

A CRITIQUE OF PHILOSOPHICAL CONVERSATION

MICHAEL WALZER

I

I am not concerned in this paper with the fact that philosophers talk to one another; there is nothing to worry about in that. Nor am I concerned with the fact that ordinary people sometimes talk about "philosophical" questions—necessity, freedom, justice, the meaning of life and death. I assume that conversations of these sorts are normal and innocent. They go on for a while; they are sometimes interesting and sometimes not; they do not reach any firm conclusions; and at some point they just stop. People get tired or bored, or they want to eat lunch, or they think of something else they have to do or someone else to whom they want to talk. These conversations have no authoritative moments, and they generate no authoritative claims; they lie outside my interests here. I want to examine constructed or designed conversations, where the whole purpose of the construction or design is to produce conversational endings, finished arguments, agreed-upon propositions—conclusions, in short, whose truth value or moral rightness the rest of us will be obliged to acknowledge.

Implicit in the constructed conversation is the value of agreement. There may be stronger foundations for truth or rightness claims, but this is the most obvious one—indeed, how would we know that any other was stronger unless we (or some of us, talking things through) agreed that it was? Even the agreement of one other person, who had begun by disagreeing, makes a strong impression; for we know how hard it is to get two intelligent people fixed on one conclusion. The force of Plato's dialogues derives in part from this knowledge. The dialogues begin with contention and end with a virtually total agreement. At the end, they have hardly any dialogical qualities; they are monologues interrupted by the affirmations of a one-man chorus—here played by Glaucon in the *Republic,* responding to a succession of arguments presented at some length by Socrates:

Certainly.
Of course.
Inevitably.
Yes, that is bound to be so.
It must.
Well, that is certainly a fact.
Yes.
No, tell me.
I entirely agree.[1]

Affirmations of this sort add to the force of a philosophical argument or, at least, they make the argument seem more forceful (why else would philosophers write dialogues?) because the acquiescent interlocutor speaks not only for himself but for the reader as well. Plato has built our agreement into his discourse, and while we can always refuse to agree, we feel a certain pressure to go along, to join the chorus. And yet we know that philosophical dialogues do not really end in this way, with one of the protagonists on his verbal knees, desperately searching for new ways to say yes. Agreements do arise among philosophers and, more generally, across societies; they develop very slowly, over long periods of time; they are always rough and incomplete; and the processes through which they arise are only in part conversational. I shall have more to say about these processes later on; right now I need only note that the conversations they include never really end. Choral affirmations make nothing firm.

Still, there is something engaging in the spectacle of the philosophical hero who triumphs over his opponents by reducing them to helpless agreement (the philosophical equivalent of surrender and captivity in time of war). More give and take in the dialogue would make for greater realism but probably not for greater persuasiveness. If we are not wholly persuaded, it is because of our own experience of argument where, even when we think we have done very well, we do not reach to, we only dream about, Platonic triumphalism. Certain sorts of arguments in the real world do have conventionally fixed endings, and these endings often represent victories of one sort or another; but these are not victories that carry philosophical certainty with them. Consider, for example, the debates that go on in a political assembly (where the right policy is at issue) or the deliberations of a jury (where truth itself is at issue). The debates end at some point with a vote, and the policy that commands majority support is then enforced; but its opponents are unlikely to concede that it is the right policy simply because the majority supports it. They will concede only that it is, for the moment, the policy that it is right to enforce. The deliberations of a jury are closer to philosophical argument, in part because the jurors (unlike the members of the assembly) are supposed to have no direct or material interest in the

183

outcomes they determine. They deliberate until they reach a *verdict,* that is, a true speech, and we enforce the verdict as if it were really true. In fact, it is true only by convention (in virtue of previous agreements). It is not the truth of the verdict which lends authority to the jury system, but the system that makes the verdict authoritative. We know that juries make mistakes even when their deliberations are genuinely disinterested and their conclusions unanimous.[2] And, similarly, we know that philosophers, even when they succeed in persuading their immediate opponents, are often wrong—at least, other philosophers always come along who tell us so.

Plato's mistake, we might say, was to write dialogues which lay claim to versimilitude—with real locations and well-known protagonists—but which do not in fact resemble our own arguments about philosophical (or any other) questions. Anyone who writes a dialogue (rather than a design for a dialogue), anyone who imagines and reports an argument between or among philosophical characters, faces a difficult dilemma. For literary if not philosophical reasons, he must make some claim on his readers' sense of what good talk is really like, and then either his conclusions and choral affirmations will not ring true or he must end inconclusively. There are not many examples of inconclusive endings, but David Hume's *Dialogues Concerning Natural Religion* demonstrate the possibility. Hume's skepticism seems to create a kind of "negative capability"—a readiness to resist philosophical triumph and forgo choral affirmation. The result is that people come away from reading the *Dialogues* unsure who it is among the characters who speaks for Hume.[3] His readers resemble men and women in an actual conversation who disagree the next day about who said what, and with what intent. It is obvious that no sure truths about natural religion have been delivered to them.

Is there some way of delivering truth (or moral rightness) through conversation? Not, I think, through actual and not through literary conversations. Real talk, even if it is only imagined, makes for disagreement as often as for agreement, and neither one is anything more than temporary. Moreover, the motives for the one are as suspect as the motives for the other: if people often disagree only because of interest, pride, or spite, they also often agree only because of weakness, fear, or ignorance. Agreement in actual conversations is no more definitive, no more foundational, than disagreement. What we require for the sake of truth is a hypothetical (which is not the same as a literary) conversation whose protagonists are protected against both bad agreements and bad disagreements. Hence the need for a design, a set of rules which will determine who exactly the protagonists are and what they can say. Working out the design is a major enterprise in contemporary moral and political philosophy. Curiously, once one has a conversational design, it is hardly necessary to have a conversation.

II

There are by now a number of available designs. I want to write about them in general terms, though also with some particular references. I acknowledge in advance that the particular references will not do justice to the complexity and sophistication of the theories involved. It takes a big theory to replace real talk. In one way or another, each of the theories must cope with the chief causes of disagreement—particular interests, relationships, and values; and it must cope with the chief causes of inauthentic or false agreement—inequality and misinformation. Since all these causes occur regularly in the real world, theorists are driven to design an ideal conversational setting and then an ideal speaker and/or an ideal set of speech acts. Consider now the possible forms of this idealism.

The setting obviously cannot be the assembly or the jury room or any other actual social or political environment. All these presuppose some institutional arrangements, but what institutional arrangements are morally preferable is one of the things that the conversation is supposed to decide. What is necessary is a change of venue, as when a jury moves from the neighborhood of a crime to some more distant place, where the jurors will be less exposed to rumor, prejudice, and fear. In this case, however, no known venue is suitable. Hypothetical conversations take place in asocial space. The speakers may be provided with information about a particular society (and a particular historical moment: "a given stage," as Jürgen Habermas says, "in the development of productive forces"[4]), but they cannot *be there,* even hypothetically, lest they gather information for themselves and make mistakes. As with jurors, ideal speakers are denied access to newspapers, magazines, television, other people. Or, rather, only one paper or magazine is allowed, which provides the best available account of whatever the speakers need to know—much as a certain set of facts is stipulated by the opposing attorneys in a courtroom (though these facts do not necessarily add up to "the best available account").

The speakers themselves are also idealized, designed or programmed in such a way that certain words, and not others, will come naturally to their lips. First of all, they are one another's equals, and they must know themselves to be one another's equals; arrogance and pride of place, deference and humility, are rooted out of their minds. This can be accomplished by stipulation: they are to speak as if (with the understanding that) all relationships of subordination have been abolished. Conversational equality reflects a hypothetical social equality (but is not the conversation supposed to produce, among other things, an argument for or against social equality?). Alternatively, the equality of speakers can be accomplished without the "as if," by dropping the Rawlsian "veil of ignorance" and denying them any knowledge of their own standing in the actually existing hierarchy of class and status. They are then equally ignorant of

185

their sociological place and of the feelings that it engenders.[5] Or equality can be given effect later on, as we will see, by policing what they can say once the conversation begins.

Second, the speakers are fully and identically informed about the real world—about what Habermas calls "the limiting conditions and functional imperatives of their society."[6] One body of knowledge, uniform and uncontroverted, is possessed in common by all speakers; now they are equally knowledgeable; they share a sociology, perhaps also a cosmology.

Third, they are set free from their own particular interests and values. This is the most complex of the idealizations, and its precise form varies with the philosophical goal of the hypothetical conversation. In Rawls's model, the ideal speakers know that they have interests and values of their own and that they will want to assert them, but they do not know anything at all about the content of these interests and values. Their conversations will therefore produce a world safe for individual men and women who plan a life of self-assertion, who intend, that is, to maximize their own interests and values, whatever these are. In Habermas's model, by contrast, the ideal speakers have full self-knowledge but are internally committed to assert only those interests and values which can be universalized; all others are somehow repressed. Their conversations will produce something more like a sense of the general interest or the common good and then a set of principles for a community of cooperating citizens. The contrast suggests the dominance of design over discourse. "One extracts from the ideal speech situation," writes Seyla Benhabib of the Habermasian model, "what one has . . . put into it."[7] The case is the same with the original position.

Whatever one does not "put into" the speakers one must put into their speech. Before anyone says anything, the speech act must be described so as to fix limits on what can be said. Habermas argues for "unconstrained communication," but he means only (!) to exclude the constraints of force and fraud, of deference, fear, flattery, and ignorance. His speakers have equal rights to initiate the conversation and to resume it; to assert, recommend, and explain their own positions; and to challenge the positions of other speakers. But the universalization requirement is a powerful constraint. Habermas insists that it is not more than the mutually understood requirement of actual speech—"demanding," indeed, but also "pre-theoretical."[8] In fact, universalization has a theoretical purpose, which stands in sharp contrast to the purpose of many actual conversations: it is intended to rule out bargaining and compromise (the negotiation of particular interests) and to press the speakers toward a preordained harmony. Justice is not, on Habermas's view, a negotiated settlement, a *modus vivendi*, fair to all its egoistic and rational subjects. It is a common life, the terms of which are fixed by the general will of a body of citizens—"what all can will in agreement to be a universal norm."[9] Habermas defends a position that is very much like Rousseau's, though Rousseau wisely renounced the hope that one could reach that position conversationally. We discover the general will, he wrote, if, when the people deliberate, the citizens "have no communication one with another."[10] But it probably does not make much difference whether there are no speech acts at all (but only internal reflection on the common good) or none but universalizing speech acts.

Bruce Ackerman's account of "liberal dialogue," by contrast, calls for external restraint rather than an internal commitment to universalization. Any claims his speakers make for the precedence of their own interests or the superiority of their own values are simply disallowed, stricken from the conversational record. If we control speech from the outside, he argues, then it will not be necessary to idealize the speakers or even the speech acts. The participants in his dialogues are real people (or better, they are typical people, with names like Democrat, Elitist, Advantaged, Disadvantaged, and so on—Ackerman's scripts are allegorical dramas), and they talk, more or less, the way real people talk. But their conversation is patrolled by a policewoman (whose name is Commander).[11] This is supposed to make the actual words of the speakers and their exchanges with one another more important than they are for Rawls or Habermas, who are focused on design rather than exchange. If one knows the mandate of the policewoman, however, and if one accepts the reasons for the mandate, it is easy to write the conversational scripts, just as Ackerman does. The scripts are merely illustrative, and the argument they illustrate is probably best defended monologically. But Ackerman's idea of a patrolled conversation points to an important fact about all these philosophical efforts: they are armed, one way or another, against the indeterminacy of natural conversation. The talk proceeds by design to a designated end. Agreement at the end is certain, and once it is reached it is equally certain, so long as the design is in place, that it will be sustained (or, if the conversation is resumed, that it will be reproduced). New speakers will not have much more to say than "That sounds right," or "I can think of no objections," or "I entirely agree." In an Ackermanian dialogue, the speakers might try to object, but their objections will regularly be disallowed by the Commander, and so the end will be, as it often is in Ackerman's scripts, "(silence)."[12]

III

I said earlier that the conversational project presupposes the value of agreement; it also presupposes the possibility of agreement. Acquiescence is not enough, nor a readiness to go along, make no trouble, think about other things. What is required is rational and explicit agreement; Ackerman's "silence" is an acknowledgment of philosophical defeat and so stands in for full consent to the victor's position. Rawls guarantees agreement with his veil of ignorance, which separates the speakers from any reasons they might have for disagreeing. The policewoman in Ackerman's account plays an analogous role. But Habermas takes a larger risk and makes a more radical assumption. He apparently believes that conversation subject to the universalization constraint will produce among the speakers what Steven Lukes calls "an endogenous change of preferences . . . such that preferences, tastes, values, ideals, plans of life, etc., will to some large degree (to what degree?) be unified and no longer conflict."[13] But what possible reason do we have for joining in this belief? Perhaps Habermas also thinks that there are knock-down arguments (about distributive justice, for example) just waiting to be made. Or perhaps he thinks that such arguments have already been made but not in ideal conditions, and so they have been denied their proper response, that is, the Platonic chorus of affirmation. Both these views are highly unlikely.

We can best see the unlikelihood of philosophical agreement by consulting what I have already described as the actual and inconclusive conversations of living (rather than hypothetical) philosophers. For these conversations bear some resemblance to Habermas's ideal speech: the participants think of themselves as rough equals, though some of them speak with greater authority and are listened to with greater respect than others; they share a body of information, though always with marginal disagreements; and they aim fairly steadily, except for a few renegades, at universalization. Yet they reach no agreement among themselves; they produce again and again the philosophical equivalents of hung juries. Some philosophers, earnestly carrying on an internal dialogue, reach agreement within themselves, but that does not have the weight of an external consensus. The "others" are always a problem.

Why are they a problem? I suppose that the reasons can always be met (or avoided) by further idealization. Among philosophers, for example, there is the desire to carve out one's own position, to find the way by oneself, to make an original argument.[14] So each speaker criticizes, amends, or rejects the claims of the previous speaker: What would be the point of agreeing? Perhaps Rawls's veil would conceal from the speakers this intensely felt interest in notice and praise; and then they might meekly join the chorus of support for the most persuasive speech. Habermas insists that speakers must always be bound by the better argument—the tightest constraint of all so long as we can recognize the better argument. But most speakers quite honestly think that their own arguments are the better ones. Sometimes they might acknowledge that they are not making the better argument then and there: so the conversation ends or one of the speakers walks out (like Demea in Hume's *Dialogues,* who "did not at all relish the latter part of the discourse; and . . . took occasion, soon after, on some pretense or other, to leave the company").[15] But such people are commonly saved by the brilliant afterthought, "I should have said . . ."—and that, they tell themselves, would have turned the argument around. How can it ever be certain that the better argument in any particular conversation is the best possible argument? It rarely happens among philosophers, but it is always possible to agree too soon.

Perhaps none of this matters; ideal speech is a thought experiment, and we can abstract from all human infirmities. If conversation itself serves to bring out our infirmities, we can abstract from that, too. Thus Rawls, who acknowledges that, for his purposes, no more than one speaker is necessary. What we hear from behind the veil of ignorance is really a philosophical soliloquy.[16] The argument does not depend on any exchange of views; if we in turn step behind the veil we will simply agree.[17]

But Ackerman claims to be describing the way liberals ought to talk to one another. And Habermas's conception of ideal speech is meant to be "compatible with a democratic self-understanding." This is the way citizens would talk to one another, he insists, in a fully realized democracy. So ideal speech reaches back toward actual speech.[18] But what is the strength and extent of its reach? What do we know about actual liberal and democratic speech?

The first thing we know, surely, is that agreement is less likely among liberals and democrats than among the subjects of a king, say, or a military dictator or an ideological or theocratic vanguard. That is why Ackerman's policewoman is necessary; she is a benevolent stand-in for authoritarian censors, though what she enforces is not deference to the ruler but universal deference—toleration for all (tolerant) ways of life. She presses the mass of diverse and discordant speakers toward a special sort of agreement: they must agree to disagree about conceptions of the good. But that agreement simply suspends the argument, and sometimes at least it is necessary to reach a conclusion. What we know about liberal and democratic conclusions is that they are unpredictable and inconclusive. They reflect the indeterminacy of any nonideal and unpatrolled (natural) conversation, in which rhetorical skill, or passionate eloquence, or insidious intensity may carry the day (but only the day). Or, it may be that none of these has any effect at all; the give and take of the conversation, the constant interruptions of one speaker by another, make it impossible for anyone to develop a persuasive argument, and people end where they began, voting their interests or defending an entrenched ideological position.

As Plato's dialogues suggest, the philosopher requires a largely passive interlocutor if he is to make a coherent argument. And since coherent arguments are important in democracies, too (though Plato did not think so), while democratic interlocutors are rarely passive, political debate among citizens cannot always take conversational forms. "Conversation," Emerson wrote, "is a game of circles."[19] But there are times when we need to listen to a sustained argument, a linear discourse. Then what is necessary is a certain freedom from interlocution, a suspension of dialogue, so that someone can make a speech, deliver a lecture, preach a sermon (or write a book). All these are standard forms of liberal and democratic communication—just as whispering in the ear of the prince is standard in royal courts. The speaker in front of (not in the midst of) his audience, speaking to (not with) the people, making a case: this picture is central to any plausible account of democratic decision making. The speech is public, and speakers take responsibility for what they say; listeners are invited to remember what they say and to hold them responsible. Who, by contrast, is responsible for the outcome of an ideal conversation? The author or designer, I suppose, who seeks however to implicate the rest of us. If we all agree, then there is no one who can be held responsible later on. But democratic politics in all its versions, ancient and modern, depends on "holdings" of just this sort.

If liberalism and democracy sometimes require freedom from interlocution so that arguments can be made, they also require radical subjection, so that arguments (and speakers) can be tested. Hence the importance of judicial cross-examinations, congressional hearings, parliamentary question periods, press conferences, and so on. None of these is conversational in style. They are governed by more or less strict conventions that have little in common with the principles of Habermasian ideal speech. One or more people ask questions; one person, standing alone, must answer the questions—though he can always answer evasively or claim one of the conventional exceptions: ignorance, self-incrimination, the requirements of national security. All answers and refusals to answer are subject to popular judgment.

Democratic citizens speak, listen, and ask questions; they play different roles on different occasions—not all roles together on a single occasion. We might think of communication in a democracy the way Aristotle thinks of citizenship: ruling and being ruled, speaking and listening, in turn. Ideal speech, by contrast, is more like Rousseau's understanding of citizenship, where the citizens "give the law to themselves," all of them ruling, all of them being ruled, simultaneously. I do not mean that ideal speakers all speak at once—though that is not impossible if they are reciting the same soliloquy. They speak and listen on the same occasion and in a setting that, in principle at least, rules out both the lecture and the cross-examination. We can, of course, imagine a dialogue across occasions, in which citizens take their Aristotelian turns: I write a book, you write a critique of the book, I write a response to the critique, you write a reply to the response. Let us assume an egalitarian society: there is no relation of subordination or dependency between us. And let us assume that we are honest writers, trying as best we can to get at the truth. It is still an open question whether the exchange will bring us closer together or drive us into polar opposition. Perhaps we will exchange concessions and draw closer—to one another, not necessarily to the truth. Perhaps we will defend, with growing irritation, our starting points.

In either case, our decisions will be at least partly strategic: democratic speech, in the turn-taking sense, has an adversarial quality; we take turns in front of an audience whose support is crucial to both of us. We seek popular support because it seems to confirm our account of the truth and—this is at least equally important—because it serves to make our account effective in the world.

Ideal speech abstracts from all this, creating thereby a more intimate conversation, a political version, perhaps, of Martin Buber's I-Thou dialogue. Something like this is suggested by Hans-Georg Gadamer, a defender of actual rather than ideal speech, whose defense, however, requires a fairly radical idealization:

> Coming to an understanding in conversation presupposes that the partners . . . try to allow for the validity of what is alien and contrary to themselves. If this happens on a reciprocal basis and each of the partners, while holding to his own ground simultaneously weighs the counter-arguments, they can ultimately achieve a common language and a common judgment in an imperceptible and non-arbitrary transfer of viewpoints. (We call this an exchange of opinions.)[20]

The parenthetical remark has a certain comic quality; we smile because we know that an "exchange" of the sort Gadamer describes may well leave neither partner any the wiser; also that many conversational partnerships, with the best will in the world, will not reach even this far. In any case, the resolute avoidance of antagonism which Gadamer defends hardly reflects a "democratic self-understanding." It does not usefully account for what happens or even for what might (ideally) happen in the political arena where parties and movements, not only individual speakers, confront one another. Gadamer is describing something closer to deliberation than debate, and he simply assumes the success of the deliberative encounter.[21]

IV

Common language and judgment, agreements and understandings, strong and extensive meetings of minds, are nonetheless necessary to any human society. It is not the case, obviously, that people agree on this or that policy, but they must agree at a deeper level on the rough contours of a way of life and a view of the world. Some things they must understand together or else their disagreements will be incoherent and their arguments impossible. They can have no politics unless they also have what political scientists call a "consensus" on institutional arrangements and lines of authority. They cannot sustain a common life without a set of shared conceptions about the subjects of that life—themselves—and their character, interests, and aspirations. But conversation is only one among many features of the complex social process that produces consensus and shared understandings. That process includes political struggle (settled, at best, by the force of numbers, not arguments), negotiation and compromise, law making and law enforcement, socialization in families and schools, economic transformations, cultural creativity of all sorts. The understandings that come to be shared will never have been rationally defended by a single speaker who managed to see them whole. Nor do they arise in the course of a debate among many speakers who contribute different pieces of the whole, and who argue until a conclusion is reached incorporating all the pieces. Nothing like that: for no conclusion is imaginable without authority, conflict, and coercion (socialization, for example, is always coercive). And yet the conclusions have some sort of binding force, which derives from the common life that is sustained on the basis they provide.

Ideal speech might be conceived as a way of testing these conclusions, but I am not sure that they are of a sort that can readily be tested. Consider, for example, one of our own deepest understandings: our conception of a human life (social, not biological) as a career, a project, an individual undertaking. The idea of a "life plan" is crucial to Rawls's theory of justice.[22] But that is not an idea that can be confirmed or disconfirmed in the original position. Rawls simply assumes that individuals plan their lives, and without that assumption he could not begin to tell us what goes on, what is thought and said and agreed to, by his ideal speakers as they maximize their opportunities and minimize their risks. The idea of a career is, so to speak, pre-original. We know that it has a history, but in the original position it is simply given. How could it ever be the subject of a rational agreement? We would have to imagine human beings who knew nothing at all, literally nothing, about the shape of a human life. And then on what basis would they decide to have careers rather than, say, inherited stations or a succession of spontaneous acts? The actual process through which the idea of a career came to be central to our self-understanding has its beginning in the breakup of traditional communities; it is the product of force and fraud as much as of philosophical argument. And yet, today, we can hardly begin a philosophical argument about social arrangements or theories of justice without assuming the existence of individuals who plan their lives—and who have a right to plan their lives—in advance of living them.

The case is the same with the external conditions of human existence as with its conceptual shape. Men and women who find themselves in the original position or the ideal speech situation will not be able to argue coherently with one another unless they share some understanding of what the world is like and where they are within it. How does their economy work? What are the constraints of scarcity in their particular time and place? What are their political options? What opportunities are offered, what choices are posed, by the current state of science and technology? These are some of the questions covered by Habermas's claim that, for any effort to construct a society or morality through discourse, there are "limiting conditions" and "functional imperatives" that must be taken into account. If the speakers start by disagreeing about the social and economic parameters within which the meaning of justice, say, is to be worked out, they are unlikely to reach an agreement, later on, about what justice means. Hence, any philosopher who wants to design an ideal conversation will have to assume the existence of, perhaps he will have to specify, a single body of knowledge: the best available social scientific information, certified, I suppose, by the most authoritative economists, psychologists, political scientists, and so on.[23] But how is such knowledge generated? By what means does it come into the philosopher's hands?

The production and delivery of knowledge is, again, a complex social process. Conversation certainly plays a part in that process; we like to imagine that it plays the largest part. In the community of scholars, good talk is all-important; argument is the essential form of scholarly communion. Maybe so; but scholarly communion is not the whole of knowledge production. No one who has sat on a university committee, helped to edit a scholarly journal, fought with colleagues over the content of the curriculum, or reviewed proposals for funding research, will doubt the centrality of politics even in the academy. Here, too, negotiation and compromise precede agreement; here, too, authority has its prerogatives, pressure can be brought to bear, patterns of dominance emerge; here, too, there are interests at work besides the interest in truth. Michel Foucault, who is wrong about many things, is surely right to argue for the symbiosis of power and knowledge.[24] The constitution of professional authority and the development of scientific disciplines go hand in hand.

None of this, obviously, produces definitive results, but knowledge production does have *results*. In some academic fields, some of the time, there is a professional establishment and a reigning wisdom (sometimes the reign is brief). In other fields, in other times, there is a determinate set of competing doctrines, each with its expert advocates who, since they cannot reign, reluctantly share power. The competition will always be encompassed within a larger agreement that establishes the boundaries of power sharing. So men and women in the original position or the ideal speech situation will be told, for example, that there are systematic connections between the economy and the political order. But what will they be told about the nature of the connections? That capitalist markets make for a liberal and democratic politics? Or that a really democratic politics is incompatible with market-generated inequalities? Each of these claims is urged with considerable force by rival authorities, who assemble much the same sort of historical and sociological evidence. They are in fact working within a single "paradigm." Ideal speakers will hardly be able to test the paradigm— they have to be given *some* authoritative view of the politics/economics relation.

193

And it is not clear that they could resolve the debate about markets and democracy (though they could certainly join it) unless they were also presented with a single set of historical and sociological "facts." But whoever made them such a present would thereby determine the resolution of the debate, and that resolution would determine, in turn, the shape of whatever agreement they reached about, say, distributive justice.

The pre-original idea of a career goes a long way toward explaining Rawlsian outcomes. In much the same way, the pre-ideal theory of society (whatever it is) will go a long way toward explaining Habermasian outcomes. Once again, the end of philosophical conversation depends on its beginnings. To say this is not to deny the value of conversation, but only the value of conversational design; it requires us to repudiate the dream of endings that are anything like full stops. We will never be brought to the point where the only thing we can do is to play the part of the Platonic chorus. Design cannot help us, since all its elements, formal and substantive, necessarily precede hypothetical speech; they have to be worked out (and are worked out) independently of any ideal procedure. We can and should talk about the elements; they have an immediate importance; they raise deep questions about freedom and equality and the nature of a human life and the structure of social arrangements. But this is real talk, not hypothetical talk, not ideal speech, not philosophical soliloquy. Hypothetical talk can only begin when real talk has been concluded, when we know what free speech is and in what way ideal speakers are one another's equals and what kind of a life they will have and how their social arrangements work. But real speech is always inconclusive; it has no authoritative moments. I began by saying that I was not interested in speech of this sort. It may be the case, however, that nothing else is more interesting.

But if ideal speech cannot serve as a test of received ideas, perhaps it can serve as a test of the processes (including the real talk) through which such ideas are generated. Should we aim, for example, at a more open debate and a more egalitarian politics? Probably we should, but the reasons for doing so precede ideal speech rather than emerge from it; the freedom and equality of all speakers is the first assumption of Rawls, Habermas, Ackerman, and, so far as I know, of every other philosopher who has written along similar lines.[25] At the same time, all these writers also assume the existence of scientific authorities, policewomen, and speech designers like themselves—who must also have their real life counterparts. Exactly what the role of such people should be is something we are likely to disagree about and to go on arguing about for as long as we argue about anything at all. And that means that there is no safe and sure conversational design that will protect us against bad agreements and bad disagreements. The continuing argument provides our only protection.

Real talk is the conscious and critical part of the processes that generate our received ideas and reigning theories—reflection become articulate. Arguing with one another, we interpret, revise, elaborate, and also call into question the paradigms that shape our thinking. So we arrive at some conception of a just society (say) through a conversation that is constrained, indeed, by the ordinary constraints of everyday life: the pressure of time, the structure of authority, the discipline of parties and movements, the patterns of socialization and education, the established procedures of institutional life. Without any constraints at all, conversation would never produce even those conventional (and temporary) stops which we call decisions or verdicts; because of the constraints, every stopping point will appear, to some of the speakers, arbitrary and imposed. They will seek to renew the conversation and, despite the constraints, will often succeed in doing so. In another sense, however, these same conversations are radically unconstrained, for while there may be ideas that are taken for granted by all the speakers, there are no stipulated ideas, none that has to be taken for granted if the conversation is to proceed (nor are the constraints taken for granted). There is no design. Real talk is unstable and restless, hence it is ultimately more radical than ideal speech. It reaches to reasons and arguments that none of its participants can anticipate, hence to reasons and arguments undreamt of (for better and for worse) by our philosophers.

Institute for Advanced Study

NOTES

1 *The Republic,* F. M. Cornford, trans. (New York: Oxford, 1945), pp. 312-315 (585c-588a).

2 At the same time, we support the jury system, because we believe that disinterested jurors are more likely to get at the truth than anyone else. So why not make this a model for all truth-seeking and even for all right-seeking inquiries? The replacement of political debate with an idealized version of judicial deliberation is in fact the goal of a number of contemporary philosophers.

3 See Henry David Aiken's "Introduction" to Hume, *Dialogues Concerning Natural Religion* (New York: Hafner, 1951), pp. vii-xvii. On "negative capability," see *The Letters of John Keats,* M. B. Forman, ed. (London: Oxford, 1952 [4th edition]), p. 71.

4 Habermas, *Legitimation Crisis,* Thomas McCarthy, trans. (Boston: Beacon, 1975), p. 113.

5 Rawls, *A Theory of Justice* (Cambridge: Harvard, 1971), pp. 136-142.

6 *Legitimation Crisis,* p. 113.

7 *Critique, Norm, and Utopia: A Study of the Foundations of Critical Theory* (New York: Columbia, 1986), pp. 292–293.

8 Habermas, "A Reply to My Critics," in *Habermas: Critical Debates,* John B. Thompson and David Held, eds. (Cambridge: MIT, 1982), pp. 254-255.

9 This is Thomas McCarthy's formula, accepted by Habermas in "Reply," p. 257.

10 *Social Contract,* bk. II, ch. 3.

11 Ackerman, *Social Justice in the Liberal State* (New Haven: Yale, 1980), p. 24.

12 See, for example, *Social Justice*, p. 169.

13 Lukes, "Of Gods and Demons: Habermas and Practical Reason," in *Critical Debates*, p. 144.

14 Cf. Descartes's account of his desire "to build on a foundation which is wholly my own." *Discourse on Method*, F. E. Sutcliffe, trans. (Harmondsworth: Penguin, 1968), p. 38.

15 *Dialogues*, p. 81.

16 "Therefore we can view the choice in the original position from the standpoint of one person selected at random." *A Theory of Justice*, p. 139.

17 Perhaps that is why Rawlsian theory appeals so much to law professors, who imagine themselves writing briefs that judges, recognizing their impartial wisdom, will instantly accept (and enforce).

18 *Social Justice*, ch. 1; Benhabib, p. 283, describing Habermas's program.

19 Ralph Waldo Emerson, "Circles," in *Complete Essays and Other Writings*, Brooks Atkinson, ed. (New York: Modern Library, 1940), p. 284.

20 Quoted in Georgia Warnke, *Gadamer: Hermeneutics, Tradition, and Reason* (Stanford: University Press, 1987), p. 101.

21 For a description of what "democratic talk" is like, see Benjamin Barber, *Strong Democracy: Participatory Politics for a New Age* (Berkeley: California UP, 1984), pp. 173-198.

22 *A Theory of Justice*, pp. 92–93, 407-416.

23 "It is taken for granted," writes Rawls, that the persons in the original position "know the general facts about human society. They understand political affairs and the principles of economic theory; they know the basis of social organization and the laws of human psychology." *A Theory of Justice*, p. 137.

24 See Foucault, *Power/Knowledge: Selected Interviews and Other Writings, 1972-1977*, Colin Gordon, ed. (New York: Pantheon, 1980).

25 For example: Agnes Heller, *Beyond Justice* (New York: Blackwell, 1987), ch. 5.

RAWLS, HABERMAS, AND REAL TALK: A REPLY TO WALZER*

GEORGIA WARNKE

In "A Critique of Philosophical Conversation," Michael Walzer criticizes an approach to political theory which relies on what he calls constructed or designed conversations. The point of such conversations, he claims, is the foundational one of justifying claims to truth and rightness by showing them to be the conclusions of a rationally motivated consensus. Legitimate norms and beliefs, in other words, are those which all would agree to under ideal conditions precluding both disagreement and the use of fear or force to achieve agreement. Hence, John Rawls drops a veil of ignorance in front of the parties to his original position; they are conceived of as having no knowledge of their particular goals or circumstances and thus as having no reason to disagree over the principles of justice appropriate to the basic structure of society. Jürgen Habermas constructs an ideal speech situation specifying the rules and relations that would have to hold between participants to a conversation if the consensus achieved were to be won through the rational force of the better argument alone. Finally, Bruce Ackerman employs the device of a benevolent policewoman who enforces strict political neutrality on questions of morality by monitoring "liberal" conversation so that it cannot encompass those ultimate goals and values on which we disagree.

Walzer's general objection to these strategies is that they abstract from the actual political, historical, and social context in which norms and principles are conceived of, assessed, and put into practice. In the first place, he argues, such shared understandings are not the result of conversation alone, but also of political struggle, negotiation, economic transformation, cultural creativity, and so on. Moreover, these historical processes lead to the very social and political understandings on which constructed conversations themselves rely for the principles of their own design. The idea of rational life-plans to which Rawls refers, for example, is not one his original position can validate, but is rather simply presupposed as a crucial factor in choosing principles of justice. Furthermore, Rawls, Habermas, and Ackerman all presuppose the equality of the speakers involved in the constructed conversations; surely, however, the moral or political belief that speakers ought to be considered equal is one of the beliefs the conversations are intended to justify. Finally, according to Walzer, in abstracting from the actual social and political conditions that affect the possibility of agreement over norms and beliefs, constructed conversations also abstract from any practical force a consensus of those involved might have. "Who," he asks, "is responsible for the outcome of an ideal conversation?" If the answer is "the author or designer who seeks to implicate the rest of us," then "there is no one who can be held responsible later on. But democratic politics in all its versions . . . depends on holdings of just this sort."[1]

These criticisms of constructed conversations, considered as philosophical fictions for grounding norms and beliefs, seem to me well-taken, but I am not sure this is the only way of understanding them. I want to begin by looking briefly at Rawls's recent restatements of his position, since they seem to me to have already incorporated some recognition of the problems with which Walzer is concerned. I shall then turn to Habermas's formulation of a communicative ethics which also seems to me to have a different intention than the one Walzer attributes to it. I shall argue that Walzer and Rawls share roughly the same interpretive approach to political theory and that Habermas's concern is the limits of interpretation. The question confronting communicative ethics is whether it can answer this concern while avoiding the pitfalls of constructed conversations which Walzer has located.

According to one interpretation of *A Theory of Justice,* the consensus that emerges in the original position among the parties behind the veil of ignorance is meant as a foundational consensus; it is the agreement about principles of justice to which all rational agents would come under similar conditions and, hence, the principles of justice are principles for any community. But *A Theory of Justice* is open to another interpretation as well, according to which it is meant *not* to uncover an unconditioned standpoint for assessing principles of justice but, instead, to articulate a conception of justice which conforms to *our* deepest moral and political convictions. This account of the task of a theory of justice seems to resemble the one Walzer himself adopts in his *Spheres of Justice.* There he claims that the question of the justice of distributive practices within a society is the question of whether or not these practices are faithful to the understandings members of the political community share about the different social goods to be distributed. Political philosophy therefore has the task of interpreting what these social understandings are. In his essay, "Kantian Constructivism in Moral Theory," Rawls argues along similar lines that the point of political philosophy is "to articulate and to make explicit those shared notions and principles thought to be already latent in common sense."[2] Indeed, just as Walzer criticizes foundationalist attempts in political theory, Rawls claims that:

What justifies a conception of justice is not its being true to an order antecedent to and given to us, but its congruence with our deeper understanding
of ourselves and our aspirations and our realization that, given our history and
the traditions embedded in our public life, it is the most reasonable doctrine
for us.[3]

These remarks seem in large measure to obviate Walzer's objection to the idea
of a constructed conversation in Rawls's theory. In the first place, as Rawls
himself regards the original position, it is not meant to serve as an asocial space
for conceiving of the basic structure of society; rather, it is meant as "a device
of representation"; that is, it is supposed to articulate and clarify what for us are
already our own deep understandings and fundamental convictions.[4] Second,
then, the circularity Walzer recognizes in the idea of a constructed conversation
has less significance. The fact that the original position presupposes a specific
notion of rational life planning or of equality is less important because, as a
device for representing our deep understandings, the original position is meant to
be dependent on them. Finally, if Rawls's constructed conversation is explicitly
derived from our social understandings, then we can retain Walzer's insistence
that democratic politics depends upon holding those involved, rather than the
political theorist, responsible for political practices and social arrangements. The
point of Rawls's theory of justice can be viewed as similar to that of Walzer's
theory of complex equality: to help clarify to the political culture to which both
belong *what* its deepest convictions and hence its responsibilities are.

But the methodological convergence here between Rawls and Walzer seems to
raise a problem; although Rawls and Walzer now seem to agree on what one
might call a hermeneutic approach to political theory, their *substantive* accounts
of the deep convictions and responsibilities of democratic political culture still
radically differ. Rawls begins with a conception of moral persons with capacities
both for a conception of the good and for a sense of justice. The principles of
justice follow from the highest-order interests in exercising these capacities and
from a higher-order interest in forming and pursuing a determinate conception of
the good.[5] As a result, there are two such principles:

(1) Each person has an equal right to a fully adequate scheme of equal basic
liberties which is compatible with a similar scheme of liberties for all.
(2) Social and economic inequalities are to satisfy two conditions. First, they
must be attached to offices and positions open to all under conditions of fair
equality of opportunity; and second, they must be to the greatest benefit of the
least advantaged members of society.[6]

For Walzer, however, freedom does not consist solely in the right "to form, to revise and rationally to pursue a conception of the good''[7] consistent with a similar right on the part of all others; nor does equality require the partial compensation for unequal talents and abilities which Rawls writes into his second principle. Instead, freedom involves the possibility of participating in the common life of a community, a possibility, therefore, which must be actively supported by whatever governmental means necessary. For its part, equality means that the significance of inequalities in talent and abilities is made secondary to what Charles Taylor calls the ''balance of mutual indebtedness'' in sustaining this community and its way or ways of life.[8] Hence, rather than delineate two principles of justice, Walzer explores the ways in which various social goods would have to be distributed to encourage and sustain membership and participation in a community.

But if Rawls and Walzer both now see themselves as interpreters of our way of life and its shared understandings, what are we to make of these substantive differences in what they take those understandings to be? Walzer has distinguished deep and inclusive accounts of social meaning from shallow and partisan ones,[9] but the problem here seems to be that of deciding between equally deep and inclusive accounts. Both interpretations are clearly rooted in our moral and political traditions, in Kantian ideas of autonomy, on the one hand, and in Hegelian notions of community, on the other; hence, it seems implausible to insist that one or the other analysis conforms to what we really mean or to our truly deepest understandings.

This substantive disagreement between Rawls and Walzer may, in fact, indicate one point of political conversation. In *Spheres of Justice,* Walzer undertakes a defense of a communitarian position in light of a criticism of the Kantian strategy that Rawls pursues in *A Theory of Justice.* In recent essays, Rawls has tried to interpret his own theory so that the conception of justice it articulates can also withstand communitarian objections. These approaches suggest that, if we were simply to adopt one of these alternative liberal or communitarian interpretations over the other as the proper account of our political understandings, the strength of each might be diminished. The cogency of each position, in other words, seems to depend upon the extent to which it has appropriated what it takes to be the insights of the other and protected itself against what it takes to be the other's mistakes. In order to discover what errors and insights are possible, however, each must continually engage the other in conversation.

One might argue, then, in general, that political traditions survive and develop because they are not monolithic, because they include diverse self-interpretations and self-conceptions, and because these opposed self-understandings can educate one another. Traditions may acquire their power precisely through the interplay of competing interpretations in which the limits and merits of each can appear. In assessing the view of our political heritage offered by either Rawls or Walzer, then the crucial question might not be which has captured the essence of our self-understanding; it might rather be whether either has exhausted it and how we might broaden our view of ourselves to include both the image of individual life planners and that of participatory citizens. That is, perhaps we should accept both (and even others) as part of a multifaceted tradition and extend the practical implications of each to incorporate what we have learned in conversation with the others.

This view of political conversation seems close to Walzer's own conception of "real talk,"[10] but it also raises an obvious problem, as Walzer himself indicates: Why should we start with the premise that political conversation can be educational? Why not begin with the evident facts of ideological distortion and power relations in political dialogue? There are certainly political positions and historical perspectives from which we should not learn as well as social groups whose voices we have not always heard. Such cases seem to point to the need for an account of the potentials for constraining and perverting the process of self–educational dialogue itself.

At least this is Habermas's claim. In his debate with Gadamer, he argues that a strictly interpretive approach to social inquiry runs the risk of a "linguistic idealism," in other words, that it can elucidate the content of a social consensus but is incapable of uncovering the social relations of power and the economic conditions affecting it. What is required, he claims, is thus a critical social theory which can combine an interpretive access to social meanings with an explanatory analysis of causes and conditions. As he writes:

> A hermeneutics that is critically enlightened about itself and which differentiates between insight and delusion incorporates meta-hermeneutic knowledge of the conditions of the possibility of systematically distorted communication. It connects understanding to the principle of rational discourse according to which truth would be guaranteed only by that consensus which was achieved under idealized conditions of unlimited communication, free from domination and which could be maintained over time.[11]

Habermas's reference here to idealized conditions as well as his more famous—or infamous—reference to an ideal speech situation are the ideas that lead Walzer to amalgamate his political method with the foundationalist account of Rawls's approach in *A Theory of Justice*. Further consideration of Habermas's approach, however, indicates that it is rather different. In recent works, he has spoken neither of idealized conditions nor of an ideal speech situation, but rather of the "idealizing"[12] and "partly counterfactual presuppositions"[13] that participants in argument actually make. In Habermas's view, Rawls's recourse to the fiction of the original position is, in fact, unnecessary because, in engaging in argumentations in which we are concerned to come to an understanding with others over disputed truth claims, practices, or norms of action, we necessarily make certain pragmatic presuppositions that have a normative content. Participants in argument cannot avoid presupposing that the structure of their communication both excludes all force other than that of the better argument and neutralizes all motives other than the cooperative search for truth. These presuppositions may be counterfactual; still, the cost of giving them up is what Habermas, following Apel, calls a performative contradiction. If one is to convince others through argument that discourse does not have this anticipatory structure, one has nonetheless to rely on it in making one's claim. That is, one has to suppose that this is the conclusion which could be reached with others in a cooperative search for truth because it reflects the force of the better argument.

The principle of communicative ethics follows from this analysis. It states that only those social norms and principles can claim validity which could find acceptance by all those concerned as participants in a practical discourse. Walzer criticizes Habermas for restricting participants in discourse to the expression of universalizable interests; but this restriction is not meant to issue from an artificial design. Habermas's point is rather that the structure of moral-practical argumentation itself constrains all who engage in it to a kind of ideal role taking: it presupposes an ability on the part of all participants to take the place of the others and to understand the perspective they bring to the moral conflict at hand. Through discourse, all have to be convinced that each person could give well-founded assent to a proposed principle or practice from her own perspective.[14] Again, the constraint at issue here is obviously as often violated as it is upheld. But Habermas's claim is that the normative implications of the idealizing premises we always already make in arguments themselves provide a standard for assessing the agreements we come to in real talk.

Of course, even if one understands ideal discourse not as an artificial construct but as a set of normative premises arising out of actual argumentation, the kinds of questions Walzer poses with regard to it remain important. Is the force of the better argument always clear, and on what grounds? How do we get from the power of reasons to political change? Does any appropriate application of the results of argument require capacities for judgment which cannot themselves be validated? The aim of these remarks has not been to deny the differences in the answers Rawls, Habermas, and Walzer might give to such questions. Still, these differences seem to be on a level other than that involving the distinction between constructed conversations and real talk. All seem to agree that we need no longer look for the ultimate foundations of our norms and beliefs; but in arguing over the meaning of our traditions and in exploring the standards embedded in our discourse we may find a way of providing some guarantee for the rationality of our political conversation without eliminating the diverse perspectives that make it possible.

Yale University

NOTES

* Michael Walzer, "A Critique of Philosophical Conversation," included in this volume.

1 *Ibid.*

2 John Rawls, "Kantian Constructivism in Moral Theory," *Journal of Philosophy*, LXXVII, 9 (September 1980), p. 518.

3 *Ibid.*

4 Rawls, "Justice as Fairness: Political not Metaphysical," *Philosophy and Public Affairs*, XIV, 3 (Summer 1985), pp. 237–238.

5 See "Kantian Constructivism in Moral Theory."

6 Rawls, "The Basic Liberties and Their Priority," in *Liberty, Equality and Law*, Sterling M. McMurrin, ed. (Salt Lake City: Utah UP, 1987), p. 5.

7 "Kantian Constructivism in Moral Theory," p. 518.

8 Charles Taylor, "The Nature and Scope of Distributive Justice," in his *Philosophical Papers*, vol. 2, *Philosophy and The Human Sciences* (New York: Cambridge, 1985), pp. 299-300.

9 "Spheres of Justice: An Exchange," *The New York Review of Books* (July 21, 1983), p. 43.

10 "A Critique of Philosophical Conversation."

11 Habermas, "The Hermeneutic Claim to Universality," in Josef Bleicher, ed., *Contemporary Hermeneutics* (Boston: Routledge and Kegan Paul, 1980), p. 205.

12 Habermas, "Justice and Solidarity: On the Discussion Concerning Stage 6," included in this volume.

13 Habermas, "Morality and Ethical Life: Does Hegel's Critique of Kant Apply to Discourse Ethics?" in *The Northwestern Law Review* (forthcoming), p. 4.

14 Cf. "Justice and Solidarity."

SOCIAL INTERPRETATION AND POLITICAL THEORY: WALZER AND HIS CRITICS

GEORGIA WARNKE

In *Spheres of Justice,* Michael Walzer[1] offers a theory of distributive justice based upon the social meanings of different goods. He argues that an examination of the understanding a given community shares about its goods already indicates the principles according to which those goods ought to be distributed. The theory is explicitly pluralistic. Walzer argues both that different cultures have developed different distributive arrangements and that within cultures such arrangements can vary with the good to be apportioned. Indian caste society, for example, has traditionally adhered to a single distributive principle valid for all social goods and based on birth, while democratic societies, Walzer claims, have developed more complex criteria. Commodities, for instance, are supposed to be distributed through the market, while offices are meant to be allocated according to talent or qualification. Walzer denies that such variations in distributive rules—either within or among cultures—can be easily disputed. Rather, philosophical attempts to avoid pluralism, to unify distributive criteria according to the rules of an unsituated "justice-in-itself," will necessarily fail. Not only do they disregard the different ways in which autonomous communities create and understand their goods; they also ignore the distinct internal distributive principles this understanding already involves. Social goods belong to "spheres" that have their own distributive principles. Unjust distributions occur not when cultures disagree on distributive rules and not when they apply different rules to different goods; it occurs rather when the autonomy of culturally conditioned distributive spheres is violated, and when rules appropriate to one sphere are brought to bear on another. As Walzer explains:

> Every social good or set of goods constitutes, as it were, a distributive sphere within which only certain criteria and arrangements are appropriate. . . . In no society, of course, are social meanings entirely distinct. But, relative autonomy, like social meaning, is a critical principle—indeed . . . a radical

204

principle. It is radical even though it doesn't point to a single standard against which all distributions are to be measured. There is no single standard. But there are standards (roughly knowable even when they are also controversial) for every social good and every distributive sphere in every particular society; and these standards are often violated, the goods usurped, the spheres invaded, by powerful men and women (SJ, 10).

Much of the criticism of Walzer's book focuses on claims articulated in this paragraph. In specific, its critics have raised three objections. They object, first, to the very idea of social meanings and claim that the members of a community often share no social understanding. They argue, second, that even where shared social meanings do exist Walzer's interpretations of them are "arbitrary and tendentious."[2] Finally, they deny that social meaning can serve as a "critical principle," and Joshua Cohen even argues that Walzer's method works against the substantive political vision of democratic socialism that Walzer himself wants to promote. On Cohen's view, in fact, any attempt to derive principles of justice from the way in which social agents understand the goods of their society is either empty or conservative, since it cannot go beyond the self-understanding of the society itself. Along with Ronald Dworkin and Norman Daniels, he therefore defends the kind of political theory that Walzer criticizes: substantive political views can be supported only through arguments in principle, arguments about what justice in general requires, and not by conventionalist arguments about how social agents understand their goods.[3]

The force of these criticisms seems to me largely to derive from a disregard for the hermeneutic basis of Walzer's position, and I therefore want to try to defend it by referring to insights that have emerged within hermeneutic schools of social and literary interpretation. I examine the three objections to Walzer's view noted above, in turn.

I. SOCIAL MEANING

In disputing Walzer's reliance on the social meanings of different goods, his critics have focused on his analysis of health care in the United States. According to Walzer, the common understanding of health care identifies it as a need and consequently places it within the sphere of what he calls security and welfare. Goods within this sphere are subject to distributive rules derived simply from their meaning as needs. As Walzer points out, if a good is considered a need, this means that one does not have to "stage a performance, or pass an exam, or win an election" in order to acquire it (SJ, 75). Rather, those goods are identified as needs which members of a community consider essential and the provision of which serves as at least one basis for their establishing themselves and continuing as a community. Walzer argues that the relationship between political community and the satisfaction of needs is reciprocal: political communities form to satisfy the shared needs of their members and are sustained by the mutual indebtedness and solidarity that the provision of needs occasions.[4]

If medical care is commonly defined as a need, what are the distributive rules derivable simply from its meaning as a need? Walzer argues that, if a community undertakes to provide some good to its members as a shared need, then it must provide the good to all of its members equally, in proportion only to their need. In other words, if a good is socially recognized to be a need, then the only relevant criterion for its allocation is that an individual or group needs it. Hence, considerations of wealth, birth, or the like are external to the sphere of needs and their intrusion upon it constitutes an injustice.

This analysis of the logic of provision allows Walzer to criticize the distribution of medical care within the United States as just such an injustice. On the one hand, Americans support medical research through taxes; they provide some care to the poor through the Medicaid program and underwrite an insurance system for the old in the form of Medicare. These arrangements point to a belief in the necessity of decent health care and to some commitment to providing it for those who need it. On the other hand, health care is also offered privately through the market. This means that wealthier citizens tend to receive much better care than the poor and hence, according to Walzer, that the distribution of health care contradicts the logic of the sphere to which it belongs. Care is not provided to all citizens equally in regard only to their need; instead, "the most telling statistic about contemporary medicine is the correlation of office visits with social class rather than the degree or incidence of illness" (SJ, 89). The discrepancy between the health care provided for the poor and that available to the rich is a "double loss" (SJ, 89). Not only are poorer citizens sicker; Walzer argues that, if the community did not provide for any medical care and hence did not at all regard health care as a need, this greater incidence of illness alone could not signal the presence of any injustice. But the United States *does* allocate some of its resources to protect against disease and, because it does so, the unequal distribution of that protection is an injustice that affects both the health of the poor and their status as full members of the community. As Walzer puts the point: "Doctors and hospitals have become such massively important features of contemporary life that to be cut off from the help they provide is not only dangerous but also degrading" (SJ, 89).

To Walzer's critics, the example of health care in the United States reveals at least two problems with his analysis. First, it starts at too late a point. Walzer's concern is how health care ought to be distributed *if* a community perceives it as a need and provides it at all. The answer to the question of whether provision can *itself* be morally required, however, is entirely a matter of the meaning of health

206

care within particular societies, according to Walzer, and cannot be determined in any universally applicable way. But his critics suggest that the question of whether provision is morally necessary is *already* a question of distributive justice; I shall consider this issue in the third section of this paper. Second, even if one begins at the point at which Walzer begins, his critics argue, the example of the American distribution of health care is a poor one for him to have picked; if his attempt is to tie just distributions to social meanings, precisely here such shared social meanings do not appear to exist. One can point to publicly supported medical research and care as evidence that some Americans understand health as a need and have successfully lobbied for a level of communally funded support. But, as Dworkin points out, such support remains very controversial; moreover, "[e]ven those who agree that some medical care must be provided for everyone disagree about its limits."[5]

This objection illuminates the issue at hand: What is meant by a social understanding? Do individuals not have a variety of different opinions on what needs should be communally supported, and are not social distributions a result of political compromise rather than shared understanding? What, then, does Walzer mean by positing one unified social meaning? If he allows for pluralism in the meaning of a particular social good among cultures, why does he not allow for it within cultures? Why assume that members of a community share any view of their goods?

In view of the importance Walzer attaches to the idea of social meaning or of a shared social understanding, he is, in fact, oddly circumspect about its foundations. He does claim that goods are first conceived and created before they are distributed and that such conception and creation is a social process (SJ, 7). Goods, in other words, do not fall from the sky as goods but are rather determined culturally. Whether education is valued, what goods are considered common necessities, what political office involves—all these questions are matters that are decided in the course of a society's development in historically and culturally specific ways. Still, can individuals or groups within a society not have different ideas about these matters? Do we all relate to education, health care, and political office in the same way? What does Walzer mean in claiming that "conception and creation are social processes"?

The first point to be made in response to these questions is that the idea of a shared social meaning or understanding does not preclude differences of opinion. Dworkin contends that the occurrence of social disputes over distributive justice already indicates the absence of a shared understanding; as he puts it, "[t]he fact of the disagreement shows that there is no shared social meaning to disagree about."[6] But, in his reply to Dworkin, Walzer distinguishes disagreements that individuals or groups may have *within* a culture or society from disagreements *between* cultures and societies.[7] The example he gives is of affirmative action programs. Here, he contends, the problem is not that Americans share no understanding of the goods to be distributed or of the relevant distributive criteria; it is rather that this understanding is complicated by its entanglement with others, partially at odds with it. American beliefs, he claims, underwrite a meritocracy at least insofar as they attach importance to the qualifications of office seekers. But Americans are also interested in promoting an equality of opportunity and in overcoming the historical effects of racial discrimination. Some may consider certain of these values and concerns more important than others, and Americans may therefore come to different assessments of the merit of affirmative action programs. But to make this claim is not to say that they share no social understandings. Indeed, reversing Dworkin, one might argue that it is only because they share certain premises and a common mode of discourse that they can argue about affirmative action at all. Some may emphasize qualification and others compensation for past discrimination; moreover, among those emphasizing qualification, there may be different reasons for doing so: utilitarian reasons, for example, as opposed to strictly meritocratic ones. Nevertheless, while Americans may ultimately weigh their convictions against one another in different ways and embed them in different systems of moral and metaphysical belief, it is arguable that they share a vocabulary which makes debate possible. Differing solutions to a history of discrimination all belong within a common semantic universe in which individual rights, qualification, and equality are the concepts relevant to the discussion.

The second point to be made in response to Dworkin, then, is that the notion of a shared social understanding cannot be refuted simply by pointing to individuals who disagree. Dworkin understands the possibility of social meanings only as explicit agreements.[8] But the social meanings at issue are not supposed to be a consensus of the thoughts and opinions in every person's head. Rather, they reflect "deep" assumptions and premises that are contained in various social practices and in the very terms used to debate them. The shared understandings with which Walzer is concerned are in a common tradition and common language of action and practice; they are reflected in what Bernard Williams[9] calls "thick" moral concepts such as "prostitution," which indicates certain shared sexual norms even though their validity is commonly debated, and in the term 'bribery', which indicates certain rules about office holding no matter how many officials ignore them. With regard to community provision, they are in the language and action of concern: in terms such as 'abuse' and 'neglect', in phrases about 'adequate nutrition', in the office of the Surgeon General, in welfare agencies, the activities of social workers, and so on. Cohen puts the relevant point quite well: "Shared values . . . do not exist in a collective mind separate from institutionalized social action, nor do they exist simply in the separate minds of individual agents. Rather they exist in an ongoing way of life."[10]

This point is one that theorists from Hegel on have made in more detail. From this point of view, the objections Walzer's critics raise with regard to shared social meanings or understandings mirror objections more typically rooted in an atomistic social science. The supposition is that social norms and traditions of thought are simply collections of individual opinions and perspectives: individuals have various views; they define health care and office in idiosyncratic ways and the values the sociologist attributes to the society as a whole are simply sums of these individual views. But such a conception of social meaning is contestable. Individuals are already members of a society before they form opinions about its arrangements, and the opinions they form are about goods that already have specific meanings. Social meaning is contextual, as is literary meaning; it is not a matter of individual opinion but of the nexus of social values, norms, and practices about which individuals have opinions. To use an example Cohen offers, it is not necessary that every member of a certain society have individualistic values for its practices and institutions to embody them; nor is it necessary for every member to be individualistic to claim individualism as a social meaning. An anthropological account of the meaning of witchcraft in Zande society would not necessarily be undermined by the discovery of an Azonde or group of Azonde who did not believe in witches. Charles Taylor's "Interpretation and the Sciences of Man"[11] is perhaps clearest about the methodological assumptions underlying both Walzer's analysis and the criticism of it and is therefore worth quoting at length:

> The inter-subjective meanings which are the background to social action are often treated by political scientists under the heading "consensus". By this is meant convergence of beliefs on certain basic matters, or of attitude. But the two are not the same. Whether there is consensus or not, the condition of there being one or the other is a certain set of common terms of reference. A society in which this was lacking would not be a society in the normal sense of the term. . . . Some multinational states are bedeviled by consistent cross-purposes. . . . But convergence of beliefs and values is not the opposite of this kind of fundamental diversity. Rather the opposite of diversity is a high degree of inter-subjective meanings. And this can go along with profound cleavage. Indeed, inter-subjective meanings are a condition of a certain kind of profound cleavage, such as was visible in the Reformation, or the American Civil War, or splits in left-wing parties, where the dispute is at fever pitch just because each side can fully understand the other.[12]

From this point of view, it looks as if Dworkin makes too much of the fact of disagreement. If one focuses on the example of health care he finds so trouble-some, it is clear that Walzer cannot deny the existence of diverse opinions on it. But the shared understandings at issue are not supposed to reflect agreement on a national health-care policy; they rather refer to other shared assumptions about medicine and disease. Because we share a view that disease is preventable or curable through appropriate intervention, we also assume certain obligations and these already suggest certain social conclusions.[13]

Of course, even if sense can thus be made out of the idea of social meanings or shared social understandings, the question remains as to what justifies Wal-zer's interpretations of them. If common terms of reference allow different opinions, what supports either Walzer's opinions or the social conclusions to which he points? In particular, what methodological premises allow him to emphasize such practices as Medicaid and Medicare while disregarding others in articulating the implications of the shared social meaning of health care? This is the second question I raised earlier and the one to which I shall now turn.

II. SOCIAL INTERPRETATION

Even if we allow for shared or intersubjective meanings, how do we decide what their proper interpretation is? With regard to health care, Dworkin does not only contend that social disputes cast doubt on the supposition of a shared social meaning; he also argues that, even if we assume that there is a shared social meaning, the record on health-care distribution in the United States does not permit us to pick any one interpretation of it over any other. Depending on whether one focuses on Medicare and Medicaid or on the private distribution of care or, indeed, tries to combine both, one will be able to formulate quite different understandings of the social meaning at issue:

> Shall we say that our traditions assign medicine to the market, with some inconsistent exceptions that should now be abandoned? Or that they assign medicine to the sphere of need but with inconsistent backsliding in favor of wealth and privilege? Or that they express the more complex principle that justice requires leaving medicine to the market but insists on just the quali-fications and exceptions that we have made? What could make one of these interpretations superior to the others?[14]

The question Dworkin poses here is one that is familiar to the hermeneutic tradition in the philosophy of the social sciences. If the interpretation of shared social meanings is as crucial as Walzer makes it out to be, what makes one interpretation of meaning better than another? In regard to issues of textual interpretation, hermeneuticists have stressed context. Understanding, they contend, moves within a circle of part and whole. One has to see how the various parts of a text connect with one another into a coherent whole, how one's interpretation of one section allows one to make sense of another and how both support one's interpretation of the whole. At the same time, one has to see how one's interpretation of the whole lends credence to one's view of the various sections. Conversely, if the meaning one attaches to a part contradicts the meaning one has elicited from the combination of other sections of the text, one has to revise one's understanding of either the part or the whole. Which way one moves and how often revisions are required are a matter of accommodating both so that a unified textual meaning can emerge.

The same condition might be said to hold of social meaning: once again, the adequacy of interpretation depends upon the extent to which it makes sense of a given meaning as part of a larger context so that it illuminates this context and is in turn directed by it.[15] The meaning of social values, practices, and institutional arrangements is constituted by what hermeneutically oriented philosophers of social science have variously called language games, semantic fields, and traditions. Their common contention is that social phenomena cannot be understood apart from the social wholes in which they are involved and that their relations to other social phenomena—values, practices, institutions, and so on—rather contribute to their particular social and historical meaning. The meaning that the activity of voting has in our society involves the notions of individual autonomy, choice, and democratic decision making. Where such conceptions are not part of the political tradition—where, for example, only one choice exists or votes can be bought and sold—voting as we know it cannot occur. In this sense, social meaning, like textual meaning, exists as part of a context and can be understood only in terms of this context.

When Walzer distinguishes "deep and inclusive accounts of our social life" from "shallow and partisan accounts,"[16] it is this attention to context which he seems to have in mind. In fact, he claims that his procedure follows that which Dworkin himself proposes for deciding hard cases in law: one has to try to uncover the principles underlying statutes and legal precedents by exploring the larger legal and political culture of which they are a part. As Walzer sees it, the point is to get at the deep understanding that informs the precedents and legal opinions or, in other words, at the assumptions and goals behind them so that one can understand how they ought to be applied in a particular case. In the same way, Walzer's various social interpretations seek to get below the practices and institutions at issue to the historical and cultural contexts that give them their meaning.[17] For this reason it misses the point to claim, as Daniels does, that Walzer's historical accounts are "exotic presentations," the intent of which is simply to make his view "palatable."[18] Instead, these accounts are crucial to the plausibility of his interpretations, since they claim to place the meaning of social goods within appropriate frames of reference.

To return to the issue of health care as an example, Walzer does not examine only current health-care distributions in the United States, but rather offers a historical and sociological analysis. He claims, first, that the medical profession has always had a "bad conscience" about the link between health care and the market. In this regard, he notes that there have always been doctors who have accepted charity cases along with their paying patients and that the call of "Is there a doctor in the house?" reflects a moral expectation that doctors will respond to emergencies without first investigating a victim's financial situation. Both facts indicate some acknowledgment of the maxim that care should be available to those who need it. Walzer investigates, second, the way in which the Western conception of medical care has changed. Medieval Christians had little faith in the cure of the body and were more concerned with the cure of the soul. There was therefore a concern with easily accessible churches, regular services, the teaching of the catechism, and so on. Medical care, in contrast, was considered a luxury. As confidence in the cure of the body grows, however, and that in the cure of the soul wanes, health and longevity come to be considered necessities. They begin to reflect a "want so widely and deeply felt that it is the want not of this or that person alone, but of the community generally" (SJ, 88). The idea develops that disease can be cured or prevented and, moreover, that, since it can be, it ought to be. The licensing of physicians, establishment of state medical schools, public-health campaigns, and similar phenomena already signal the growing commitment of the community to providing for the health of its members and this commitment is further developed through health education, compulsory vaccinations, and the like.

This social and historical contextualization of current health-care practices may provide some justification for Walzer's interpretation of their social meaning. Nevertheless, it does not entirely resolve the issue in question; for, even if one decides that a historical and social approach is necessary to the interpretation of social meaning, one can still ask whether *contrasting* historical and social accounts are not possible. Why is Walzer's particular contextualization the proper one? Although his critics do not offer fully worked-out counterhistories to buttress their objections to this contextualization, Dworkin does refer to a mixed understanding of health care, according to which its social meaning is a combination of need and commodity, and thereby suggests one alternative to Walzer's account. Walzer himself points to an older view according to which medical care is a luxury available only to the very rich. Might it not be this view which survives in the market dimension of current health-care distributions? On this interpretation, the present pattern of distribution reflects two competing traditions: a newer tradition of collective concern for the health of citizens and an older tradition for which health care is not yet a socially recognized need. But if both traditions survive, why is a mixed interpretation of the American understanding of health care not correct? One could argue that such an interpretation is as historically plausible as Walzer's own but that it shows that health-care distributions reflect at least a two-dimensional tradition. If this is the case, however, it would seem that the principles of distributive justice must be similarly complex. Dworkin writes:

> We cannot just rule out, in advance, the possibility that though justice requires the state to intervene in the market for medicine in order to ensure that the poor have some care, it does not require that the poor be provided with the same medical care that the rich are able to buy.[19]

The problem raised here, then, is that, if interpretation requires some integration of whole and part, it may nonetheless be possible to integrate them in radically different ways and it is not clear how one decides between these ways. Walzer may offer us one means of viewing the dynamics of medical care but there also seem to be others that, if worked out in detail, might prove equally convincing. He himself denies that any interpretation can be "final and definitive,"[20] but then the initial question of this section returns at a higher level: If the interpretation of meaning must be "deep and inclusive," how does one choose between equally "deep and inclusive" accounts?

This problem has received extensive hermeneutic treatment. In an appendix to his *Validity in Interpretation,* E. D. Hirsch[21] points to conflicting interpretations of Wordsworth's "A Slumber Did My Spirit Seal" and argues that they stem from different ways of integrating part and whole. Thus, Cleanth Brooks[22] interprets the poem as an expression of inconsolable grief at the death of a loved one and emphasizes both the negativity expressed in the lines, "No motion has she now, no force;/She neither hears nor sees," as well as the lifelessness contained in the image of being "Rolled round in earth's diurnal course." F. W. Bateson,[23] in contrast, sees the poem as an affirmation of a pantheistic immortality and emphasizes the similarity between the dead Lucy and the "rocks, and stones, and trees" of the last line. Both interpretations are equally attentive to context and equally committed to finding a meaning that integrates individual lines; yet this process of contextualizing and integrating does not seem to lead to any definitive understanding. The question that arises, then, is whether any adjudication between interpretations of meaning is possible or whether the focus on meaning—whether textual or social—inevitably leads to subjectivism, arbitrariness, and tendentiousness, as Walzer's critics fear.

Hirsch tries to resolve the problem of contrasting textual integrations by introducing an author's *intentions* as inferred from direct inquiry or from a knowledge of the author's life, typical concerns, beliefs, and so on. This strategy is not open to the interpreter of shared social meanings, however, since the meanings at issue are not necessarily thoughts or intentions in anyone's head. Shared meanings are not subjective impressions *about* social phenomena but perspectives and conceptions already embodied in them.[24] But even if one could succeed in reducing shared meanings to individual intentions, Hirsch's solution fails to consider how evidence about intentions is to be understood. The problem is that such evidence seems itself to be subject to the so-called hermeneutic circle. If the question is how to fit whole and part together, then intentional evidence will also have to be interpreted, integrated with our understanding of other textual or extratextual evidence, and formed into a coherent unity. But if there is more than one way of doing this, then the solution Hirsch proposes will simply reiterate the problem with which we began: How do we decide between equally plausible integrations?

The difficulty here is that there appears to be no way out of interpretation. If we try to resolve ambiguities in the meaning of a text by going beyond the text, we still have to interpret the meaning of the external evidence to which we appeal. We will take certain aspects of the life or work of an author to be more important than others, emphasize those statements which we think are indicative of her real concerns, and rely on those experiences which support our interpretations. To some critics' dismay, Walzer does precisely this in arguing for his conception of the meaning of health-care practices. He views our social understandings and traditions from a particular perspective—that of a pluralistic democratic socialism—and emphasizes the way in which our conceptions "tend to proscribe the use of things from the purposes of domination" (SJ, xv). This analysis certainly ignores other features of our conceptions. But the crucial question here is whether any mode of understanding does not emphasize and select dimensions of its subject matter while disregarding others. Were one to offer an alternative history of the practices and institutions Walzer examines, would this account be any less interpretive?

At issue here are what the contemporary hermeneutic philosopher, Hans-Georg Gadamer, calls "prejudices": to understand *anything*—whether event, natural phenomenon, literary text, or social activity—is inevitably to view it in one particular, and by no means the only, way. One sees it *as* something, highlighting certain features, downplaying others, and finding similarities and dissimilarities to other events, phenomena, texts, or activities with which one is familiar. This selective approach to texts and "text analogues" is conditioned by the interpreter's circumstances, concerns, assumptions, and expectations. Moreover, such circumstances and concerns are historical; we are situated at a certain point in history and affected by much of that which that history involves.[25] This is an insight which has become prominent not only within the hermeneutic tradition but also within Anglo-American philosophy following W. V. O. Quine, Nelson Goodman, and others. The argument is that understanding always partakes of a particular vocabulary, focuses on particular social, literary, or scientific problems, and leaves certain assumptions unquestioned. The same holds of the attempt to adjudicate between interpretations; it can appeal to no ultimate evidence or uninterpreted, "brute data"[26] because the point about such evidence is that it is already interpreted. It has already been approached from a certain perspective and within a certain vocabulary or frame of reference.[27] To this extent, Walzer is in fact somewhat confused about his approach when he contrasts "deep and inclusive accounts of our social life" to "shallow and partisan accounts." If one is to make sense of this approach, it is, instead, deep, inclusive, and partisan at once.

Following Gadamer, Dworkin himself makes very similar remarks about interpretation in the legal context. In a criticism of Hirsch, he argues against the equation of the meaning of laws with a legislator's intentions about them on the grounds that these intentions can be described in different ways:

> Suppose a delegate to a constitutional convention votes for a clause guaranteeing equality of treatment, without regard to race, in matters touching people's fundamental interests; but he thinks that education is not a matter of fundamental interest and so does not believe that the clause makes racially segregated schools unconstitutional . . . the delegate intends to prohibit discrimination in whatever in fact is of fundamental interest and also intends not to prohibit segregated schools. These are not isolated, discrete intentions; our descriptions . . . describe the same intention in different ways. But it matters very much which description a theory of legislative intention accepts as canonical. If we accept the first description, then a judge who wishes to follow the delegate's intention, but who holds that education is a matter of fundamental interest, will hold segregation unconstitutional. If we accept the second, he will not.[28]

Dworkin argues that no choice can be made between the two descriptions by further reflection on the delegate's "true" intention and that the choice is rather political: it depends upon which description better fits what a given judge takes to be "the best theory of representative democracy."[29] He adds that this is the reason we find "distinctly liberal or radical or conservative" constitutional opinions.[30] In Gadamer's words, we are prejudiced even in our descriptions of intention by our own situation and commitments. Our descriptions will never square with all the "facts" or legal precedents. Indeed, Dworkin argues that a deep interpretation of a community's "constitutional morality" may condemn its "discrete" judgments on certain issues such as its objection to abortion.[31] Moreover, he proposes a "doctrine of mistakes" to cope with legal precedents moving in opposed directions.[32] But if these claims represent Dworkin's view, his objection to Walzer's procedure becomes difficult to assess. In articulating the social meanings underlying, say, current medical-care practices, Walzer seems to pursue exactly the same course. His interpretation does not "fit" all dimensions of our practices, but it need not claim to. It rather examines social meaning from a particular, inevitably "prejudiced" point of view. How, then, do the positions of Dworkin and Walzer differ?

A partial answer lies in how Dworkin interprets the idea of a "best theory of representative democracy" or, in general, the notion of what he calls "abstract justice." Dworkin's claim is not simply that legal interpretations present political glosses on legal precedents, opinions, and the like; it is rather that they present interpretations in tune with ideas of abstract justice and, moreover, that they thereby rely on an idea of justice "independent of the conventional arguments of any particular society."[33] But it is not clear what Dworkin can mean here. On the one hand, he emphasizes the openly political nature of our interpretations. On this view, the "best theory of representative democracy" or the judgment of what abstract justice requires are themselves political. On the other hand, we are meant to infer from our conservative, liberal, or radical ideas of abstract justice "that justice is at bottom independent of the conventional arguments of any particular society." That is, it is independent not merely of a particular political view within the society but of the political views the society shares. But if we know that our particular interpretations are conditioned by our political views, why should we not recognize that our views of representative democracy or abstract justice are also conditioned? And if we do recognize this, in what sense are they independent of the conventional beliefs and arguments of a particular society? Dworkin states that, if Walzer were to claim that justice is a matter of social convention, "his argument that one interpretation comes closer to abstract justice would be wholly circular and wholly ineffectual."[34] But it is worth pointing out that, as Dworkin knows, Walzer never makes this argument. *Dworkin* is concerned with abstract justice; but if he admits the political nature of interpretation, what is the force of his appeal to abstract justice? He seems to combine a recognition of the conditioned character of social beliefs with the claim that this recognition is without consequences.[35] This combination raises issues with which we shall be concerned in the third section of this paper. Before concluding the present section, however, I would like to make one more crucial point about social interpretation.

To maintain that Walzer's readings of social meanings are necessarily selective, that they present only one gloss on social meaning, is not to adopt the criticism Cohen makes of them that they are therefore "arbitrary and tendentious." Walzer offers a particular slant on our shared social meanings, a slant that can claim no more than any other to be either neutral, unprejudiced, or exclusionary. But the slant is not idiosyncratic or one peculiar only to him. Indeed, it would be odd if it were; for this would imply that, although shared social meanings are possible, interpretations of them are so prejudiced as to be unshared. But not only do we share social meanings in the sense given above, we often share understandings of them. Put otherwise, the range of plausible understandings of social meanings is itself limited by shared assumptions and prejudices embedded in our institutions and practices and in the culture and tradition to which we belong.

Interpretations of our conception of medical care are a case in point. We may have differing views of the legitimate place of Medicare and Medicaid in our society. Moreover, an interpretation of social meaning which focuses on these programs will differ from one which focuses on private care or, indeed, on hospitals that try to make a profit. But not *any* interpretation of our understanding of medical care will make sense to us. We may differ in our interpretations and, indeed, differ along political lines, as Dworkin suggests. But there will nonetheless be limits to the positions we can take and still remain intelligible to our adversaries. Although we take a liberal, conservative, or radical view of a given practice, we will also share a vocabulary that makes it possible for us to describe one another's perspectives and argue with them. In any case, the question of whether Walzer's interpretation is uniquely correct misdirects the inquiry. The relevant question is not whether he presents the only possible interpretation of our social meanings, but whether he offers one that we would like to adopt. It is arguable that the relevant criteria here are pragmatic: How well does a specific interpretation cohere with other values, norms, and self-interpretations we hold? How well does it suit our conception of what we are and would like to be? Certainly we can have debates about this, but they might prove more fruitful than debates over which interpretation of social meaning is "objectively" right.

III. SOCIAL CRITICISM

As I noted earlier, Walzer's critics have reservations not only about the notion of social meanings and not only about his interpretations of them, but also about the critical implications of social meaning and interpretation. If principles of distributive justice are to be derived from interpretations of shared social meanings, this way of proceeding seems to tie such principles to an analysis of the way in which a community understands itself. Not only can such an analysis be inadequate. Walzer's critics suggest that, even if his interpretations are not "arbitrary and tendentious," they still do not allow for social criticism and fall prey to the circularity with which Dworkin is concerned. Cohen connects this objection to what he calls the "simple communitarian dilemma":

If the values of a community are identified through its current distributive practices, then the distributive norms, subsequently derived from those values, will not serve as criticisms of existing practices. . . . On the other hand, if we identify values apart from practices, with a view to assessing the conformity of practices to these values, what evidence will there be that we have the values right?[36]

The problem as Cohen sees it is that Walzerian social criticism has only two options: it can either uncover the values embodied in social practices or determine what practices certain values require. If it derives social values from social practices, however, it is not clear how these values can be used to criticize the practices. Alternatively, if it determines the values of a society independently of its practices and claims that the practices fail to conform to the values, it is unclear what evidence it can use to justify the interpretation of the values. Interpretation is thus imprisoned within the circle of a society's self-understanding and, because it is, one cannot move from the interpretation of social meaning to social critique.

The reflections above do much to obviate this criticism, for they suggest that, while a given society may share a vocabulary for addressing questions of politics and justice, this shared vocabulary need not reflect a monolithic self-understanding. Walzer uses Indian caste society to make roughly this point. On the one hand, he claims that, although distributions in this society are unequal, they are not for this reason unjust. Rather, this distribution follows principles internal to shared social meanings. For Indians, the idea of an equality of opportunity refers to the whole of an individual's different incarnations rather than simply to the current life span. Hence, even if a person is treated unequally in this life, this fact does not entail any violation of the norm of equality in the long run; it means only that he is receiving what is proper given his current birth status. To the extent that the distribution of goods is faithful to this shared understanding, it remains just and it would be unjust only if it violated the shared understanding: for example, if it followed rules of the market instead of those of religious doctrine.

On the other hand, Walzer does not think that no criticism of Indian caste society is possible. First, the understanding embodied in a practice may be under attack within the society itself. One might be able to attribute norms and values to a subsection of the society which work against the entrenched understandings. Thus, Walzer claims that a subservient group might be "angry and indignant" (SJ, 314) about caste-directed distributive processes and that this anger and indignation might reflect either incipient values influenced by the West or, indeed, a different shared understanding which the distributive practices at issue violate. Either case would provide a foothold for criticism within the society's self-understanding and the point here, then, is that this self-understanding neither precludes internal dissent nor remains necessarily static. Different weightings and emphases will, as I stressed earlier, surely lead to differences in opinion. To this extent, Cohen seems unwittingly to agree with Walzer when he claims that "political philosophy can adopt a perspective that is 'internal' to the society, even if it is 'external' to its institutions and values."[37]

But, second, Walzer also accepts the legitimacy of social criticism that is "external" to one society because it is immanent to another. In the event that the understandings which justify an unequal distribution of goods are unquestioned within the caste society itself, for example, criticism can still depend upon the shared understandings of a different system. A visitor to India might even try to argue its citizens out of their conception of social goods and Walzer calls this an "entirely respectable activity" (SJ, 314).[38] The crucial difference between Walzer and his critics on this point is Walzer's insistence that social criticism is always situated or, in other words, always issues from particular cultural and historical assumptions even where it refers to the standards of abstract justice. If one criticizes a caste society, one does so either from the point of view of assumptions it shares or from the point of view of the beliefs about equality of another society and tradition. In neither case, however, is one appealing to universal norms that are unrelativized to one society or another. In this regard, Walzer shares Richard Rorty's antifoundationalist political assumptions: there is no ultimate court of appeal or nonconventional account of "abstract justice" which could legitimate our political beliefs against those of others or those of others against our own; rather, both sets of beliefs flow from situated social meanings, and this means that criticism, whether external or internal, is inevitably "prejudiced."

Even if this Walzerian-Rortian account of social and political critique resolves the worry that Cohen voices, it clearly leads to difficulties of its own. First, if we assume that all social criticism is inevitably prejudiced by one set of social and political assumptions or another, does it not lose its force? If we acknowledge that our notions of justice and equality are based simply on shared understandings peculiar to our culture or tradition, why should we object to the inequalities of a different system? More importantly, why should members of that system object to it? In trying to convince members of a caste society to change their social understanding, we can only be asking them to move from one "local account" (SJ, 314) to another, and it might be understandably unclear to them why they ought to do so.

A second difficulty is related to this first. If we have no basis for defending our principles of justice except that they issue from our shared understandings, why should we defend rather than oppose them? Why should we engage in the task Walzer sets himself of pushing certain interpretations of our shared social meanings to their logical conclusions? In *Interpretation and Social Criticism,* Walzer argues that the best social critics are those who remain connected to their societies and cultures and exhort their members to live up to the ideals and standards their shared social meanings entail. But suppose we are Fascists or members of a caste society? Should we still try to realize norms and values internal to our social meanings?

Rorty answers such questions essentially by conceding the difficulties involved. A self-acknowledged or "frankly ethnocentric"[39] political philosophy cannot hope to show that its point of view is correct, since there is no set of facts or brute data about which it could be correct; there are only the distinct meanings and interpretations of diverse societies. Such a political philosophy can, however, enter into open conversation with alternative meanings and interpretations, thereby becoming "edified." Indeed, a convergence of positions is not impossible; Rorty's contention is only that, if it occurs, it will not be because the views of the parties involved have got closer to the "truth" or to the "real" meaning, say, of equality or justice. It will rather be because the parties begin to make sense to one another for whatever reason. Rorty is aware of the obvious objection to this view, namely, that, if a Fascist begins to make sense to us, we are in deep trouble;[40] still, he denies that retreat to an Enlightenment position is possible. There are no uninterpreted principles of justice to which we can appeal to test the validity of our beliefs and values; we are culturally and historically parochial and if we are to retain our non-Fascist understanding of justice, we must do so by means of a commitment to our tradition which is without extratraditional support.

If Rorty's position thus reduces to a conventionalist defense of our tradition, it is not clear that Walzer follows him. Daniels has noted what he views as three contradictions within *Spheres of Justice* in which Walzer appears to give up the immanent character of his analysis of criticism and move to a more universalistic view. First, he claims that political expertise has its limits in democratic decision making and therefore rejects Plato's claims about the role of experts in guiding the ship of state (SJ, 285ff). Here Walzer's point appears to be that philosopher-kings are wrong not simply for Athens but for any society. Second, he argues that, if "ownership, expertise, religious knowledge and so on" are located in their proper spheres, "there is no alternative to democracy in the political sphere" (SJ, 303). Finally, he argues that the rule of one citizen/one vote is "the functional equivalent, in the sphere of politics, of the rule against exclusion and degradation in the sphere of welfare, of the principle of equal consideration in the sphere of office, and of the guarantee of a school place for every child in the sphere of education" (SJ, 305–306).

It is not clear that these positions are as contradictory to the spirit of immanent social criticism as Daniels supposes. Walzer explicitly relativizes his comments on political expertise and decision making to conceptions we, as heirs of Athens and citizens of democracies, have of state power. The relevance of his remark about democracy in the political sphere is limited to societies with a differentiated conception of social goods and his claim about the principle of one citizen/ one vote holds, again, only for democracies. In all three of these cases, then, Walzer's views follow not from supposedly universal norms but from social meanings that are said to be embedded in democratic political culture. Even if these apparent contradictions in Walzer's analysis can be reconciled, however, Daniels does seem correct in pointing to the nonconventionalistic elements in his point of view. These can perhaps best be clarified by first re-examining his analysis of the sphere of security and welfare and then turning to the general account of complex equality which is supposed to follow from the differentiation of spheres. Both cases illuminate the distance between Rorty and Walzer despite the obvious similarities in their positions.

As we saw, Walzer claims that needs are socially determined. Health care, for instance, only gradually becomes a socially perceived need in the West and may not be considered a need in a different kind of society. Similarly, while food might be considered a general human need, how much, of what kind, and how far one is entitled to go in order to obtain it are all social questions. Hence, caste societies that distribute food unequally, according to considerations of birth, are not for that reason alone unjust. But Walzer also writes, "in any community where resources are taken away from the poor and given to the rich, the rights of the poor are being violated" (SJ, 83). This assertion seems to entail the strong claim that, regardless of the shared understandings of a community, its withholding resources from the poor in favor of the rich is a violation of universal human rights. But if, for example, Untouchables are the poor of Indian society, what difference does it *now* make that they may adhere to the religious doctrines that justify an unequal distribution of the society's resources? The community cannot take resources away from them without violating their *rights*. One might try to claim that resources are not being taken away from them; according to their own self-understanding, they are simply being withheld until they are reborn into a higher caste. But this solution to the apparent contradiction seems to make a mockery of Walzer's original declaration of rights. If a violation of rights can be made to disappear by simply reinterpreting the concept of "taking away," what is the point of referring to *any* community and to the general rights of the poor?

The apparent problem here is the following: on the one hand, an absolute violation of rights seems to occur whenever resources are taken from the poor and given to the rich; on the other hand, all social meanings are conventional. This means that the determination of what counts as rights, resources, or poverty depends upon particular societies. But if Walzer's declaration refers simply to our notions of rights, resources, and poverty, it has no necessary significance for the different notions of a different society; alternatively, if societies are allowed to hold to their own, possibly opportunistic definitions, the declaration has little force. Now it simply means that, if a society forthrightly "takes" what it considers "resources" from those it considers "poor" to "give," as it defines 'give', to those it considers "rich," such a society is "violating rights" as it itself understands this action. But societies are rarely dumb enough to describe themselves in these terms.

Rorty might understand our repugnance to Indian caste society as a reflection simply on the parochial character of our beliefs, while Walzer's critics might see his recourse to rights as confirmation of the tension between his "conventionalist" method and his overt political goals. Walzer, I think, understands the recourse somewhat differently, as becomes more fully clear in his discussions of complex equality.

Complex equality requires that differentiation of types of social goods which we have been considering and the distribution of goods according to the internal principles of autonomous spheres. Thus, citizens will receive money in accordance with their success in the market, offices according to talent and qualification, education according to their desire for it, power according to their persuasive abilities, and so on. But complex equality also requires a strict delimitation of spheres: someone who has acquired great wealth through the market is not to be given political power simply on that basis; nor can those with power and wealth monopolize other social goods, such as education. Monopolies are tenable only within spheres so that, although the talented monopolize offices without having to share them with the less talented and the wealthy monopolize certain luxuries without having to give them up, these prerogatives are not convertible into others.[41] Complex equality will allow "many small inequalities" (SJ, 17) but not their multiplication across distinct spheres:

> The argument for complex equality begins from our understanding—I mean our actual, concrete, positive and particular understanding—of the various social goods. And then it moves on to an account of the way we relate to one another through those goods. Simple equality is a simple distributive condition, so that if I have fourteen hats and you have fourteen hats, we are equal. . . . On the view that I shall take here, however, we simply have the same number of hats. . . . Equality is a complex relation of persons mediated by the goods we make, share, and divide among ourselves; it is not an identity of possessions. It requires then, a diversity of distributive criteria that mirrors the diversity of social goods (SJ, 18).

What is initially confusing in this statement is whether the argument for complex equality simply begins from our understanding or begins and ends there. A conventionalist position would require the latter. It would argue that contemporary America is a differentiated society, that it distributes different kinds of goods differently, and that it relies on diverse standards to adjudicate the justice of those distributions. In institutionalizing these differentiations, complex equality "promises a society at peace with its own traditions,"[42] as Dworkin puts it. But is this Walzer's view? Is complex equality preferable to simple equality merely because it more easily coheres with our traditions? Walzer does argue that enforcing simple equality would require restrictions on individual freedoms. But are these unwarranted restrictions absolutely, or restrictions that violate Americans' shared understandings? If merely the latter, the question I raised earlier seems to arise again: Why not at least try to jettison our traditions? We may not be able to eliminate as many as we like or, indeed, any tradition completely since we are social and historical beings; we have grown up *in* our traditions and our identities are largely formed *by* them. But Walzer himself points out that less differentiated societies leave less room for the tyranny that results from processes of conversion (SJ, 315). So why should we not at least be skeptical of our traditions and shared meanings instead of formulating a theory to match them?

This is the question to which Walzer's critics continually return in one form or another. In their view, the contradictions and tensions in Walzer's account merely point up the inadequacies of his approach to political philosophy. But there is another dimension to his position. His argument for complex equality is *neither* the Rortian one that it simply corresponds to our social self-understandings *nor* that of his critics, namely, that it conforms to the requirements of abstract justice. Instead, he thinks that complex equality resolves the age-old problem of both belonging to a community and yet retaining a sense of one's individuality. Against Aristotle, he therefore argues the following:

> What a larger conception of justice requires is not that citizens rule and are ruled in turn, but that they rule in one sphere and are ruled in another—where "rule" means not that they exercise power, but that they enjoy a greater share than other people of whatever good is being distributed. The citizens cannot be guaranteed a turn everywhere. . . . But the autonomy of spheres will make for a greater sharing of social goods than will any other conceivable arrangement. It will spread the satisfaction of ruling more widely, and it will establish what is always in question today—the compatibility of being ruled and respecting oneself (SJ, 321).

For Walzer, then, the merit of a notion of complex equality is that it sustains community while allowing for the individual's pursuit of her own good. On the one hand, individuals can enjoy the fruits of their accomplishments in line with the meanings of the goods in question. To this extent, complex equality respects the distinctness of individuals and the integrity of their own lifeplans.[43] On the other hand, since the individual's accomplishments in one sphere are not convertible into prerogatives in another, they do not affect the full membership of others in the community. Many different social arrangements and levels of economic inequality are compatible with sustaining membership. But this is the limit on permissible differences which Walzer establishes. A just society is one that has a common life in two senses. Not only is "its substantive life . . . lived . . . in a way faithful to the shared understandings of its members." Moreover, its institutions and practices support the full participation and self-respect of individuals.

Walzer, then, takes democratic political culture seriously, not simply because it is *our* culture, as Rorty suggests, but because, even if it has yet to realize community fully, it still allows for it. But the criterion of community does not derive from universal principles; it is rather rooted in our traditions and reflects an interpretation and evaluation of what is significant in them. This view of our heritage can be accepted or rejected but, I think, only on its merits. In focusing on the alleged inadequacies of his method and its supposed tension with his aims, his critics largely miss the point.

Yale University

NOTES

1 *Spheres of Justice: A Defense of Pluralism and Equality* (New York: Basic Books, 1983) [hereafter SJ].

2 See Joshua Cohen's review of *Spheres of Justice,* in *Journal of Philosophy,* LXXXIII, 8 (August 1986):457-468.

3 See *ibid.;* Dworkin, "To Each His Own," in *New York Review of Books* (April 14, 1983), pp. 4-6; and Daniels, "The Roots of Walzer's Relativism," APA Western Division (Chicago: April 26, 1985).

4 The vocabulary I am using here is that of Charles Taylor in "The Nature and Scope of Distributive Justice," in his *Philosophy and the Human Sciences, Philosophical Papers,* 2 vols. (New York: Cambridge, 1985). It seems to me to articulate what Walzer means with his remark: "Political community for the sake of provision, provision for the sake of community" (SJ, 64).

5 "To Each His Own," p. 4.

6 "To Each His Own," p. 6.

7 Walzer and Dworkin, " 'Spheres of Justice': An Exchange," in *The New York Review of Books* (July 21, 1983), p. 44.

8 For further confirmation of this point, see Dworkin, *Law's Empire* (Cambridge: Harvard, 1986), pp. 65ff.

9 *Ethics and the Limits of Philosophy* (Cambridge: Harvard, 1985), pp. 129-130.

10 Cohen's review, p. 462.

11 Reprinted in *Philosophy and The Human Sciences,* pp. 15-57; originally published in *Review of Metaphysics,* xxv, 1(1971):3-51.

12 *Ibid.,* pp. 36–37.

13 Dworkin seems to voice a very similar criticism of "methodological individualism" in *Law's Empire,* arguing that interpretive claims about the practice of courtesy, for example, are not claims about what "the citizens of courtesy" think about the practice but rather claims about what courtesy is (p. 65). Still, he does not sufficiently stress that the practice is itself an interpretation or social understanding. He tends, instead, to see it as a thing in the world about which people can disagree. To this extent, he remains confused about that connection between social practices and the vocabulary used to talk about them which Taylor emphasizes. The practice of courtesy is not simply a series of bodily movements that individuals can describe in different ways; it is rather bound up with a certain vocabulary of action and description without which it would not be the practice that it is. Dworkin points to certain uncontroversial aspects of courtesy—its connection to respect, for instance. But the important point here is not that, if polled, we would all answer "yes" to a question linking courtesy to respect. Rather, the vocabulary of respect cannot be stripped off of the practice without also eradicating the practice as we know it. This is not to deny that differing interpretations of it are possible; but it is to claim that all partake of a particular language and that this language reflects social meaning. The same holds of arrangements for distributing goods; they have a social meaning no matter what we may think about it.

14 " 'Spheres of Justice': An Exchange," p. 45. Dworkin does not clearly distinguish the question of social meaning from that of social interpretation; "To Each His Own" rather uses differences in the *account* of the social meaning of health care to instance differences in its meaning; but there are two separate issues: whether social meanings exist and what the adequate interpretation of them is.

15 It is not clear that deconstructive criticisms of hermeneutics affect the point at issue here. One might argue that, for deconstruction, the part and whole of a text continue to illuminate one another; it is just that what is now illuminated is the way in which the text deconstructs itself, how the part subverts the ostensible meaning of the whole and leads to a different interpretation of it.

16 " 'Spheres of Justice': An Exchange," p. 43.

17 Walzer thus cites Dworkin's claim that the judge searches for the political morality presupposed by the laws and institutions of the community [*Taking Rights Seriously* (Cambridge: Harvard, 1978), p. 126] and asserts "That is exactly the procedure I too would recommend" (" 'Spheres of Justice': An Exchange," p. 43.).

18 "The Roots of Walzer's Relativism," p. 1.

19 "To Each His Own," p. 6.

20 " 'Spheres of Justice': An Exchange," p. 43.

21 (New Haven: Yale, 1967), pp. 227ff.

22 "Irony as a Principle of Structure," in *Literary Opinion in America,* M. D. Zabel, ed. (New York: Harper, 1951 [2nd ed.]), p. 736.

23 *English Poetry: A Critical Introduction* (New York: Barnes and Noble, 1966 [2nd ed.]), pp. 29ff, and p. 59.

24 In declaring that an individual's degree of commitment to shared social meanings is a problem for Walzer, Cohen seems to miss this point. See his review, p. 462.

25 See Gadamer, *Truth and Method* (New York: Seabury, 1975), pp. 235ff.

26 Taylor, "Interpretation and the Sciences of Man," p. 28.

27 This is what Heidegger refers to as the "fore-structure" of understanding. See *Being and Time,* John Macquarrie and Edward Robinson, trans. (New York: Harper & Row, 1962), pp. H151ff.

28 Dworkin, "How Law is Like Literature," in *A Matter of Principle* (Cambridge: Harvard, 1985), p. 163.

29 *Ibid.*, pp. 163–164.
30 *Ibid.*, pp. 164–165.
31 *Taking Rights Seriously*, p. 126.
32 "How Law is Like Literature," p. 161.
33 " 'Spheres of Justice': An Exchange," p. 45.
34 *Ibid.*
35 See *Law's Empire*, p. 78ff.
36 Cohen's review, pp. 463–464.
37 Cohen's review, p. 463. See Walzer's further reflections on internal criticism in *Interpretation and Social Criticism* (Cambridge: Harvard, 1987), pp. 40ff. Here Walzer identifies social criticism with what the Marxist tradition calls "immanent critique" without seeming to acknowledge the difficulties Marxists themselves have found with its application to advanced societies. Here a faith in technology and scientific progress seems to have replaced traditional bourgeois values of freedom and equality, thereby rendering ineffective any attempt to appeal to shared social norms to criticize social practices. See, for example, Habermas, "Technology and Science as Ideology," in *Toward a Rational Society* (Boston: Beacon, 1970); and "The Place of Philosophy in Marxism," in *Insurgent Sociologist*, v (Winter 1975):41-48.
38 He seems more troubled by this kind of activity in *Interpretation and Social Criticism*, however; see pp. 62ff.
39 Rorty, "Habermas and Lyotard on Postmodernity," in *Habermas and Modernity*, Richard Bernstein, ed. (Cambridge: MIT, 1985), p. 166.
40 *Ibid.*, pp. 172, 174.
41 Walzer thinks that the case of American Blacks who have been disadvantaged is a partial exception to this rule, but that it is historically specific and limited. See SJ, 151ff.
42 "To Each His Own," p. 4.
43 Indeed, it might be argued that it corrects Rawls's difference principle in this respect. Although Rawls, too, begins with the distinctness of individuals and criticizes utilitarianism on this basis, critics have charged that, in limiting benefits to individuals to those which also benefit the least advantaged, he takes the individual's talents and capacities away from the individual and transforms them into social assets. See Michael Sandel, *Liberalism and the Limits of Justice* (New York: Cambridge, 1982), pp. 66ff.

MODELS OF FREEDOM IN THE MODERN WORLD

ALBRECHT WELLMER

I

The question how freedom can be realized in the modern world has inspired and haunted European political philosophy for centuries. This is true at least if we only regard those political thinkers who belong to the tradition of the Enlightenment in the broadest sense of the word, and leave aside those antimodern and antiliberal theories which belong to the tradition of counter-Reformation and counter-Enlightenment. Political philosophers in the tradition of the Enlightenment, as I understand it, are, e.g., Locke, Rousseau, Kant, Hegel, Marx, Mill, Tocqueville, and, in our day, Jürgen Habermas, Charles Taylor, and John Rawls. Freedom, for these philosophers, has been a universalist concept, i.e., a concept that is inextricably intertwined with a universalist conception of human rights. But here the agreement ends; the basic disagreements concern the question of whether the idea of freedom should be explicated primarily from the point of view of the individual or from the point of view of the collective. Depending on which orientation is dominant in a political philosophy, we might distinguish between "individualist" and "collectivist" conceptions of freedom in modern political theories. Since the term 'collectivism' has come to be used to designate a specifically modern form of *repression* of individual freedom, however, I would prefer to talk about individualist and "communalist" conceptions of freedom, respectively.[1] Individualism and communalism are not simply opposed, they are rather in some important sense complementary to each other; correspondingly, most important political theories of modern Europe contain elements of both of these orientations. Radical individualism and radical communalism are extreme cases that are hard to come by. Perhaps Marx could be called a radical communalist, and Robert Nozick a radical individualist. Usually, however—although not in the case of either Hobbes or Nozick—individualist theories lead up to some conception of democratic self-organization of the collective (a "communalist" element), while communalist theories *eo ipso* must

227

claim to provide a more adequate conception of individual freedom than individualist theories can do—this is clear, e.g., in the case of Marx, whose idea of a realm of freedom represents a communalist conception of an almost unlimited freedom of the individual.

Although the dividing lines between individualist and communalist theories of freedom are not always clear, there is, I think, a rather sharp dividing line between the basic *underlying* orientations. For individualism and communalism represent two sharply opposed anthropological conceptions, as e.g., Taylor[2] has pointed out. Individualist theories take isolated individuals, characterized by certain natural rights and a goal-oriented rationality, as their starting point: they try to construe political institutions—as far as they can be considered to be legitimate—as the result of a contract between autonomous individuals. Needless to say, the term 'contract' must not be taken too literally here; what is at stake is not the real genesis of political institutions, but their legitimacy: they are legitimate if they can be thought of as being the result of a contract between free and equal individuals. Freedom here is basically the freedom to do what I want to do—whatever it is that I want to do—and natural rights can be understood in the sense of Kant's definition of right at the beginning of his *Metaphysical Elements of Justice:* "Each action is right which—or the maxim of which—is such, that the freedom (*Freiheit der Willkür*) of each individual can coexist with the freedom of everybody else according to a universal law."[3] Freedom in the sense of Kant's *Freiheit der Willkür* is what is often called "negative" freedom. Negative freedom, restricted by means of a general law which guarantees equal freedom for everybody, is the basic content of natural rights; and the basic achievement of the social contract is that the universal law mentioned in Kant's definition becomes a *positive* law, enforced by a political authority which has the power to punish whoever violates the rights of others. Needless to say, the basic paradigms of these "inviolable" rights have always been property rights (but, of course, also the right to one's own life).

Communalist theories, in contrast, do not only question the basic anthropological premise of individualist theories, but, together with this premise, the individualist notion of individual freedom as such.[4] The anthropological premise which is questioned is that the notion of a human individual outside society, an individual who is not constituted *as* an individual by becoming socialized as a member of an intersubjective form of life, is an adequate starting point for political theory. If, however, human individuals are essentially *social* individuals, if, in their very individuality, they are constituted and, as it were, permeated by the culture, traditions, and institutions of the society to which they belong, then their freedom as well must have a social character. Even as *individual* freedom this freedom must have a *communal* character, or at least an essentially communal aspect, expressing and manifesting itself in the way in which the individual participates in and contributes to the communal practices of his society. The originary locus of freedom, then, would not be the isolated individual, but a society that is the medium of individuation through socialization; freedom would have to be thought of as ultimately residing in the structures, institutions, practices, and traditions of a larger social whole. But since this larger social whole is what it is only through being kept alive, "reproduced," and interpreted by the individuals who are part of it, individual and "public" freedom now become inextricably intertwined; and this means, as again Taylor has pointed out, that the very concept of freedom assumes a normative meaning that it does not have in individualist conceptions. For this conception no longer merely signifies the absence of external obstacles that might prevent an agent from doing what he wants to do, it rather now also signifies a specific way in which agents come to decide upon *what* they want to do. The idea of freedom as the idea of individual-cum-collective self-determination has an irreducibly normative dimension, because it is conceptually linked up with the idea of rationality. By 'rationality' I do not just mean "strategic" or "means-ends" rationality; rather, following Habermas, I take the notion of rationality in a broad sense, signifying a way of dealing with intersubjective validity claims of all sorts. Rationality in this sense manifests itself in the practices of deliberation, argumentation, and critique, where what is argued about may be empirical, evaluative, moral, aesthetic, or hermeneutic truth claims. For communalist conceptions of freedom, not only the very idea of freedom but also the idea of rationality becomes a "communal" notion; we cannot explain what rationality is except by referring to the intersubjectivity of forms of life which is prefigured in the intersubjectivity of the symbolic medium—language—through which forms of life are constituted.

Individualist and communalist conceptions of political freedom are thus opposed to each other with regard to their respective conceptions of those "rational" agents whose freedom is at stake. The individualist conceptions, the first classical representative of which is of course Hobbes, may be characterized by an anthropological "atomism"[5] and an "instrumentalist" conception of rationality; epistemologically, they have close affinities with the objectivist ("mechanist," "physicalistic") and anti-Aristotelian tradition of modern science; politically, they reflect the perspectives, interests, and self-interpretations of that revolutionary class which came to dominance in modern Europe: the bourgeoisie. The communalist conceptions, in contrast, have roots in the Aristotelian tradition, which had been widely abandoned in modern individualist theories of natural right, as well as in the radical critique of modernity which started with Rousseau and early romanticism. Although these two traditions—the Aristotelian one and what might be called the "romantic" tradition of a radical moral and aesthetic critique of modern society—are in many respects incommensurable, they have certain points of convergence which become manifest in the paradigmatic role which the Greek polis—or an idealized memory of the Greek polis—has played in the communalist tradition. Whereas individualist conceptions have been rather firmly associated with the great bourgeois revolutions and therefore also with the legitimation of modern capitalist economy, communalist conceptions almost invariably were *critically* related not only to the anthropological premises of modern natural-right theories, but also to the *reality* of modern bourgeois society. This shows, of course, that not the *philosophical* but the *political* critique of "possessive individualism"[6] was their main concern; and what this means is that for them the anthropological premises of individualist conceptions, though being deeply wrong, had to some extent *become true* in modern bourgeois society. The controversy between individualists and communalists therefore always was—and still is—a political controversy about the role that bourgeois society has played with respect to the advancement of freedom in the modern world.

II

In my ideal-typical sketch of two mutually opposed types of political philosophy, I have already indicated that, as far as anthropological and epistemological premises go, I am taking the side of the communalists. Every communalist, however, as long as he unmistakably wants to side with the Enlightenment tradition, has to come to terms with the fact that modern bourgeois society is the paradigmatic society of the Enlightenment in the modern world: the only society in which human rights, the rule of law, public freedom, and democratic institutions have to some extent become safely institutionalized. It must have been an experience like this which led Hegel, who started as a radical romantic communalist, to become a communalist defender of what he called "civil society." Since Hegel's exposition of the question of how freedom can be realized in the modern world is—notwithstanding the faults of his specific answers—in some sense still unsurpassed, I want to say a little more about his attempt to bridge the gap between individualist and communalist conceptions of freedom.

Hegel's basic strategy was, as is well-known, to incorporate the tradition of natural-right theories into a communalist conception of "ethical life" (*Sittlichkeit*). What Hegel calls "civil society" is, in its basic characteristics, a society of property owners who, notwithstanding their religious, racial, political, and other differences, are equal before the law, and who, in accordance with general laws, are permitted to pursue their personal interest and their idiosyncratic ideas of happiness, and who, finally, are free to choose careers, professions, employments, or places for living and working. This "civil society" is intrinsically linked with a market economy which might be called "capitalist" in Marx's sense; it is a society which roughly corresponds to the picture of modern society sketched out by natural-right theorists like Locke and political economists like Adam Smith. It is a society in which "negative" freedom has been institutionalized, a society of universal human rights and of universal social antagonism. Morally, i.e., from a communalist perspective, this society must appear as deeply ambiguous: as a society of universal human rights, it is the realization of that *conditio sine qua non* which every modern conception of ethical life (i.e., which every communalist conception of freedom in the modern world) must respect, if it is not to drift away into counter-enlightenment, repression, or terror. As a society of universal social antagonism, however, this society is, at the same time, the negation not only of specific—e.g., premodern—forms of ethical life, but the negation of the very category of ethical life. For where this society is in "unhampered progression"—and Hegel describes this "unhampered progression" in terms very similar to those which Marx later used—no communal bonds between the individuals, no concern for the public good, and no moral scruples stand in the way of social devastation, whose victims are those who are the losers in the general race after wealth, power, and happiness.

Hegel's communalist response to this deep ambiguity of modern civil society is his theory of the state. The state signifies for Hegel that sphere of ethical life in which the antagonism of civil society is "sublated"—not annihilated, but overcome by being *relativized*. Hegel's basic idea here is that civil society—contrary to what the theorists of natural right thought—cannot be understood and could not possibly exist on its own terms. Actually, Hegel claims that civil society is always already more than it appears to be as long as it is seen only in its own terms, which are also the terms of natural-right theories and classical political economy. For the very idea of a society of equal individuals, who as property owners strategically interact in the market in accordance with general laws, does not only presuppose that these individuals morally recognize each other as free and equal, it rather also—and by the same token—presupposes the existence of political and juridical institutions whose functioning can*not* be explained in terms of the strategic rationality which is characteristic of the individuals as members of civil society proper. It is in these institutions of *political* society that rational freedom in the communalist sense of the word has its place: rational freedom as it is connected with a concern for the common good, the virtues of citizens, communal action, public debate, and the political control of the economy. Civil society now appears as only *one dimension* of the substantive ethical life of the modern state, namely, that dimension through which the right of particularity, the "negative" freedom of the individual, has become an institutional reality. This dimension of negative freedom with its universalist connotations is an essential aspect of any viable modern notion of political freedom; but the emancipated individuals can be free in the full sense of rational freedom only as citizens of a political community, as citizens of the state.

Before I come to the shortcomings of Hegel's construction, I want to say a few words more about the "right of particularity" in Hegel's view of the modern state. For Hegel, as for many of his contemporaries, the Greek polis had always been an exemplary model for the political institutionalization of freedom. At the same time, the Greek polis provided him with a model for illustrating his thesis that political freedom can be real only as a form of ethical life (*Sittlichkeit*). Hegel used the term 'ethical life' to characterize the normative structure of an intersubjective form of life. The ethical life of a people—in contrast to what Hegel called "morality"—is inseparable from its institutions, its collective interpretations of the world, its ways of self-understanding, its customs, traditions, and values. If the individuals are what they are only as participating in a specific form of ethical life, as understanding themselves and their social relations in accordance with this form of ethical life, then even their individual concerns, their ambitions, their sense of self-respect and dignity, their feelings of shame or guilt must in their depth structure be formed by the "objective spirit" of their society. Turned the other way round, this means that the idea of freedom can only take a foothold in a society if it becomes a form of ethical life. This is precisely what happened in the Greek polis and above all in the great period of Athenian democracy. For here the spirit of the whole is, at the same time, the spirit of the individuals who are free; the polis, law, and religion as general concerns are, at the same time, concerns of the individuals, and the individuals, as Hegel says, are only individuals through these concerns.[7]

Hegel has called the Greek form of ethical life "beautiful." This is a tribute to the unique coalescence of myth, art, and politics in the Greek polis; it is, however, also an indication of the essential *limitations* of the Greek form of freedom. These limitations become manifest for Hegel in the institutions of the oracle and of slavery.[8] If we consider Hegel's objections against these institutions, we shall better understand what, for Hegel, is involved in the right or the emancipation of particularity.

As far as slavery goes, the objections are familiar; they have become obvious for us and they had, of course, already become obvious for most people in Hegel's time. Slavery goes against our conception of human beings as rational beings. The correlate of this objection is a universalist conception of human rights, which, as we saw, was for Hegel an essential ingredient of any viable modern conception of ethical life, and the legal and institutional explication of which he took over to an important extent from the tradition of natural-right theories. Human rights in this tradition are centered around property rights and their legal and moral implications. The right of particularity is for Hegel not exhausted by these types of rights, however. This becomes clear if we consider his objections against the institution of the oracle. In Hegel's view the institution of the oracle signifies a structural limitation concerning the scope of possible rational discourse in the Greek polis. By basing their decisions in important political or private matters on what the oracle says, individuals do not yet take full responsibility for their own decisions. Full self-determination requires—as Hegel puts it—a determination of the will by prevailing *reasons;*[9] consequently, the type of self-determination which was realized in the Greek polis was not yet rational self-determination in the full sense of the word. These limits of rational self-determination in the polis, however, only reflect an irreducible dogmatic aspect of Greek ethical life; they are conceptually linked up with a still mythological form of world- and self-interpretation which as such was not an object of rational critique or rational evaluation, i.e., with precisely those aspects of Greek ethical life which to us make it appear as beautiful. For this reason the Greek enlightenment, which culminated in the figure of Socrates, meant doom for the Greek polis, for it introduced an element of reflexive and discursive scrutiny into the ethical life of the polis to which it could not stand up. Once the idea that nothing must be accepted as valid which cannot be justified by arguments gained credence, the grounds on which the Greek polis was built proved to be shaky. And it was not only the Sophists but Socrates himself who contributed to the dissolution of the foundations of the polis; in this sense, the Athenians were right in putting Socrates to death. In the spirit of Socrates, however, the very "principle of self-reliant particularity," as Hegel calls it,[10] shows itself from its other side, namely, as the "right, not to recognize anything as valid which I do not recognize as reasonable."[11]

This right demands a form of legitimation which was not accessible within the boundaries of the Greek polis; for this reason, Plato's attempt to restore once more the beauty and truth of Greek ethical life in the medium of philosophical thought was paradoxical from the beginning and could only lead to a highly repressive conception of an ideal society. "Plato in his Politeia," Hegel says, "represents the substantial ethical life [of the polis] in its ideal *beauty* and *truth;* but the only way in which he could come to grips with the principle of self-reliant particularity, which in his time had intruded into Greek ethical life as a disaster, was to oppose to it his only substantial state and to exclude it from his state up to its very origins in private property and in the family."[12]

The principle of self-reliant particularity has for Hegel, as we can see now, an internal and an external aspect. Taken in its full sense it is, as Hegel says, "the principle of the self-reliant and in itself infinite personality of the individual, of subjective freedom," a principle which, according to Hegel's philosophical vision of history, made its world-historical appearance with the emergence of Christianity, on the one hand, and with Roman law, on the other.[13] It exploded the boundaries of the Greek world.

III

Given what I have said so far about the premises on which Hegel tried to construct the idea of the modern state, one might have assumed that he would try to develop a conception of a democratic, universalist, and secular form of ethical life for modern societies. As is well-known, however, this is not what he did. In some respects he comes close to such a conception in those parts of his theory of the state where he talks about the self-government of communes and corporations, about public opinion and the freedom of the press, or about parliamentary representation. Hegel's partial concessions to the democratic spirit of the modern Western world are always connected, however, with principled objections to the idea of democracy as applied to the modern world. What Hegel rejects is the *political* interpretation of the principles of natural right as principles of democratic participation and democratic decision making in modern societies. Hegel's philosophical reasons for this are rather complex but, in the end, not very convincing. Hegel's basic arguments are: (1) a "communalist" objection against the individualist anthropology of natural-right theories; and (2) an argument concerning the differentiation and complexity of modern societies. According to the first argument, the idea of democracy, as developed in theories of natural right, is "abstract," because the anthropological assumptions and the principle of negative freedom which go into the construction of a social contract are too weak to support the idea of democracy as a form of ethical life. According to the second argument, the complexity and functional differentiation of modern societies and, in particular, the emergence of a depolitized sphere of civil society do not allow for anything like an all-pervasive *direct* democracy in the modern state. Whereas the first argument pins the complexity of a form of ethical life against the simplicity of a principle of "abstract" right, the second argument pins the complexity of modern societies against the simplicity of direct democracy; but these two "premises," together with Hegel's "conclusion," do not yield a valid syllogism: Hegel by no means shows why it should not be possible to "translate" the universalist principles of natural right into a viable conception of a *democratic* form of ethical life for modern societies. This is the blind spot in Hegel's *Philosophy of Right*. I think that this blind spot can be partly *explained* by the fact that Hegel, though a "communalist" political philosopher, ultimately conceived of "spirit" as *subjectivity* and not as *intersubjectivity*.[14] Another part of the explanation certainly is, however, that Hegel's owl of Minerva started its flight a little too early: Hegel did not have any first-hand experience of democratic traditions, and America was still very far away. The Prussian monarchy, even in its idealized version, obviously was not the last word of European history.

Accordingly, in his critique of Hegel's theory of the state, Marx was right in insisting on the *democratic* principle of modern European history. "Democracy," he says, "is the essence of all constitutions." And "[d]emocracy is related to all other constitutions as to its old testament."[15] Unfortunately, however, Marx's articulation of this idea remained "abstract" precisely in Hegel's sense. His idea of a free association of the producers, who collectively regulate their metabolism with nature once capitalism has been overcome, signifies the utopian perspective of a collective life process, the unity and harmony of which would spontaneously emerge from the social interaction of fully emancipated individuals. This honorable anarchist utopia represents a *transpolitical* interpretation of the idea of democracy; against this interpretation, however, Hegel's arguments, which I have mentioned above, still appear as quite compelling. In Marx's conception, neither "negative" freedom, nor political institutions, nor functional and systemic differentiation have a place; consequently, one might say that Marx, instead of *solving* the problem of an institutionalization of freedom in the modern world, which ultimately had been left unsolved by Hegel, simply *exorcized* it.[16] What he turned upside down was not Hegel but Rousseau. The price that had to be paid for the neglect of the political dimension of freedom in Marxist thought has been high, as we know; the states that tried to put his utopia into practice became much more repressive than the state as conceived by Hegel ever could have been.

It was not Marx but Tocqueville who took up the Hegelian problem of how to conceive of a democratic form of ethical life. Of course, the term is not Tocqueville's; nor is his analysis of American democracy a response to Hegel's *Philosophy of Right*. As far as the understanding of an underlying historical problematic and the exposition of the problem of freedom goes, however, Tocqueville's *Democracy in America* may very well be considered to be a democratic counterpart to Hegel's *Philosophy of Right*. For both authors, the French revolution with its internal dialectics of emancipation and repression was the crucial historical experience. And the basic concern of both authors was how a political institutionalization of freedom could be found for the egalitarian civil society, which both of them considered to be an irrevocable outcome of bourgeois revolutions. For both Hegel and Tocqueville, civil society represented the destruction of the old—feudal or aristocratic—political order; both considered it to be the institutionalization of an egalitarian order of negative freedom centering on property rights; both acknowledged the emancipatory content of civil society with its universalization of human rights; and both of them saw clearly that the egalitarianism of civil society not only was not yet equivalent to an institutionalization of political freedom, but that, on the one hand, it was still compatible with various forms of despotism: e.g., the bureaucratic despotism of a centralized modern state, the despotism of an unconstrained majority rule, etc.; and, on the other, that this egalitarianism taken all by itself would amount to a dissolution of all social solidarity. Hegel articulated this insight in terms of his objections to a political, i.e., democratic interpretation of natural-right theories; the core of these objections being that a rational common will could not possibly emerge from the coming together of atomistically conceived property owners, whose social relations were basically characterized by the dissolution of all communal bonds of solidarity which had tied them together in previous societies. Tocqueville, although less theoretically-minded than Hegel, used essentially the same argument, the only significant difference being of a terminological kind: for the term 'democracy' for him signified above all the egalitarian realization of "negative" freedom in modern civil society, so that the problem for him became how *freedom* can be realized in a *democratic* society. Although the historical experience of the decline of the spirit and the institutions of political freedom in postrevolutionary France was the starting point for both Hegel's and Tocqueville's reflections, they turned in opposite directions to look for alternatives: Hegel thought that he had found a viable alternative in a somewhat idealized Prussian monarchy; Tocqueville, by contrast, turned to a study of the second great revolutionary society of his time: the American society. And here he found something that was lacking not only in postrevolutionary French society, but in all the great Continental states of his time: a spirit of freedom that had become a form of ethical life.

I have called this form of ethical life "democratic" before; the term can here be taken in Tocqueville's as well in the more traditional Hegelian sense: for it is a form of ethical life for egalitarian societies ("democratic" societies in Tocqueville's sense); and it is a form of life based on a universalist principle of individual and collective self-determination. What has still to be explained is what it means to say that democracy has become a form of *ethical life* in Hegel's sense. Let me try to give this explanation by reminding you of certain crucial aspects of Tocqueville's analysis.

First let me say a few words about Tocqueville's conception of freedom and its relationship to what I call democracy. Tocqueville's conception of freedom is a "communalist" one. It is inseparable from (1) the idea of individuals acting in concert to deal with and to decide upon matters of common concern; (2) the idea of public discourse as the medium of clarification, transformation, and critique of personal opinions, choices, and interpretations; and, finally, (3) the idea of an equal right of the individuals to participate in the process of shaping and determining their collective life. The "negative" freedom embodied in the structures of civil society is here transformed into the "positive" freedom of citizens acting in concert; this "positive" or "rational" freedom amounts to a form of restoration of those communal bonds between the individuals, the absence of which defines their existence as mere independent property owners. "Freedom alone," Tocqueville says, "can draw the bourgeois out of their isolation which is a consequence of the independence of their situation, and force them to come closer to each other; freedom . . . unites them every day anew by the necessity, to converse with each other in dealing with matters of common concern, to convince each other, and to do favors to each other . . . freedom alone offers nobler objects to ambition than the acquisition of wealth and creates the light in which the vices and virtues of men can be seen and judged."[17]

Now, this much seems obvious: freedom in this sense can exist *only* as a form of ethical life; i.e., as a communal practice pervading the institutions of society on all levels and habitualized in the character, the customs, and the moral sentiments of its citizens. It is precisely something like this which Tocqueville discovered in the institutions and everyday life of postrevolutionary America. I think that Tocqueville is right when he attributes the deep-seated differences between the course of the French and the American revolution to the fact that the *Constitutio Libertatis* in the United States did not start at the top, like the revolution in France, but, as it were, at the bottom of society. The American revolution, after all, had only been a revolution against a colonial power, i.e., against the British crown, while the political and social structures that had been formed on a local and regional level during the period of the colonial regime represented the most radical libertarian traditions of the colonial motherland itself. Thus, the democratic republic had for a long time been a reality on the level of townships and regional associations before it became the principle of the federal association of the American states. A long tradition of self-government in the townships had generated those political experiences, attitudes, and insights, without which the American revolution could not have led to the constitution of an egalitarian democratic republic. "The American revolution," Tocqueville says, "broke out and the doctrine of the sovereignty of the people, came out of the townships and took possession of the state."[18] And it "was the result of a mature and reflecting preference of freedom."[19]

I shall not go into any of the details of Tocqueville's fascinating analysis here; so I shall not say anything about the institutions of self-government on the local level, about Tocqueville's reflections on the educational role of the jury system, or about the division and decentralization of power in the American constitution. Tocqueville, as is well-known, was not uncritical of American democracy, and he did not see it as a model simply to be imitated by European states. Moreover, one and a half centuries after the publication of Tocqueville's book, there are plenty of reasons not to idealize American democracy: the history of American democracy has *also* been the history of the political, social, and economic exclusion of minorities, and it has *also* been a history of imperialist exploitation and interference. Yet it has to be added that Hegel's dictum about civil society—"Human beings are recognized *as* human beings, not as Jews, Catholics, Protestants, Germans, Italians etc.''[20]—has nowhere in the world become true to a greater extent as a principle of citizens' rights, i.e., as a principle of *political* freedom, than in the United States of America. All of this, however, is in some sense irrelevant with respect to the *philosophical* questions I am posing here. For I have referred to Tocqueville to show only that—Hegel's objections notwithstanding—there is no reason to claim that the universalist principles of natural right are not "translatable" into a communalist conception of political freedom; what Tocqueville actually shows is that freedom in the modern world is conceivable *only* as a democratic form of ethical life.

Tocqueville's analysis has one particularly interesting consequence. If one should try to "re-translate" this analysis into the more systematic conceptual framework of Hegel's *Philosophy of Right,* it would become obvious that the boundary lines between civil and political society, which already in Hegel's analysis are by no means clear-cut, must be seen as rather fluid. For the spirit of a democratic form of ethical life, if it exists at all, will pervade all the institutions of society; consequently, no sharp line of demarcation could be drawn once and for all which would separate the sphere of "negative" freedom from that of "positive," public freedom. To put it in different terms, a democratic form of ethical life will affect the way in which the negative freedom of property owners is exercised and can manifest itself. To take the most obvious example: socialization of the means of production is always—and must always be—a possible option for a democratic polity. Does this mean that a communalist conception of political freedom contains in itself all the truth content of natural-right theories? Or should we assume that Hegel's conceptual strategy—which *de facto* (although in a less systematic sense) is also that of Tocqueville and even of Mill, and according to which the "negative" freedom of the bourgeois individual is a sphere of rights *sui generis* which is not at the disposal of a democratically conceived common will—has a distinct concept of right of its own? It is with these questions that I want to come back to my initial reflections concerning the alternative of individualist versus communalist conceptions of freedom in the modern world.

IV

To sharpen my questions, I first want to contrast two recent paradigms of an individualist and a communalist conception of freedom, respectively. I take Nozick as my protagonist for the individualist case, and Habermas as my protagonist for the communalist case. I have chosen Habermas because his theory is the most profound and original reconstruction of a communalist conception of freedom which exists today, and I have chosen Nozick because his book, *Anarchy, State, and Utopia,* although perhaps not the most profound, is the most radical defense of an individualist conception I know. I do not want to discuss any details here, and I shall not discuss the anthropological and epistemological premises of the two authors; as far as the latter are concerned, I think that Habermas is basically right and Nozick deeply wrong. What I want to discuss is merely an interesting formal analogy between the two theories. Both Nozick and Habermas are concerned with certain *meta*principles of freedom, i.e., with principles that only define the formal conditions of a free society and not any specific content—in terms of institutional structures, forms of life, forms of association, etc. In Nozick's case, these metaprinciples are principles of negative freedom, centered on property rights; in Habermas's case, they are principles of rational discourse. In both cases, the metaprinciples of freedom do not define a utopian state of society, but, as Nozick put it, a "framework for utopias," a "meta-utopia."[21] The formal conditions of freedom in both cases define the conditions of an essentially pluralist society; the metaprinciples spell out which conditions must be fulfilled if *specific* contents are to be called legitimate. And *as far* as these conditions *are* fulfilled, any content—institutional arrangements, forms of life, individual choices, forms of actions, etc.—*would* be legitimate.

At this point the analogy ends; for, obviously, form and content will be linked with each other in very different ways, depending on whether they are linked in accordance with principles of rational discourse or in accordance with principles of property rights. The metaprinciples of rational discourse are, above all, principles for an institutionalization of public freedom and democratic decision making; from the perspective of these metaprinciples, property rights appear as a possible *content* of a *democratic consensus.* The metaprinciples of individual rights, in contrast, are, above all, principles of negative freedom; from the perspective of these metaprinciples, participatory democracy appears as a possible *content* of an *agreement* (contract) among the members of a specific group of society. As Nozick puts it: "Visionaries and crackpots, maniacs and saints, monks and libertines, capitalists and communists and participatory democrats, proponents of phalanxes (Fourier), palaces of labor (Flora Tristan), villages of unity and cooperation (Owen), mutualist communities (Proudhon), time stores (Josiah Warren), Bruderhof, kibbutzim, kundalini yoga ashrams, and so forth, may all have their try at building their vision and setting an alluring example."[22] Compared with Habermas, Nozick's vision, which is a postmodernist version of a liberal utopia, represents a puzzling reversal of form and content. But why is it puzzling and not just absurd? I think it could be easily shown that it is absurd in many respects, absurd in terms of the underlying anthropology, sociology, and theory of rationality, and particularly absurd because Nozick does not even ask the question how the citizens of his utopian state are to make sure that the metaprinciples of their freedom are put into practice in the right way. It is at this point that Locke or Kant would have developed a conception of representative government (and Hobbes a conception of the state as a Leviathan). Prima facie, and from a philosophical point of view, all the odds are against Nozick's liberal utopia; it seems obvious that a communalist perspective in the sense of Habermas is much more coherent if a formal conception of freedom is to be delineated. The reason why I nevertheless find something puzzling for a communalist (and not *just* absurd) in Nozick's construction is that it could be understood as an account of *civil society* in Hegel's sense; however, if it is understood in this way, i.e., as the legitimation of a sphere of negative freedom in the modern state, a sphere of negative freedom which is structurally distinct from and in *some sense* independent of the communal sphere of public debate and democratic will formation, then one might begin to ask whether a construction like Nozick's might be seen in the way in which Hegel saw the theories of natural right: as the articulation of one basic dimension of freedom in the modern world, namely, a negative freedom which, by disrupting the bonds of solidarity between the individuals, is, at the same time, a precondition for that reflective—universalist and democratic—restoration of solidarity which is the only adequate one for the modern state. The question to be asked, then, would be whether a communalist conception of freedom in Habermas's sense can take account of this dimension of negative freedom all by itself, or whether the liberal ideology has an independent truth content that needs to be explicitly *incorporated* ("sublated") into a communalist conception of freedom.

To explain what is at stake, let me distinguish between three different possible ways in which the problem of legitimation concerning a sphere of negative freedom may be taken up from a communalist perspective. The first two kinds of legitimation do not question the primacy of the communalist perspective, i.e., the prerogatives of a democratically understood common will; it is only with regard to the third kind of legitimation that the primacy of the communalist perspective, though not being put into question as such, is put into a new light.

The first kind of legitimation concerns the steering capacities of a free market. The only alternative to the economic steering mechanism of the market we know is bureaucratic regulation, and there seems to be an almost universal consensus today that the market mechanism is far superior as far as economic efficiency goes; by 'economic efficiency' I mean efficiency with respect to the production and distribution of goods (use values) from the point of view of the needs of the potential *consumers* of these goods. In the economic "subsystem" of modern (Western) societies, money as a "generalized medium of communication" determines a type of interaction and decision making with respect to the production and distribution of material goods which has proved far more flexible and efficient than any "political" type of interaction and decision making could be. Since this has become almost part of economic common sense in modern societies, one might easily construe it as the content of a real—or at least potential—democratic consensus. The primacy of the communalist perspective is maintained here in a straightforward sense, since the delegation of steering functions to the market—as a sphere of negative freedom—can be seen as at least potentially resulting from—and being limited by—a democratic process of decision making. This kind of legitimation of a sphere of "strategic" economic action is the one which is built into Habermas's theory of communicative action.

The second kind of legitimation is rather closely related to the first one, although it is directly concerned only with the problem of distributive justice. What I have in mind here is something like Rawls's second principle of justice, according to which an unequal distribution of wealth and opportunities is legitimate ("just") if it is to the benefit of the least advantaged.[23] Because this principle obviously has a particular relevance with regard to those inequalities connected with market systems, above all with capitalist economy, it might again be seen as (part of) a communalist justification of a sphere of negative (economic) freedom.

It is only with the third kind of argument for a sphere of negative freedom that a particular problem is posed for a communalist perspective. I am thinking of the kind of argument which Hegel used, referring directly to the tradition of natural-right theories. This kind of argument, although not incompatible with the other two kinds of argument I have mentioned, is distinct from them in that it focuses, to put it paradoxically, on the *positive* side of negative freedom. Negative or, as Hegel would call it, "abstract" freedom is seen here as a "moment"—and therefore also as a precondition—for that kind of communal freedom which is based on the recognition of the rights of the individual; it is that kind of freedom to act (Kant's *Freiheit der Willkür*) which must be conceptually presupposed if communal freedom—i.e., rational freedom—is to be possible as a form of freedom which is based on insight and voluntary agreement. Negative freedom—in the sense of a universalist institutionalization of abstract right—is the precondition of communal freedom in the modern world to the same degree as it is also the condition under which the individuals have a right *not* to be fully rational. For only if they have a right not to be fully rational in the sense of a communal notion of rationality can their communal rationality become their own achievement, their own work, and can communal freedom become an expression of their *individual* freedom. Negative freedom as a human right of self-determination includes the right to be—within certain limits—selfish, crazy, eccentric, irresponsible, deviant, obsessive, self-destructive, monomaniac, etc.; what needs to be added is only that what at some point *appears* to others as crazy, eccentric, deviant, etc.—and even as selfish—may at some other point appear, even from the point of view of communal rationality, as reasonable and justified.

For Hegel, civil society—as the sphere of institutionalized negative freedom—was ethical life lost in its extremes. It represented for him that aspect of *disunification (Entzweiung)* in modern life which, being the big scandal of modernity in the eyes of Rousseau, the early romantics, and, later on, Marx, he considered to be the price to be paid for the restoration of communal freedom under conditions of modernity: i.e., under conditions of a fully emancipated human individuality, of universal human rights, and of an emancipation of science, art, and professional life from the political and religious constraints of premodern society. As a price to be paid it was, at the same time, the *precondition* for that modern form of communal freedom which, in contrast to the classical Greek form of ethical life, would not tolerate any limitations of rational discourse and rational investigation. For civil society as the sphere of disunification was for Hegel, at the same time, a sphere of learning, of the education (*Bildung*) of individuals in a practical, cognitive, moral, and aesthetic sense; consequently, it had also a *positive* role with regard to the formation of individuals who would have the intellectual and moral qualifications as citizens of a modern state. What Hegel actually claims is that the loss of ethical life embodied in the antagonistic structure of civil society is ultimately, i.e., from the point of view of the ethical life of a fully rational state, only an appearance.

Now, as far as Hegel's own theory goes—Marx was correct in pointing this out—he was certainly begging the question with this last claim. Marx, however, by reversing the order of reality and appearance—according to Marx, civil society was the reality, and the element of communal freedom only an appearance within the modern state—was missing the point of Hegel's metacritique of the romantic critique of modernity. For the validity of this metacritique is independent of Hegel's particular construction of the modern state. Even a radical democratic conception of ethical life as the form of communal freedom in the modern state has to incorporate the truth content of Hegel's critique of romantic utopias of reconciliation. The truth content of this critique is that no communal freedom in the modern world is conceivable which is not based on the institutionalization of an equal negative freedom for all.

V

Two questions still remain to be answered: (1) What is the relationship between negative freedom and property rights? (2) How does the third argument concerning negative freedom affect a communalist understanding of a democratically conceived common will?

(1) As to the first question, the relationship is quite clear in Hegel's construc-

tion: negative freedom can exist only if it has an external sphere of reality with regard to the individual person;[24] therefore, it can exist only in the form of an individual right concerning objects which are exclusively *mine*. If human rights are to be attached to individuals *as* individuals, property rights must be individualized—this is the gist of Hegel's argument. This is far from being a justification of anything like a capitalist economy; arguments of a different sort, e.g., those corresponding to the first and second kinds of legitimation I mentioned, would have to be added to justify a specific form of organization of the economy. For this reason, it would be extremely difficult to draw a sharp boundary line between those individual property rights which seem to be implied in the very conception of negative freedom, on the one hand, and those property rights, on the other, the recognition and institutionalization of which could be seen as the content of a democratic consensus in a particular society. Moreover, as Nozick correctly points out, it is a legitimate way of exercising individual property rights for individuals to give away property or abrogate property rights in favor of, let us say, a communal form of property. Does this mean that voluntary agreement, i.e., "rational consensus," is after all the ultimate criterion concerning the legitimate scope of individual property rights? And, if it is, would this not amount to an unconditional affirmation of the primacy of a communalist perspective after all? It is with these questions that I want to turn to the problems concerning the primacy of the communalist perspective, i.e., to the second question I raised at the beginning of this section.

(2) What my previous considerations show is that there are no clearly defined limits to the possible content of a rational consensus about the institutionalization of property rights—at least as long as we keep in mind that, of course, no consensus can be called rational which would put into question the very conditions under which a rational consensus among citizens can be brought about. One could try to formulate these conditions in terms of the metaprinciples of rational discourse. What is interesting about this way of securing the primacy of the communalist perspective is that at least the metaprinciples of rational discourse are not up for debate in the same sense as are the principles concerning the distribution of property rights. Consensus on these principles is not a criterion of their validity; rather, since these principles can be justified independently, a consensus which would amount to a negation of these principles could not—a priori—be called rational. Now, I think, and I have tried to show elsewhere,[25] that the kind of metaprinciples of rational discourse which actually *can* be justified a priori—i.e., by using the argument of "pragmatic self-contradiction"—are too weak to account fully for the universalist content of a modern conception of communal freedom. This means, however, that no purely formal account—not even an account in terms of a procedural conception of rationality in Habermas's sense—is sufficient to render all by itself the univer-

salist core of a modern conception of communal rationality or of communal freedom. That is, as far as I can see, the universalist demand of equal human rights does not follow *directly*—in any transparent sense of 'following'—from a priori principles of rational discourse. And it is precisely with respect to the universalism of basic human rights that Hegel, following a long tradition, emphasizes the importance of a sphere of "negative" freedom. But then there must be additional conditions of the possible rationality of a democratic consensus, which, like the metaprinciples of rational discourse themselves, cannot derive their validity *from* a democratic consensus. I think that an argument rather similar to this one is at the heart of Hegel's antiformalist strategy. If the argument is correct, it would imply that we need more than the "abstract" concept of rational argumentation or of a rational consensus to spell out the basic conditions of a possible rational consensus in modern societies. So Hegel might have been right after all about natural-right theories in a twofold sense: (1) in trying to save a truth content in the "atomistic" conception of natural rights; and (2) in refusing simply to transform the idea of natural rights into a transcendental principle of communal rationality and communal freedom. The reason why from the latter kind of principle—even if it is spelled out as a procedural conception of rationality—a universalist conception of negative freedom cannot be read off directly is that the rights of negative freedom in some sense are, as I have indicated before, rights even *against* the demands of communal rationality. If this sounds paradoxical, it will appear less so if we only take into account that the demands of communal rationality in any specific context and at any given point of historical time will have some kind of public definition in terms of institutions, moral beliefs, public opinion, etc., a kind of public definition which must be open for critique and possible revision and which must leave a space for dissent. Negative freedom seen from this angle would be at least the freedom to dissent and to act as a dissenter. It seems obvious, however, that the recognition of corresponding rights must be an essential ingredient of any viable conception of communal freedom in the modern world. Of course, a "communalist" like Habermas would easily grant this. The only *controversial* question, therefore, would be whether the kinds of "intermediary" philosophical arguments, which I have tried to sketch here, following Hegel's strategy, are necessary if we want to give a philosophical account of our widely *uncontroversial* intuitions concerning freedom in the modern world; i.e., whether my thesis is correct that a universalist principle of negative freedom can*not* conceptually be considered to be part of a communalist conception of rationality in Habermas's sense. To support this thesis, I want to make two further comments on it.

(1) From the point of view of a procedural conception of rationality, we could understand universalist principles of human rights *either* as moral norms that *we* consider to be the content of a possible rational consensus, *or* as already implied

in the metaprinciples of rationality themselves. In the first case, we would have to grant the possibility that our universalist moral intuitions may turn out to be wrong, since a rational consensus might be brought about which *negates* these principles. Apart from being deeply counterintuitive, I think that this interpretation could never be accepted by Habermas. Consequently, universalism, according to the logic of his position, *must* be built into the "unavoidable normative presuppositions" of rational discourse, i.e., must be part of the metaprinciples of rationality. But how could a principle of rationality, even if it is a principle of "communicative" and/or "discursive" rationality, say anything about a *right not* to be rational? The point of a principle of rationality is to delimit the sphere of rational communication and rational discourse, as it were, *from within;* it reminds us that we have *no* "right" *not* to be rational and it spells out *what* it is that we have no right to be (what the norms are which we have no right to violate). Now, if this principle is an a priori principle, it must be valid for any possible speaker at any time; it cannot possibly allow for exceptions. Consequently, if there is anything like a right *not* to be rational, it must be a different *sort* of right. It could not be, e.g., a moral right that a speaker might claim to violate the demands of communal rationality (for there can be no such rights). So, if a moral right is involved at all, it must be a moral right that can be explained only in terms of the moral obligations that *other* human beings have concerning *my* sphere of negative freedom, i.e., a moral obligation to respect my sphere of negative freedom—even if I exercise the corresponding rights in an irrational way. A corresponding principle of negative freedom cannot be part of a metaprinciple of rationality, although it would be highly plausible to argue that a rational consensus on a principle like this must be possible. As we have seen, however, this way out seems not to be acceptable from the point of view of a procedural conception of rationality. Interestingly enough, it *is* a possible way out only if we conceive of the relationship between the principle of negative freedom and the possibility of a rational consensus in a different way. This brings me to my second comment.

(2) Rawls has interpreted his first principle of justice—which can be understood as a universalist principle of negative freedom—as the content of a rational consensus among individuals, who in what he calls the "original position"— i.e., behind a "veil of ignorance"—and on the basis of purely strategic calculations would try to figure out what kind of basic social arrangement would be the most advantageous for them. The concept of the "original position," which is a conceptual fiction, is the device that Rawls uses to make sure that the strategic calculations of the individuals are made under the constraints of a universalist morality.[26] For this reason, Rawls's first principle of justice is very close to Kant's definition of "right" which I quoted earlier, and still rather close to Hegel's conception of "abstract right." Now, the interesting point is that the

consensus which is at stake here is a "transcendental" consensus: given that there is a plurality of individuals, each single individual rationally calculating her own interests behind a veil of ignorance would arrive at the same conclusion. No rational discourse *between* the individuals is necessary. This is a "transcendental" argument of a different sort than that which is involved in the justification of the metaprinciples of rational discourse in Habermas's sense; i.e., the principle that Rawls is looking for is *neither* a metaprinciple of rational discourse in Habermas's sense, *nor* a specific moral norm that might be the content of a possible rational consensus (in Habermas's sense). It is rather a metaprinciple of justice for individuals who want a maximum sphere of negative freedom for themselves and are prepared to grant an equal sphere of negative freedom to everybody else. These individuals are "abstract" individuals, their freedom so far is an "abstract" freedom.

Now, it is interesting to see that Rawls tries to follow a procedure that is in some sense analogous to the one chosen by Hegel. For what Rawls tries to show is that his "thin" conception of justice, if one thinks through all its "implications" concerning a possible *institutionalization,* will lead to a universalist conception of *communal* freedom in the sense of what I have called a democratic form of ethical life. Of course, if it comes to the particular "transition" which leads from "abstract right" to "concrete ethical life," Rawls's procedure differs sharply from Hegel's; the most important difference being that for Rawls the first principle of justice, i.e., the principle of equal liberty, directly leads to a principle of equal rights of political participation.[27] I do not want to defend any of the details of Rawls's construction here; but what I find intriguing about it is that for such a construction there seems to be no inherent limit concerning the possible conceptual and anthropological *enrichment* of the "abstract" conception of justice which is its starting point; one might even introduce a notion of communicative rationality at some point. Consequently, there seems to be no problem *coming back* to a communal conception of freedom; what is guaranteed from the start, however, is that this conception of communal freedom will be one for the *modern* world—for the construction starts at the heart of modern consciousness, with Kant, as it were, i.e., with a universalist conception of right and of morality. Therefore, there will be some kind of dualism of civil society and state built into this construction from the very beginning, a kind of dualism which has a normative content. And this normative dualism might be also the common truth content in the political philosophies of Hegel, Mill, and Tocqueville. A conception of communal freedom, by contrast, which is built exclusively on a conception of communicative rationality, does not contain such a normative dualism precisely because no principle of negative freedom is built into it. This, of course, is also the reason why the "atomistic" aspects of civil society find their legitimation in Habermas's theory only from the point of view of a necessary "reduction of complexity," i.e., in terms of a "steering problem" for complex societies. One might argue, however, that from the point of view of a principle of negative freedom not the *reduction,* but the *creation* of complexity is the redeeming feature of that aspect of "disunification" which is built into modern civil society.

My reservations concerning the possibility of grounding a modern conception of freedom exclusively on a procedural notion of "communicative" or "discursive" rationality should not be misunderstood. For I think that Habermas is right to consider such a conception of rationality as the normative core of any possible postmetaphysical idea of reason. In an important sense this conception does capture the basic normative structure of modern consciousness. What I have argued is only that it is not *sufficient* in itself to give a *full* account of the normative content of a modern conception of freedom. A universalist principle of equal human rights is a moral principle, which, one might argue with Rawls *and* Habermas, is the only possible content of a universal rational consensus concerning human rights. Since the very category of "abstract" or "negative" freedom, and therefore an important aspect of what we mean by human rights, cannot be part of a principle of rationality, however, it appears that a principle of human rights cannot be directly implied in a principle of rationality: a principle of human rights is a substantive moral principle, the justification of which must be different from that of the principle of rationality itself. At the same time, a principle of rights is not one of those specific norms which might be justified by a rational democratic consensus: as a *meta*principle of rights it is rather close to a metaprinciple of morality and therefore defines a limiting condition of what the legitimate content of a democratic consensus might be. It is precisely in this sense that a principle of human rights defines a condition of the possible rationality of a democratic consensus. This, it seems to me, is the hard core of truth in the tradition of modern natural-right theories from Hobbes to Rawls. This hard core of truth must indeed be supplemented by a concept of "communicative" and "discursive" rationality if it is to become the "abstract" nucleus of a modern conception of "positive," communal freedom, i.e., of a universalist conception of a democratic form of ethical life. The principles of equal liberties and of communicative rationality "demand" each other, but they do not, in any simple sense, "imply" each other. It is in this sense that freedom and reason do *not* coincide in the modern world—even if the *demand* for freedom is a rational demand and if the telos of negative freedom is a rational, communal freedom.

VI

So far I have presupposed rather than argued that there is an internal link between Habermas's notions of communicative and discursive rationality, on the one side, and the idea of communal freedom, on the other. Of course, in some sense the link is obvious: the idea of democratic self-determination demands a public space of unconstrained communication and discourse as well as institutional forms of discursive will formation. Individual liberty rights are here "translated" into rights of political participation, negative freedom is "sublated" into collective self-determination. One might therefore argue that communal freedom is simply discursive rationality that has become a form of "ethical life," to use Hegel's term once more. Let me first show in which sense this is a plausible idea and then show in which sense it is not. (That things must be more complicated follows already from my argument about negative freedom.)

The plausibility of the idea that a procedural conception of rationality in Habermas's sense already contains an idea of communal freedom is due to the fact that it defines a post-traditional type of "ethical" agreement—namely, an agreement on the *meta*norms of rational argumentation—*and,* by the same token, a form—the only form—for restoring ethical agreement among free and equal individuals once traditional ethical substance has dissolved. Through the procedure of argumentation, freedom would be linked with solidarity and rationality; a procedural conception of rationality would therefore define the normative core of a post-traditional form of communal freedom. Consequently, my somewhat paradoxical suggestion that a *formal* conception of rationality might determine the *substance* of a democratic form of ethical life would appear to be justified.

I argued before, however, that no universalist principle of "negative" freedom is really, in any perspicuous sense, "implied" in a procedural conception of rationality. If this is true, such a conception cannot provide us with a postconventional idea of solidarity ("brotherhood") either. Solidarity in a postconventional sense demands that we *want* a space of negative freedom for everybody else: a space of negative freedom which is the precondition for determining and taking responsibility for one's own life, and which, by the same token, is a space of freedom to say "no" and to act accordingly. Only on the basis of such freedom are symmetrical forms of mutual recognition voluntary agreements, and a rational consensus among equals conceivable. Only if a procedural conception of rationality contained in itself an anticipation or "projection" of a form of life which would be an embodiment of communicative and discursive rationality in an *ideal* sense (an "ideal community of communication") could we ground a conception of communal freedom solely on the idea of rationality. I believe and have tried to show elsewhere,[28] however, that such an idealization does not make sense. What I want to say is not that the idea of rationality contains a transcendental illusion—as, e.g., Jacques Derrida would argue—i.e., that it rests on idealizations which are as unavoidable as they are illusory. What I want to say is rather that those idealizations, being conceptually incoherent, are not really implied in the concept of rationality. For this reason, the idea of communal freedom, though it needs to be delineated and supported by rational arguments, and though it will give rational argumentation a privileged place with respect to the restoration and continuation of ethical agreement, cannot be reduced to a procedural conception of rationality.

Communal freedom is freedom that—through the institutions and practices of a society, through the self-understanding, concern, and habits of its citizens—has become a common *objective*. Negative freedom changes its character when it becomes a common concern. For then it is not only our own freedom we want but a maximum of self-determination for each individual and collective. Such a common—and commonly recognized—space of self-determination can exist, however, only if a space of public freedom is institutionalized in which *we,* constrained by the demands of rationality and justice, collectively, i.e., in the medium of public debate and by "acting in concert," exert our right of self-determination as a *political* right. And whereas negative freedom is transformed into communal freedom through the institutions and practices of collective self-determination, such communal freedom, where it exists, is necessarily self-reflexive: it becomes its own objective. This was already true in some sense for the Greek polis, at least if we believe those philosophers from Hegel to Hannah Arendt, for whom the Greek polis provided the first paradigm of political freedom. The institutions, practices, and habits of communal freedom become their own objective by becoming part of the self-interpretation, the identity, and the practical orientations of the individuals; for when this happens, the content of democratic will formation is no longer determined only by those prepolitical concerns, interests, and conflicts which enter the political sphere from the outside (as a matter for "just" regulations); it is rather communal freedom itself which becomes a content of politics—not only in the revolutionary act of the *constitutio libertatis,* which for Arendt always was the paradigm of political action, but also in the praxis of securing, of re-interpreting, of defending, of modifying, and of widening the space of public freedom. The *constitutio libertatis* is an ongoing concern of political action under conditions of public freedom; this is the element of truth in Arendt's otherwise paradoxical belief that the sphere of political action has itself as its content.[29]

What distinguishes this form of self-reflexivity of communal freedom, which we may already attribute to the Greek polis, from the self-reflexivity of any modern form of communal freedom, is not only that the latter must rest on a (universalist) recognition of the "rights of particularity," but that it is self-reflexive still in another sense; namely, in the sense of an awareness that no specific normative contents, nor the specific interpretations on which they may rest, are immune to the possibility of rational critique. In some sense—and this is the truth content of Habermas's interpretation of communal freedom—any particular normative content, any specific institutional regulation, and any particular system of interpretations is open for debate and rational revision. Consequently, a procedural conception of rationality *does* define an important structural condition of any modern form of communal freedom. That it only defines a condition and does not give us a "definition" of communal freedom could now also be put by saying that a procedural concept of rationality can only tell us what *rational* freedom would be, but not what rational *freedom* would be.

VII

If freedom in the modern world rests on a normative dualism of "negative" versus "positive," i.e., communal freedom, then a dialectical tension is built into the universalist idea of freedom itself. I think it is this dialectical tension between negative and positive freedom with which both Hegel and Tocqueville tried to come to grips. We may interpret this tension as a tension between individualism and communalism in the modern idea of democracy. While negative freedom is a precondition of communal freedom in the modern world, it is also a potential cause of disintegration, a source of conflicts, a potential threat of the bonds of solidarity between the individuals. Negative freedom represents, as Hegel saw it, the element of disunification which is constitutive for any modern form of communal freedom. This, I believe, is also the basic truth content of Hegel's critique of romantic ideas of reconciliation, a critique which retrospectively can be read even as a metacritique of Marx's critique of bourgeois individualism. The "project of modernity," the truth content of Hegel's critique, has no utopian telos. Hegel, however, was deeply wrong to reject a political interpretation of the principles of natural right; for a democratic form of ethical life is, as Tocqueville shows, the only possible form of "reconciliation" for modern societies. The project of modernity in some sense *is* the project of such a reconciliation between negative and communal freedom. Against Marx *and* Hegel, it has to be said that this project is an *ongoing* project without ultimate solutions, a project which occasionally transforms utopian energies into concrete new solutions. Against liberalism, it has to be said that, without the realization of a rational, communal freedom, of a democratic form of ethical life, negative freedom must become a caricature or turn into a nightmare.

The project of modernity as I have understood it here is intimately linked up with a universalist idea of freedom. Freedom, however, is not the sort of thing that could ever be realized in a definitive or perfect sense; the project of modernity, therefore, is not the kind of project that could ever be "completed." The only way in which this project could ever be completed is through exhaustion or through the self-annihilation of humanity—a possibility which, as we know, is no longer inconceivable. The open-ended character of the project of modernity implies the end of utopia, if utopia means "completion" in the sense of a definitive realization of an ideal or a telos of history. The end of utopia in this sense is not the insight that we shall never be able to realize fully the ideal, but the insight that the very idea of a definitive realization of an ideal state does not make sense with respect to human history. An end of utopia in *this* sense, however, is not equivalent to an end of the radical libertarian impulses, the moral universalism, and the democratic aspirations that are part of the project of modernity. The end of utopia should rather be understood as the beginning of a new self-reflection of modernity, of a new understanding of the radical aspirations of the modern spirit; it should be understood as modernity entering its postmetaphysical stage. This end of utopia would not be the blocking of utopian energies; it would rather be their redirection, their transformation, their pluralization; for no human life, no human passion, no human love seems to be conceivable without a utopian horizon. It is only the objectification of this utopian horizon of human life into a conception of an ultimate state of reconciliation which may be called "metaphysical." And as far as utopian radicalism in the sphere of politics is linked up with such objectifications, it may be called "metaphysical" as well. In the political sphere only "concrete" utopias have a legitimate place. A universalist idea of communal freedom, however, is neither an "abstract" nor a "concrete" utopia. It rather signifies a normative horizon for concrete utopias; for it defines a precondition of what might be called a good life under conditions of modernity.

Konstanz University

NOTES

1 My distinction between individualist and communalist conceptions of freedom has, naturally, some affinity with Isaiah Berlin's distinction between "negative" and "positive" conceptions of freedom. Since, however, my conceptual strategy is rather different from that of Berlin, the two distinctions are also, to some extent, incommensurable. See Berlin, "Two Concepts of Liberty," in *Four Essays on Liberty* (New York: Oxford, 1969).

2 "Atomism," in *Philosophy and the Human Sciences. Philosophical Papers, vol. 2* (New York: Cambridge, 1985).

3 Immanuel Kant, *Metaphysik der Sitten*, in *Werke in sechs Bänden*, W. Weischedel, hrsg., vol. IV (Darmstadt: Wissenschaftliche Buchgesellschaft, 1956), p. 337 (AB 33) (my translation).

4 See Taylor, *op. cit.*

5 The term is taken from Taylor; see *op. cit.*

6 C. B. MacPherson, *The Political Theory of Possessive Individualism* (New York: Oxford, 1962).

7 Hegel, *Vorlesungen über die Geschichte der Philosophie, Werke in zwanzig Bänden, vol. 12* (Frankfurt: Suhrkamp, 1970), p. 275.

8 *Ibid.*, pp. 310–311.

9 *Ibid.*, p. 310.

10 Hegel, *Grundlinien der Philosophie des Rechts,* in *Werke in zwanzig Bänden, vol.* 7 (Frankfurt: Suhrkamp, 1970), §185, p. 342.

11 *Ibid.*, §132, p. 245.

12 *Ibid.*, §185, p. 342.

13 *Ibid.*

14 As Vittorio Hösle has shown, Hegel had made the transition to a conception of spirit as intersubjective only on the level of "Realphilosophie," but not in his *Logic.* This, according to Hösle, would explain the unresolved tensions and discrepancies between Hegel's *Logic* and "Realphilosophie." But it might also explain why on the level of "Realphilosophie" itself, i.e., in the *Philosophy of Right,* the sphere of intersubjectivity remains subordinated to the constraints of a philosophy of an *absolute* subject, and therefore cannot be spelled out in terms of a democratic conception of ethical life. See Hösle, *Hegels System,* 2 *vols.* (Hamburg: Meiner, 1987).

15 Karl Marx, "Kritik des Hegelschen Staatsrechts," in *Werke-Schriften-Briefe,* H.-J. Lieber and P. Furth, hrsg., vol. 1 (Darmstadt: Wissenschaftliche Buchgesellschaft, 1962), p. 293 (my translation).

16 See my "Reason, Utopia, and the Dialectic of Enlightenment," *Praxis International,* III, 2 (July 1983).

17 *Der alte Staat und die Revolution* (Hamburg: Rowohlt, 1968), p. 13 (translation from the German edition).

18 Tocqueville, *Democracy in America* (New York: Random House, 1945), p. 58.

19 *Ibid.*, p. 73.

20 Hegel, *Grundlinien der Philosophie des Rechts,* §209, p. 360 (my translation).

21 Nozick, *Anarchy, State, and Utopia* (New York: Basic Books, 1974), p. 312.

22 *Ibid.*, p. 316.

23 Rawls, *A Theory of Justice* (Cambridge: Harvard, 1971), pp. 60, 302.

24 Hegel, *Grundlinien der Philosophie des Rechts,* § 41, p. 102, passim.

25 *Ethik und Dialog* (Frankfurt: Suhrkamp, 1986), p. 69, passim.

26 "My suggestion is that we think of the original position as the point of view from which noumenal selves see the world"; *A Theory of Justice,* p. 255.

27 *Ibid.*, p. 221.

28 *Ethik und Dialog,* sects. VII and VIII.

29 See, e.g., Arendt, *On Revolution* (New York: Viking, 1963). Actually, Arendt did not really (always) take the extreme position I am ascribing to her. See her interesting replies to a series of questions about this issue addressed to her during a conference on her work in Toronto in 1972 [in Melvyn A. Hill, ed., *Hannah Arendt: The Recovery of the Public World* (New York: St. Martin's, 1979), pp. 315-318]. Arendt here comes to define as "political" those matters of common concern for which no clear-cut technical solution exists and which therefore are a suitable subject for public debate (p. 317).

ON THE CONCEPTION OF THE COMMON INTEREST: BETWEEN PROCEDURE AND SUBSTANCE

CAROL C. GOULD

I

The concept of the common interest, which, together with such concepts as the common good and the general will, was a cornerstone of traditional political philosophy, fell into disuse after Joseph A. Schumpeter's[1] 1942 critique of what he called the classical theory of democracy. The classical theory, according to him, asserted that (1) there exists a common good; (2) every normal person can be made to see it by means of rational argument; (3) from this conception of the common good there can be derived judgments about every social fact and every measure taken as "good" or "bad"; and (4) (quoting his account) "all people, having therefore to agree in principle at least, there is also a Common Will of the people (= Will of all reasonable individuals) that is exactly coterminous with the common good or interest or welfare or happiness" (*ibid.*, p. 250). Schumpeter attempted to undercut this notion by several arguments: first, to the effect that there is no uniquely determined common good or interest that all people could be made to agree on by force of rational argument; second, even if a sufficiently definite common good—e.g., the utilitarian view of maximizing economic sat-isfaction—proved acceptable, it still would not imply equally definite answers on different issues; and consequently, third, there is no will of the people or *volonté générale*. As is well known, Schumpeter's alternative to this mythical account was to understand democracy as the competition of elites for political power through elections, in which an equilibrium was maintained among a plurality of conflicting interest groups.

Whether Schumpeter interpreted the classical theory of democracy correctly or not has been an open question. (Carole Pateman,[2] for one, has argued that he got it wrong.) In any case, in recent political philosophy, the pluralist and descrip-tivist equilibrium theories of Schumpeter, the early Robert A. Dahl, and others have been rejected in favor of a range of normative theories, emphasizing par-ticipatory, communal, universalist, consensual, contractualist, or rational-choice models of political and social decision-making. These include such contemporary

253

theories as those of C. B. Macpherson, Pateman, John Rawls, Jürgen Habermas, Michael Walzer, and Kenneth Arrow. It is interesting that there has been surprisingly little attention in these recent theories to the concept of the common interest. Thus, for example, where one would expect it most, in participatory or communal approaches, it is barely dealt with or taken for granted. And where it is specifically at issue, e.g., for Habermas, as a "generalizable interest," or for Rawls, as the interest of the "representative man" or, more recently, as an "overlapping consensus," as a condition for a well-ordered society, the concept remains problematic and unanalyzed. Rational-choice theories often do operate with a conception of collective choice and collective goods, where these suggest a conception of the common interest, but in general this remains undeveloped.

I would like to consider therefore whether the concept of the common interest is of any interest; or whether it is redundant, hopelessly vague, and hence well lost.

In fact, in my recent book *Rethinking Democracy,*[3] I make hardly any explicit use of a concept of the common interest. Instead, I offer an argument in which what I call common activity plays an important part. Specifically, I argue that democracy, as equal rights of participation in decision-making, is required not only in the political sphere but more generally in economic and social contexts as well, and this argument depends in part on a conception of common activity understood as the activity of a group of individuals which is defined by shared goals. I show that engaging in such common activity is one of the conditions for self-development, where such self-development is understood to be the meaning of freedom. I argue that all agents have prima facie equal rights to the conditions of self-development (that is, what I call the principle of equal positive freedom). Since engaging in common activity is one of these conditions, and freedom requires determining one's activity, each person engaged in such common activity has an equal right to participate in determining the goals and course of this activity. This suggests that, in any such joint activity with common goals, all those engaged in it have a common interest both in the successful achievement of those goals, and more generally, a common interest in participating in such common activity as a condition for their self-development. Further, insofar as freedom or self-development is a universal norm of agency, this suggests that there is an overarching common interest in self-development that characterizes all human action, where, however, the modes of self-development are understood as individually differentiated.

But here, several questions arise. For example, is such a common interest an objective property of a group of agents, or is it an interest only if it is recognized as such by the agents? Is it common in the sense that each agent individually has it as an interest, or does its being common require that it is the interest of some organized group as a whole or of some supraindividual entity? Indeed, is the common interest simply an ideological myth, covering up domination (by class, party, or church) under the guise of some universal interest? Or is the term 'interest' itself so loaded with utilitarian connotations that it inevitably dictates a narrowly utilitarian method for its determination?

These reflections open the door to a range of conceptual problems. Yet there is no fixed and univocal concept of the common interest to which one can appeal to resolve such problems. Rather, there is a need to clarify alternative conceptions of the common interest; and indeed, even to examine the genealogy of the term and of the social or political phenomena that it is intended to designate. I do not intend to pursue this genealogy or history here. (One might mention that Habermas does this in a related context in examining the historical emergence and transformation of the "public sphere" or *Öffentlichkeit*.[4]) Instead, I want to ask whether there is a sense of common interest that is useful for democratic theory and, if so, what it is.

There are four conceptual problems concerning our understanding of the common interest which I shall focus on here: first, what is the domain of the common interest? Is it appropriately understood as applying only to the domain of politics alone, where the requisite unit is the state or perhaps society as a whole? Or instead, can any group or association of any size be said to have a common interest if it is characterized by shared values or ends or if it is engaged in coordinated activity? Second, is the common interest a matter of procedure or of substance? That is, is what is in the common interest defined by whatever results from a procedure that is mutually accepted by members of a group, regardless of the content of that decision? Or are there normative constraints on decisions such that only certain outcomes can be in the common interest, while others, even if procedurally legitimated, may be said to be against it? A related issue is whether the common interest is defined subjectively or objectively; that is, can something be in the common interest of the members of a group even if none of them recognizes or acknowledges it to be so? Or is the common interest intentionally constituted? Third, to whom can the common interest be assigned? Should one say that the common interest exists only as the sum of the interests of individuals; or instead, is the common interest a property only of a supervening group or whole? Or is there a third view possible here? Fourth, how is it possible for there to be a common interest if in fact what is characteristic of society and political life is not only a plurality of interests but conflicting interests? Would 'common' in this context entail simply compromise between conflicting interests? There is an important fifth question which I shall bracket here, and that is, what is the role of rationality in determining the common interest or in providing its normative justification, and how should such rationality be characterized?

II

I shall begin by laying out three alternative models of the common interest in both the traditional and contemporary literature, followed by a critical consideration of some current approaches, namely, those of social-choice theory, Rawls, and Habermas. In this critical discussion, I shall take up some aspects of the four conceptual problems listed above and then thematize them directly in the last part of the paper, in the context of the development of my own views.

Both traditional and contemporary theories of the common interest may be schematically represented in terms of three main approaches, which I will call the *aggregative,* the *objectivist,* and the *constructivist.* In the first, the common interest is defined as an aggregative interest, i.e., as the sum of individual private interests. As Jeremy Bentham[5] classically defines it, "[t]he interest of the community then is . . . what? The sum of the interests of the several members that compose it" (*ibid.,* ch. 1, sect. IV). In its older traditional form—e.g., in Adam Smith's *Wealth of Nations* or in Bernard Mandeville's *The Fable of the Bees*—the autonomous pursuit of private interest was sanctioned as the optimal method for satisfying the common interest, by the operation of a blind rationality, behind the backs of the actors, as in Smith's "invisible hand." In contemporary forms of individualist or aggregative social-choice theory, which derive from utilitarianism, this background rationality is dispensed with and the common interest is seen as the outcome of a process of aggregating individual preference orderings. These approaches typically define rationality as instrumental, that is, in terms of choices or decisions that would lead to the satisfaction of these private or individual interests and, in the case of social choice, to an optimal distribution of such satisfactions. Since in contemporary theories the common interest is implicitly defined by such an aggregation of choices, and is determined by whatever they happen to be, this may be characterized as a relativist approach. One may say that most social-choice theories fall within this framework.

An important qualification should be mentioned here, however, and that is Arrow's theorem which argues that under certain intuitively plausible constraints there is no way to arrive at a general or common interest or a coherent expression of the popular will by any aggregation of ordinal preferences where there is a choice between more than two alternatives. Nevertheless, this does not deny that there are aggregative decision procedures that are better or worse than others in contexts of collective choice. It does deny, however, an easy reading of aggregative outcomes as expressing a common interest, such as characterized the classical utilitarian view.

A second perspective, and perhaps the most traditional one, takes the common interest as an objective social good, existing independently of the knowledge, belief, or desires of individuals, and thus takes it to be a supervenient interest which imposes itself as a rational imperative. The form of rationality that is cognate to this characterization of the common interest is typically a Platonic or deontic rationality, in which knowledge of the good or the right is the product of dialectical reason or immediate intuition. In political thought, this view is exemplified in those approaches which claim some privileged epistemological access to the knowledge of this objective social good, as in the notion of the infallible historical understanding of the Party, or the infallible eschatological understanding of the Church. This second approach grounds the common interest on a foundation that transcends the subjective choices of individuals emphasized in the first approach, and in this sense, this view may be characterized as foundationalist.

The third approach interprets the common interest as constructed by a consensual procedure. By contrast to the aggregative approach which requires no agreement or even social interaction among the separate individuals, this view sees the common interest as the product of a common choice or a mutual understanding. The form of rationality that is operative here is largely procedural, i.e., one that specifies the ways in which agreement about the norm of the common interest can be reached. In some versions, this approach tends to be relativist because of the emphasis on consensus as the sole basis for determining the common interest. Other versions propose a foundationalism of a rationalist sort, i.e., one grounded on the nature or structure of reason itself, as the presupposition of any process of agreement whatever. This third, constructivist approach to the determination of the common interest is exemplified in different ways in Rawls's theory of justice and in Habermas's theory of communicative action.

This schema of three alternative models is too simple and abstract to capture all the conceptions of the common interest. There are what one may call mixed models that do not fall neatly or exclusively into these categories. For example, in some contemporary communitarian views, there are both constructivist and objectivist elements, insofar as tradition becomes a warrant for something more than simply contemporary choices or preferences. Similarly, some contemporary social-choice theories propose models of situated rationality and of extrarational and nonegoistic determinants of social choice and thereby introduce elements of a constructivist sort into the aggregative model. Nonetheless, the schema does mark off the fundamental differences that characterize existing theories.

I want now to turn to a critical consideration of three leading contemporary theories, namely, those of social choice, Rawls, and Habermas, in order to see what bearing they have on the question of the common interest.

III

The dominant approach within contemporary social-choice theory remains the aggregative approach, that is, one in which the social choice of a group or a collective is determined by some method of aggregating the individual choices or preferences as expressions of the individuals' interests. Whatever the virtues of such an approach, it may be criticized for dealing with the common interest by reducing it to no more than a sum (or a vector sum) of individual interests or by eliminating it altogether as impossible to determine. In the case of reduction, the individuals are regarded as sharing no interest in common except the meta-interest that they all may be said to have in each one's satisfaction of her own interest. Such an interest is common in the distributive sense only, but is not a shared social interest.

Classically, in such an aggregative approach, the individuals are taken as atomistic entities aiming at the satisfaction of egoistic interests. Correlatively, the social policy of the state that would be in accordance with an aggregation of such individual interests would be the utilitarian maximization of these individual interests as the greatest happiness for the greatest number, that is, as a conception of the general welfare. In either case, there is no interest that the individuals share in common or cooperate with each other in order to satisfy. Therefore, what remains of the "common interest" is either the most minimal procedural rule—that each individual is free to pursue her own individual interest—or the minimal welfare policy that permits the greatest satisfaction of the greatest number of individual interests. Any sense of a social or common interest beyond this, in terms of shared goals or common activity toward a shared end, is left out of account.

On the presupposition that there may be some genuinely shared interest among members of a group, a community, or a polity, such a reductive individualist approach would certainly be inadequate. If, alternatively, it is shown that it is impossible to determine a common interest on the basis of such an aggregative method of combining individual preferences, then it may reasonably be asked whether it is not just this methodological supposition about the nature of decision-making which eliminates the possibility of a common interest. And on the reasonable supposition that a people gathered together in some social group do have some shared interest in common, one could argue that the aggregative approach simply fails to represent the richer facts of social choice.

In addition, one can argue as critics have (e.g., Amartya Sen and Frederic Schick), that the concept of rationality at work in traditional social-choice theory is too narrowly conceived as simply instrumental to the satisfaction of private self-interest. That is, agents also act with regard to the interests of others; or for social reasons that are not strictly rational; or on grounds of sympathy; or in terms of commitments, where one may subordinate one's own welfare to ideals, or promises, or the needs of others.

In recent social-choice theory, there has been an attempt to include a notion of cooperation as a factor in rational social choice. That is, in acting to satisfy one's own interests most fully, it is shown that the optimal procedure is to follow a policy of reciprocity, understood in terms of "tit for tat" or of equal exchange or of equal return for benefits received. Thus, agents may be said to have a common interest in such a procedure of social cooperation as the best way to satisfy their individual interests. But such a common interest remains at the level of instrumental reciprocity or means rationality and ultimately therefore remains at the level of individual self-interest. An adequate conception of the common interest, though it would not eliminate individual self-interest, would also articulate a conception of shared interest that extends not only to means but to ends as well, and would also include the common interest that arises from common activity, namely, that activity in which people work together to realize common goals.

There are, however, two other contexts of social-choice theory in which the notion of a common interest seems not only unproblematic but is indeed presupposed in a certain sense, and where the determination of this common interest is not by aggregation of individual preferences but is a priori. The first such context deals not with the interest of individuals but of groups or of those collections of individuals defined as interest groups. Thus, on such a view, environmentalists, anti-abortionists, and trade unionists are defined, groupwise, by an interest they already share. In such a case, it may be said that the individual members all have the same individual interest in achieving a common goal through collective action which benefits them all or which satisfies their desires. But where there are such interest groups, there are likely to be other groups that have conflicting or divergent interests. And in the resolution of such differences in determining policy or in social decision, we either have a zero-sum game or we are back to aggregating preferences once again, except that this time, these are group rather than individual preferences. Thus, for example, in a multiparty system, where each of the parties represents a particular interest group, the members of each of the several parties have their common interest defined by the party's platform, but the determination of a national common interest would either be by the aggregation of the various political preferences of the groups or by a zero-sum determination of political victory of the program of one group over all the others.

The other context of common interest related to this one has to do with what are called pure public goods, namely, those "that *must* be provided in equal quantities to all members of the community."[6] Examples are police and fire protection, and national defense. Presumably, all members of a community have a common interest in these goods, but their interest may be distributive, and thus no more than the expression of the private interests taken together.

Two things more should be said here about interest groups, common interest, and public goods in social-choice theory. First, in some approaches, where the characterization of common interest is taken to refer to the limited domain of a given interest group (as it is, for example, in Mancur Olsen's work on the logic of collective action), it is implied that the domain of the common interest need not be only that of a whole society or nation, nor that of a universal humankind. It may be local and limited (as in the model of interest groups that was discussed above). Second, the common interest shared by such a group or by society as a whole in what are called public goods presents a conceptual problem: though a share in the public good which is assured to all members of the group is an equal benefit, in large groups individuals who receive this benefit willy nilly will be encouraged to decide rationally not to share in paying the voluntary cost. Anonymity—a version of Gyges's ring—combined with rational self-interest entails getting something for nothing when you can. This is the so-called free-rider problem. It means that the common interest may not command a common responsibility from members of a group and that the kind of rationality that is presupposed by social-choice theory seems to lead to situations of unfair advantage—precisely what it was intended to eliminate in the ideal model. This means that, unless the model of rationality is revised, the anticipated symmetry between a common interest and a common or joint activity to realize this interest may not hold.

IV

Rawls, in his *A Theory of Justice*[7] and in later writings, including his most recent essays, does not develop any systematic or central conception of the common interest. He uses the concept explicitly in certain important contexts of his theory, however, and he suggests implicitly and analogically its relevance in a number of other contexts where he does not use the term. The more explicit concept of the common interest is discussed only in *A Theory of Justice* but not in his most recent work. He takes the common interest to concern that which is equally necessary for everyone as a condition for furthering their aims. Thus, he writes:

> . . . There are matters which concern the interests of everyone and in regard to which distributive effects are immaterial or irrelevant. In these cases, the principle of the common interest can be applied. According to this principle institutions are ranked by how effectively they guarantee the conditions necessary for all equally to further their aims, or by how efficiently they advance shared ends that will similarly benefit everyone (TJ, p. 97).

The common interest, then, is the interest shared from "the standpoint of the equal citizen" (TJ, p. 97), where the requisite ground for commonality is not necessarily equal benefit—for example, the rich benefit more from public order and security than the poor, because they have more to lose, in Rawls's example—but rather equal membership in a state. Again, in discussing limitations on liberty that the state may impose in the interests of public order, Rawls refers to the common interest as the principle legitimating such restriction, and as the one that would be chosen in the original position. For "each recognizes that the disruption of these conditions is a danger to the liberty of all. This follows once the maintenance of public order is understood as a necessary condition for everyone's achieving his ends, whatever they are . . . (TJ, p. 213).

This seems both clear and classical: the common interest is the public interest, where its scope is defined in terms of the state, or the political institution whose members *as* members have that interest. There is no appeal here to common interests in a general human or universal sense. (This would seem to exclude from the common interest the needs of all those in a polity who are *not* citizens, which raises the question of what share they would have in public goods.)

Past this point, however, instead of speaking about the common interest, Rawls uses notions of shared interest or shared final ends (for those shared goods which are good in themselves). These operate over different domains or have a different scope than does the common interest. [In his later work, he sharpens the distinction between (or in fact dichotomizes) the political institution of the state and all other associations, assigning the common interest only to the political sphere.[8]]

In *A Theory of Justice,* then, the common interest seems to take as its object public or collective goods. Specifically, he writes, "Public goods consist largely of those instrumentalities and conditions maintained by the state for everyone to use for his own purposes as his means permit, in the same manner that each has his own destination when traveling along the highways" (TJ, p. 521). Thus, public security or adequate health facilities are such public goods, in everyone's interest, and suggest such shared ends as freedom from harm and alleviation of suffering, among other things, as conditions for each and every person's activities. But not all shared ends are objects of the common interest in the sense thus far given. Thus, in discussing self-respect, which Rawls takes as "perhaps the most important primary good" (TJ, p. 440), he argues that what is necessary for such self-respect is that a person belong to "at least one community of shared interests . . . where he finds his endeavors confirmed by his associates" (TJ, p. 440). Such communities "provide a secure basis for the sense of worth of their members" (TJ, p. 440). Now, as a primary good, self-respect may be said to be a common interest in some uncomplicated sense: everybody needs it, and it is a condition for achieving whatever ends we may have. But it is not a public good, i.e., it is not the political institution that is the domain of this shared end, but any of a variety of particular associations—which Rawls later identifies as *communities*—which fit the particular needs of endorsement and confirmation of the worth of different individuals with different talents and aspirations. *Each* such community has its shared ends and particular goods, but these are not, severally or collectively, *the* common interest. So it would seem that for Rawls, *the* common interest is one whose domain is exclusively the state.

In his recent writings, Rawls suggests that the state, as a well-ordered society supported by an overlapping consensus, has as its shared values and final ends only those which are connected with a political conception of justice (PR, p. 269, OC, p. 10–17). In accordance with this conception, the state's constitution and the related values that its institutions embody are supported by the citizens as their common aim. At other points, however, Rawls seems to suggest that there are indeed other shared ends to be realized through the political cooperation of citizens which are not only those strictly required by justice. Thus, he writes:

> A well-ordered society, as thus specified, is not, then, a private society; for in the well-ordered society of justice as fairness citizens do have final ends in common. While it is true that they do not affirm the same comprehensive doctrine, they do affirm the same political conception of justice; and this means that they share one very basic political end, and one that has high priority—namely, the end of supporting just institutions and of giving one another justice accordingly, not to mention many other ends they must also share and realize through their political arrangements (PR, p. 269).

Now, what exactly are the shared final ends that are *not* part of the common interest by contrast with those shared final ends which *are* and which define it? Rawls is not entirely clear about this. The distinction he repeatedly draws is one between what he calls on the one hand, "comprehensive" philosophical, moral, or religious conceptions that commit members of a community who share these ends to certain beliefs and practices, and, on the other, the "political" conception of justice as fairness which he thinks requires no such commitment but abides a variety of such alternative and even mutually exclusive commitments as the fact of pluralism in a democratic society (see, e.g., PR pp. 269, 270–1; OC, pp. 6–7, and DP, p. 242). Those associations which have such comprehensive shared ends are in Rawls's term "communities" and the state is not a community precisely because it does not have a shared comprehensive doctrine (PR, p. 269; OC, p. 10). Yet it has a shared final end—justice. What it has in addition as shared ends is in one place characterized as the constitution and its political values as required by justice, but in another place as "the other ends they must also share and realize through their political arrangements (PR, p. 269). It seems to me that these other ends include things that are not derivable from justice, though of course they must be compatible with justice. But if this is the case then it cannot, strictly speaking, be true, as Rawls states earlier, that in a state citizens share no ends except justice.

Although Rawls does not use the term 'common interest' at all in his recent work, he does introduce a conception of what people with different particular ends and values would nevertheless agree about politically, given the fact of pluralism and the rejection of coercion in imposing the view of one comprehensive doctrine upon those who hold alternative ones. Rawls calls this kind of agreement about what is in the common interest of such plural views ''an overlapping consensus.'' It is not clear that this is the same idea as the common interest he spoke of earlier in *A Theory of Justice*. Yet it has some similarities: it is essentially an agreement about justice, which in turn entails support for a constitution that preserves basic liberties and a limitation of the domain of the state's exercise of justice to the political: that is, not only a sharp separation of church from state but of philosophy, morality, and other ''comprehensive'' views from the state's jurisdiction and concern. The ''overlapping consensus'' is thus a free agreement entered into by people who regard themselves as free and equal, rather than a comprehensive doctrine. The state is saved from becoming a community; it remains a *Gesellschaft* and not a *Gemeinschaft*.

Without attempting a full-scale critique of Rawls, one may raise some further questions about his account. One question here is the limitation of the consensus to ''people like us,'' i.e., who take themselves to be free and equal. Although Rawls at one point denies that his conception is relativist [because it has certain implications for relations among nations, and therefore has some universal import (DP, pp. 251, 251–2n46), the presupposition of freedom and equality is ungrounded. There is no account given of why we should view ourselves in this way, or take other human beings outside our society as free and equal. His argument depends entirely on whether we accede to his premise about what people like us would choose, and thus to a consensual agreement about what justice ought to be. This yields a very restricted account of what the common interest could be, for not only does it *not* apply to associations and the other institutions within society, it also does not apply to human beings generally. There are no common interests that all human beings share, since the scope of the common interest on his account is necessarily limited to a political society.

Furthermore, though it would seem that Rawls's idea of overlapping consensus, and thus the interest in justice, emerges from the procedure of coming to agreement, he necessarily appeals to substantive characterizations of the interest, a move which would seem to be unsupported by his own account.[9] Thus, he talks about basic conditions of human life or basic human needs that have to be taken into account in the original position (PR, p. 254), most notably individuals' common interest in equally having the necessary conditions for the realization of their aims or shared ends. So, too, the conception of ''primary goods,'' as what anyone would need for the realization of her ends, constitutes a concept of the common interest that is substantive and preexists the agreement.

Thus, what appears to be based on a procedure or a way of coming to agreement in fact presupposes a substantive content in the premises of the original position. "People like us" who take themselves to be free and equal, and who are reasonable besides, function like the rational choosers in social-choice theory: they are hypothetical constructs from which inferences can be made by some presumed valid reasoning. But Rawls's representative men or citizens are not simply the maximizing choosers of standard social-choice theory. They are substantively different, that is, they operate from different premises about who they are and what their goods and final ends are. They are the individuals of the liberal democratic state which Rawls plausibly describes and whose interests he realistically maps. *A Theory of Justice* may be taken as a report on their behavior and their choices. But then the sense of justice and the political good which is their highest shared end is not proposed normatively by Rawls but only proposively and descriptively to see if it conforms to our own moral and political intuitions. If it does, then Rawls is right about us but without any grounds for why we ought to be the way we are or whether in fact it makes any normative difference if we happen to be radically different or had different shared ends. If we read Rawls in this way, then a procedural interpretation of the theory of justice simply masks this core of substantive-normative presuppositions in Rawls's model of the person or citizen. The peculiar twist seems to be that Rawls increasingly shies away from making any normative argument on behalf of this person and therefore reads his own theory of justice as simply one model that may be entertained among others. My view by contrast will be seen to offer a normative argument for some of the same things that Rawls proposes but grounds the account in a nonessentialist social ontology of individuals-in-relations.

V

Habermas's conception of the common interest may be described in terms of his account of the construction of what he calls a generalizable interest. By contrast with social-choice views, the generalizable interest is not any sort of aggregation of individual interests; and by contrast with Rawls's view, its domain is not limited to the political sphere, and its reference is not exclusively to the principles of justice. Nevertheless, there are strong similarities to Rawls's project, with respect to the aim of reaching consensus on the common interest by means of a process of reasonable agreement. Both also intend that the common interest in this sense should be theoretically described in a procedural way. Thus, both place emphasis on how the common interest would be arrived at, rather than directly on what it is or what it ought to be. Of the two, Habermas is more stringent in insisting on giving a purely procedural account. He criticizes Rawls for introducing substantive and normative presuppositions into his account, e.g., the characterization of primary goods, especially the idea that everyone would want more income and wealth, and his introduction of a concept of the person with normative content.

Habermas's systematic framework for introducing the notion of a generalizable interest is distinctive, however. It concerns the general theory of communicative action in which one of the domains of discourse and practice concerns reaching agreement about norms of action, where these norms are contested. He looks to the validity claims which he sees in any communicative act as the basis for a discourse aimed at coming to agreement about these norms. The process of such agreements proceeds through what he calls "vindicating or criticizing" these claims, that is, through rational argumentation. As is well known, Habermas introduced the concept of an ideal speech situation of undistorted communication as the counterfactual norm of such argument. The forms of such an ideal situation may be seen to be presupposed by the very nature of communicative action. The speakers take themselves and each other to be free and equal in entering into the dialogue; they stand in relations of symmetry and reciprocity; they presuppose that the dialogue is aimed at understanding and agreement.

A crucial feature of the participants is that they are not simply bound to their own egoistic standpoints and interests as they are in some classical models of social choice. Rather, they are capable of adopting the perspective of the other, of decentering, and in terms of practical reason, listening to the other with understanding and respect. Once this standpoint of the other can be generalized as what the others could understand or agree to along with me, then this construction of a generalized other provides the ground for the constructon of a generalized interest. According to Habermas, a norm is justified only when "the consequences and side-effects for the satisfaction of the interests of *every* individual, which are expected to result from a *general* conformance to that norm can be accepted *without compulsion* by all."[10]

By contrast to the Kantian model in which the universalizability could be carried out formally, that is, by rational analysis and by a single individual representing universal reason, or equally monologically in the Rawlsian version (at least in *A Theory of Justice*), Habermas's universalizability requires the actual discursive practice of argumentation and criticism where the voices of all those who are affected by the acceptance of a norm can be heard. Nonetheless, as in the Kantian and Rawlsian models, Habermas's focus has been on justice and equal treatment. Yet in his version, there is also an emphasis on needs and on their generalizability as a common interest in this discursive context. Thus, in *Legitimation Crisis*,[11] he writes:

> The interest is common because the constraint-free consensus permits only what *all* can want; it is free of deception because even the interpretation of needs in which *each individual* must be able to recognize what he wants becomes the object of discursive will-formation (*ibid.*, p. 108).

More recently, Habermas has been concerned to argue that included in this context of the discursive justification of norms is a presupposition concerning the social commitment which the participants have to their common form of life and that what is at stake is not only justice but also solidarity. Thus, he writes:

> Justice conceived deontologically requires solidarity as its reverse . . . Justice concerns the equal freedoms of unique and self-determining individuals, while solidarity concerns the welfare of consociates who are intimately linked in an intersubjectively shared form of life . . . and thus also to the maintenance of the integrity of this form of life itself. Moral norms cannot protect one without the other: they cannot protect the equal rights and freedoms of the individual without protecting the welfare of one's fellow man and of the community to which the individuals belong.[12]

Furthermore, he argues that

> the fundamental notions of equal treatment, solidarity, and the general welfare, which are central to *all* moralities, are (even in premodern societies) built into the conditions of symmetry and the expectations of reciprocity characteristic of every ordinary communicative practice, and indeed, in the form of universal and necessary pragmatic presuppositions of communicative action (*ibid.*, pp. 47–8).

A few brief critical remarks about Habermas's view of the generalizable or common interest: first of all, one may ask, can Habermas in fact have it both ways, i.e., as a nonfoundationalist consensus theorist and as a theorist of the deep structures of communicative practice? If consensus as a counterfactual norm is the ultimate appeal in the determination of a common interest, then it is not clear whether there are any constraints on what such a decision procedure could lead to. For example, it would not be excluded that the common interest could be the setting up of a totalitarian state if people agreed to it—obviously not an outcome Habermas would countenance; and indeed he has told me that it would be excluded a priori. But if such outcomes are to be excluded on a priori grounds, namely, by the very definition of undistorted communication, then the ultimacy of the consensus, even as a counterfactual norm, is not clear. Habermas could respond that the condition that such a decision be freely acceptable to all affected by it would prevent any such imposition of totalitarian rule. But this would require that *all* who are affected participate in the consensus and this is an impossible condition, since we cannot know all who may be affected because of unintended consequences of action and we cannot speak for the future generations and others who are absent from the discourse. Furthermore, actual participants may at a given time fail to recognize such an outcome as a violation of their own interest or of the common interest even after long discussion.

I would suggest that the structure of the ideal speech situation is not by itself strong enough to block such unwanted consensual outcomes. Habermas does introduce some substantive constraints which he does not recognize as substantive but which he claims are part of the procedure—namely, the freedom and equality of the participants in the discourse. But his interpretation of such freedom and equality is not strong enough to generate a theory of the rights of these participants beyond the discursive practice itself. I think what is needed here is a stronger theory of human beings and an account of their rights which can serve as a constraint on any consensual or democratic decisions that can determine common interests.

A related point concerns Habermas's treatment of the relation between social interests and individual interests. Although I would agree with Habermas's attempt to introduce the social dimension strongly into the deliberations about norms—that is, his dialogical model, the emphasis on reciprocity and solidarity, and his recognition of a common interest as more than an aggregate interest—I think that he goes too far in this direction.

Most generally, despite corrections he has introduced recently, it seems to me that Habermas's model does not provide enough room for the recognition and preservation of individual differences and interests within the generalizable interest. The very emphasis on agreement as the implicit and overriding norm of discursive practices neglects the role of difference and the specificity of individuals. In his theory, these individuations are relegated to the domain of the expressive and the aesthetic. Indeed, Habermas sometimes even speaks as though these individuated expressions can themselves be subject to common agreements. Thus, in his discussion cited earlier where he states that "even the interpretation of needs, in which *each individual* must be able to recognize what he wants, becomes the object of discursive will-formation," he seems to suggest that the determination of individual needs themselves are subject to some process of consensus, and that the group can decide best what individuals need.

A final criticism, to be no more than noted here, is that Habermas restricts the framework for the emergence of a common interest to an exclusively linguistic or communicative one. Because of his separation of strategic action oriented to the realization of aims from communicative action oriented to understanding and the validation of norms, common interests are taken out of the context of practical action and common activity, that is, the ongoing practices that are the objects of reflection in the discursive framework, but are not reducible to it. Common activity, which I would like to propose as a basic context for the common interest, has both communicative and goal-oriented dimensions.

VI

I would like now to propose an alternative conception of the common interest which draws upon this notion of common activity. What I can offer here is a preliminary sketch of a more systematic approach to this question. It proceeds from my discussion and criticism of the other views.

By common activity I mean the activity of a group of individuals acting together in some coordinated way to achieve shared or common goals. These goals may either be explicitly chosen by the members of the group themselves; or be imposed on them to varying degrees by others; or be presupposed as defining that kind of activity or implicit in it (as, for example, playing to win is presupposed as defining the activity of a team in competitive sports, or making music defines the activity of an orchestra). By common activity in the fullest sense I shall refer specifically to the case where the goals are explicitly chosen by the members of the group and where they also have joint control over the conditions or means of their common activity.

In general, all of these various types of common activity may be institutional or not. For example, it may be the common activity of citizens in a state or workers in a firm, or of people in a voluntary association or even an ad hoc one, e.g., members of a pick-up softball team or a shared child-care arrangement. The common interest in such cases is, in the first place, clearly identified with the goals of the activity, and with what it would take to achieve these goals, namely, with the means or conditions of the activity. (I am excluding here the questionable case where one's participation in the activity is coerced and the goal totally externally imposed, as in the case of slave labor. Even here, however, there may be common interests that the slaves share in the activity but they are not identified with the goals of the masters.) In common activity, there is also usually a common interest in the quality of the relationships within the group, that is, in the reliability or mutual support that members afford each other, or in the quality of interaction on the job, or socially, etc., and there may indeed be common interests of this sort shared by some members of the group and not by others. Finally, individuals may be said to engage in the common activity as a condition of their own self-development or as a mode of the expression of it, and therefore may have a common interest in such self-development through their participation in the group.

This last case suggests also a more general context for the common interest which extends beyond membership in groups and may be seen to be a universally common interest. This is the interest that human beings have in freedom, which I argue should be understood as an activity of self-development, and correlatively, an interest in the conditions for such self-development. These conditions are both material and social, and entail both what has been called negative freedom as freedom from constraint (including, therefore, civil liberties and political rights) and positive freedom as access to the means needed for the realization of purposes. The full argument for this view of freedom as self-development is given in my *Rethinking Democracy*. I argue there further that there is a systematic connection between the interest in freedom as self-development and the equal rights that each individual has to the differentiated conditions for such self-development; and that this latter constitutes what I call the principle of equal positive freedom as a principle of justice (RD, pp. 31–71, 127–32). From these principles of freedom and equality and from the idea that engaging in common activity is itself one of the conditions for self-development, it follows that there is an equal right to participate in decision-making concerning the common activities in which one engages. This is the principle of democracy.

I offer this extremely schematic account only as background for the present discussion. Nevertheless, these normative considerations have an import for how we should define the common interest and further will help make clear that the common interest is not simply procedurally definable but requires a substantive normative content for its definition.

The common interest, therefore, has been considered here in two main senses: first, as an interest shared by members of a designated group engaged in a common activity (namely, an interest in the realization of the goals of the group and correlatively an interest in the conditions that are required for the achievement of these goals); second, more generally, as an interest shared by all human beings in freedom as an activity of self-development and in the conditions for it. This raises questions about the proper scope of the concept of the common interest which I shall take up shortly.

The principle of democracy has import for the normative constitution of the common interest within a common activity. On my view, the common interest is not an objective given, existing independently of the choices of the agents whose interest it is, nor is it simply constructed ad hoc by any decision procedure whatever or by a mere aggregation of individual interests. It is, so to speak, a normative construct, though one based on the concrete ongoing activity in which the members of the group are engaged. Common interest in the full sense emerges through a democratic process of decision-making about the goals and the conditions for this common activity, where this decision-making is carried out by the members of the group. Of course, democratic process here does not necessarily connote a voting procedure but more generally a deliberative process in which all have an equal right to participate and which operates by consensus where possible and by voting where necessary.

On my view, however, there need to be some constraints upon this procedural determination of the common interest. These are the rights of individuals to freedom, equality, and participation which are derived from the substantive conceptions of freedom and of the nature of agency. Therefore, not every decision democratically arrived at will be in the common interest. In this respect, my view differs from both that of Rawls and of Habermas in limiting the consensual determination of what is just or what is the generalizable interest. This conception which I propose of the common interest is therefore explicitly substantive in that it is constrained by what is required by the freedom and equality of individuals, where this freedom and equality are themselves taken as grounded in a conception of human beings as agents, and are therefore not procedurally defined concepts.[13]

Thus, this interpretation of the common interest sets certain limits for procedurally democratic determination of what this interest is, limits that derive from the recognition of basic human rights required by the conceptions of freedom and equality.[14] What is determined to be in the common interest must respect such basic rights. In this way, the second sense of the common interest presented above—namely, the universally common interest in freedom—establishes limits for what could be determined to be in the common interest in the first sense, namely, the joint interest in the goals of common activity and in the conditions for their realization. This consideration bears upon respect for the rights both of the members of a group engaged in common activity, and equally, of all those who are not members of the group. This means that the common interest of a group defined in this substantively normative way cannot be such as to ignore or violate the basic rights of those either inside or outside the group.

We may observe that there is another substantive feature of the common interest as it is presented here, that is, the positive content of any common activity as defined by its goal or in terms of the good at which that activity aims. This content goes beyond the procedural matter of participation in the choice of the goals by members of the group. Thus, it is substantive in the sense that, for example, the content of the Supreme Court's desegregation decision or an environmental group's aim to end pollution of the waterways is substantive by contrast to the particular procedures by which the group chooses its goals or modes of realizing them.

I proposed earlier that the conception of the common interest ranges over two contexts: first, that of common activity and, second, that of the general human interest in freedom and its conditions. These two aspects of the conception of the common interest may be interpreted as connoting a collective sense in the case of common activity and a distributive sense in the case of the general human interest. What I mean by this is that, in the first case, the common interest based in common activity is an interest of all in what is a collective end or goal achieved by cooperative means, even if it is ultimately always individuals who jointly determine the goal and jointly utilize the means. By distributive common interest in general I mean one that pertains to every individual, taking them severally. The universal interest in freedom is distributive in this sense in being an interest of each individual. Yet, since the realization of such freedom as self-development requires cooperation and is often expressed through forms of common activity, it may be said to have some collective aspects as well.

For the sake of analysis, one may distinguish among at least four types of common interest, along the lines of the distributive/collective contrast. The first type may be characterized as a distributively common interest, namely, one that a group of people share, but only as individuals and without any commitment to common activity in achieving it. Thus, for example, individuals may all be interested in happiness distributively, that is, they may all wish for the same thing for themselves without posing this happiness as a collective end. Such an interest may be designated as a nominal common interest in the sense that only the name of the interest is common whereas the interest itself is always particular or individual.

The second, and stronger, form of the common interest is one in which the ultimate end of the activity of individuals is their own private benefit or good but where the achievement of this requires the cooperation or at least the forbearance of others. For example, in economic exchange, each individual in seeking his or her own profit or benefit, requires what another has, and is freely willing to exchange at some agreed upon rate. The common interest here is in maintaining the structure of free and equal agency on the part of the partners in such exchange, therefore an interest in the conditions of contract. A common interest in this second sense, then, is based on reciprocity or cooperation of an instrumental sort among individuals for the sake of their separate and private interests.

A third conception of the common interest is one in which individuals in order to satisfy their own private interest must choose a common or collective goal for their activity, since it is only in this way that their private interest can be satisfied. Thus, it is not only that they act reciprocally in an instrumental way, but that they are required to join in a common project as well. For example, if individuals in a community want clean air and the elimination of environmental pollution, they cannot act to satisfy this desire only for themselves individually but must at the same time provide this same condition for others. Clean air is a collective rather than a distributive good.

The fourth and fuller sense of common interest is the collective interest of a group engaged in a common activity, as described earlier. (It will be recalled that this was distinguished from the universal interest in freedom.) Here, the interest is in the realization of a common goal which is determined collectively by democratic or participative procedures, and which is undertaken by the joint activity of those who choose it. This common interest has these four necessary and jointly sufficient conditions: that it involves common activity directed toward a common goal; that this goal and the means toward its achievement be determined democratically by those whose goal and activity it is; that these decisions are compatible with their basic rights as free and equal individuals; and that these decisions also be compatible with the basic rights of others not engaged in the common activity and the recognition of them as free and equal individuals.

An example of such a common interest involving both common activity and joint determination of goals and procedures is that of a worker self-managed enterprise, in which those who engage in a common activity of production at the same time have the right to determine the goals and the means of this activity, either directly or through the power to appoint managers. This kind of model may also be seen to apply both to smaller scale activities and on a large (for example, national) scale. On this definition, it may be seen that the common interest cannot be reduced to its merely procedural component; nor can it be constituted simply by the blind or involuntary collective action toward a goal not chosen by the agents themselves.

It may be observed that the universal interest in freedom, which I have also characterized as a common interest and as in the first place a distributive one, does not fit neatly or exclusively within any of these four types, nor does it constitute a fifth type. Rather, as suggested above, it shares in some aspects of the first three and may also be expressed in common activity oriented toward a common goal, as in the fourth type.[15]

Finally, it may be useful to comment on the scope of the common interest, a question that I raised earlier with respect to both Rawls and Habermas. My difference with Rawls is that I regard his view that the common interest is exclusively concerned with the domain of the political and of the state as too restrictive. By contrast, it seems to me that Habermas's account of generalizable interest by means of consensual agreement among a host of indeterminate others is too broad, at least in its import for political philosophy. My own choice is to offer a generous interpretation of scope as wide in its inclusiveness at the limit as is Habermas's—namely, in my case, in terms of the universal interest in freedom—but also more specifically situated in the contexts of common activity, not only at the institutional level of the state (as in Rawls) but also at other levels of association and institution as well.

NOTES

1 *Capitalism, Socialism, and Democracy,* 3rd edition (New York: Harper, 1950).
2 *Participation and Democratic Theory* (New York: Cambridge, 1970).
3 New York: Cambridge, 1988 [hereafter RD].
4 *The Structural Transformation of the Public Sphere: An Inquiry into a Category of Bourgeois Culture,* Thomas Burger, trans. (Cambridge: MIT, 1989).
5 *An Introduction to the Principles of Morals and Legislation,* in *Collected Works of Jeremy Bentham,* J. H. Burns, J. R. Dinwiddy, and F. Rosen, eds. (New York: Oxford, 1968).
6 Dennis C. Mueller, *Public Choice II* (New York: Cambridge, 1989), p. 11.
7 Cambridge: Harvard, 1971 [hereafter TJ].
8 See, for example, "Justice as Fairness: Political not Metaphysical," *Philosophy and Public Affairs* (Summer 1985), pp. 225, 231ff.; "The Idea of an Overlapping Consensus," *Oxford*

Journal of Legal Studies, VII, 1 (1987), pp. 4–5, 10, 10n17 [hereafter OC]; "The Priority of Right and Ideas of the Good," *Philosophy and Public Affairs* (Fall 1988), pp. 263, 268ff. [hereafter PR]; "The Domain of the Political and Overlapping Consensus," *New York University Law Review,* LXIV, 2 (May 1989), pp. 241–3, 253 [hereafter DP]. The "common interest" in the political sphere is constituted as what Rawls characterizes as an "overlapping consensus."

9 Recently, however, Rawls writes: "Justice as fairness is not, without important qualifications, procedurally neutral. Clearly its principles of justice are substantive and express far more than procedural values, and so do its political conceptions of person and society" (PR, p. 261). But it turns out that the substance here consists in what would be procedurally elicited by an overlapping consensus that is the practical support for Rawls's political conception of justice. Hence, this "common ground" or "neutral ground," as Rawls calls it, whatever substance it may contain, depends finally on the outcome of a procedure of agreement beyond which there is no further recourse.

10 *Moralbewusstsein und kommunikatives Handeln* (Frankfurt: Suhrkamp, 1983), p. 103, as cited in Stephen K. White, *The Recent Work of Jürgen Habermas* (New York: Cambridge, 1988), p. 49.

11 Boston: Beacon, 1975.

12 "*Justice and Solidarity,*" in this volume, p. 47.

13 This is not to imply that democracy, by contrast to freedom and equality, is simply a procedural concept. For the equal right to participate in decision-making concerning common activity by those engaged in it, which constitutes the principle of democracy, is normatively grounded in the equal freedom of agents and the related principle of equal rights to the conditions of self-development. These are substantive concepts whose content is carried over into the meaning of democracy itself. For example, on this view, equal voting rights entail recognition by each of the equal freedom of the others and are not simply a matter of acting in accordance with a rule. Also, since the principle of democracy is grounded in a substantive conception of freedom, it should be exercised within the constraint of respect for this equal freedom of individuals, if it is to be consistent with its own ground. For a further development of this conception of democracy, see my RD.

14 It should be noted that these rights include not only the traditional negative rights against bodily harm or interferences with liberty but certain positive rights as well. For a discussion of the human rights both basic and nonbasic, see my RD, ch. 7.

15 For a full discussion of the universality of freedom and its relation to cooperation and to common activity, see my RD, chs. 1 and 2.

NOTES ON CONTRIBUTORS

Kenneth Baynes, Assistant Professor of Philosophy at the State University of New York at Stony Brook, is the author of articles on Kant's political philosophy and the liberalism/communitarianism debate, and the co-editor of *After Philosophy* (Cambridge: MIT, 1987). His first book, *From Social Contract Theory to Normative Social Criticism: Kant, Rawls, and Habermas,* will be published by SUNY Press in 1990.

Seyla Benhabib, Associate Professor of Philosophy at the State University of New York at Stony Brook, is the author of numerous articles in critical theory and of *Critique, Norm, and Utopia: A Study of the Foundations of Critical Theory* (New York: Columbia, 1986); she is also co-editor of *Feminism as Critique* (Minneapolis: Minnesota UP, 1987) and of *Praxis International.*

Carol Gould, Professor of Philosophy and Chair of the Humanties Department at Stevens Institute of Technology, is the author of *Marx's Social Ontology* (Cambridge: MIT, 1978) and *Rethinking Democracy* (New York: Cambridge, 1988), editor of *Beyond Domination* (Totowa, NJ: Roman & Allen Held, 1984) and *Information Web* (Boulder: Westview, 1989), and co-editor of *Women and Philosophy* (New York: Putnam, 1976).

Jürgen Habermas, Professor of Philosophy at Frankfurt University, is the author of numerous books; the most recent are, in English, *The Theory of Communicative Action, 2 volumes* (Boston: Beacon, 1984, 1987) and *The Discourse of Modernity: Twelve Lectures* (Cambridge: MIT, 1988); and, in German, *Moralbewusstsein und kommunikatives Handeln* (Frankfurt: Suhrkamp, 1983) [to be published in English soon by MIT] and *Nachmetaphysisches Denken* (Frankfurt: Suhrkamp, 1988).

Agnes Heller, Professor of Philosophy at the New School for Social Research, is the author of many books, including *The Power of Shame: A Rational Perspective* (Boston: Routledge, 1985), *Beyond Justice* (New York: Blackwell, 1987), *General Ethics* (New York: Blackwell, 1988), and *A Philosophy of Morals* (New York: Blackwell, 1990).

Michael Kelly, Adjunct Assistant Professor of Philosophy at Columbia University and Managing Editor of the *Journal of Philosophy*, has written articles on Gadamer, Habermas, hermeneutics, and ethics, and is currently writing a book on models of ethical critique.

Thomas McCarthy, Professor of Philosophy at Northwestern University, has taught at Boston University and the University of Munich. He is the author of *The Critical Theory of Jürgen Habermas* (Cambridge: MIT, 1978); co-editor of *Understanding Social Inquiry* (Notre Dame: University Press, 1977) and *After Philosophy* (Cambridge: MIT, 1987); and General Editor of the series, "Studies in Contemporary German Social Thought" (MIT).

Rudolf Makkreel, Professor of Philosophy at Emory University, is the author of *Dilthey: Philosopher of the Human Studies* (Princeton: University Press, 1975), and of *Imagination and Interpretation in Kant: The Hermeneutic Import of the Critique of Judgment* (Chicago: University Press, 1990). He is also editor of the *Journal of the History of Philosophy*.

Adi Ophir, Assistant Professor of Philosophy at the Institute for the Philosophy and History of Science and Ideas at Tel Aviv University, has written several articles on Foucault, social criticism, and other topics. His first book, *Plato's Republic: The City and the Space of Discourse,* will be published by Routledge in 1990.

Michael Walzer, Professor of Social Science at the Institute for Advanced Study, is the author of numerous books, most recently *Spheres of Justice: A Defense of Pluralism and Equality* (New York: Basic, 1983), *Interpretation and Social Criticism* (Cambridge: Harvard, 1987), and *The Company of Critics: Social Criticism and Political Commitment in the Twentieth Century* (New York: Basic, 1988); he is also co-editor of the journal *Dissent.*

Georgia Warnke, Assistant Professor of Philosophy at Yale University, is the author of articles on hermeneutics and social theory, and of *Gadamer: Hermeneutics, Tradition, and Reason* (Stanford: University Press, 1987); she is also co-editor of *Habermas and Philosophy: A Reader* (forthcoming) and translator of Karl Otto Apel's *Understanding and Explanation: A Transcendental-Pragmatic Perspective* (Cambridge: MIT, 1984).

Albrecht Wellmer, Professor of Philosophy at the University of Konstanz, is the author of *The Critical Theory of Society* (New York: Continuum, 1971) and, more recently, *Zur Dialectik von Moderne und Postmoderne* (Frankfurt: Suhrkamp, 1985), and *Ethik und Dialog: Elemente des moralischen Urteils bei Kant und in der Diskursethik* (Frankfurt: Suhrkamp, 1986).

INDEX

Ackerman, Bruce, vi, 187–89, 194, 197
Action
  communicative, in Habermas, 122, 128–29, 135, 137
  as criterion of those in moral community, 6–8, 48, 134
  existential choice of, 59–61
  rational explanation of, 5–6, 123–33
    by Davidson, 126–30
    by Habermas, vi, 125–26, 128–29
    by Weber, 127
Adorno, Theodor, 145n, 151, 159
Aesthetics, Kant's, 173–77
Affirmative action programs, 208
After Virtue (MacIntyre), 70, 72, 78
Aggregative model of common interest, 256
American Revolution, 237
Anabaptists, 17
Anarchism
  Derrida and, 162
  Foucault accused of, 113
  Marx and, 235
Anarchy, State, and Utopia (Nozick), 239
Apel, Karl-Otto, 202
  communicative ethics of, 1, 2, 6–7, 19, 48, 110
Aquinas, Thomas, 42, 72
Arendt, Hannah, 24–25, 169, 179, 249
Argumentative justice, 110–11
Aristotle, 2, 23, 42, 49, 59, 70, 72
  discourse on friendship of, 160, 161
  on existential choice, 60
  Walzer on justice in, 223
  See also Neo-Aristotelianism
Arrow, Kenneth, 254, 256
Aufklärung. See Enlightenment
Augustine, 72, 94
Authentic persons, 64
Autonomy, 1
  developmental psychology and, 51
  freedom and, 43, 45
  gender bias in concepts of, 21–22
  of the spheres, 97

Baier, Annette, 20
Baier, Kurt, 1
Bateson, F. W., 213
Baynes, Kenneth, vi, 274
Belief, Kant on, 171

Benevolence
  under "equal respect for all," 35
  in Kohlberg, 35, 42–46
Benhabib, Seyla, iv, 76–77, 80, 81, 186, 274
Bentham, Jeremy, 111, 119n
Berlin, Isaiah, 251n
Blanchot, Maurice, 161
Bloom, Allan, 3
Blum, Lawrence, 20
Bourgeoisie, deontological ethics and, 41
Boyd, Dwight, 35
Brooks, Cleanth, 213
Browning, Robert, 59
Buber, Martin, 119–20n, 191

Capitalism, late, 2–3
Caste society, Indian, 218–19, 221–22
Categorical imperative
  each person as end in, 45
  as principle of justification, 35
  See also Universalizability
Character
  in communicative ethics, 20–23
  deontological ethics and, 41
  existential choice of actions to form, 59–61
  "Choosing oneself"
  as "knowing oneself" rather than "making oneself," 58–59
  See also Existential choice
Cicero, Marcus Tullius, 174
Cognitivism, ethical, 1, 20, 22, 34
  value skeptics and, 51
Cohen, Joshua, 205, 209, 216–19
Collective learning, in Habermas, 139, 141
Commodity fetishism, 139
Common activity, 254, 257, 259–60, 267–72
Common interest, 253–73
Common sense, Kant on, 173–74
Common will, communalist democratic
  property rights and, 242–43
  when a common concern, 249
Communalist ideas of freedom, 227–30
  Habermas's paradigm, 238, 240–42, 244–45, 247, 248, 250
Communication
  by contingent persons on contingency, 57
  ideal community of, 1, 7, 19–20, 48
  systematic distortions to, 139
  universal conditions of ("ideal speech situation"), 6–7, 73–76, 81

276